New Directions in Judicial Politics

Edited by Kevin T. McGuire

Routledge
Taylor & Francis Group

NEW YORK AND LONDON

First published 2012
by Routledge
711 Third Avenue, New York, NY 10017

Simultaneously published in the UK
by Routledge
2 Park Square, Milton Park, Abingdon, Oxon OX14 4RN

Routledge is an imprint of the Taylor & Francis Group, an informa business

Library of Congress Cataloging in Publication Data
New directions in judicial politics / edited by
Kevin T. McGuire.
   p. cm.
   1. Judicial process—United States. 2. United States. Supreme
Court. 3. Political questions and judicial power—United
States. 4. Courts—United States. I. McGuire, Kevin T.
KF8775.N48 2012
347.73'1–dc23   2011043302

ISBN: 978-0-415-89331-2 (hbk)
ISBN: 978-0-415-89332-9 (pbk)
ISBN: 978-0-203-80571-8 (ebk)

Typeset in Minion
by Wearset Ltd, Boldon, Tyne and Wear

Printed and bound in the United States of America
by Edwards Brothers, Inc.

Contents

Contributors

Michael A. Bailey is the Colonel William J. Walsh Professor of American Government in the Georgetown University Department of Government and the Georgetown Public Policy Institute. He is co-author (with Forrest Maltzman) of *The Constrained Court: Law, Politics and the Decisions Justices Make* from Princeton University Press. Bailey's work covering the Supreme Court, trade, Congress, elections, and methodology has been published in the *American Political Science Review*, the *American Journal of Political Science*, the *Journal of Politics*, *World Politics*, the *Journal of Law, Economics, & Organization* and elsewhere. He received his Ph.D. from Stanford University.

Sara C. Benesh is Associate Professor of Political Science and Director of Graduate Studies at the University of Wisconsin–Milwaukee. Her primary research interests include decision-making in lower state and federal courts, and public opinion about the power and legitimacy of courts. Her research has appeared in *American Journal of Political Science*, *Journal of Politics*, *American Politics Research*, and *Justice System Journal*, among others, and has been supported by the National Science Foundation. She is the author of *The U.S. Court of Appeals and the Law of Confession: Perspectives on the Hierarchy of Justice* and co-author of *The Supreme Court in the American Legal System* and contributed to *The Pioneers of Judicial Behavior*. She teaches courses on the Supreme Court, constitutional law, American government, and political methodology. She received her Ph.D. in 1999 from Michigan State University.

Ryan C. Black is Assistant Professor of Political Science at Michigan State University. He has published on the Supreme Court's decision-making process in the *Journal of Politics*, *Political Research Quarterly*, *Journal of Law, Economics, & Organization*, *American Politics Research*, and *Justice System Journal*. He is also the co-author of two forthcoming books about the Court: *Oral Arguments and Coalition Formation on the United States Supreme Court* and *The Solicitor General and the United States Supreme Court: Executive Branch Influence and Judicial Decisions*.

Chris W. Bonneau is Associate Professor of Political Science at the University of Pittsburgh. He has published widely in such journals as the *American Journal of Political Science*, the *Journal of Politics*, *Political Research Quarterly* and others on the topic of judicial selection and the election of judges. He is co-author of *In Defense of Judicial Elections* and *Strategic Behavior and Policy Choice on the U.S. Supreme Court*.

Brent D. Boyea is Associate Professor of Political Science at the University of Texas at Arlington. His primary research and teaching interests include American political institutions, judicial politics, state politics, and elections. He has published articles in several journals, including the *American Journal of Political Science*, *Social Science Quarterly*, and *American Politics Research*. He received his Ph.D. from Rice University.

Damon M. Cann is Assistant Professor of Political Science at Utah State University. His research on judicial elections has been published in a variety of scholarly journals including *Journal of Politics*, *American Politics Research*, and *State Politics & Policy Quarterly*. He has also written extensively on Congress and congressional elections, including his award-winning book *Sharing the Wealth: Member Contributions and the Exchange Theory of Party Influence in the U.S. House of Representatives*, and authored articles in journals including *Political Research Quarterly* and *Political Analysis*. He holds a Ph.D. in Political Science from Stony Brook University.

Tom S. Clark is Associate Professor of Political Science at Emory University. He has published on judicial politics in political science and law journals, including the *American Journal of Political Science*, the *Journal of Politics*, the *Journal of Law, Economics & Organization*, *Political Research Quarterly*, the *Journal of Theoretical Politics*, the *Journal of Empirical Legal Studies*, and the *Wisconsin Law Review*. His book, *The Limits of Judicial Independence*, was published by Cambridge University Press in the Series in the Political Economy of Institutions and Decisions. Professor Clark received his Ph.D. from Princeton University.

Paul M. Collins, Jr. is Associate Professor of Political Science at the University of North Texas. He has published extensively on interest group litigation in journals such as *American Politics Research*, *Journal of Empirical Legal Studies*, *Judicature*, *Law & Social Inquiry*, *Law & Society Review*, *Political Research Quarterly*, and *Social Science Quarterly*. Professor Collins is also the author of *Friends of the Supreme Court: Interest Groups and Judicial Decision Making* (Oxford University Press), which received the 2009 C. Herman Pritchett Award from the Law and Courts Section of the American Political Science Association for the best book on law and courts written by a political scientist. He received his Ph.D. from Binghamton University.

Scott A. Comparato is Associate Professor of Political Science at Southern Illinois University. He has published on courts and compliance in several journals, including the *American Journal of Political Science* and *American Politics Research*. He is also the author of *Amici Curiae and Strategic Behavior in State Supreme Courts*. His current research addresses lower court compliance with U.S. Supreme Court precedent, and he has a book on the topic forthcoming with Scott D. McClurg.

Shane A. Gleason is a Ph.D. student at Southern Illinois University, Carbondale, where he studies public law and methodology. Currently his research focuses on executive level attorneys, in particular the Solicitor General.

William Haltom is Professor of Politics and Government at the University of Puget Sound. He wrote *Reporting on the Courts* and, with Professor Michael McCann, *Distorting the Law* as part of his ongoing study of how modern mass media render disputes and litigation. On popular culture he has written about *Cool Hand Luke* and Bruce Springsteen. His major current project, with Professor Hans A. Ostrom, concerns updating George Orwell's essay "Politics and the English Language" for the twenty-first century. Dr. Haltom earned his Ph.D. at the University of Washington in Seattle, his native city.

Virginia A. Hettinger is Associate Professor of Political Science at the University of Connecticut. She has published articles on the U.S. courts of appeals and the U.S. Supreme Court in several journals, including the *American Journal of Political Science, Legislative Studies Quarterly, Political Research Quarterly,* and *American Politics Research.* With co-authors Stefanie Lindquist and Wendy Martinek, she published a book on dissenting behavior in the courts of appeals, *Judging on a Collegial Court: Influences on Federal Appellate Decision-Making.* She received her Ph.D. from Emory University.

Timothy R. Johnson is Morse Alumni Distinguished Teaching Professor of Political Science at the University of Minnesota. He received his Ph.D. from Washington University in St. Louis in 1998. He has published articles on the U.S. Supreme Court in the *American Political Science Review, American Politics Research, Congress and the Presidency,* the *Journal of Politics, Law & Society Review, Loyola University Law Review, Political Analysis, Political Research Quarterly, University of Illinois Law Review, University of Minnesota Law Review, Washington University Law Review,* and *Washington University Journal of Law and Policy.* He is also the co-editor of *A Good Quarrel* (University of Michigan Press, 2009, with Jerry Goldman), the author of *Oral Arguments and Decision Making on the U.S. Supreme Court* (SUNY Press, 2004), and the co-author of *Religious Institutions and Minor Parties in the United States* (Praeger Press 1999, with Chris Gilbert, David A.M. Peterson, and Paul Djupe).

Jonathan P. Kastellec is an Assistant Professor in the Department of Politics at Princeton University. He studies American politics, with a focus on judicial politics, particularly the federal judicial hierarchy and the nature of political influence on three-judge panels of the courts of appeals. His research has appeared in the *Journal of Politics*, the *Journal of Law, Economics & Organization*, and *Political Research Quarterly*. His current projects include "Racial Diversity and Judicial Influence on Appellate Courts."

Jeffrey R. Lax is Associate Professor of Political Science at Columbia University. He studies American politics, specializing both in judicial politics and in the influence of public opinion on policy and legislative behavior. His recent work has appeared in the *American Political Science Review*, the *American Journal of Political Science*, and the *Journal of Politics*. His current papers include "The Democratic Deficit in the States" (forthcoming in the *American Journal of Political Science*), winner of the Pi Sigma Alpha Award for Best Paper at the 2010 Annual Meeting of the Midwest Political Science Association, and "Political Constraints on Legal Doctrine: How Hierarchy Shapes the Law" (forthcoming in the *Journal of Politics*).

Stefanie A. Lindquist is the A.W. Walker Centennial Chair in Law at the University of Texas Law School, where she is also Associate Dean for Academic Affairs. She has taught political science and law at Vanderbilt University and at the University of Georgia. In addition, she has practiced law at Latham & Watkins in Washington, DC, and has worked as a Research Associate at the Federal Judicial Center in Washington, DC. Professor Lindquist's research focuses on judicial behavior in the federal and state appellate courts. She has authored *Judging on a Collegial Court: Influences on Federal Appellate Decision Making* (University of Virginia Press, with Wendy Martinek and Virginia Hettinger) and *Measuring Judicial Activism* (Oxford University Press, with Frank Cross). Other research has been published in numerous political science and law journals. She holds the J.D. from Temple University School of Law and the Ph.D. in Political Science from the University of South Carolina.

Forrest Maltzman is a Professor of Political Science at George Washington University. He earned his Ph.D. from the University of Minnesota and his B.A. degree from Wesleyan University in Connecticut. From 1991 through 1992, he held a Hartley Fellowship at the Brookings Institution. His research has focused on the factors that shape decision-making within Congress and the Supreme Court. He has contributed articles to the *American Political Science Review, American Journal of Political Science, Journal of Politics, Legislative Studies Quarterly, Political Research Quarterly, Judicature,* and is the author of *Competing Principals: Committees, Parties, and the Organization of Congress* (University of Michigan Press,

1997). He is also the co-author of *Crafting Law on the Supreme Court: The Collegial Game* (Cambridge University Press, 2000, with James Spriggs and Paul Wahlbeck), *Advice and Dissent: The Struggle to Shape the Federal Judiciary* (Brookings, 2009, with Sarah Binder), and *The Constrained Court: Law, Politics, and the Decisions Justices Make* (Princeton University Press, 2011, with Michael Bailey).

Wendy L. Martinek is Associate Professor of Political Science at Binghamton University (SUNY). She studies law and courts and is particularly interested in the application of small group theories to appellate court decision-making, the politics of judicial selection, and decision-making in state courts of last resort. Her work has appeared in numerous outlets, including *American Journal of Political Science, American Politics Research, Journal of Politics, Judicature, Justice System Journal, Law and Society Review,* and *Political Research Quarterly.* She is the co-author (with Virginia A. Hettinger and Stefanie A. Lindquist) of *Judging on a Collegial Court,* which examines separate opinions and reversal behavior in the U.S. courts of appeals. She received her M.A. from the University of Wisconsin–Milwaukee and her Ph.D. from Michigan State University.

Michael McCann is Gordon Hirabayashi Professor for the Advancement of Citizenship at the University of Washington. He has served as founding Director of the Law, Societies, and Justice program and as chair of the Political Science Department. He is the author of *Rights at Work: Pay Equity Reform and the Politics of Legal Mobilization* (Chicago, 1994) and (with William Haltom) *Distorting the Law: Politics, Media, and the Litigation Crisis* (Chicago, 2004). Professor McCann is also editor and lead author for *Law and Social Movements* (Dartmouth/Ashgate, 2006); and co-editor, with David Engel, of *Fault Lines: Tort Law as Cultural Practice* (Stanford, 2009). He is currently co-authoring two books on law and struggles for egalitarian change as well as serving (2011–2013) as President of the Law and Society Association.

Scott D. McClurg is an Associate Professor of Political Science and Sociology at Southern Illinois University. His research interests focus on elections and voting behavior, as well as political methodology. His published work on state courts has appeared in *American Politics Research.* He is finishing a book on state courts with his co-author, Scott Comparato. He earned his Ph.D. from Washington University in St. Louis.

Kevin T. McGuire is Professor of Political Science at the University of North Carolina at Chapel Hill. He is the author of *Understanding the U.S. Supreme Court* (McGraw-Hill) and co-editor of *Institutions of American Democracy: The Judiciary* (Oxford University Press), and his research on the U.S. Supreme Court has appeared in a variety of journals, including the *American Political Science Review,* the *American Journal of Political*

Science, the *Journal of Politics*, *Political Research Quarterly*, and *Law & Society Review*. He was also a Fulbright Scholar at Trinity College, Dublin. He received his Ph.D. from The Ohio State University.

Christine L. Nemacheck is the Alumni Memorial Distinguished Associate Professor of Government at the College of William & Mary. Her research focuses on judicial selection and the role of the courts in a separation-of-powers system. Her book, *Strategic Selection: Presidential Selection of Supreme Court Justices from Herbert Hoover through George W. Bush* was published in 2007. She is also a co-author of *Government by the People*, with David Magleby and Paul Light. Her work has appeared in political science and law review journals. Her research, which is primarily archival, has been funded by numerous grants and awards from presidential library foundations. Professor Nemacheck has received a number of awards for her teaching and research activity, including the Alumni Fellowship Award for excellence in teaching at the College of William & Mary, a Coco Faculty Fellowship, and she was named a Dean's Distinguished Lecturer in 2010. She is the co-faculty adviser of the Pi Sigma Alpha Undergraduate Journal of Politics, which will be housed at the College of William & Mary through the spring 2013 semester. She received her Ph.D. from the George Washington University.

Ryan J. Owens is a Lyons Family Faculty Scholar and Assistant Professor of Political Science at the University of Wisconsin. Previously, he taught at Harvard University. His current book project (along with Ryan C. Black) examines how the United States Solicitor General influences the Supreme Court. Owens's work has appeared in the *American Journal of Political Science*, the *Journal of Politics*, *William & Mary Law Review*, the *New York Times*, the *National Law Journal*, and elsewhere. Owens received his Ph.D. from Washington University in St. Louis and his J.D. from the University of Wisconsin.

Justin Phillips is an Associate Professor of Political Science at Columbia University. He has published articles on public opinion in several journals, including the *American Political Science Review*, *American Journal of Political Science*, and the *Journal of Politics*. His current papers include "The Democratic Deficit in the States" (forthcoming in the *American Journal of Political Science*), winner of the Pi Sigma Alpha Award for Best Paper at the 2010 Annual Meeting of the Midwest Political Science Association. He also has a forthcoming book with Cambridge University Press, entitled *Gubernatorial Power*. His book explores the determinants and limits of executive power in the U.S states.

Richard Sander is an economist and Professor of Law at the University of California, Los Angeles, where he studies the interaction of law, social policy, and social problems. He is the author of "A Systemic Analysis of

Affirmative Action in American Law Schools," published by the *Stanford Law Review* in 2005, and is currently working on a book about affirmative action with Stuart Taylor for Basic Books. He has been active in developing and implementing policies related to fair housing, living wages, and ETIC utilization. He is a co-founder of UCLA's Empirical Research Group and its Program in Public Interest Law and Policy. He earned degrees at Harvard and Northwestern Universities.

James F. Spriggs, II is the Sidney Souers Professor of Government and Chair of the Department of Political Science at Washington University in St Louis. He is the co-author of *Crafting Law on the Supreme Court: The Collegial Game* (Cambridge University Press) and *The Politics of Precedent on the U.S. Supreme Court* (Princeton University Press). The former book won the C. Herman Pritchett Award for the best book in the field of Law and Courts from the American Political Science Association in 2001. His articles on judicial politics have appeared in numerous political science journals—such as the *American Political Science Review, American Journal of Political Science, Journal of Politics,* and *Political Research Quarterly*—and various law reviews—such as *The Georgetown Law Journal, Emory Law Journal,* and *University of Illinois Law Review.* He is currently researching the dynamics of legal change and the role of *stare decisis* using empirical analyses of judges' citations to court opinions.

Isaac Unah is Associate Professor of Political Science at the University of North Carolina at Chapel Hill. He teaches courses on the Supreme Court, judicial process, and constitutional interpretation. His research focuses on judicial politics, punishment politics, and the interaction of law and judicial expertise. His research has been published in several political science, law, and interdisciplinary social science journals, including the *American Journal of Political Science, Political Research Quarterly, Law & Policy, Business and Politics, South Carolina Law Review,* and *Michigan Journal of Race and Law,* among others. He is the author of *The Courts of International Trade: Judicial Specialization, Expertise, and Bureaucratic Policymaking* (University of Michigan Press, 1998), which examines the role of specialized courts in U.S. trade policy implementation, and *The Supreme Court in American Politics* (Palgrave Macmillan, 2009), which explains from an evolutionary perspective how the Court generates its enduring power and impact in American society. He is currently working on a book project on the death penalty in the United States. From 2005 through 2007, he served as Program Director for the Law and Social Sciences Program at the National Science Foundation. He received his Ph.D. from Stony Brook University.

Paul J. Wahlbeck is Professor of Political Science at George Washington University. His research and teaching focus on judicial politics and research methods. He has conducted research on legal change, oral argument before the Supreme Court, strategic interaction among justices, and institutional development. He is co-author of *Crafting Law on the Supreme Court: The Collegial Game* (Cambridge University Press, 2000). His work has appeared in many journals, including the *American Political Science Review*, *American Journal of Political Science*, *Journal of Politics*, and *Political Research Quarterly*. He served as Director of the Law and Social Sciences Program at the National Science Foundation from 2001 through 2003 and Director of the Political Science Program at the NSF in 2006.

Preface

In one way or another, courts are at the center of American life. Judges are regularly called upon to settle legal problems that touch upon all kinds of policy concerns, from child custody, divorce, personal injury, traffic violations, and landlord/tenant relations to labor disputes, the protection of intellectual property, and the regulation of energy, telecommunications, and transportation. Courts hear criminal cases and impose sentences. Courts address questions of anticompetitive business practices. Courts settle conflicts over immigration law. Courts interpret the meaning of tax law. Courts decide cases relating to environmental protection. Courts consider violations of voting rights. Courts resolve questions of terrorism. This, of course, is just a sample.

In each of these areas, courts engage in dispute resolution, but they also engage in policy-making. Many seemingly mundane matters can become transformed into major questions of public policy; what starts out as a routine criminal prosecution, for example, might evolve into an important question of a defendant's constitutional rights, racial equality, state autonomy, or perhaps even congressional power.

It is scarcely a wonder, then, that Americans are fascinated with courts, judges, and the work of the legal profession. Appointments to the U.S. Supreme Court, of course, command substantial attention from the news media, and the various groups within society that stand to lose or gain by its decisions care deeply about who gets to serve on the nation's highest court. Quite apart from the Supreme Court, courts more generally are an integral component of popular culture. Authors such as John Grisham and Scott Turow have captivated the American consciousness with their legal thrillers. Sensational accounts of the legal problems of celebrities are featured prominently on the airwaves. The popularity of such television programs as *Law & Order*, *CSI*, and *Boston Legal*—to name just a few of relatively recent vintage—are testament to the American public's enduring interest in law and courts. And sooner or later, it seems, everyone goes to law school; some 40,000 new lawyers enter the ranks of the legal profession each year.

Such interest notwithstanding, the judiciary remains quite mysterious to many. Courts employ vague legal concepts, such as jurisdiction, substantive due process, and strict scrutiny. (In fact, even the term "vagueness" itself denotes a specific legal doctrine.) Moreover, courts operate according to a variety of peculiar procedures, including discovery, estoppel, pleadings, and peremptory challenges. Courts, therefore, can be highly enigmatic.

Happily, scholars have shed substantial light on the business of judging. Even a cursory glance through the principal journals of political science, history, economics, and sociology, as well as law reviews and other legal periodicals reveals that there is a great deal of systematic knowledge about the institutions, actors, processes, and consequences of judicial decision-making. This book features some of that knowledge. Addressing a wide variety of interesting and important research questions and featuring many of the leading scholars of law and courts, the chapters in this book illustrate how the various tools of social science can be used to illuminate judicial politics.

The book is organized under five general headings. It begins by addressing several questions related to the selection of judges. In Chapter 1, Christine Nemacheck considers the difficulties that presidents face when selecting individuals to serve on the U.S. Supreme Court and the strategies that they employ to minimize the uncertainty about the choices an individual might make if elevated to the Court and the prospects of that nominee's confirmation. Viewing the selection of justices from the perspective of the Senate, Jonathan Kastellec, Jeffrey Lax, and Justin Phillips test the idea that senators approach the confirmation of justices as republican representatives, that is, with an eye towards satisfying the preferences of their constituents. These scholars muster an impressive array of polling data to show that members of the Senate pay a good deal of attention to their constituents when deciding who gets to serve on the nation's highest court. In Chapter 3, Damon Cann, Chris Bonneau, and Brent Boyea turn their attention to the selection of state judges, many of whom are chosen through competitive elections. Like many election campaigns, the quest for judicial office requires candidates to raise substantial amounts of money. These scholars investigate the linkage between campaign contributions and judicial behavior by testing whether attorneys who contribute to supreme court candidates enjoy any special advantages when arguing cases before the judges whose campaigns they help to underwrite.

The second section of the book examines the politics of trial courts, both criminal and civil. In Chapter 4, Isaac Unah inquires about the fundamental fairness of one of the most serious decisions the state can make: the imposition of capital punishment. His data reveal that, despite efforts to ensure that the death penalty is applied in an even-handed fashion, the sentencing decision of jurors in capital cases is strongly influenced by both the race of the victim and the race of the defendant. William Haltom and Michael McCann, in Chapter 5, explore how different interests use civil litigation as a means of achieving social reform. In their fascinating analysis, they examine the media coverage of litigation of four consumer products: tobacco, firearms, breast implants, and junk food. They find that, while the lawsuits against these industries have often failed in court, the media's portrayal of these courtroom conflicts have had more broad effects by casting the industries in a less favorable light in the public consciousness.

Part III of the book is devoted to the politics of appellate courts and the determinants of their decisions. In Chapter 6, Scott Comparato, Scott McClurg, and Shane Gleason explore the decision-making of state supreme courts, examining the puzzle of why they occasionally defy the mandates of the U.S. Supreme Court. They discover that many judges on state supreme courts are motivated by their policy preferences and as such are willing to disobey the Supreme Court's mandates. These decisions, though, are tempered by how closely they are monitored by the justices in Washington; state courts that are particularly recalcitrant are frequently overturned by the Supreme Court, and they respond to these rebukes and adjust their behavior accordingly. Virginia Hettinger and Stefanie Lindquist also examine the supervisory role of appellate courts, but they focus their attention on the federal courts of appeals. In explaining the decision of courts of appeals to reverse the decisions of federal district courts and federal agencies, they find that a complex set of forces is at work, including the political preferences of appellate judges and their professional experience, as well as the substantive issues, litigants, and organized interests involved in a case.

The next three chapters in this section each examine a distinctive facet of decision-making on the U.S. Supreme Court. In Chapter 8, Ryan Black and Ryan Owens investigate one of the most significant features of the Supreme Court, its ability to set its own agenda and to decide what to decide. The analysis shows that the justices act in accordance with their ideological orientations, voting to review lower court decisions when doing so will advance their policy goals. At the same time, their evidence suggests that the justices are sensitive to the need to address issues of national importance, particularly when lower courts have difficulty resolving those issues in a consistent fashion. Most important, they discover that a justice's responsiveness to legal considerations has a lot to do with whether she believes the case will help advance her policy ambitions. In Chapter 9, Timothy Johnson, James Spriggs, and Paul Wahlbeck explore one of the enduring issues of judicial politics, the reliance upon precedent as a basis for decision-making. Approaching this issue from a longitudinal perspective, they survey the Supreme Court's reliance upon precedent over time, and their analysis reveals that the professionalization of the legal system as well as the justices' need to promote institutional legitimacy have combined to create the norm of *stare decisis* on the Court. Tom Clark probes another critical element of decision-making on the Supreme Court. In Chapter 10, he focuses on the collegial nature of the Court by asking which justice determines the substantive content of the Court's legal policy. Since justices must frequently bargain with and accommodate one another, the majority opinion can reflect the view of a number of different justices. But which justice predominates? Using a complex method to measure the content of the Court's opinions, he finds that it is the justice who is at the ideological center of the majority coalition—not the author of the opinion or the "swing justice" at the center of the Court—who governs the Court's policies.

The fourth section of the book illustrates the importance of the various publics with whom courts come into contact. Michael Bailey and Forrest Maltzman, for example, survey inter-branch relations at the national level. They examine important features of the separation of powers and their potential consequences for the Supreme Court. As they explain, the appointment process affords the president and the Senate the formal opportunity to mold the policy choices of the Court, just as congressional pressure to defer to popular decision-making serves as an informal mechanism for reining in the policy ambitions of the justices. Furthermore, the considerable policy expertise possessed by the executive branch as well as the ability of Congress to reverse the justices both temper the choices the justices make. In Chapter 12, Paul Collins offers an assessment of the influence of the various organized interests that are affected by the Court's decisions. As he explains, interest groups of various kinds recognize that they have a stake in the outcomes of cases and, even though they are not directly involved, file *amicus curiae* briefs as a means of advocating their preferred policies. His data show that all manner of interests now take advantage of this opportunity, and he discusses the very real consequences that these briefs have on the shape and direction of judicial policy. In Chapter 13, I investigate the external pressures that can be brought to bear upon judges of state supreme courts. Examining decisions in church–state litigation, I show that these judges are acutely aware of the need to come to terms with the preferences of the population within their states. In particular, the brand of fundamentalist Christian conservatism that is common in southern states as well as the political preferences across the states more generally affect how judges—especially those who must campaign for re-election—craft their policies.

The last part of the book is devoted to exploring the consequences of judicial policy-making. As Sara Benesh and Wendy Martinek explain in Chapter 14, the reaction of lower courts to the decisions of the U.S. Supreme Court can be quite varied. They mine a deep vein of scholarly research to demonstrate that the reaction of lower court judges cannot be explained simply by the obligation that they have to abide by the principles of *stare decisis*. To be sure, judges on lower courts usually attempt to implement conscientiously the dictates of the Court. At the same time, though, these judges can and do exhibit independent judgment, usually as a function of different characteristics of the Court's decisions. Benesh and Martinek also add an important cautionary note; because there is not widespread agreement about how best to gauge compliance with the Supreme Court, the specific measure used to tap that concept often has implications for the findings of researchers. Chapter 15 addresses some of the practical effects of judicial policy. In this chapter, Richard Sander looks at the effects of two of the U.S. Supreme Court's most important decisions concerning racial equality, the University of Michigan's affirmative action cases. He explains that, on the face of it, the Court's affirmative action policy severely limited the discretion of public universities when it comes to using the race of applicants as a basis for increasing the diversity of their student populations. He examines a large trove of admissions data and comes to a surprising conclusion: the Court's affirmative action decisions have not only failed to have their desired effects but have produced precisely the opposite results of those that the Court intended. Instead of eliminating reliance upon race as the central factor in promoting campus diversity in favor of a broader set of characteristics, the race of applicants has taken on *greater* weight in admissions decisions. Instead of abandoning a system that routinely gave automatic preference to minority applicants, admissions officers have actually become more rigid in their use of racial preferences.

Taken together, these chapters offer a rich and detailed understanding of courts, judges, and the legal process. They underscore the considerable complexity that distinguishes the institutions and actors that are involved in judicial policy-making. Aided by the care and creativity of the contributors to this volume, readers will gain a deeper understanding not only of the important questions that comprise the study of judicial politics but also the interesting ways in which scholars set about answering them.

Acknowledgments

Working on this volume was a pleasure, thanks to the support that I received from a number of people. The staff at Routledge merits particular praise. Michael Kerns was a splendid editor; he provided valuable direction and was the source of many excellent ideas. Mary Altman was remarkably efficient, patient, and good natured in shepherding the manuscript to publication. I am particularly indebted to Allie Waite and Gail Welsh for their stellar efforts in managing the production of the book.

As the book was taking shape, several scholars offered useful insights about its scope and content. John E. Finn, Wesleyan University; Banks Miller, University of Texas at Dallas; Susan Haire, University of Georgia; and one anonymous reviewer provided thoughtful and detailed guidance in the book's early stages. Lawrence Baum helped fill several gaps in my knowledge, responding to my questions with his customary care and thoroughness. At my home institution, Georg Vanberg generously made himself available to discuss the book and made a number of recommendations for improvement. Stephen Gent paid a heavy price for having an office located next to mine.

Naturally, the principal strength of a book such as this one derives from the quality of its contributors. So I am grateful that so many outstanding scholars whose work I respect were willing to feature their research here. Recruiting them turned out to be a remarkably simple and painless process. I sat down and drew up a list of the individuals whom I most wanted to be a part of the volume, and then I contacted them. To my amazement and delight, they all agreed.

Finally, my wife Nancy and my daughters gave me the time that I needed to work on the book—often at times very inconvenient to them—and they did so without (much) complaint.

Permissions

Comparato, Scott A., and Scott D. McClurg. 2007. "A Neo-Institutional Explanation of State Supreme Court Responses in Search and Seizure Cases." *American Politics Research* 35(5): 726–754. Reprinted in part by permission of Sage Publications.

Kastellec, Jonathan P., Jeffrey R. Lax, and Justin Phillips. 2010. "Public Opin-
ion and Senate Confirmation of Supreme Court Nominees." *Journal of
Politics* 72(3): 767–784. Reprinted in part by permission of Cambridge
University Press.

Nemacheck, Christine L. 2007. *Strategic Selection: Presidential Nomination of
Supreme Court Justices from Herbert Hoover through George W. Bush.*
Charlottesville: University of Virginia Press. Reprinted in part by permis-
sion of University of Virginia Press.

Part I

Selecting Judges

Chapter 1

Selecting Justice

Strategy and Uncertainty in Choosing Supreme Court Nominees

Christine L. Nemacheck

On May 10, 2010, President Barack Obama formally nominated then Solicitor General Elena Kagan to be an associate justice of the United States Supreme Court. Almost three months later, the United States Senate voted to confirm the president's nominee by a 63–37 vote. Much of the media coverage of the Kagan appointment focused on the confirmation process—the Senate Judiciary Committee's hearings, debate among political pundits over the kind of justice Kagan might be, the possibility of a Republican-led filibuster, and the final vote on Kagan's nomination. While the confirmation stage of judicial nominations is certainly an interesting process fraught with partisan politics, many of the most important considerations in the judicial nomination process happened before President Obama officially nominated a candidate to take the seat being vacated by Justice John Paul Stevens.

Presidents care a great deal about their nominations to the Supreme Court. When, in May 2009, President Obama announced that Justice David Souter would be retiring from the Court, he told White House reporters that "the process of selecting someone to replace Justice Souter [was] among [his] most serious responsibilities as President" (Gibbs 2009). President George W. Bush compared Supreme Court appointments to other appointments presidents make by saying that "[w]hile White House staff and Cabinet appointments are crucial to decision making, they are temporary. Judicial appointments are for life" (Bush 2010). Because Supreme Court justices serve lifetime appointments, presidents are able to use appointments to influence the Court's decisions long after they leave office. Although a president can only serve two terms in office, Supreme Court justices routinely serve two or three times as long as that, and many have served much longer (McGuire 2005). For example, Justice Stevens, who announced in April 2010 that he would retire at the end of that Court's term, was appointed by President Ford in 1975, nearly 35 years earlier. Justice Stevens' near record-setting tenure on the Court is certainly not the norm, but the potential for Supreme Court justices to affect policy long after a president leaves office makes such appointments opportunities presidents relish.

Presidents Obama and Bush (43) are not alone in the importance they attribute to Supreme Court nominations. Throughout our nation's history presidents have realized the crucial nature of these appointments. Appointments to the Court can have even greater implications for law and policy when the Court itself is closely divided and case outcomes might be affected by a change in one or two justices. Even justices themselves have made comments that reveal the weight of such changes on the nation's high bench. Justice Stephen Breyer's dissent in a prominent affirmative action case decided by the Supreme Court in 2007 is illustrative of that impact. Just four years after the U.S. Supreme Court had upheld affirmative action in university admissions by a 5–4 vote (*Grutter v. Bollinger* 2003), it struck down the use of race in student assignment to public schools in Seattle, Washington (*Parents Involved in Community Schools v. Seattle School District No. 1* 2007). In his dissent to the Court's 2007 decision, Justice Breyer referred to the abrupt change in the Court's holdings on affirmative action as a result of the changing membership on the Court. He wrote, "It is not often in the law that so few have so quickly changed so much" (*Parents Involved v. Seattle*, Breyer, S., dissenting). As the proportion of cases decided by a one vote margin grows, as has been the case in the 1990s and 2000s (Epstein *et al.* 2007b), it is increasingly likely that even a single appointment to the Supreme Court will have important legal and political implications.

Thus, presidential appointments to the Supreme Court matter a great deal. That there is agreement on the importance of these appointments begs the question of how presidents actually choose their nominees to the Court. Why does one candidate rise to the top of the president's list? Although nominees to the Supreme Court do not win confirmation as easily as do high executive branch appointments (as will be discussed in the following pages), the fact is that the great majority of presidential nominees to the Supreme Court are confirmed by the Senate. As a result, it is important to understand the politics of the selection stage of the nomination process—the point from which a vacancy on the Court exists until the president officially nominates his candidate for the Court.

In this chapter, I focus on the president's choice of a nominee to the U.S. Supreme Court. As mentioned above much of the attention to the appointment process centers on the Senate's decision to confirm the president's nominee. This is not only true in the case of the media; it is also true of much of the scholarly research on appointments (Cameron, Cover, and Segal 1990; Overby *et al.* 1992; Ruckman 1993; Segal 1987; Segal, Cameron, and Cover 1992; Shipan and Shannon 2003). But, there has been some examination of the "selection stage" of the nomination process.

Much of the research on the selection stage has focused on the choices of individual presidents or has been historical accounts of particular nominations. Such research has suggested that appointments are idiosyncratic and unsuitable for systematic empirical research (Abraham 1999; but see Yalof 1999). This research has provided important insight on a myriad of factors that might affect any one nomination to the Court; and to that end, it has shed light on the appointment process. It is undoubtedly true that any appointment to the Supreme Court, or any other position for that matter, is affected by factors unique to the candidate being appointed and to the context in which the appointment occurs. However, rather than focusing on an individual nomination, or even the nominations of one particular president, we can approach the process of Supreme Court nominations by examining commonalities that exist for every president making such appointments (Nemacheck 2007; Yalof 1999). We can develop a theoretical framework to analyze the factors that shape the selection process and the conditions under which those factors are influential. Such an approach provides a lens through which we can better understand the dynamics of choosing nominees who, along with their colleagues on the Supreme Court, will have the final word on many of our most important constitutional debates.

This systematic, theoretical approach work draws heavily on Henry Abraham's seminal research in which he identified common threads across presidential appointments to the Court (Abraham 1999). Abraham analyzed the history of Supreme Court appointments from Presidents Washington through Clinton and found that four themes emerge as important to presidents in making nominations to the Court: objective merit, political and ideological compatibility, representation, and personal friendship (Abraham 1999). Abraham's work provides an important step in understanding of the commonalities among those whom the president chooses to sit on the Court. However, it does not get us as far in determining why a particular candidate is chosen for the Court in the first place, rather than other potential candidates for the position.

It has become commonplace for presidents to develop a "shortlist" of candidates they might consider for appointment to the Supreme Court, often before a vacancy on the Court exists. President George W. Bush did just that when he asked his White House Counsel, Alberto Gonzales, to begin developing a list of potential candidates for the Supreme Court shortly after the 2000 election was decided (Bush 2010). Of course President Bush would not have the opportunity to make an appointment to the Court until his second term in office, but his list was ready should a vacancy have occurred. By analyzing why the president chose Chief Justice John Roberts or Justice Samuel Alito instead of other candidates included on the shortlists for those positions on the Court we can better understand factors that affect the president's choice and the make-up of the Supreme Court more generally.

An advancement of more recent research on the selection process is its focus on systematically analyzing the determinants of presidents' choices of nominees for the Court. In the following pages, I will discuss a framework through which we can analyze presidents' choices of Supreme Court nominees. I contend that although there are undoubtedly idiosyncratic factors that affect presidential appointments to the U.S. Supreme Court, there are patterns that underlie the selection of justices. I will first give a very brief overview of the process of Supreme Court appointments. Since I argue that the institutions are important in constraining presidents' choices, it is important to have a clear understanding of the institutional requirements. I will then discuss the importance of uncertainty in shaping the way presidents think about Supreme Court nominations. Then, I will focus on the political and institutional constraints that affect all presidents when making appointments to the Supreme Court. After laying out the framework within which these appointments take place, I will then present evidence showing that presidents act strategically in their choice of nominees.

A Brief Overview of the Supreme Court Appointment Process

Article II, Section 2 of the U.S. Constitution vests the appointment power in both the president and the Senate. Presidents can nominate "and by and with the Advice and the Consent of the Senate" appoint justices to the U.S. Supreme Court. The process of appointing a justice to the U.S. Supreme Court typically begins when a vacancy becomes available on the Court. This might happen because a justice chooses to retire, as Justice John Paul Stevens did at the end of the Court's term in 2010, or it might occur as a result of a sitting justice's death, as was the case when Chief Justice Rehnquist passed away in September 2005.

In some cases, presidents may get notice of the justice's intention to retire before the justice officially announces his or her retirement. This was the case, for example, in 1986 when Chief Justice Burger retired from the Court. He told President Reagan that he would retire and the President was able to conduct his search for a replacement without the press being aware of the process. During the same press conference in which Reagan announced Chief Justice Burger's retirement, he announced that then Associate Justice William Rehnquist would become the next chief justice and that Antonin Scalia, a judge on the Court of Appeals for the District of Columbia Circuit, would become an associate justice.

However, presidents might also receive notice of a justice's retirement in the same way the press and the public do. For example, on June 30, 2005, President Bush (43) was notified by the Supreme Court that a letter was being forwarded from one of the justices. Because Chief Justice Rehnquist had been battling cancer, the administration thought it was likely a letter from Rehnquist announcing his retirement. But, that was not the case. Instead, the letter was from Justice Sandra Day O'Connor; in it she announced her own retirement from the Court (Bush 2010, 97). Though the administration may have anticipated some retirement from the Court at the end of the Court's term in 2005, it was not the vacancy they had expected to fill.

Once presidents are aware of a vacancy on the Court, they generally direct officials in the White House Counsel's office and/or the Justice Department to begin researching possible candidates. For presidents who have come into office with some list of possible nominees, this typically means considering those candidates and winnowing it down to a shortlist of candidates to seriously consider for the particular appointment. For presidents who do not have such a list to begin with, and this is more likely the case historically than in the last 30 years, they begin compiling a list of names for consideration.

During the process of developing a shortlist, presidents have typically consulted with a number of political actors both within and outside of their administrations. It is quite common for presidents to consult with members of Congress and for those members to formally recommend candidates for the president's consideration. It is also not unusual for presidents to consult with former or current members of the Supreme Court itself, as well as with friends and personal advisers.[2]

Presidents typically continue to consult with advisers as they consider candidates on the shortlist. Again, they may well consult with Members of Congress, in particular they may vet names with key senators, such as the Senate leadership and those on the Senate Judiciary Committee, as they will play important roles in the confirmation process. Once the president chooses a candidate (the process I will discuss below), the nomination is sent to the Senate for consideration.

In the Senate, the nomination is first sent to the Senate Judiciary Committee. The Committee holds hearings on the nomination, often requesting testimony from individuals who have worked with the candidates and from the candidates themselves.[3] Upon closing the hearings, the Senate Judiciary Committee then makes a recommendation on the candidate to the Senate as a whole. Although in lower federal court confirmation proceedings, a negative vote by the Judiciary Committee kills the nomination, that is not true of Supreme Court nominations. The nomination is still sent to the Senate floor with the Committee's recommendation, but a negative vote certainly indicates poor prospects for the vote on the floor.

Supreme Court nominees are confirmed by a majority vote on the floor of the Senate. Although the great majority of nominees are confirmed, the possibility of rejection is very real. As mentioned above, Supreme Court nominees do not enjoy the same degree of success in the confirmation process as do other presidential appointees. For example, approximately 95% of nominees to executive branch positions are confirmed (McCarty and Razaghian 1999). Nominations to the Supreme Court have not enjoyed the same level of success. Since 1789, presidents have nominated 154 candidates to become Supreme Court justices and the Senate has failed to confirm 31 of those nominations,[4] a success rate just under 80%.[5] Thus, with one in five Supreme Court nominees failing to garner Senate confirmation, presidents have reason to choose their candidates carefully.

Once a nominee is confirmed by the Senate, he holds his position "during good Behaviour."[6] Essentially, justices of the United States Supreme Court, as well as lower federal court judges, hold their positions for life. It is only when they choose to resign or retire, or die in office, that the president has the opportunity to appoint a replacement. If, on the other hand, the nominee is rejected, the process begins again. In such circumstances, presidents typically have returned to their ealier shortlists for another candidate, perhaps with some modification, and chosen a new nominee to fill the vacancy.

Uncertainty and the President's Choice

President Obama, like all other presidents before him, faced two types of uncertainty in choosing his nominees to the U.S. Supreme Court. First, he was uncertain about how someone he nominated to the Supreme Court might behave once he or she took the position. Presidents, of course, face this kind of uncertainty with almost any nomination they make. However, unlike their nominees to head an executive department or agency who can be removed if the president is unsatisfied with their service, a Supreme Court justice cannot be removed from office because the president disapproves of the decisions he or she makes. So, even more than in the case of executive appointments, it serves a president well to choose judicial nominees about whose future behavior he can be most assured.

Beyond the uncertainty presidents face over the nominee herself, presidents also face uncertainty surrounding the Senate's confirmation decision. Presidents do not have the power to appoint candidates to the judiciary on their own. They enter the fray of judicial nomination politics knowing that any candidate they might appoint to the Supreme Court will have to garner Senate approval. This institutional feature confronts all presidents regardless of their individual goals in naming a candidate to the Court.

Supreme Court nominations are particularly vulnerable to Senate confirmation difficulties during divided government—when the Senate is controlled by the party opposite the President.[7] Under those circumstances, Presidents face even greater degrees of uncertainty over the Senate's confirmation decision. Under conditions of divided government, Supreme Court nominees have been confirmed only 55% of the time, compared with an 88% success rate when the President's party has also controlled the Senate (Maltese 1995). When President Obama faced the prospect of filling the seat left vacant by Justice Stevens, he enjoyed a positive confirmation environment. Democrats held 58 seats in the U.S. Senate and two Independent senators, Sanders of Vermont and Lieberman of Connecticut, more often than not voted with Democrats. Republicans held only 40 seats. Thus, if Senate Democratic leaders were able to hold together this coalition of 60 votes, President Obama could choose his nominee for the Court with near certainty of getting his nominee confirmed.

Another important factor prominent in the nomination and confirmation of Supreme Court nominees is the ideology or policy preferences of the candidates. From the first Supreme Court nomination to our most recent, presidents have focused on the preferences of their nominees. President George Washington suggested a number of factors were important in his consideration of Supreme Court nominees, but chief among them was the candidate's support of the new Constitution, and indeed, each of his appointees was a strong advocate of the Federalist viewpoint (Abraham 1999). More recently, President George W. Bush expressed the importance of selecting candidates espousing the view of judicial restraint. On this point Bush has written that he "subscribed to the strict constructionist school; I wanted judges who believed the Constitution meant what it said" (Bush 2010).

Although there is debate about the role that the justices' policy preferences play in making decisions and writing opinions on the Supreme Court (as you'll read about elsewhere in later chapters), political scientists widely agree that preferences matter (Epstein and Knight 1998; Maltzman, Spriggs, and Wahlbeck 2000; Segal and Spaeth 2002). The debate typically concerns the degree to which ideology matters, when it matters, and its effects on outcomes. As evidenced both by their own statements, as well as by the often difficult and increasingly bitter confirmation battles, presidents and senators recognize this as well.

These two types of uncertainty, and the importance of ideology, structure the selection stage of the nomination process. All presidents, regardless of their other goals in nominating justices to the U.S. Supreme Court, must deal with the uncertainty over their nominees' future behavior on the Court as well as the uncertainty of the Senate confirmation decision. However, presidents can act strategically in the selection process to lessen their uncertainty. Strategic action implies that political actors make decisions based on how they perceive other actors will behave. Judicial politics scholars often discuss strategic action in analyzing judicial decision-making (Murphy 1964; Wahlbeck, Spriggs, and Maltzman 1998). Just as judges might behave strategically by anticipating the response of other members on the Court or those who will implement their decisions, presidents can act strategically in the selection process by choosing a candidate for the Court with an eye toward senators who will vote on confirmation and by considering how the candidate herself is likely to act once she is a justice of the Supreme Court free from the president's reach.[8]

Prior to his tenure on the U.S. Supreme Court, Felix Frankfurter advised President Franklin Roosevelt on a number of issues, including nominations to the Supreme Court. His comments regarding Roosevelt's ability to influence court decisions reflect his understanding of strategy in the selection process. He said, "I assume that a strategist like you will select time and circumstances most favorable for victory. I suspect that events may give you better conditions for battle than you have even now" (Frankfurter 1935). Indeed, President Roosevelt's appointments to the Court went further than perhaps any other modern president in affecting changes in law and politics.

Lessening Uncertainty in the Choice of a Nominee

Since George Washington's appointment of 10 Federalist justices to the Supreme Court during his two terms in office, presidents have had a number of goals and have encountered a variety of circumstances in making such appointments. However, regardless of those goals, each of our 44 presidents can be thought of as trying to lessen their uncertainty in achieving them. As mentioned above, presidents face uncertainty over the behavior of future justices once they have been confirmed to the bench. Thus, presidents, aware of the impact their nominations can have on the judiciary and on their own legacy, might act strategically so as to choose candidates about whose future behavior they are most certain.

There are several factors presidents might consider to limit their uncertainty over nominees' likely positions once on the Supreme Court. When presidents consider such factors, they are pursuing what I refer to as an informational strategy. They choose nominees about whose future judicial behavior they have the greatest degree of certainty. Given that presidents lack the ability to rein in justices who write opinions out of line with their own views, the need to appoint those about whom they have the best information is particularly acute.

Stories about presidents who have been disappointed by their Supreme Court appointments are memorable and are often repeated. President Eisenhower's reference to his appointments of Earl Warren and William Brennan as "mistakes" (Richardson 1979) and President Truman's statement that his nominee to the Court, Tom Clark, was "the dumbest man I think I've ever run across" (Abraham 1999, 186) are well known. And, indeed there is evidence that these mistakes can affect presidents' ability to influence law and policy made through Supreme Court decisions (Lindquist, Yalof, and Clark 2000). But, by using an informational strategy, presidents can strategically select candidates about whose future behavior they are most certain and thus lessen the potential for such surprises.

There are a number of factors presidents can use to minimize their uncertainty regarding the kind of justice a particular candidate is likely to be. First, presidents might consider potential nominees' ideological preferences. Although presidents cannot reprimand a justice who decides cases contrary to the way a president might like them decided, he can consider candidates' preferences *before* making an appointment and choose a candidate who most closely approximates his own preferences (Baum 1998; Chase 1972; Dahl 1957; Hulbary and Walker 1980; Moraski and Shipan 1999; Watson and Stookey 1995). I expect that presidents will choose ideologically proximate nominees.

Presidents might also lessen their uncertainty by choosing nominees they know well. There is a long history of presidents choosing friends and colleagues to sit on the Supreme Court (Baum 1998; Chase 1972; Scigliano 1971). President Bush's (43) selection of Harriet Miers to fill Justice O'Connor's seat in 2005 would seem to fall into this category. Miers was the legal counsel in Bush's 1993 Texas gubernatorial campaign, was later his outside counsel as governor, and served in a variety of positions in his presidential campaign. Prior to becoming his White House Counsel, she joined the administration as the president's staff secretary during the transition (Draper 2007, 343). In short, President Bush knew her very well and felt strongly that she would be a Supreme Court justice in line with his own interpretation of the Constitution and the proper role of the judiciary.

Beyond knowing a candidate personally or through a working relationship, presidents might also become more certain about future behavior by considering their previous judicial or public service (Baum 1998; Hulbary and Walker 1980). If candidates were politically active, presidents might form even clearer ideas of a candidate's true preferences. It is, perhaps, not surprising that, up until President Obama's nomination of Solicitor General Elena Kagan to be a justice in 2010, every Supreme Court justice since 1986 had experience as a federal court judge. And while Kagan had never served as a judge, she had public sector experience in both the Clinton and Obama administrations and thus was hardly an unknown quantity.

Thus, I suggest that presidents pursuing an informational strategy are more likely to choose ideologically proximate candidates with whom they have been colleagues, who have relatively more judicial experience or public sector service, and who have been politically active. Presidents can simply be more certain about such candidates' future behavior. However, in choosing candidates about whom he is more certain, the president does not lessen only his own uncertainty. He also minimizes the uncertainty of the opposition party.

When the president's own party controls the Senate, the president has a somewhat freer hand in making his choice, knowing that his co-partisans in the Senate are likely to support his nominee. However, as discussed above, when the opposition party controls the Senate, the institutional constraint posed by the requirement of Senate confirmation is more keenly felt by the president; the likelihood of confirmation substantially declines. Under the more restrictive constraint of divided government, a strategic president might be willing to risk greater uncertainty surrounding a candidate's future behavior as a means of creating a more promising confirmation environment. Indeed, a president may even moderate his choice in terms of the ideological preferences of his candidate in a less certain confirmation environment.

President George H.W. Bush's (41) appointment of Justice David Souter is an example of a president pursuing a political strategy. Facing a Senate controlled by the Democrats, President Bush seriously considered two candidates for the nomination to replace retiring Justice William Brennan. The first was Judge Edith Hollan Jones of the Fifth Circuit Court of Appeals. Jones was a well-known, conservative judge thought to be closely in line with the president's preferences (Nemacheck 2007). However, Jones' attributes were also her liabilities. She had a substantial paper trail of well-known conservative decisions. It was true that the president had a great degree of certainty over her future behavior on the Court, but so did Senate Democrats. And, unlike the president, they were not comforted by that clarity.

David Souter, on the other hand, was a lesser known commodity. President Bush was assured by White House Chief of Staff John Sununu that Souter would "uphold conservative values on the Supreme Court" (Apple 1990) and decide cases in line with President Bush's views. But, his paper trail was much shorter than Jones' and many in Bush's base were unsure about this "stealth" nominee. A Jones nomination was certain to ignite a confirmation battle and, in the end, President Bush went with the lesser known judge from New Hampshire. Judge Jones even seemed to acknowledge the president's political strategy in a letter she wrote to White House Counsel C. Boyden Gray after Bush's decision was made. Jones wrote that based on her "reading in the newspapers, it appears that the President had very good reasons for making his selection yesterday. Houston news reports indicate that Judge Souter may be virtually invulnerable on controversial issues" (Jones 1990).

In addition to illustrating how the confirmation environment can shape the president's strategy in choosing a nominee to the Court, the factors surrounding Justice Souter's appointment to the Court also inform discussions of presidents being surprised by a justice's behavior on the bench. In the case of Souter, President Bush *knew* he was less certain about Souter's future decisions on the bench. But, due to the institutional constraints he was under, he chose to pursue a political strategy—one that gave him greater certainty over the confirmation environment at the expense of certainty over his nominee's future decision-making. Had Republicans controlled the Senate, it is possible that President Bush would have pursued an informational strategy resulting in Judge Jones' nomination.

Presidents may well pursue a political strategy when the opposition party controls the Senate. If the political strategy does help to explain selection choices during divided government, then we should expect to see different factors affecting the president's choice than hypothesized by the informational strategy. Under conditions in which the opposition party controls the Senate, I expect that presidents seeking to avoid allegations of cronyism (as President Johnson suffered from in his failed attempt to elevate his good friend Abe Fortas to become chief justice in 1968) are less likely to choose friends or colleagues. Presidents may also have to moderate their ideological preferences and choose candidates who are more palatable to the opposition. Because there is also a belief that candidates with political experience are more likely to be "political activists" than are those without such experience (Baum 1998), presidents pursuing a political strategy may be less willing to appoint those with experience in public office or those who have been political activists. However, since it is comparatively easy for senators to base their opposition to a nominee on a lack of qualifications (Cameron, Cover, and Segal 1990; Massaro 1990), presidents are more likely to appoint justices with judicial experience than those without.

Another factor that might be important to presidents pursuing a political strategy is the support for a candidate being considered for appointment. For as long as presidents have been making appointments to the Court, they have consulted with Members of Congress on that process. Given the important role the Senate in particular plays in the process (Massaro 1990), this should not be surprising. As discussed above, members of Congress often make formal endorsements of candidates for appointment to the Court. I expect that strategic presidents will be more likely to choose a nominee that, all else equal, has greater support from Members of Congress.

The prior literature on Supreme Court appointments points to two other factors that I would expect to affect presidents' choices if they pursue a political strategy in the appointment process. Although the political strategy encompasses those factors important in garnering confirmation, presidents might also pursue other political goals in making appointments to the Court. For example, historically presidents paid attention to the geographic composition of the Court so as to provide each region of the country with some representation (Hulbary and Walker 1980; Marshall 1993; B. Perry 1991; Scigliano 1971). Over time geography has come to matter less, but presidents might still give it some consideration in terms of their re-election prospects. Some scholars have suggested that presidents might use nominations to induce or reward support from a region or group (Chase 1972; Hulbary and Walker 1980). Presidents pursuing a political strategy might take electoral support into consideration when choosing a nominee.

Lastly, I contend that presidents pursuing a political strategy would be especially sensitive to the age of the nominee. Presidents hope to appoint justices who will serve on the Court long after they leave office. For that to be a possibility, presidents will need to choose candidates who are relatively young enough to have a long judicial career ahead of them. However, presidents will not want to choose someone too young for fear that they will come under criticism for being unqualified (Walker and Epstein 1993). Indeed, the average age for all candidates included in presidents' shortlists was just under 55 and this is consistent with the literature that suggests presidents are likely to appoint candidates in their fifties (Hulbary and Walker 1980; B. Perry 1991, 12). This leads to the hypothesis that presidents are likely to select nominees who are old enough to avoid critiques that they lack the experience to serve on the Supreme Court, but young enough to have the potential for a long career on the Court.

The need to overcome uncertainty confronts all presidents who nominate candidates to serve on the U.S. Supreme Court. As such, it provides a lens through which to understand presidents' choices and the political and institutional conditions that constrain them. This is not to say that this framework completely explains each and every appointment to the Court. However, much of the literature to date on Supreme Court nominations has focused on the unique aspects of Supreme Court nomination politics. By systematically examining the nomination process using a theoretically driven model, we can better understand those factors shaping the selection of justices to the nation's highest bench.

Developing the Shortlist and Analyzing the Choice

In order to systematically examine a president's choice of a Supreme Court nominee, we need to know whom he seriously considered for the position. Several scholars have discussed presidents' "shortlists" and candidates that were considered to be on them (Abraham 1999; Yalof 1999). But, in order to quantitatively analyze the factors that shape a president's decision, I needed to systematically develop presidents' shortlists for each of their nominations to the Supreme Court.[9]

I developed shortlists for presidents' nominations to the U.S. Supreme Court beginning with President Herbert Hoover's appointment of Chief Justice Charles Evans Hughes in 1930 through President George W. Bush's selection of Justice Samuel Alito in 2005.[10] With the exception of Presidents Clinton's and Bush's (43) shortlists, I relied exclusively on the presidents' own papers to construct the lists.[11] Utilizing these rich archival resources allowed me a first-hand account of the presidents' deliberations to document the presidents' choices. An accurate compiling of these lists is crucial given that the empirical analysis depends on comparing the nominee chosen to the other candidates seriously considered by the president.

It was rare that a single sheet of paper with an exhaustive list of the candidates seriously considered for appointment existed in the papers (though President Ford did have such a list when he selected Justice John Paul Stevens in 1975) (Nemacheck 2007, 56). Instead, for most appointments to the Court, I assembled a list of serious contenders by examining memos between the president and his senior advisers, as well other materials such as presidential diaries and oral histories.

Once I established shortlists for each of the nominations, I empirically analyzed the factors that affected a president's decision on a nominee from the list of potential candidates (Greene 2000; Maddala 1983). In doing so, I used a type of regression model that allows us to determine the probability that a president would choose any one of the seriously considered candidates on the shortlist, conditioned on the likelihood that he would choose every other candidate. Using a model like this and the theoretical underpinnings discussed above, we can determine the circumstances under which each of the independent variables are significant factors in the presidents' decisions.

Strategically Selecting Supreme Court Nominees

In my analysis of presidents' choices of nominees to the Supreme Court, I found support for presidents' use of both the informational and political strategies. The analysis included 39 nominations to the Court and 240 candidates considered for these nominations. In some cases, candidates were considered for more than one nomination. The results of the analysis can be found in Table 1.1.

As is evident from Table 1.1, three of the five variables supporting an informational strategy are significant. Presidents do aim to lessen their uncertainty regarding a candidate's future behavior when they are under relatively looser institutional constraints. However, the political strategy is also supported. When presidents experience relatively more stringent constraints, particularly during divided government, they are more likely to pursue a political strategy to improve their candidates' confirmation prospects. Presidents do indeed act

Table 1.1 Choosing a Supreme Court Nominee (Conditional Logit Model)

Variable	Coefficient	Standard error
Informational strategy variables		
Preference differentiation	−3.069*	1.437
Colleague	−0.242	0.628
Federal Court experience	−0.559	0.652
Public Sector experience	0.138**	0.046
Political activism	−3.097**	1.106
Political strategy variables		
Colleague interaction (colleague × Senate opposition)	0.291	1.078
Federal Court interaction (court experience × Senate opposition)	1.285	1.295
Public sector interaction (public sector experience × Senate opposition)	−0.211**	0.078
Preference differentiation interaction (preference difference × Senate opposition)	0.119	2.642
Congressional recommendations	1.073*	0.632
Electoral college votes	0.009	0.023
Presidential support interaction (electoral college × presidential support)	−0.002	0.002
Age	0.102*	0.061
Number of cases	240	
Log likelihood	−50.174	
Chi-squared	27.92**	
Pseudo-R^2	0.218	

Notes
* $p < 0.05$ (one-tail test), ** $p < 0.01$ (one-tail test).

strategically to choose candidates who are both more likely to clear the hurdle of Senate confirmation and are also acceptable to the president himself.

The model used to analyze the president's choice from a list of candidates yields coefficients that can be difficult to interpret. Rather than discussing the size of the coefficients, it can be helpful to consider the statistical impact of each variable on the president's choice of an actual nominee. In discussing the analysis, we can use President Reagan's elevation of Justice William Rehnquist to the position of chief justice in 1986, upon Chief Justice Warren Burger's decision to retire.

When President Reagan deliberated on a candidate to fill Burger's vacancy, he seriously considered three candidates: Associate Justice of the Supreme Court William Rehnquist, and two judges from the U.S. Court of Appeals for the District of Columbia Circuit, Robert Bork and Antonin Scalia. The selection model correctly predicts that Justice Rehnquist would be Reagan's choice with a baseline probability of 0.452. To examine the effects of the significant independent variables, we can manipulate Justice Rehnquist's characteristics while holding the other variables constant and examine the probability that he would still be President Reagan's choice.

From the results in Table 1.1, we can see that presidents do choose candidates with an eye toward lessening their uncertainty about their nominee's future behavior. Consistent with the predictions of the informational strategy, presidents choose candidates who are more ideologically proximate than the other members of the shortlist. William Rehnquist was President Reagan's most ideologically proximate candidate included on the shortlist. But had his

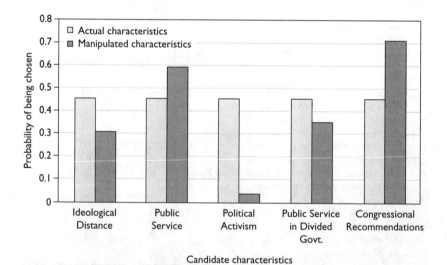

Figure 1.1 Probability of William Rehnquist being chosen as chief justice.

ideology been at the mean distance of all candidates from all presidents included in the data set, the likelihood that he would have been the president's choice drops more than ten percentage points, to 31%.

A candidate's experience in the public sector has a similar effect on the president's choice. Justice Rehnquist had two years of public sector service (in the Justice Department). This was lower than the average candidate considered across all nominations included in the data set. Had he instead served the average number of years in the public sector (six) the likelihood that President Reagan would have chosen him for the chief justice's position is even greater—a nearly 60% probability.

As one can see from Table 1.1, whether a candidate had a history of prior political activism was a significant factor in presidents' choices. However, contrary to my expectation if presidents pursued an information strategy, politically active candidates were much *less* likely to be appointed. The variable is statistically significant but in the opposite direction than what I expected. It seems that strategic presidents do see political activism as a telling characteristic, but it is perhaps too revealing in terms of making the candidate susceptible to confirmation difficulties. Thus, the way in which political activism is important seems to support a political rather than an informational strategy.

The analysis also provides support for the theory that when presidents are under relatively greater institutional constraints, they lessen their uncertainty over the confirmation environment by pursuing a political strategy. When the opposition party controls the Senate and the president is faced with relatively more stringent institutional constraints, they are more likely to choose candidates strategically so as to improve the nominee's confirmation prospects. They are willing to risk greater uncertainty over a candidate's future behavior to gain greater certainty of garnering confirmation.

For example, if President Reagan had considered Justice William Rehnquist's two years of public service during a period of divided government he would have been less likely to choose Rehnquist as the next chief justice. Although Rehnquist's service lessened Reagan's uncertainty over his future judicial behavior, it also would have lessened the uncertainty of senators who might have opposed that future behavior. The probability that Reagan would have chosen Rehnquist would have fallen from the baseline of 45% to 31%.

Another factor also bears a significant influence on presidents' nomination decisions. Consistent with my expectation of presidents pursuing a political strategy, they are more likely to choose candidates who have been recommended by Members of Congress. Given the institutional requirement for Senate confirmation, this seems quite reasonable. Presidents concerned with clearing the confirmation hurdle might improve their candidate's prospects by listening to recommendations made by Members of Congress. Had Justice Rehnquist been recommended by Members of Congress, the likelihood he would have been chosen would have increased to over 70%.

The lack of one particularly prominent variable in the literature on judicial nominations, judicial experience, to achieve statistical significance is worth mentioning. For appointments to the U.S. Supreme Court, judicial experience is typically thought to be important in selection decisions. However, according to this analysis, it is not a significant factor in the president's choice of a nominee from the shortlist. We should be cautious, however, in thinking that judicial experience does not matter. As mentioned above, Elena Kagan's nomination in 2010 was the first in nearly 30 years in which the candidate did not have federal court experience. However, in that time period presidents have also greatly restricted their serious consideration of candidates to those with federal court experience. For example, since 1975 over 75% of the candidates on presidents' shortlists had federal court experience. Thus, the likely explanation for this somewhat surprising finding is that a candidate's experience on the federal bench did little to set him apart from his colleagues on the president's shortlist.

The Final Choice

In the end, it should not be surprising to us that presidents act strategically to appoint candidates about whom they have the most certainty in terms of future behavior on the Supreme Court and about whose confirmation prospects they feel most confident. When presented with the relatively fewer institutional constraints that accompany appointments made under unified government control, presidents seek to maximize their certainty of candidates' future behavior. However, under the more restrictive condition of garnering confirmation by an opposition-controlled Senate, they are more likely to focus on securing the candidate's confirmation. However, this analysis is unique in the literature on presidents' selection decisions in that it pursues a theoretical framework to empirically analyze the determinants of the presidents' choices. Utilizing data from presidential archives provides rare insight into presidents' deliberations and the context in which these choices are made.

There are certainly distinctive and idiosyncratic aspects of each of the selection decisions discussed above. But that fact need not prevent us from using a theoretical lens to systematically examine the ways that institutional and political conditions shape all presidents' selection decisions. Doing so gives us greater leverage on how and why certain candidates emerge as the presidents' choices for the Court. For example, it seems clear that our current political landscape would look quite different had Judge Bork been President Reagan's choice for chief justice in 1986 instead of William Rehnquist. Given the importance of the Court's membership for the legal and policy decisions that emerge, understanding why one candidate is chosen over another is crucial for understanding our broader political system.

Notes

1 For a more fully developed explanation and analysis of this theoretical approach, see Nemacheck (2007).

2 For an extensive discussion of the process of developing a shortlist, see Nemacheck (2007, chapter 4).

3 Although hearings are now so commonplace as to seem required, this has not always been the case. Harlan Fisk Stone was the first nominee to testify at his own confirmation hearing in 1925 and open public hearings were not considered the norm until the mid-1940s (Rutkus and Bearden 2006). It was not until 1981, with Justice O'Connor's confirmation, that a hearing was televised (Comiskey 2004).

4 Of these 31 nominations, the Senate rejected 19 through votes, 11 of the nominations were withdrawn or postponed, and there was one nomination on which the Senate took no action.

5 Epstein *et al.* (2007b, Table 4–15, update by the author).

6 United States Constitution, Article III, Section 1.

7 Here I am only concerned with power division between the White House and the Senate, not the House of Representatives, since the latter does not have a constitutional role in the judicial appointment process.

8 See Nemacheck (2007) for a fuller discussion of strategy in the selection process.

9 For a very detailed discussion of this process, see Nemacheck (2007, chapter 3).

10 A compilation of these shortlists can be found in Nemacheck (2007, appendix).

11 The importance of relying on presidents' papers or first-hand accounts of the shortlists instead of relying only on press reports is illustrated by the recent memoir by President Bush and his discussion of whom he considered for the Court. Though it was frequently reported that the president's former White House Counsel and then Attorney General Alberto Gonzales was under consideration for appointment to the seat left vacant by Justice O'Connor, President Bush does not include his name under the list of those candidates seriously considered even though he discusses consulting with Gonzales on the decision (Bush 2010).

Chapter 2

The Role of Public Opinion in Supreme Court Confirmations[1]

Jonathan P. Kastellec, Jeffrey R. Lax, and Justin Phillips

The judiciary is the branch of the federal government most insulated from the public. Unlike the president or Members of Congress, federal judges do not have to stand for election—they are appointed to the bench and serve lifetime terms. Justices on the Supreme Court do not even worry about securing a promotion to a higher court. This leaves them largely unconstrained in their decision-making, which ultimately reaches into some of society's most important and controversial policy areas.

Judicial independence has obvious advantages. It leaves the justices free from improper influence, free to make impartial decisions, and free to protect the rights of unpopular minorities. "Too much" independence, however, could work against the democratic principle of popular rule. If Supreme Court justices frequently overturn the actions of the elected branches or issue decisions that are opposed by the people, concerns will inevitably be raised that the Court is thwarting public will and undermining the responsiveness of the American political system.

Scholars of political science have long debated whether Supreme Court justices are influenced by public opinion (Flemming and Wood 1997; Giles, Blackstone, and Vining 2008; Mishler and Sheehan 1993). If they are, concerns about the counter-majoritarian nature of the Court would be mitigated somewhat. There is another, but less noticed, way in which these concerns could be allayed: if the public could influence not only how the justices vote, but who sits on the Court in the first place. The decision to seat a justice is in the hands of the president and the Senate, but electoral incentives, particularly for senators, can tie the Court back to the public. Senators must eventually stand for re-election, which gives them an incentive to pay close attention to the views of their constituents, especially when casting a high profile roll call vote for or against a nominee to the Supreme Court.[2]

In this chapter, we ask whether public opinion influences the votes of individual senators when they vote on Supreme Court nominees, and thus whether it affects who ultimately sits on the Court. Using national public opinion surveys and advances in estimating opinion at the state level, we generate measures of state-level public support for 11 recent nominees. With the help of regression analysis, we then see if constituent opinion is a significant predictor of senators' confirmation votes. We find that it is, even when accounting for well-known influences on roll call voting, such as partisanship and ideology. Our results establish a strong and systematic link between constituent opinion and voting on Supreme Court nominees. These results have important implications for confirmation politics specifically and more generally for larger debates about representation and responsiveness in legislatures.

Linking Constituent Opinion and Confirmation Votes

One might wonder whether the public can actually play the meaningful role in confirmation politics that we suggested above. There are three elements that are necessary to create a meaningful connection between the American public and the identity of those individuals who sit on the Supreme Court: knowledge, salience, and attention.

First, does the public know enough to play a role in confirmation politics, particularly with respect to senatorial voting? It is commonly thought that the American public has only very minimal knowledge of the Supreme Court. Indeed, surveys often find that large majorities of respondents cannot name a single justice. We now know that this conclusion is overstated, if not simply incorrect. Citizens tend to know about court decisions that affect them or issues they care about. They are also able to able to answer basic knowledge questions about the Court as an institution, such as the method by which justices are selected, the length of their terms, and whether or not the Court has the "last say" when it comes to interpreting the Constitution (Gibson and Caldeira 2009a).

Of course, general knowledge is less important than whether citizens actually pay attention to Supreme Court nominations—in fact they do. By the time a nominee comes up for a roll call vote, most Americans can say where they stand on her nomination. For instance, in the days prior to the confirmation votes of Justices Clarence Thomas and Justice Samuel Alito, 95% and 88% of survey respondents, respectively, held an opinion either for or against confirmation (Gibson and Caldeira 2009c; Gimpel and Wolpert 1996). Importantly, these opinions appear to be reasonably well developed. Research shows that they are shaped by a survey respondent's ideology, partisanship, and policy preferences as well as the whether the respondent views the nominee as having the characteristics of a good judge (Gibson and Caldeira 2009a). The public's views on nominee confirmation seem connected to the very same influences as opinion on many other political issues from voting to policy support.

The second element is salience: if the public did not care about confirmation votes, then lawmakers might not pay attention to their constituents' views. However, many Americans do care about such votes. For example, during the Alito nomination, 75% of Americans thought it important that their senators vote "correctly" (Gibson and Caldeira 2009a). Using 1992 Senate election data, Wolpert and Gimpel (1997) showed that voters nationwide factored their senator's confirmation vote into their own vote choice. Such findings suggest that Americans know far more about the Court, pay far more attention to confirmation politics, and hold their senators far more accountable for confirmation votes than has often been assumed.

Finally, the third element is attention: do senators monitor and care about what the public thinks? Theories of legislator responsiveness to constituent opinion would suggest that the answer is "yes." While the goals of Members of Congress are multifaceted, the desire for re-election has long been established as a powerful driver, if not the primary driver, of congressional behavior (Mayhew 1974). Although six-year terms provide senators with greater insulation than representatives, a re-election-minded senator will constantly consider how his votes, particularly highly visible ones, may affect his approval back home. While the outcomes of many Senate votes, such as spending bills or the modification of a statute, are ambiguous or obscured in procedural detail, the result of a vote on a Supreme Court nomination is stark: either the nominee is confirmed, allowing her to serve on the nation's highest court, or she is rejected, forcing the president to name another candidate. In this process, note Watson and Stookey (1995, 19), "there are no amendments, no riders and [in recent decades] no voice votes; there is no place for the senator to hide. There are no outcomes where everybody gets a little of what they want. There are only winners and losers." Accordingly, a vote on a Supreme Court nominee presents a situation in which a senator is likely to consider constituent views very carefully.

Indeed, history contains ominous warnings for senators who ignore what their constituents want. In 1991, Senator Alan Dixon of Illinois was one of only 11 Democrats who voted for the confirmation of Clarence Thomas, who was narrowly confirmed by a vote of 52 to 48. The next year, Carol Moseley Braun, despite being virtually unknown, defeated Dixon in the Democratic primary, principally campaigning against his vote to confirm Thomas (McGrory 1992). That same year, Senator Arlen Specter of Pennsylvania, a Republican at the time, nearly lost his Senate seat when liberal women's rights organizations mobilized to defeat him after he voted to confirm Thomas.

Even when an unpopular vote does not lead to immediate retribution by the voters, it can still arise as a campaign issue years later. For instance, in a bid to unseat Specter in the 2004 Republican primary, challenger Pat Toomey invoked Specter's vote against Robert Bork 17 years earlier. Specter was one of only six Republican senators to cast a vote against Bork, a nominee of President Reagan who was defeated after a highly combative nomination fight between, on one side, the Republican administration of President Reagan and its Republican allies in the Senate, and Democratic senators on the other.

Of course, senators can only follow public opinion if they know what the public thinks. How do senators take the pulse of their constituents on

Supreme Court nominees? Public opinion polls help inform senators, as do more direct forms of communication such as phone calls and letter writing. Interest groups also play an important role both in shaping constituency preferences and informing senators of these preferences: "Interest groups attempt to mold senators' perceptions of the direction, intensity and electoral implications of constituency opinion" (Caldeira and Wright 1998). They organize letter-writing campaigns and encourage the public to contact their senator. As part of their lobbying efforts, interest groups also directly convey information about the direction and intensity of constituent opinion. It is thus likely that most senators will have a good idea of where their constituents stand when voting on a Supreme Court nominee.

Given this, it is no surprise that presidents often "go public" in the hope of shifting public opinion on their nominees (Johnson and Roberts 2004). For example, in 1969, Richard Nixon's White House actively worked to shift public opinion on Clement Haynsworth and Ronald Reagan's White House launched a "major (though largely unsuccessful) public relations offensive to build support for [Robert Bork]" in 1987 (Maltese 1995, 87–88). Indeed, "one of the crucial elements in confirmation strategies concerns how public opinion will be managed and manipulated" (Gibson and Caldeira 2009c).

Measuring Constituency Opinion

While there are reasons to believe that constituent opinions matter when it comes to confirmation votes it has been very difficult for scholars to evaluate this prediction. The reason is straightforward: most polls that gauge public support for a Supreme Court nominee are conducted by national survey organizations and are only designed to measure public sentiment at the national level. These polls do not sample enough respondents from each state to make cross-state comparisons possible or even to say anything meaningful about public opinion in a given state. Indeed, an average-sized national survey is likely to include just a few people from smaller population states, such as New Hampshire, Vermont, and Wyoming.

Fortunately, we are able to overcome this limitation by using a new methodological technique. Our first step was to gather national survey data. We began by seeing how much polling data exists on Supreme Court nominees, going back as far as possible. To accomplish this, we searched the Roper Center's *iPoll* electronic archive, which is a terrific resource for finding survey data on almost any topic.[3] As it turns out, while Supreme Court nominations have been high salience events throughout U.S. history, not until very recently were polls systematically conducted on Supreme Court nominees. Indeed, we could not find a single poll conducted on the nomination of Justice Antonin Scalia—a fact that is very surprising considered in hindsight, given Scalia's rather notable and controversial tenure on the Court.

The survey questions we rely upon directly ask each respondent whether he or she supports confirmation. An example is the following question from a CBS/*New York Times* poll (2006) conducted after President Bush had nominated Samuel Alito to the Court, but before the Senate vote on his nomination: "Should the Senate vote to confirm Samuel Alito as a Justice of the U.S. Supreme Court, or vote against Alito, or can't you say?" Our search left us with us 11 nominees for whom sufficient polling data are available. Sandra Day O'Connor, William Rehnquist (his nomination for chief justice in 1986), Robert Bork, David Souter, Clarence Thomas, Ruth Bader Ginsburg, Stephen Breyer, John Roberts, Samuel Alito, Harriet Miers, and Sonia Sotomayor. Of these, all but Miers received a vote on the floor of the Senate (Miers withdrew before her nomination came up for a vote). For nominees who are featured in only a handful of polls, we gathered every poll that asked about respondents' views on the nominee and contained suitable information on individual respondents. For nominees with a large number of such polls, we retained polls as close to their confirmation vote as possible. This procedure helped ensure as much as possible that our estimates would tap state opinion as it existed at the time a senator cast his vote.

Our goal was to estimate support for confirmation for every state-nominee pair—that is, state-level opinion for each of the 50 states for every nominee. All of these polls we found, however, were conducted on the national level, so we are still left with the problem of how to develop accurate *state-level* estimates of public opinion on the nominees. To accomplish this, we use statistical models to translate the data from the national polls into state-level estimates. Specifically, we use a technique known as multi-level regression and poststratification or MRP (Gelman and Little 1997; Park, Gelman, and Bafumi 2006). While the underlying method relies on fairly sophisticated statistical techniques, the idea behind MRP is fairly intuitive. Basically, this method uses the information we have in the survey data and from other sources to build an accurate picture of what is going on in each state. After all, in a survey, we do not just know *how many people* hold a certain opinion—we know *which people* hold that opinion. We know their demographic characteristics such as age and education. MRP makes use of this information in a particular way.

MRP proceeds in two stages. In the first stage, individual survey responses and regression analysis are used to estimate the opinions of different types of people. This is the "multilevel regression" part of MRP, which is a version of traditional regression analysis, except that the hierarchical nature of the data is explicitly modeled (for example, citizens are one level of analysis but citizens are grouped into different states, which are another level of analysis). These opinions are treated as being a function of individuals' demographic and geographic characteristics. That is, we evaluate Americans' support for a given nominee, or the "dependent variable" in MRP, as function of these characteristics, or the "independent variables."

The demographic variables we employ are age, education, gender, and race; for geography we employ a respondent's state and region (and some extra information about state demographic composition). The estimates from this regression tell us the probability that a particular type of person will want to confirm a given nominee. For example, for Justice Alito, our model estimates that among white males in Utah who were older than 64 and had a college degree, 76% supported the confirmation of Justice Alito (among those who had an opinion). By contrast, our model estimates such support at only 23% among black females in New York of age 18–29 with a college degree. For every "type" of person in the United States (specifically, there are 4,896 "demographic-geographic" types in our analysis), we can estimate the probability of support.

The second stage of MRP is poststratification, which is just a fancy word for taking the weighted average of a series of numbers generated through some process. Based on data from the U.S. Census, we know what proportion of a given state's population was comprised by every demographic-geographic type in a year relatively close to a particular nomination. For example, the subset of Utah residents mentioned above comprised 1.6% of the state's total population in 2000, while the subset of New York residents comprised 0.2%. Within each state, we simply take the level of support for a nominee across every demographic-geographic type, and weight each level by the frequency of the type in the population. So the Utah subset would count about eight times as much in estimating Utah's overall support for Alito as does the New York subset for estimating that state's overall support. Finally, we add up these weighted estimates in each state to get a measure of overall state-level support for a nominee. Thus, even though our polls asking about support for Justice Alito polled only 17 people in Wyoming, for example, we can still get a reliable estimate of his support in that state.

Visualizing State-level Opinion

We now have estimates of public opinion in every state for each of our nominees. Before turning to regression models (which we do below), it is always a good idea to simply look at one's data. We do this in Figure 2.1, which depicts the distributions of estimated state support for each nominee. To be clear, each histogram is based on 50 state estimates of support for the nominee. The vertical dashed lines show the average support for each nominee. Both plots reveal that Bork and Miers were the two most unpopular nominees on average, while Souter, O'Connor, Ginsburg, and Breyer enjoyed widespread support. O'Connor, for example, had roughly 90% support across the board, while Bork received much greater support in more conservative states than liberal states. In addition, Bork was the only nominee for whom the balance of public opinion in a significant number of states was opposed to his nomination. Thus, among voters with an opinion, all but one nominee received broad public support on average. The bottom histogram depicts support for

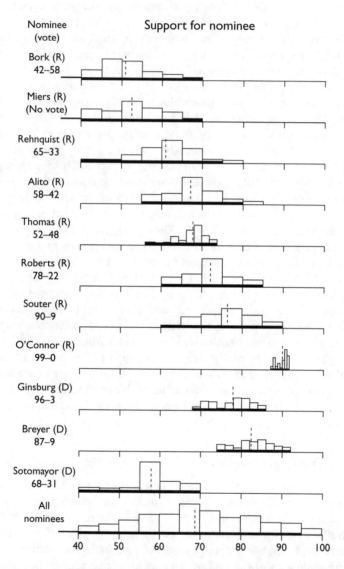

Figure 2.1 The distribution of nominee support (nominees are ordered by party and then increasing mean support. The dashed vertical line depicts mean support).

all nominees combined, revealing that most of the distribution of opinion falls between 60% and 80% support. Despite the overall tendency toward support, the histograms show widespread variation in estimated state support for several nominees. This means for most nominees, senators will be faced with varying levels of support among their constituents.

Roll Call Voting and State-level Opinion

Our next task is to evaluate whether there is a systematic relationship between public opinion and senatorial voting on Supreme Court nominees. From this point on, we exclude Harriet Miers from our analyses, since her nomination was withdrawn before she received a Senate vote (though we return to her below). The remaining 10 nominees in our sample were each voted on by the full Senate, for a total of 990 confirmation votes (10 senators abstained, in total), 74% of which were to approve the nominee. We are studying a dichotomous outcome: senators vote either "yes" or "no" on a nominee. Given this, we are interested in estimating the *probability* of a yes vote and how that probability varies across different levels of public support for a nominee. A good statistical technique for estimating the probability of events is logistic regression, or simply "logit" analysis.

Like all forms of regression, logit has the advantage of being able to assess the impact of one explanation (like public opinion), while taking other confounding explanations into account. After all, many things that influence roll call voting, such as a senator's party affiliation and ideology, could also correlate with public opinion. Thus, we need to see whether public opinion has an *independent effect* on roll call voting, after accounting for other possible influences on senators' voting. If there is a significant relationship between public opinion and votes, even after taking other factors into consideration, we can be confident that public opinion really does "matter."

Previous research in this area (see, e.g., Cameron, Cover, and Segal 1990; Epstein *et al.* 2006) suggests the following variables are important in Supreme Court nominations:

Quality: nominees to the Court can and do vary in quality. A nominee who is deemed to be more qualified is likely to receive more votes for confirmation. (Harriet Miers' nomination, for example, foundered in large part due to concerns over her lack of legal experience.) The measure of quality we use is based on a content analysis of newspaper editorials written during a nominee's confirmation process (Segal and Cover 1989).

Ideological distance between the senator and a nominee: a senator is more likely to support a nominee who is "closer" to him ideologically. We use a measure of distance that uses an institutional bridging technique that combines "ideal point" estimates of senators and nominees to place them on the same scale (Epstein *et al.* 2006).

President's party: coded 1 if the senator is a co-partisan of the president. Senators are more likely to approve a nominee appointed by a president of the same party.

Presidential capital: to measure presidential capital we use public approval of the president, based on the most recent Gallup poll taken before a nominee's confirmation vote.

Table 2.1 Explaining roll call voting (the table presents two logistic regression models of roll call voting. The first number in each pair is a logit coefficient; the number in parentheses is the standard error of that coefficient. '*' indicates that the coefficient is statistically different from zero (at p<0.05))

	Model (1)	Model (2)
Opinion	3.7* (0.5)	3.5* (0.5)
Quality	2.0* (0.4)	2.0* (0.4)
Ideological distance	−2.5* (0.4)	−2.5* (0.5)
Same party	3.2* (0.5)	3.3* (0.5)
Presidential approval	1.4* (0.4)	1.4* (0.4)
Reelection	−	0.1 (0.3)
Opinion x re-election	−	0.6 (0.8)
Intercept	1.3 (0.2)	1.2 (0.2)

Results

The results of the full regression analysis appear in Table 2.1. Before turning to the specifics of the model, however, we graph the basic statistical relationships between key variables of interest. We focus on the relationships between confirmation votes and constituent opinion, a senator's partisanship, and the ideological distance between a senator and a nominee. Figure 2.2 depicts constituent opinion on the x-axis (the share of a state's voters who support confirmation) and ideological distance on the y-axis; the open circles denote "no" votes, while the dark circles denote "yes" votes. From the top panel, which depicts this information for all senators, it is evident that few senators vote against nominees who have high levels of public support. For nominees with less public support, senators are likely to vote "yes" when nominees are ideologically close. By contrast, a senator facing a nominee who is less popular in his state and is ideologically distant from him will usually vote against confirmation. "Yes" votes and "no" votes can be roughly divided by a diagonal cut-line: the dashed line in each plot is the estimated cut-line, based on a simple logistic regression invoking distance and opinion as predictors, showing where the estimated probability of a positive confirmation vote is 50%.

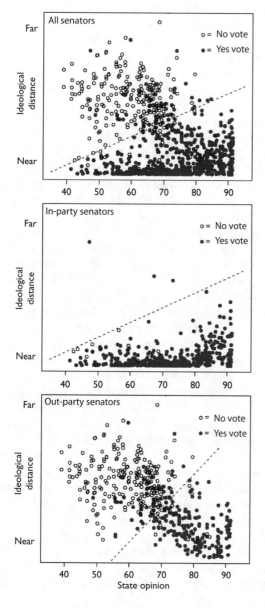

Figure 2.2 Public opinion, ideological distance, partisanship, and roll call voting on Supreme Court nominees (the open circles denote "no" votes, while the closed circles denote "yes" votes. The dashed line shows an estimated cut-line between "yes" and "no" votes (based on a logistic regression using just distance and opinion as predictors)).

How does partisanship affect these relationships? The second panel in Figure 2.2 depicts only senators of the president's party (sometimes referred to as "in-party" senators). As the graph makes clear, "no" votes by in-party senators are very rare, but are undertaken only when the nominee is relatively unpopular in the senator's home state. The voting patterns of out-party senators exhibit a starker pattern than that seen for all senators. Senators from the opposition party almost always reject unpopular nominees. For moderately to highly popular nominees, ideological distance is crucial: more moderate members of the opposition party do support nominees with moderate support, while more ideologically distant members often vote "no."

We now turn to a multiple logistic regression analysis to systematically assess the influence of opinion, while also accounting for the variables mentioned above. Table 2.1 presents two regression models. We are first interested in evaluating the sign of each coefficient in the model, which tells us in what direction the dependent variable moves as the independent variable associated with that coefficient increases.[4] For example, the coefficient of 2.0 on *Quality* indicates that as a nominee's quality increases, a senator is more likely to vote for that nominee. (Because we are working with a logit regression model, which is non-linear, as opposed to a linear model, like ordinary least squares regression, the coefficient is not directly interpretable in terms of its magnitude. Because of this, we take additional steps below to show the substantive effect of opinion.) We are also interested in the statistical significance of each coefficient. The numbers in parentheses depict the standard error for each coefficient. If a coefficient is accompanied by an asterisk (*), that means it is large enough relative to its standard error that we can say it is "statistically significant," or statistically different from zero (these are equivalent). This means that if the true relationship between the independent variable of interest and roll call voting were actually zero, it is highly unlikely (less than 5%) that we would see a coefficient that large, relative to the size of its standard error.

In our regression results, the coefficient on *Opinion* is statistically significant, and, as it turns out below, of a sizable magnitude in terms of its substantive effect. This result demonstrates that public opinion has a robust influence on Supreme Court confirmation politics—as public support of a nominee increases, senators are more likely to support her, even after controlling for well-known predictors of the vote. The estimated coefficients on the other predictors match results from previous studies. A senator is more likely to support a nominee appointed by a president of the same party, ideologically near to him, and of higher quality. Increased presidential approval also increases the chances of a "yes" vote.

Before turning to the substantive importance of public opinion on Supreme Court confirmation votes, we consider whether the effect of opinion varies across the electoral calendar. The main reason senators care about public opinion is that they care about re-election. Thus, we might expect opinion to matter more when a nomination occurs close to a senator's re-election date. Model 2 in Table 2.1 investigates this possibility by including an interaction between state opinion and an indicator variable, *Re-election*, coded 1 if a vote on a nominee took place within two years of the senators' next re-election. Interpreting coefficients when there is an interaction term in a model is tricky, and requires careful evaluation of the "main effects," the independent variables that go into the interaction term, and the interaction itself. The coefficient on *Opinion* in Model 2 now tells us the effect of opinion when the senator is *not* nearing re-election (that is, when *Re-election* equals 0). That coefficient is unchanged from Model 1, meaning opinion matters even early on in a senator's term. If the coefficient on *Opinion* × *Re-election* were positive and statistically significant, that would mean that opinion matters *even more* as an election approaches. The coefficient on the interaction term, however, is small and not statistically different from zero, meaning there is no interactive effect between opinion and re-election. Thus, we can conclude that the effect of opinion is more related to senators' long-term interests in maintaining constituent support, rather than a more short-term focus on whether a vote contrary to such support will have immediate negative consequences.

Substantive Importance of Public Opinion on Votes

To flesh out our findings about the role of public opinion in confirmation politics, we use a technique known as generating predicted probabilities. Based on the results of our logit models, we can get the predicted probability that a senator votes yes under any possible combination of the independent variables that we specify. Figure 2.3 does this in four ways, with each plot highlighting a shift in a different independent variable of interest. In all panels, public opinion is the x-axis and ranges from 35% to 95% support (the approximate range of our opinion estimates). The non-shaded regions depict the range of public opinion between low opinion (one standard deviation below the mean) and high opinion (one standard deviation above)—that is, the range where most observations fall. The predicted probability of voting yes is shown on the y-axis. Across curves, at a given level of opinion, we can compare the effect of changing the predictor noted in the panel description.

Public Opinion and Nominee Quality

In the top panel of Figure 2.3, we show how the effect of public opinion varies across nominee quality. One might suspect that public opinion simply mirrors nominee quality. While the two are positively correlated, the graph shows that the probability of a "yes" vote varies substantially across public opinion levels even for nominees of similar quality. (In addition, recall from Figure 2.1 that there is substantial variation in state-level opinion *within* each nominee; this variation, of course, cannot be explained by nominee quality.) For popular nominees, quality has almost no effect, as the probability of a "yes"

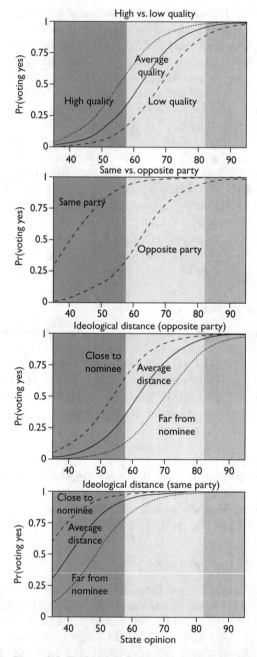

Figure 2.3 The predicted effects of opinion on roll call voting (each panel shows the predicted probability of a senator voting yes on confirmation, across the range of state-level public opinion, for different levels of the other predictors. All curves

vote is near one. For less popular nominees, however, the difference in probability of a "yes" vote is substantial. Low-quality and unpopular nominees are much less likely to be supported than either popular or high-quality nominees. Quality levels also affect the impact of opinion. For a high-quality nominee, roughly 50% public support in a state yields a 50–50 chance of a "yes" vote from that state's senator. A low-quality nominee needs roughly 65% support to have the same chance.

Public Opinion and Partisanship

The second panel in Figure 2.3 shows the predicted probabilities for same- and opposite-party senators, with respect to the president. Same-party senators are already highly likely to support a nominee, at least over the central range of opinion. There is a drop-off in same-party senator support only once the nominee is significantly unpopular in the state. For opposite-party senators, however, public opinion strongly influences the probability of a vote to confirm over the central range of opinion; a "yes" vote only approaches certainty among more popular nominees. To put this another way, same- and opposite-party senators (holding ideological distance constant) react similarly to high-opinion nominees, but low-opinion nominees are very vulnerable to senator opposition, especially among members of the opposition party.

Public Opinion and Ideological Distance

The last two panels of Figure 2.3 display the impact of ideological distance, first among opposite-party senators and then among same-party members. Beginning with the former, it is clear that public opinion is most important for ideologically distant senators, who are only likely to support distant nominees who are popular in their state. More moderate senators of the opposition party, on the other hand, are likely to support nominees with weak to moderate public approval. The effects of opinion over its typical range illustrates this difference. When the senator and nominee are ideologically close a swing from low opinion to high simply increases the probability of a yes vote from 85% to nearly 100%. For ideologically distant senators/nominees, the spread

derived from Model I in Table 2.I. The default value of each continuous variable is its mean. "Low" values are one standard deviation below this; "high" values are one standard deviation above. We assume unless otherwise noted that the senator is of the opposite party, that the president is weak, and that the nominee is otherwise average (random effect set to zero). The non-shaded regions depict the range of public opinion between low opinion (one standard deviation below the mean) and high opinion (one standard deviation above)—that is, the range where most observations fall).

is from under 10% to nearly 80%. Thus, ideologically distant senators of the opposition party are very sensitive to public opinion, average-distance senators are still sensitive, and ideologically compatible ones are less so. For same-party senators, we see that ideological distance only influences their votes among very unpopular nominees. As a nominee's state approval exceeds 60%, a "yes" vote by an in-party senator approaches certainty.

Counterfactuals

One additional way to assess the importance of public opinion in confirmation politics is to make counterfactual "predictions" had the public felt differently about the nominees. We ask three questions based on such counterfactuals.

Should Bork Blame the Public?

Robert Bork received far less public support for confirmation than did Samuel Alito (see Figure 2.1). What if Bork had received as much public support as Alito? We applied the coefficients from a more comprehensive model (not reported here) to predict votes for each of the senators who voted on Bork's confirmation, but using the state-by-state opinion estimates from Alito instead of from Bork (leaving all else the same). Bork received only 42 votes in his favor. If he were as popular as Alito, however, with the state-by-state popularity of Alito, we predict that he would have been confirmed with 53 votes.

Justice Alito's confirmation too seemed at risk, at least for a time. He eventually received 58 votes, the same number of votes cast *against* Bork. We asked whether Bork would have been confirmed if as popular as Alito—what about the reverse? With state-by-state opinion at Bork's levels, we would predict that Alito would have lost some support, but still would have been confirmed with 54 votes. This suggests that attempts by the Democrats to investigate Alito further and shift the public's stance on confirmation might have proved futile. Bork and Alito had similar quality levels and, on average, were roughly as compatible ideologically with the senators, but otherwise the situations were quite different. Alito faced a Senate with 12 more Republicans than did Bork, giving him a larger base of support against any opinion drops. In terms of confirmation (rather than individual senator votes), the partisan distribution of the Senate trumped the effects of opinion—Alito's nomination might have suffered a different fate if it had taken place after the Democrats took control of the Senate following the 2006 elections.

Did the Public Confirm Justice Thomas?

Justice Thomas also faced a tough confirmation fight, eventually being confirmed with 52 votes after Anita Hill's allegations nearly derailed him. Thomas was more popular a nominee on average than was Bork, and a bit more popular than Alito. Did this make a difference in his confirmation vote? What if he had been as unpopular as Bork? Our prediction, applying Bork's state-by-state opinion level instead of his own, is that Thomas would have received only 40 votes—a "landslide" vote against confirmation. Public opinion, it seems, was crucial to his successful confirmation.

Could Harriet Miers Have Won Confirmation?

The nomination of Harriet Miers was unique in many ways, particularly in the manner in which senators of the president's party signaled their opposition. Nevertheless, her nomination is still useful for exploring the potential magnitude of opinion effects. In October 2005, President Bush nominated Miers to replace Justice O'Connor. Three weeks later, he withdrew the nomination, after vocal opposition from Republicans. Miers was one of the least popular nominees in our sample; her average state-level support was 52% among those with an opinion, ranging from a low of 38% in California to 65% support in North Dakota. On average, her support was similar to Bork's, with less variation across states. Her quality score was 0.36, lower than any of our other nominees. Neither her quality nor opinion levels would be good omens for a successful confirmation, as compared to Alito, for example. On the other hand, because she was more ideologically moderate than Alito, her average ideological distance from senators (0.14) was slightly less than the average across our nominees (0.18) and clearly less than the average for Alito (0.21) (her distance was on par with Souter or Ginsburg's average ideological compatibility with the senators). This factor would push in her favor in comparison to Alito who, recall, wound up with 58 votes.

First, assume that Miers was an otherwise average nominee. Our best prediction is that she would have squeaked by with 51 votes, all from Republican senators. Of course, the opposition from members of her own party, as well as her poor performances in meetings with senators (Greenburg 2007, 278–281), indicate that Miers was a well below average nominee. We take this weakness into account by assuming she was a relatively "weak" nominee, while keeping her actual public opinion as is. Given this, our best prediction would be that she would only have received 32 votes—a landslide against confirmation.

Could greater public opinion have saved her nomination? To answer this, we next predicted senator votes assuming the public had supported Miers to the same extent they did Alito, while still assuming she was a weak nominee. We predict she would have gained confirmation with 53 votes. The gain in public opinion would approximately offset the negative nominee effect.

These counterfactuals clearly illustrate the pivotal role of public opinion in confirmation politics. Shifts in public support can mean the difference between a Justice Bork and a Justice Kennedy. And had the former taken the bench instead of the latter, it is certain that Supreme Court doctrine in several areas would look a lot more conservative than it does today, particularly on hot-button issues like abortion and the death penalty.

Conclusion

Political scientists have long known that legislators tend to follow public opinion, for fear of going against the public will and risking being thrown out of office. But despite the importance of Supreme Court nominations, little attention has been paid to the relationship between the public, nominees, and senators on these crucial votes. Our research has sought to remedy this comparative neglect.

Our answer to our main question—does public opinion drive senatorial confirmation voting?—is a resounding yes. Constituent opinion, measured at the state level, is a strong predictor of a senator's roll call vote even after controlling for other known influences. Indeed, public opinion is important for all nominees, including those that are high-quality and those named by strong presidents. Senators clearly worry that election returns may follow Supreme Court confirmations. This means that a process which has traditionally been thought to be driven largely by political elites is responsive to the mass public as well. Even the six-year terms of senators do not make them invulnerable to public pressure on issues of this magnitude and salience. Of course, senators do respond to other forces besides public opinion, most notably their own preferences and partisanship. That senators respond to these forces suggests that they are sometimes willing to partially "shirk" the desires of their constituents, in pursuit of their own ideological or other goals.

Still, these results tie the Supreme Court back to majority will. The public's influence over justices *after* confirmation may be unclear, but we find strong evidence of influence over confirmation itself. This means that the Court is even less likely to fall outside the mainstream of American public opinion than would be the case if the public's influence over the Court's membership were realized solely through the blunt instrument of election of senators and the president.

Our work, however, is not done. Like most sciences, political science is an incremental discipline, in which researchers continually build on prior findings (as we did here) to advance the current state of knowledge on a particular subject. Answers to one question often lead to a subsequent question. We have shown that senators respond to public opinion. This naturally leads to the question of *whose* opinions senators follow, since different citizens within a state are likely to hold different views on a range of policy questions, including Supreme Court nominations. In subsequent work, we have sought to break down public opinion by partisan subgroups: that is, examining how opinion varies across Democrats, Independents, and Republicans in the electorate. This has revealed that opinion across party identification frequently diverges, as citizens from the same party as the president are much more likely to support a nominee than citizens not of the president's party.

We have next investigated whether, when opinion diverges, senators are more likely to follow the views of the state as a whole (which can be captured by the opinions of independents), or of their constituents in their own party. We find that when independents and the constituents of the senator's party disagree, senators vote with their party constituents a full 75% of the time, meaning they vote with the state as a whole only 25% of the time. So far, we have also found that senators seem to pay more attention to their fellow partisans even controlling for other influences. (Recall our stories about primary politics earlier to see why they might.)

As a result, the conclusion we have drawn herein about the effect of public opinion tying the Court back to majority may not be so simple, as some opinions may be represented more than others. Thus, while the link between public preferences and confirmation votes is very real, it may also be imperfect. The quality of representation is one of the key questions in political science, and we and other scholars will continue to research it in the years to come.

Notes

1 This chapter is adapted from our article: Kastellec, Lax, and Phillips (2010).
2 For a good overview of the nomination and confirmation process, see Epstein *et al.* (2006). For studies of the relationship between public opinion and senators' votes on the Supreme Court's only African-American justices in history, Thurgood Marshall and Clarence Thomas, see Overby *et al.* (1994) and Overby *et al.* (1992).
3 The archive can be accessed at www.ropercenter.uconn.edu/data_access/ipoll/ipoll. html.
4 Note that we have rescaled the continuous predictors (distance, quality, and approval) by centering them at zero and dividing by two standard deviations. We do this because this makes the coefficients for all continuous and binary predictors comparable on roughly the same scale.

Chapter 3

Campaign Contributions and Judicial Decisions in Partisan and Nonpartisan Elections

Damon M. Cann, Chris W. Bonneau, and Brent D. Boyea

The days of judicial elections being low-salience, sleepy affairs has long passed. In recent years, candidates for judicial office have spent increasingly large sums of money to win elective office. These circumstances led former Solicitor General Ted Olson to refer to judicial fundraising as a "financial arms race" (Biskupic 2009).

Examples of the rising costs of judicial campaigns are abundant. Like contributions to campaigns for other offices, rising costs are tied to efforts to mobilize voters and to fund increasingly expensive advertising campaigns. The result of states using both partisan and nonpartisan judicial elections has been the emergence of increased electoral competition between judicial candidates. Relating to the expense of judicial elections, research shows that the costs of judicial campaigns almost doubled between 1990 and 2004 (Bonneau and Hall 2009). While judicial campaigns in a few states remain low-key affairs, for most states the difference between a generation ago and today represents a stark contrast. To survive a judicial campaign and to pay for expensive television and print ads, judicial candidates now raise considerable amounts of money from larger groups of contributors.

Among contributors, however, the rising tide of judicial campaign costs has not displaced the traditional role of attorneys. Recent studies report that attorneys provide more than a quarter of judicial campaign contributions, with pronounced variation throughout the states (Goldberg *et al.* 2005). As those familiar with judges, candidates, and a state's judicial system, attorneys likely donate money to create access between themselves, their firm, and their state's judges (Bonneau *et al.* 2010). Responding to the expense of judicial campaigns, attorneys in all likelihood seek to remain on even footing with their competition. While evidence of judicial responsiveness has been difficult to consistently uncover (see Cann 2007), the correlation between attorneys and judicial decisions has emerged in several studies (Cann 2007; Champagne 1988; Waltenburg and Lopeman 2000). For attorneys in this period of costly judicial elections, activity in campaigns likely symbolizes concern about the balance between success and failure in the courtroom.

Regarding the costs of judicial campaigns, some scholars have noted the possible benefits of greater campaign spending in judicial elections. One study suggests that voter participation in judicial elections increases as spending increases (Hall and Bonneau 2008), while another shows that these vigorous, expensive campaigns serve to inform voters (Hojnacki and Baum 1992). Nevertheless, there is some evidence that the campaign spending in these elections may diminish the legitimacy of state high courts (Cann and Yates 2008; Gibson 2008; but see Gibson *et al.* 2011). This is likely, at least in part, because of the appearance of quid pro quo exchanges between judges and the individuals who support their campaigns.

A national survey conducted in 2004 by the Justice at Stake Campaign found that 71% of citizens believe that judicial decisions are influenced in some measure by campaign contributions; these high levels of concern among citizens have been confirmed by other scholars (Geyh 2001; Schotland 2001). While citizens' perceptions of courts are important in their own right, we contend that the relationship between dollars and decisions is fundamentally an empirical question, albeit one that proves difficult to answer. This difficulty springs from three primary sources. First, the scope of state judicial systems is broad. The 22 state high courts that select judges by competitive election hear thousands of cases each year. Moreover, campaign finance records reveal that the justices who staff these courts received contributions from tens of thousands of donors, making nationwide data collection a daunting task. Second, the system is no less diverse than it is broad. Some elective states use partisan elections while others employ nonpartisan selection methods. Some state high court justices are elected from districts that constitute only a portion of their state's geography while judges in other states are elected statewide. Term lengths and the requirements for office vary across states, as do procedures for case flow and standards of judicial conduct. Any number of these nuances of state justice systems could amplify, attenuate, or even preclude a hypothesized relationship between campaign contributions and judicial decision-making. As such, studies that seek to reduce the data collection efforts by limiting their investigation to a single state will have results that are fundamentally nongeneralizable.

Perhaps it is the third problem, which we refer to as the problem of reciprocal causality, that has proven the most vexing to scholars. While it is possible that the campaign contributions cause judges to support their benefactors' preferred positions, it is equally plausible that donors simply give to judges who are already ideologically disposed to rule in the contributor's favor. Either of these situations is enough to generate a correlation between contributions and judges' decisions, but the presence of both possibilities makes it more difficult to define the direction of causality. This problem has been eloquently stated by Madhavi McCall (2008) as a question of whether "decisions follow dollars" or "dollars follow decisions." Even if scholars are able to overcome the sizable obstacles of data collection, even for a single state, they must also address the chicken-and-egg problem of whether contributions drive decisions or if the propensity to decide cases in a particular way attracts contributions in order to make a compelling empirical case for the quid pro quo hypothesis.

One approach to resolving these issues involves an instrumental variables statistical approach (e.g. Cann 2007). While potentially useful, that approach requires finding a variable that can be assumed to be related to campaign contributions but unrelated to judges' decisions, a non-trivial problem. We proceed here with a different, but analytically similar, approach, comparing judges' votes and behavior in cases where campaign contributions are present and in cases where they are not.

We first review existing literature on contributions and state high court judges' decisions and then move to three different tests that suggest that in some circumstances, the causal arrow runs from dollars to decisions rather than a judge's propensity to decide in a particular direction causing him/her to attract contributions from donors of a particular ideological bent.

Campaign Contributions and Judicial Decisions

Naturally, we are not the first to consider the relationship between campaign contributions and state supreme court decision-making. One can classify existing empirical studies into several groups based on the nature of the evidence they use to assess the contributions–decisions link. The first set of studies simply shows that campaign contributors frequently appear in the courtroom before the very judges to whom they contributed (Dubois 1986; Hansen 1991). While the actual parties to the case generally do not know in advance that they are likely to have a case before their state high courts, attorneys can typically predict whether they are likely to face a judge during the course of her term, making attorneys (rather than parties to cases) the more likely entity to enter quid pro quo exchanges with judges. While it is true that a substantial percentage of state high court cases involve at least one attorney who contributed to at least one of the judges, the possibility (or even the appearance) of impropriety is not sufficient to show an actual association between contributions and decisions.

A second group of studies strives to provide evidence of a correlation between contributions and decisions. Some of these studies rely primarily on anecdotal evidence. For example, Anthony Champagne (1988) evaluates actions taken by the Texas Commission on Judicial Conduct in cases involving attorneys who had given money or gifts to two state supreme court justices. While such instances are a matter of concern, they by no means demonstrate a widespread influence of money in state courts. Other studies in this vein use larger-scale data collection efforts. For example, Stephen Ware (1999) evaluates the outcomes of arbitration decisions from the Alabama Supreme Court, finding a correlation between judges' funding sources and their rulings. Several other studies show a correlation between campaign contributions and the decisions of judges in the Texas Supreme Court (McCall 2008; McCall and McCall 2006). Still other studies find evidence of a correlation between contributions and decisions in Kentucky, Ohio, and Alabama (Waltenburg and Lopeman 2000), but not in Wisconsin (Cann 2002). While these studies are interesting, they still fall victim, in varying degrees, to the three major obstacles we outlined above that have prohibited scholars from convincingly establishing a causal relationship between contributions and decision-making. With one exception, these studies consider only a single court. While this decision is typically made out of convenience, single-state studies neglect the nuances of interstate institutional variation that could be consequential for the relationship between contributions and decisions. More critically, while the establishment of no correlation rules out the possibility of causality, the studies that find a correlation are unable to demonstrate the direction of causality.

A final group of studies uses aforementioned instrumental variables statistical techniques in an attempt to resolve the vexing problem of causality. One study argues for the use of an instrumental variables probit model, an advanced statistical technique designed to obtain consistent estimates of the effects of variables in reciprocal causality situations (Cann 2007). Applying this method to three state high courts, Bonneau and Cann (2009) find preliminary evidence of a causal effect in some state high courts.

While we applaud the recent advanced statistical efforts as a means of circumventing the reciprocal causality problem, the major drawback of such an approach is that the results are opaque to individuals without advanced statistical training. Moreover, they require the identification of variables that can be reasonably assumed to be correlated with campaign contributions but unrelated to judges' decisions, and it is difficult to assess the validity of that assumption. While we see this sophisticated quantitative work as being useful, in this chapter we discuss several alternative approaches that, while quantitative in nature, are still intuitive and accessible for a broader audience. We present here results of a pilot study of campaign contributions and judicial decisions in three state high courts. While the results are not definitive, we discuss three "suggestive" tests that, when taken together, represent a credible effort to overcome the three major hurdles to a conclusion on the nature of the link between campaign contributions and judicial decisions we outlined above.

General Framework for the Study

As part of an ongoing project, we have gathered data on decisions during the 2005 term of three state supreme courts: Nevada, Texas, and Michigan. The states are diverse on a number of characteristics, including size of the court, partisan vs. nonpartisan selection of judges, term length, and region.

Additionally, our data balance two states where the contributions and decision-making link has not been studied in detail (Michigan and Nevada) with a state that has been the subject of much study (Texas). Collecting data on three states is not a perfect resolution to the problem of the scope of data collection; it represents only a fraction of states that select judges in competitive elections. Nevertheless, this approach represents an improvement over studies that consider this question in a single state.

Moving to a multi-state research design not only increases our sample size, but also begins to give us some leverage over the second major obstacle that studies on this subject have faced: the neglect of interstate institutional variation. While state courts vary in a number of ways, the difference we perceive as being particularly important is the distinction between partisan and nonpartisan elections. Partisan elections breed contentious campaigns marked by issue content and greater campaign spending (Bonneau 2005, 2007; Hall 2001). Under these conditions, judicial candidates seeking to raise substantial sums of campaign funds may be uniquely vulnerable to the influence of campaign contributors. While our three-state sample does not allow us to address the full range of court system variation that may mediate the possible relationship between contributions and decisions, we can assess the effect of this critical variable on the relationship between dollars and decisions. Specifically, we compare our nonpartisan state, Nevada, with a classic partisan state, Texas. Michigan is a quasi-partisan state where parties nominate candidates and campaign vigorously on their behalf but judicial candidates' party identifications do not appear on the ballot. Where individual voters are involved, Michigan is often treated as a nonpartisan state because voters do not have a partisan cue to guide their decisions (Bonneau and Hall 2009; Hall and Bonneau 2006). However, in terms of campaign style, the behavior of judicial candidates, and most critically for the purposes of this chapter the behavior of contributors, Michigan more closely resembles a partisan state. As we evaluate the effects of contributions on decisions, we will regard Michigan as a quasi-partisan state.

Our study requires the compilation and merger of two sets of data. The first is a contributor data set, which has a record for each contribution from attorneys and law firms to each of the judges sitting on the Nevada, Michigan, and Texas supreme courts in the 2005 term. For each judge, the contributions are measured from that judge's most recent election campaign. These data allow us to see who gave how much in contributions to whom. However, in order to determine whether these contributions influenced judges' behavior, we must also create a database of cases and decisions. We developed a set of all cases with full opinions heard in the 2005 terms of the Texas Supreme Court, Michigan Supreme Court, and Nevada Supreme Court. Included in this case database are the judges involved in each case and the attorneys who argued for each party. We focus on attorneys rather than litigants for two reasons. First, it is relatively rare for litigants to have made contributions to judicial candidates. In the three states we studied, 61% of cases involve at least one attorney who contributed to at least one judge who ruled on the case. In contrast, only a handful of parties to these cases made contributions. Second, attorneys have the status as long-term players necessary to make an exchange work. Many attorneys can reliably make a prediction regarding whether they will be likely to litigate a case before a given judge during a six- to nine-year term. In contrast, individual litigants are unlikely to be able to predict their likelihood of being involved in a case before their state supreme court.

While compiling the data set of court cases, we assigned research assistants who did not have access to the contribution data to review each case and determine which party to the case could best be deemed the "liberal" party and which was the "conservative" party. The criteria for coding an outcome as liberal or conservative were those used in Harold Spaeth's Supreme Court database.[1] We then merged the contributor data set with the attorney names in the case data set. We have applied this process to allow us to look at both the case as the level of analysis (the relationship between the case outcome and contributions to all judges hearing the case from all liberal party attorneys and from all conservative party attorneys) and the individual judge's vote as the level of analysis (the relationship between judge voting for the liberal or conservative party and the amount of contributions that judge received from the liberal party's attorneys and the conservative party's attorneys).

With our data in place, we now proceed to a discussion of three empirical tests intended to evaluate whether there is a genuine correlation between dollars and decisions, to determine whether that relationship is actually causal rather than simply correlational and whether that relationship is, as we hypothesized above, more likely to be observed in partisan states than in nonpartisan states.

Empirical Test 1: Less Unanimity

In general, state supreme courts issue a large number of unanimous rulings (Brace and Hall 1990). This is due in part to the absence of intermediate appellate courts in some states as well as the tendency of state supreme courts to be staffed with judges who are ideologically homogeneous. Additionally, some courts appear to have a culture of unanimity, such that dissent is a relatively rare event (Arceneaux, Bonneau, and Brace 2008).[2] However, if judges tend to favor attorneys who contributed to their campaigns, in some instances they will be required to choose between conforming to the norm of unanimity and ruling in favor of the campaign contributor. If campaign contributions influence judges' decisions, we might expect to see more dissent in cases where judges received contributions than in cases where none of the judges received contributions from the attorneys arguing the case.[3]

This test is not a perfect test of the hypothesis that contributions affect judges' decision-making and thus affect unanimity. This is because contributions could be made in a way that reinforces unanimity (e.g. a conservative attorney who gave to liberal judges but not to conservative judges would be making contributions in such a way that would increase unanimity rather than decrease it; similarly, an attorney who gave to all judges regardless of their ideology would be increasing unanimity) or they could be made in a way that diminishes unanimity (e.g. a conservative attorney who gave to conservative judges but not liberal judges would be, if anything, diminishing the chances of a unanimous ruling). Nevertheless, this approach provides a conservative test of the notion that contributions cause decisions, since the test only looks for cases where contributions work against unanimity. We must simply note that this test involves a bias against finding an effect for campaign contributions.

Table 3.1 shows the relationship between unanimity and campaign contributions. In our nonpartisan state, Nevada, there is virtually no difference in the levels of unanimity between cases that involved contributing attorneys and those that did not (this difference is not statistically significant). This supports the notion that campaign contributions are not related to voting decisions in our nonpartisan state. However, in our quasi-partisan state, Michigan, we find a moderately strong relationship between contributions and unanimity rates. In Michigan, half of cases were unanimous when there were no campaign contributions on the case. However, when contributions were present, only about 16% of cases were unanimous. In contrast to Michigan, the fully partisan Texas Supreme Court did not show a relationship between contributions and unanimity. At least in Michigan, something makes cases involving contributions very different from those without contributions in terms of the likelihood of unanimity. While this does not provide concrete proof of contributions influencing outcomes, it is certainly suggestive. It is also partially consistent with our hypothesis that states with a partisan component to their elections are more likely to show a relationship between contributions and decisions than nonpartisan states.

Empirical Test 2: Correlation Among Ideologically Similar Judges

While it is clear from our first suggestive test that judges behave differently in the presence of contributions, our second test takes a somewhat more direct tack. Here we consider the relationship between attorney campaign contributions and the decisions of individual state high court judges. To isolate the effect of contributions on decisions from the effect of ideology, we compare only judges who have the same party-adjusted ideology score (PAJID, as devised by Brace, Langer, and Hall 2000). The PAJID score is a weighted combination of the judge's party identification and the ideology of the citizens in her state at the time of selection and has been shown to be a valid predictor of judges' rulings. Judges with the same PAJID score will have a propensity to

Table 3.1 Campaign Contributions and the Incidence of Unanimous Decisions in Partisan and Nonpartisan States

	Nonpartisan (Nevada)		Quasi-partisan (Michigan)		Partisan (Texas)	
	Contributions present	No contributions	Contributions present	No contributions	Contributions present	No contributions
Unanimous decision	29 82.86%	31 88.57%	7 16.28%	2 50.00%	53 88.33%	21 87.50%
Non-unanimous decision	6 17.14%	4 11.43%	36 83.72%	2 50.00%	7 11.67%	3 12.50%
Total	35 100%	35 100%	43 100%	4 100%	60 100%	24 100%

Note
Cell entries are the number of cases in each cell with column percentages listed below. For Nevada, $\chi^2 = 0.47$, $p = 0.495$. For Michigan, $\chi^2 = 2.689$, $p = 0.101$. For Texas, $\chi^2 = 0.011$, $p = 0.915$.

rule in the same way on the same case in the absence of contributions. This test will allow us to establish the possible correlation between contributions and decisions in the three states we consider. If we find no correlation between contributions and decisions, we would be reasonably confident that contributions do not affect decisions. If we do find a correlation, further examination will be required to establish the direction of causality.

We again make use of our merged data set of contributions and cases in the 2005 terms of Nevada, Michigan, and Texas. Table 3.2 presents the percentage of liberal and conservative decisions reached by individual justices across cases where the liberal party's attorney(s) contributed more, where the conservative party's attorney(s) contributed more, or where both sides contributed the same amount (in most instances this occurs where neither party's attorney made any contributions). In our nonpartisan state, Nevada, judges who received contributions from the conservative party's attorney(s) sided with the conservative party slightly over 57% of the time while judges who received funds from liberal party attorneys still voted for the conservative party 56.5% of the time. The difference is substantively small and statistically insignificant. There is no evidence to support even a correlation between contributions and decisions (much less causality) in our nonpartisan state. In contrast, our quasi-partisan state, Michigan, shows a strong association between dollars and decisions. In cases where the conservative party's attorneys contributed more to a judge than the liberal party's attorneys, the judge voted for the conservative party about 85% of the time. In contrast, when the liberal party's attorneys out-contributed the conservative party's attorneys, the conservative side won only about 31% of the time. In our fully partisan state, Texas, a more modest connection appears, with the conservative party winning 86% of cases where their attorneys out-contributed the liberal party's attorneys. However, attorneys for the conservative party still won about 78% of cases where their attorneys were out-contributed by the liberal party's attorneys. Most importantly, this relationship is not statistically significant.

The appearance of a strong correlation between contributions and judges' decisions in Michigan does not definitively show that the contributions cause the decisions. However, the strong relationship observed in Michigan means that we cannot rule out the possibility of a causal relationship in our partisan states as we can in Nevada and Texas. Coupled with the results from Test 1, it seems that Michigan is different from Nevada and Texas in ways that are not related to method of selection. To test for causality, we advance a final test based on a matching case-control method.

Empirical Test 3: Matching and a Case-Control Approach

If one had deific power, the ideal way to assess the influence of contributions on judicial decisions would be to take a judge, ensure that the judge received

Table 3.2 Campaign Contributions and the Decisions of Individual State Supreme Court Justices in Partisan and Nonpartisan States

	Nonpartisan (Nevada) Contributions			Quasi-partisan (Michigan) Contributions			Partisan (Texas) Contributions		
	Cons. gave more	Same	Lib. gave more	Cons. gave more	Same	Lib. gave more	Cons. gave more	Same	Lib. gave more
Conservative decision	12 57.14%	83 69.75%	13 56.52%	44 84.62%	42 46.15%	6 31.58%	19 86.36%	134 69.79%	14 77.78%
Liberal decision	9 42.86%	36 30.25%	10 43.48%	8 15.38%	49 53.85%	13 68.42%	3 13.64%	58 30.21%	4 22.22%
Total	21 100%	119 100%	23 100%	52 100%	91 100%	19 100%	22 100%	192 100%	18 100%

Note
Cell entries are the number of judges' decisions with column percentages listed below. For Nevada, $\chi^2 = 1.62$, $p = 0.444$. For Michigan, $\chi^2 = 25.52$, $p = 0.001$. For Texas, $\chi^2 = 3.01$, $p = 0.222$.

more contributions from one party than the other, and observe that judge's decisions. Then, were it possible, one would "rewind" the world, replaying the same set of events with the exception that the judge would not receive any contributions. The difference in the judge's ruling between when he or she received the contribution and when he or she did not would be the causal effect of the contribution. Naturally, though, we can never observe the world both ways; we only ever observe world events unfolding such that a judge either does or does not receive a contribution in a single case. Since we can never observe the world both ways, we can never observe the true causal effect. Social scientists refer to this as the fundamental problem of causal inference.[4]

Scholars have developed a number of methods of comparison to circumvent the fundamental problem of causal inference if certain assumptions are met. The basic idea behind the method of comparison, exemplified in the context at hand, is to compare two judges that are similar to each other in all relevant respects except that one received contributions from one party to the case while the other did not. If these two judges vote differently, we have evidence of a causal effect, assuming that the judges are indeed similar in all important respects.

The problem with existing correlational studies of the contributions–decisions link lies in comparing judges where the types of contributions they are likely to receive are different. Further, these differences are correlated with the decisions they ultimately reach even if those decisions are based on their ideology or jurisprudential philosophy rather than the contributions. In other words, correlational studies compare the decisions of liberal judges (who tend to receive contributions from trial lawyers and other types of attorneys) with the decisions of conservative judges (who tend to receive contributions from corporate attorneys or other lawyers); even if the contributions have no genuine effect, the correlation between ideology and contributions could make it appear as though they were related.

We propose to resolve this problem through the application of a matching research design. Specifically, we match a judge's decision on a case only with other judges who have the same ideology. Judges with the same ideology have the same propensity to attract contributions from the same types of attorneys. Inevitably, in a specific case some of the judges will actually have received contributions from one side or the other, but because the propensity to receive these contributions is the same across judges, the results from the matched analysis are not subject to the spurious relationship that can be observed in correlational analyses. Said another way, by comparing the decisions of judges with the same ideology (and thus the same base of contributors), we can make an unbiased assessment of the effect of the campaign contributions on the decisions.

To implement this approach in practice, we match decisions of judges in the same state with the same ideology scores and on the same case and analyze those decisions with a case-control approach (this approach allows us to control for the facts of the case as well as ideology).[5] In Nevada, our nonpartisan state, five judges are rated as having the same ideology. In our partisan states, the Texas Supreme Court has five judges rated identically and Michigan has four.[6] Within each case, we compare ideologically identical judges who did and did not receive contributions. The case-control method aggregates these differences across cases to arrive at a general estimate for the effect of contributions.[7]

In the instance of our nonpartisan state, Nevada, our matched case-control analysis unsurprisingly shows no statistically significant relationship between contributions and decisions. For our fully partisan state, Texas, we similarly find no statistically significant relationship. This is consistent with our results from Test 2. In contrast, even after controlling for case facts and matching judges on ideology to alleviate the reciprocal causality problem, our quasi-partisan state, Michigan, still shows a strong association. For a judge who received $100 more from the liberal party's attorney(s), the odds of a liberal decision are more than double the odds (specifically 2.29 times greater) where the respective parties' contributions are at parity. For a judge who receives $100 more contributions from the conservative party, the odds of a liberal decision decrease by a factor of 0.44.[8]

The matched case-control design, while not perfect, is more intuitive than the instrumental variables approach used by others for resolving the reciprocal causality problem (Bonneau and Cann 2009; Cann 2007). By limiting the comparison to individuals who have the same ideology (and thus the same propensity to receive contributions from the same types of attorneys), we potentially limit the effect of the reciprocal causality problem to arrive at estimates of the actual effect of contributions on decisions. This test, perhaps the most telling of our approaches, confirms what we expected based on our first two tests: there is a meaningful relationship between contributions and decisions in Michigan, our quasi-partisan state, but not in Texas (partisan) or Nevada (nonpartisan).

Discussion

We have presented three analyses to evaluate the question of whether campaign contributions to elected judges affect the judicial decision-making process. Above, we outlined a series of questions about whether a correlation exists between dollars and decisions, about whether the direction of causality ran from dollars to decisions or in the reverse direction, and if there was a true causal relationship, about whether one is more likely to observe that causal relationship in states that incorporate partisanship in judicial elections than in those that are strictly nonpartisan. As we conclude, we wish to reflect on what our study contributes toward answering those questions.

Previous single-state studies have found differing results in terms of correlation and causality across different states. Our results similarly find a mixture of results across our sample of three states, showing evidence of correlation and suggestions of causality in Michigan, but no evidence of even a correlational relationship in Nevada and Texas. Our study, however, improves on previous explorations of the contributions and decisions link by looking at multiple states and advancing an explanation for why we might see a relationship in some states but not in others. While our results must certainly remain tentative because we only consider a fraction of states where judges face contestable elections, they represent an improvement over single-state studies.

Our analysis points out something that has been lacking in the discussion of the influence of contributions and judicial decision-making: the possibility of money's influence being conditional. Existing studies tend to posit either that money has no influence on judges or that every decision by every judge is for sale. We begin here an effort to identify the conditions under which money might make a difference. Specifically, we exploit cross-state institutional variation on partisanship to assess whether the more intense, competitive, and rancorous campaign environment in partisan elections makes it more likely for judges to trade their votes for campaign contributions. While we do not find a universal influence of money on decisions in partisan states, we do find suggestive evidence of a causal link in Michigan, one of the two states we studied that allows a partisan component in its state supreme court elections. We recognize that there are other factors that may condition whether dollars influence decisions (especially since Texas, a partisan state, shows no relationship in our tests). We suspect that a partisan election format alone is not sufficient to induce quid pro quo money-votes deals, but that it likely contributes to the type of environment where such arrangements may arise.

While we recognize that a partisan format does not guarantee that causal relationships between dollars and decisions will emerge, our results do suggest that nonpartisan elections may have an inoculating effect, protecting judges from the potentially corrosive effects of campaign contributions. These results must be taken with caution, however, because we only consider a single nonpartisan state. A number of other unique aspects of Nevada's system may also serve to limit the effect of contributions on judicial decisions. In particular, because Nevada has no intermediate appellate court, the Supreme Court of Nevada hears most cases in randomly selected three-judge panels to reduce their workload (*en banc* review—that is, review by the entire court—is reserved for the most important cases). This generates uncertainty among attorneys about whether a judge to whom they contribute will even hear the case (unless they contribute to all judges). As we expand the scope of our study, we will be able to verify these preliminary results that distinguish between partisan and nonpartisan elections.

An additional innovative contribution of our study is a number of suggestive attempts that allow us to attack the problem of reciprocal causality. Specifically, we find evidence that in Michigan the norm of unanimity is weakened in cases where judges receive contributions relative to those cases where no contributions are made. Further, when we compare Michigan judges who are alike in terms of ideology, we find that a judge who receives contributions from one party's attorney(s) is more likely to favor the contributing attorney's party than a judge who has the same ideological predisposition but did not receive a contribution (e.g. conservative judges who receive contributions are more likely to favor the conservative party's attorney than equally conservative judges who did not receive contributions from the conservative party's attorney). While none of these tests alone is a perfect solution to the fundamental problem of causal inference, when taken together, these results are certainly promising. More work is needed as this is one of the most important and unanswered topics in judicial selection.

These results have important implications for the ongoing debate over the manner in which state court judges ought to be selected and retained; they imply that reformers' concerns about the potential effects of money on the impartial administration of justice are not completely without empirical foundation. Scholars and practitioners alike should consider the very real possibility of monetary influence on judges when evaluating state court selection systems. Still, our results do not indicate that judicial elections are fundamentally flawed. Indeed, proponents of judicial elections may consider our study as evidence that well-crafted institutional structures can diminish or even eliminate the effects of money on judicial decisions. To be clear, there is nothing in this chapter that compels the conclusion that the election of judges ought to be eradicated. The results here simply suggest that, under some conditions, there may be a relationship between campaign contributions and the votes of judges. Further exploration of this relationship should be high on the list of priorities for those interested in the politics of judicial selection.

Notes

1 A number of cases had no identifiable ideological content (e.g. divorce, paternity, etc.); these cases are excluded from our analyses below.

2 Arceneaux, Bonneau, and Brace (2009) also reveal the wide variation in dissent rates in tort cases among states. For the states we discuss here, they find a unanimity rate of 73.1% in Nevada, 73.6% in Michigan, and 90.6% in Texas. Note that these figures come from 1995–1998, before the time frame of our study.

3 One may wonder if this test has its own unique reciprocal causality problem, specifically that contributors may focus inordinately on important, complex, or unique cases, which may also be less likely to be unanimous. In defense of our research design, we point out that this would require attorneys to know at the campaign phase (when contributions are made) whether they would be involved in complex or important cases several years down the road. While we recognize that attorneys can predict whether they are likely to argue cases before their state's high court at some point in the 5–7 year period subsequent to an election, we doubt that attorneys can predict the complexity or importance of the case(s) they may argue that far in advance of the case being filed.

4 For a more thoroughly developed discussion of the fundamental problem of causal inference, see King, Keohane, and Verba (1994).

5 The case-control study is implemented as a conditional logit model. Rather than presenting a table of coefficients, which is less accessible to a general audience, we describe the substance of the results in the text. Coefficients are available from the authors upon request.

6 We refer to this test as suggestive because it requires the assumption that the Brace, Langer, and Hall (2000) ideology scores accurately capture differences in the propensity of these judges to receive campaign contributions from different types of attorneys. One possibility that remains unmodeled is the collegiality within the field of law they practiced (e.g. former prosecutors who ascend to the bench may be more likely to raise funds from prosecuting attorneys even independent of their ideology).

7 This approach, common in medicine, is mathematically equivalent to models social scientists refer to as conditional logit, fixed-effects logit, or McFadden's choice model. For an elaborate discussion of the math behind the estimates, see McFadden (2004).

8 We make these estimates based on a conditional logit model grouped by case for the decisions of ideologically identical judges. The dependent variable is whether the judge made a liberal or conservative decision, the independent variable is the difference between liberal attorney contributions and conservative attorney contributions. The coefficient on the contribution differential is 0.0082 and it is statistically significant ($z = 2.11, p = 0.035$).

Part II

Trial Courts

Chapter 4

Race and Death Sentencing[1]

Isaac Unah

Robert Bacon and his girlfriend, Bonnie Clark, were each tried and convicted of first-degree murder in Onslow County, North Carolina in 1991 for the 1987 killing of Glennie Leroy Clark, Bonnie's estranged husband. According to court and other public records, the murder was suggested, planned, and instigated by Bonnie because Glennie (reportedly an alcoholic) had physically and emotionally abused her and their two children during the marriage.[2] Robert had never been involved in criminal activity before and was reluctant to help Bonnie kill her husband. But Bonnie persisted. She informed Robert that she was the beneficiary of a $50,000 life insurance policy on Glennie, which they could use together. Eventually, Robert agreed to help but only after Glennie had called him by a racial epithet during a heated encounter. Ultimately, the attack on Glennie was carried out by both defendants.

After Bacon was arrested, he quickly confessed to having stabbed Glennie. He showed contrition and cooperated fully throughout the investigation and trial proceedings. Bonnie, on the other hand, lied and prevaricated with the police about her involvement. One officer said: "She played us for dummies."

Under North Carolina law, Robert Bacon and Bonnie Clark both faced the possibility of a death sentence irrespective of who actually inflicted the fatal stab.[3] Following the penalty phase of the trial, the jury sentenced Robert (who is black) to death. In a separate proceeding and with a different jury, Bonnie (who is white) was sentenced to life in prison. In this introductory section, I shall discuss the circumstances surrounding Robert Bacon's death sentence as a way of demonstrating how, during a criminal trial, race can influence sentencing outcomes. Ultimately, my goal in this chapter is to investigate, through analysis of statistical data, whether race continues to matter in death sentencing in North Carolina, even after significant legal reforms designed to end racial bias have been implemented. I also hope to identify other factors besides race that may explain death sentencing.

Since Robert and Bonnie were tried separately and by different juries, we cannot simply conclude based solely on the different outcomes that racism determined the outcome. However, we cannot rule out the influence of race entirely. To be sure, the difference in outcomes could have been attributed to case facts such as the quality and effectiveness of defense attorneys handling the cases, the extent to which the jurors actually understood the judges' instructions, and the number of aggravating versus mitigating circumstances found in each case. When we scrutinize Robert Bacon's case closely, however, we find evidence suggesting that race did indeed play a role in his death sentence. The evidence was a notarized affidavit from a juror, Pamela Bloom Smith, who participated in the trial and had voted in favor of death.

Robert Bacon had been on death row for about 10 years and was scheduled to die on May 18, 2001. On May 9, 2001, Pamela Bloom Smith came forward and made her declaration about the nature of the jury deliberations:

> I remember during our deliberations there was discussion of the fact that Bacon was dating a white woman. This topic came up after the first vote. A female juror first brought up the issue. Some jurors felt it was wrong for a black man to date a white woman. Jurors also felt that black people commit more crime and that is it typical of blacks to be involved in crime. We talked about this for at least ten to fifteen minutes and some jurors were adamant in their feeling that Bacon was a black man and "he deserved what he got". I understood this to mean Bacon should receive the death penalty.[4]

She further declared that "she felt that the jurors who expressed these attitudes about race believed that these views justified the death penalty" and that she was "offended by the discussion" but voted for the death penalty only because of intense pressure from other jurors.

These facts raise questions of whether equal justice was served under the law and whether, under rules governing clemency, Robert Bacon's death sentence should be commuted to life in prison without parole. The United States Supreme Court established a key legal standard for handling claims of racial discrimination in death penalty cases in *McCleskey v. Kemp* (1987). McCleskey, a black male Georgian convicted of killing a white police officer, presented in his defense a comprehensive statistical study of Georgia's death penalty system conducted by Professor David Baldus and his colleagues (Baldus, Woodworth, and Pulaski 1990). The study showed significant evidence of racial discrimination by prosecutors and juries in Georgia. Ultimately, the Court rejected the study's relevance to McCleskey's case and ruled 5 to 4 that a defendant must demonstrate evidence of racial bias in his or her own case rather than rely on group-based statistical evidence when seeking material alteration of a criminal sentence.

By virtue of the *McCleskey* decision and Pamela Smith's declaration, Robert Bacon appeared to have a chance at clemency. He submitted a petition for clemency to the Office of North Carolina Governor Mike Easley through his attorneys. North Carolina's Constitution vests the authority to grant clemency in the governor.[5] It is an important discretionary power. However, for political reasons, governors in North Carolina and in other states are reluctant to grant clemencies because it is often *not* in their strategic interest. The fear is that political opponents might cast the governor as soft on crime, especially if the convict whose sentence is commuted later commits another violent crime. Despite this risk, Governor Mike Easley granted Robert Bacon's clemency petition and commuted his death sentence to life in prison without parole based largely on Pamela Smith's declaration.

In light of the contentious history of race relations in North Carolina and in the United States more generally, Bacon's case illustrates a central problem that continues to haunt the American criminal justice system: whether society should tolerate the influence of extrinsic elements such as race in death sentencing. After all, the difficult question of whether people should be put to death by the state is of great moral and political consequence and is sharply debated in both scholarly and public arenas (Bailey and Peterson 1994; Baumgartner, De Boef, and Boydstun 2008; Bedau 2004; Keil and Vito 1992).

The history of American criminal trials is filled with many pages discussing race as a most vexing aspect of the death penalty landscape. Race adds an additional layer of complication to an already difficult subject matter. Within the death penalty debate, however, no serious proponent argues that death sentencing should be racially biased. Indeed, as Justice Anthony Kennedy stated in *Edmonson v. Leesville Concrete Company* (1991), "racial bias mars the integrity of the judicial system and prevents the idea of democratic government from becoming reality" (p. 628).

Robert Bacon's death sentence is only one example in which race appears to have played a role. But we are left to wonder how many such cases go undetected. Had Pamela Smith not stepped forward with her declaration, we never would have discovered what transpired behind the closed doors of the jury room on behalf of the people of North Carolina. Because this is just one case and because it possesses unique characteristics, it would be inappropriate to generalize and say that race plays a significant role in death sentencing in North Carolina. A substantially higher threshold of evidence is required to sustain such a conclusion. In this chapter, I carefully obtain and offer ample evidence to suggest that race continues to play an illegitimate role in death sentencing in North Carolina. First, I discuss briefly the historical terrain of race and death sentencing in North Carolina and the nation.

Historical Context of Race and Death Sentencing

Research conducted in North Carolina during the era of Jim Crow segregation in the 1940s indicated that racial discrimination was playing a regular, illegitimate role in two different respects: black defendants were more likely to receive death sentences for similar crimes than white defendants, and those defendants (of whatever race) who murdered whites were also more likely to

receive death sentences (Garfinkel 1949; Johnson 1941). Similar racial disparities were identified by researchers in other states (Wolfgang and Riedel 1973),
and these disparities were sufficiently disturbing that they became one of the
features condemned by several U.S. Supreme Court justices who joined in
striking all death penalty statutes in 1972 in the *Furman v. Georgia* decision.[6]
Indeed, before *Furman*, it was considered a matter of routine in the South for
an all-white jury to convict a black defendant, especially if the victim was
white, without careful consideration of the evidence or by ignoring the evidence altogether. According to political scientists Earl Black and Merle Black,
"old southern politics was transparently undemocratic and racist" (2002, 2).

In the history of modern capital punishment, *Furman* was the climax of a
long campaign against the death penalty. The case is significant because justices temporarily halted executions to allow states some time to address defi-
ciencies in their death penalty statutes. But more importantly, *Furman*
expressed the Court's desire to eradicate racial bias in death sentencing by
introducing a structured sentencing scheme requiring *bifurcated capital trials*
and *guided discretion* for the jury. Bifurcated trials mean that before defendants can be sentenced to death, they must first be found guilty. Then in a separate sentencing phase, the sentencing authority must find at least one
statutory aggravating factor that increases the severity of the murder. These
factors are numerous, and they vary from state to state. However, they typically include the killing of a law enforcement officer, killing while incarcerated,
endangering other people besides the murder victim, and a killing that is
incidental to additional felonies such as armed robbery, burglary, or sexual
assault (Unah 2009, 143). Guided discretion requires that the jury be given a
list of aggravating and mitigating factors to help in their deliberation. Only
when aggravating factors outweigh mitigating factors that make the crime less
severe can a jury impose a death sentence. Justices expressed optimism that
these legal reforms would help channel the jury's discretion and ultimately
eliminate arbitrariness and bias in death sentencing.

After *Furman*, states such as North Carolina re-enacted capital sentencing
statutes. These states were on clear notice that it was unconstitutional for race
to play any role in determining an appropriate punishment. Those who
defended the new statutes assured the federal courts that the combined effects
of the desegregation of formerly segregated courtrooms, the coming of African Americans into capital juries, and the gradual desegregation of police, as
well as prosecutorial and judicial ranks would lead to an end of racial bias in
death sentencing. The Supreme Court, in upholding several of the new, post-
Furman capital statutes in the 1976 *Gregg v. Georgia* case, accepted these state
assurances. The justices concluded that the states' new sentencing procedures
would be sufficient to curb racial discrimination and other forms of arbitrariness that had characterized earlier capital punishment statutes.[7] The Court
therefore used *Gregg* as the vehicle for reinstating capital punishment after a
four-year moratorium. Currently, nearly all the 36 states operating a death

penalty system plus the federal government employ a bifurcated trial system and guided discretion modeled after Georgia.

Social Science Evidence and Death Sentencing

Soon after *Gregg*, social scientists began to examine the actual operation of death sentences in the post-*Gregg* era to see whether the new statutes had successfully eliminated racial bias. Many reported that racial factors, especially discrimination based upon the race of the homicide victim, remained. The most prominent of these early research efforts was the Baldus, Woodworth, and Pulaski (1990) study, which I mentioned earlier. It involved two overlapping studies on the capital system of Georgia from 1973 through 1979. After accounting for dozens of independent variables and using a sophisticated statistical methodology called logistic regression, the study found that the odds of receiving the death penalty in Georgia were 4.3 times greater in white victim cases than in black victim cases. The results of these studies were introduced as part of a constitutional challenge in *McCleskey v. Kemp* (1987), but the Court rejected McCleskey's claim that his own race and the race of his victim were key factors in his death sentence.

Writing for the majority, Justice Lewis Powell held that purposeful discrimination in capital sentencing—whether on the basis of the defendant's race or the victim's race—would violate the Equal Protection Clause, and likely the Eighth Amendment as well. (The Eight Amendment prohibits cruel and unusual punishments.) However, Justice Powell found that the Baldus study relied upon by Warren McCleskey did not offer sufficiently clear evidence that *his* capital jury had been influenced by racial considerations, and the Court suggested that statistical arguments about patterns of capital sentencing "are best presented to the legislative bodies" that "are better qualified to weigh and 'evaluate the results of statistical studies in terms of their own local conditions and with a flexibility of approach that is not available to the courts'" (p. 319). This statement has implications for current legislative efforts in many states to eliminate race in capital sentencing, including the recently enacted *North Carolina Racial Justice Act.*[8] Since the *McCleskey* decision in 1987, federal courts have been closed to virtually all system-wide claims of racial discrimination in death sentencing even though in other areas such as gender discrimination in employment, the Court continues to accept statistical evidence that demonstrate disparate treatment of groups in hiring (*Johnson v. Transportation Agency of Santa Clara County, California* 1987).

The North Carolina Death Penalty Study

Most of the earlier studies on the death penalty focused on sentencing patterns either in the immediate post-*Furman v. Georgia* period after 1972 or in the early-to-mid 1980s (Baldus *et al.* 1998). Two leading modern studies of North Carolina's capital system fit that pattern. The first study examined the first year

(1977–8) of North Carolina's experience under its new statute and was conducted by Barry Nakell and Kenneth Hardy (Nakell and Hardy 1987). That
study found both race-of-defendant and race-of-victim effects at various stages
of the capital charging and sentencing system during the new law's first year of
implementation. A later study that relied upon data submitted by North Carolina law enforcement personnel to the Federal Bureau of Investigation in the
years 1976 through 1980 found that "the race of the victim had sizable and statistically significant effects on the likelihood that a defendant would receive the
death penalty." However, only a small number of defendants had received death
sentences at that time. Therefore, "the race-of-victim effect became smaller and
statistically insignificant" when the race of the defendant was added to the analysis (Gross and Mauro 1989, 91).

Between 1980 and 1997, no thorough examination of North Carolina's
capital sentencing system was undertaken at all. Unfortunately, it was a period
that cried out for close scrutiny because, as Figure 4.1 shows, the number of
murders reached a peak in North Carolina and the nation during this period.
Since then, overall murders have been on a steady decline, as have death
sentences. My earlier study, with John Charles Boger, attempted to fill that
void in the literature by examining death sentencing in North Carolina from
1993 to 1997 (Unah and Boger 2001). I rely on rich data from that study to
answer in this chapter specific questions about the racial justice of North
Carolina's death sentencing system, and more broadly, to reflect on whether
southern states, during the 1990s—many now boasting multi-racial juries and
prosecution teams, and some significant fraction of African American
judges—have finally shed their age-old tendency of employing racial considerations in imposing the death penalty. The regrettable answer that emerges
from my study is that race remains important in the Old North State.

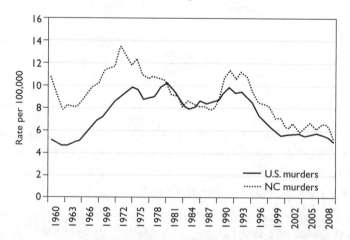

Figure 4.1 Murder rates in North Carolina and the United States,
1960–2009 (source: The Federal Bureau of Investigation).

Theories of Death Sentencing

A theory is a set of interrelated concepts that help us to understand political or social phenomena. Two groups of theories have been proposed for understanding capital punishment. The first is aimed at the motivations behind state adoption of capital punishment. The second is aimed at understanding the causal process leading to differences in death sentencing outcomes.

For motivational theories, scholars have emphasized the following perspectives: deterrence, incapacitation, retribution, public opinion, and cost (see, e.g., Bailey and Peterson 1994; Ehrlich 1975; Ellsworth and Gross 1994; Rhinestein 1995; Savelsberg 1994; Unah 2009; Wilson 1985). I do not focus on motivational explanations here, although I admit that the question of motivation is interesting and important.

Instead, I consider here process-oriented theories that address observed variance in the incidence of death sentences. I consider three such theoretical frameworks. The neoclassical theory of formal legal rationality emphasizes the importance of legal rules in sentencing (Rhinestein 1995). Socio-structural theories emphasize structural differences among social groups and the conflicts they engender based on race and socioeconomic organization as a way of understanding death sentencing (Blalock 1967; Key 1949). Institutional theories emphasize how death sentencing is embedded within the political process (Smith 2004; Yates and Fording 2005).

Under the *theory of formal legal rationality*, the process for determining criminal punishment should be based solely upon legal rules established and approved by the state to communicate the priorities and wishes of the polity (Savelsberg 1994; Unah 2009). Under this theory, law is a rule that guides behavior of both state officials and citizens, and it does not tolerate deviations from the rules as stated in the legal code. Most people can appreciate the appeal of this theory. For one thing, its mechanical nature facilitates our ability to live together in peace by fostering predictability and uniformity of behavior on the part of government officials who must enforce the rules and citizens who must abide by them. The theory therefore argues in favor of a determinate mode of death sentencing (Unah 2009, 140). For example, if an individual is found guilty of first-degree murder after a capital trial, then the process for determining a sentence should be based not on extrinsic elements such as race but on objective criteria grounded in law.

North Carolina General Statutes list several statutory aggravating factors that make a crime more severe and therefore more likely to lead to a death sentence, e.g. killing a police officer. I developed a cumulative index of aggravating factors and expect that more aggravating factors will make a death sentence more likely. In addition to aggravating factors, North Carolina law lists three murder elements that determine whether an accused can be prosecuted and sentenced to death. These elements point to the essential mental condition of the accused when the crime was committed (*mens rea*). The first element involves five actions historically recognized as especially heinous when they lead to murder: poisoning, lying-in-wait, imprisonment, torture, and starvation. The second element designates a killing that reflects malice and is implemented with willful intent, premeditation, and deliberation. The third element is felony murders, those committed in the process of committing another felony such as rape, armed robbery, or arson. I consider each of these three murder elements and predict that the death penalty will be imposed when the element is present in a defendant's case (Thornburg 1995, 61–66). See Appendix A for all variable measurements.

North Carolina law also enumerates several mitigating factors that make the crime less severe and therefore minimize the chances of a death sentence. Examples include murders where the defendant has no significant history of prior criminal activity or where the defendant was mentally impaired; and where the victim consented to the homicidal act.[9] I measure this variable by developing a cumulative index of all mitigating factors found in the case. I expect that a death sentence is less likely if more mitigating factors exist. I also include the killing of multiple victims as a possible determinant of death sentencing. Both society and the law view the killing of multiple individuals as a sure sign of depraved indifference to human life. Therefore I expect multiple victims to make the death penalty more likely.

The U.S. Supreme Court has ruled in *Lockett v. Ohio* (1978) that defendants are free to furnish mitigating evidence from whatever source, including sources not listed in the state statute. These non-statutory mitigating factors include family deprivation, such as whether the defendant was neglected as a child or raised poor. As such I expect non-statutory mitigating factors to lower the probability of a death sentence.

Studies that analyze the ways in which communities respond to crime show that criminal motives are related to punishment severity (Simon and Spaulding 1999). Indeed, the U.S. Supreme Court has upheld state laws that permit punishment enhancement for crimes motivated by hate. Unfortunately studies that rely on official government data often fail to explicitly account for motive by assuming that motive is already incorporated into sentencing guidelines. But because human motivation is fluid, jurors can assign greater severity to a crime based on their individual experiences in relation to the assailant's motive. Motive is made explicit by examining five motives typically associated with homicide: hatred, rage, sex, money, and involvement in collateral crimes. I expect each motive to enhance the chances of a death sentence. Finally, I consider other factors not stated in the statute but related to the case that might enhance sentence severity. These are called non-statutory aggravating factors and may include whether the murder victim had small children to support, which might move a jury to impose death. I also consider whether the victim's body was abused after death. I expect post-mortem abuse to increase the chances of a death sentence.

Socio-structural theories suggest that differences in death sentencing are the result of group conflict caused by political, economic, and socio-structural arrangements in society. Two categories of this theory emphasize perceived racial threat and the socioeconomic status of defendants and victims for understanding death sentencing.

The classic racial threat thesis postulates that the death penalty is a mechanism for controlling the potential threat posed by racial minorities to broader economic and social arrangements that traditionally benefit the white majority. Evidence of those structural arrangements can be found in de facto residential segregation within cities and communities, distribution of educational resources, and employment polarization between low-wage (services) and high-wage (technical) jobs. Thus under the racial threat perspective, the death penalty is one mechanism for minimizing the potential menace presented by nonwhites. Indeed political scientists Jeff Yates and Richard Fording (2005) have furnished evidence indicating a significant increase in black imprisonment relative to whites as the size of the black population in a state increases. Therefore, I expect an escalation of criminal punishment as nonwhites increase in a given county. I further expect non-white defendants who kill whites to receive more death sentences and non-whites who kill nonwhites to receive fewer (compared to whites who kill whites, the base category).

Structural theories also target the importance of socioeconomic status (SES) in death sentencing. In our capitalist culture, individual placement on the social ladder is determined by how much resources and power the individual is perceived to possess. Individuals with power and resources are placed higher than individuals without, and this often engenders class conflict and resentment. According to political scientists Anne Schneider and Helen Ingram (1993), law is a tool of the ruling class. They use it to design policies, institutional structures, and implementation patterns that disadvantage the lower classes. In that sense, class-based explanations of sentencing view the death penalty as a card game with a stacked deck unfavorable to the interests of lower SES individuals because they lack both affluence and influence relative to the powerful. Accordingly, higher SES defendants are better able to exploit the rules of the game to their utmost advantage. They are able to use legal institutions to reduce or altogether escape punishment for their criminal transgressions through their social networks and ability to hire superior lawyers. I use educational attainment as a measure of socioeconomic status of defendants and victims. I expect defendants with more education to be less likely to receive the death penalty compared to those with less education. The explanation works for victims as well. Higher SES victims possess higher social values and so are expected to command more severe punishment for their killers than low SES victims.

Juries may be more sympathetic to a certain class of defendants and victims than to others. Unfortunately, we have little information to assess which defendants or victims will elicit such sentiment. Two socio-structural factors that seem especially appropriate are age and sex. Age has been associated with sentencing in capital cases (Radelet and Pierce 1985). Society views older individuals as being better able to judge right from wrong, whereas younger individuals are viewed as impulsive and immature, yet more easily rehabilitated. Moreover, younger defendants are less likely to carry a criminal history than older offenders. Therefore, older convicts are more likely to receive a death sentence than younger ones.

One study of jury decision-making in product liability awards shows that at the extremes, age has an exculpatory quality in the justice system (Graddy 2001). Because of physical and mental infirmities associated with age, much older capital defendants (those over 75) and much younger defendants (under 20) may be perceived as being cognitively weak and consequently more likely to elicit leniency compared to middle-aged offenders.[10] This possibility suggests a curvilinear relationship between a defendant's age and death sentencing. The variable "Age^2" tests this relationship for defendants and victims. Similarly, society views very young and very old victims as "helpless" and therefore especially vulnerable to crime. I expect crimes against very old and very young victims to command more death sentences than crimes against middle-aged victims.

Empirical evidence points to a gender gap in the criminal justice system. The United States' death row is overwhelmingly male. For women the death penalty is a tale of rarity. From 1900 to 2005, 8,339 individuals were executed in the United States and only 50 (0.6%) were women. At the end of 1997, only 1.5% of death row inmates were women, even though women commit nearly 12% of all homicides (Strieb 2006). Women are underrepresented partly because of the arrangement of gender roles in society but mostly because women commit fewer violent crimes than men. Moreover, women are treated more leniently than men in both prosecution and sentencing (Spohn and Spears 1997). Research evidence also suggests that violent offenses against women are more likely to prompt a death penalty charge and conviction than offenses against men (Baldus, Woodworth, and Pulaski 1990; Songer and Unah 2006). Thus, I expect that female offenders are less likely to be sentenced to death, whereas killers of women should be more likely to receive the death penalty.

Institutional theory concerns the manner in which the death penalty is situated within the political process. Criminological research of past generations reached mixed conclusions when researchers at the time fixated on ideas, popularized by European philosophers Emile Durkheim (French) and Karl Marx (German), that unemployment (i.e., surplus labor) was the root cause of crime and that increasing the intensity of punishment was the solution to crime. Since then scholars have increasingly turned to political processes as a way of understanding criminal punishment (Garland 1990; Scheingold 1984).

Americans of a certain age would remember Richard Nixon's 1968 campaign pledge to return the nation to "law and order" through the appointment of hardnosed "strict constructionists" to the Supreme Court. In speech after speech, politicians describe our crime problem via aggressive political rhetoric to signal they are tough on crime. These speeches are a part of the political process, and they signify the strong connection that exists between politics and criminal punishment. Recent empirical studies of the impact of aggressive political rhetoric suggest that politicians do control policy implementation through words spoken from the bully pulpit (Unah and Coggins 2011; Whitford and Yates 2009). I consider here four variables related to the political process: electoral proximity of the prosecutor, partisan ideology of the prosecutor, county ideology, and defense attorney type.

Research into the accountability of judges suggests that elections have a powerful effect on the behavior of state judges. Some scholars found that in controversial issues such as the death penalty, state supreme court justices act strategically by casting votes that conform to constituency preferences (Hall 1995; Traut and Emmert 1998). One researcher reported that an Alabama trial judge up for re-election actually upgraded a jury's life sentence to a death sentence to improve his chances for re-election. Another suggested that there is much the prosecutor can do to influence the conviction rate as an election approaches: either decline many close cases, or offer steep discounts to get at least some conviction in every case (Burnside 1999; Wright 2009). Thus, there is reason to believe that prosecutors facing electoral competition do succumb to political pressure to cultivate an aggressive posture by disingenuously upgrading the crimes of, and vigorously prosecuting, accused offenders deemed easily convictable. These soft targets are typically the poor or minorities. The payoff for prosecutors includes a high conviction rate, which they can use to win support from crime-conscious voters. Electoral proximity increases aggressive prosecution and should lead to more death sentences.

Ideology is an important political asset that government officials and citizens rely upon for decisions about public policy. I consider the ideology of the prosecutor and of the county in which the crime was tried. Opinion polls consistently indicate that conservatives support the death penalty considerably more than liberals. In the wake of the Scott Peterson case, the Gallup Organization conducted a poll on attitudes toward the death penalty and found a 20 percentage point difference in support for the death penalty, with conservatives being more supportive (Carroll 2004). Conservatives believe that severe punishment is needed to deter crime, an act of individual choice. Liberals believe that crime is often the result of concentrated structural forces beyond the individual's control such as poverty, weakened family arrangements, and poor opportunities.

Beyond the polls, ideology operates at the judicial level as well. I use party identification of the prosecutor as a stand-in for ideology. Further, I use the percent vote for the Republican Party candidate for Senate in 1992 and 1996 as a measure of county ideology. Greater support for the Republican candidate signifies a more conservative county. Since jurors are selected from county voting and property tax records, I assume that this measure is valid.

I expect conservative districts to return more death sentences than liberal districts. However, I think that a more heterogeneous population is more sensitive to racial differences than a homogeneous one. Therefore, I expect the effect of county ideology to vary depending on the size of the nonwhite population in the county. I expect the direction of the effect to be negative (i.e., as the nonwhite population increases, I expect the effect of county ideology to negate death sentences).

I include the following control variables: whether the defense attorney is a public defender and whether the district attorney is male. Finally, researchers have reported significant district level variation in death penalty prosecution and sentencing (Baldus, Woodworth, and Pulaski 1990; Songer and Unah 2006). I test for possible regional effects by dividing North Carolina into three regions: the tourism-heavy counties of the coastal region, the urbanized counties of the piedmont region, and the rural counties of the mountain region, with the mountain region as the base.[11]

Research Design

From January 1, 1993, to December 31, 1997, 3,990 known defendants were prosecuted for homicide in North Carolina. My data capture homicides resulting in a murder or first-degree murder charge.[12] In addition, my data include a random sample of second-degree murder cases to account for the possibility that prosecutors may undercharge an otherwise death eligible offense (see Paternoster et al. 2004). The data then consist of the entire population of first-degree murder cases in which the defendant received a death sentence (99 cases) or life in prison without parole (303 cases). I used multistage statistical sampling to select a random sample from the remaining homicide cases designated with a "murder" charge but receiving a life sentence, a term of years in prison, or an acquittal/dismissal (118 cases). In this way the data reflect the entire population of homicides committed in North Carolina during the period examined.

Under multistage sampling, cases are selected in stages to arrive at an overall nonzero probability of inclusion in the analysis (see Appendix B). To assess the representativeness of the sample, I created a sampling weight that reflects the probabilities of the two sampling stages used.[13] I use the weighted data for reporting death-sentencing rates for various racial groups and configurations but limit the regression analysis to the unweighted sample, N= 520. As a way of controlling for case selection bias in the trial and sentencing phases, Heckman probit was used to estimate a system of two equations simultaneously.[14] The first equation estimates the decision to find the defendant guilty or not. The second estimates the decision to award a death sentence or life in prison, given a guilty verdict.

Race and Death Sentencing by the Numbers

Does race *still* contribute substantially toward death sentencing in North
Carolina during the 1990s? If progressive changes in southern racial attitudes
in recent decades are reflected in the application of criminal punishment in
North Carolina, then little evidence of racial bias in death sentencing should
emerge. By racial bias, I mean a predictable inequity in the treatment of a
racial group. That treatment need not be intentional to satisfy this definition.
Figure 4.2 reports simple *death-sentencing rates* grouped by racial category.
Overall, the death-sentencing rate for homicides in North Carolina from 1993
to 1997 is 2.5%. Coincidentally, this rate is right in line with the national average of 2.5% (see Blume, Eisenberg, and Wells 2004). Beyond the aggregate
death sentencing rate that I report, three interesting trends emerge once the
data are disaggregated and a weight index is applied.

First, I examine murder victims by race. Consistent with classic racial threat
thesis, there is a stark difference in death-sentencing rates between white and
nonwhite victim cases in North Carolina.[15] The death-sentencing rate for white
victim cases is 3.4% regardless of the race of the defendant. This is more than
double the death-sentencing rate for nonwhite victim cases (1.6%, p<0.01).
Thus the aggravated murder of a white individual is 3.4 times more likely to
result in a death sentence compared to the murder of a nonwhite individual.

Second, I examine defendants by race. The death-sentencing rate for both
white and nonwhite defendants is statistically indistinguishable from zero if

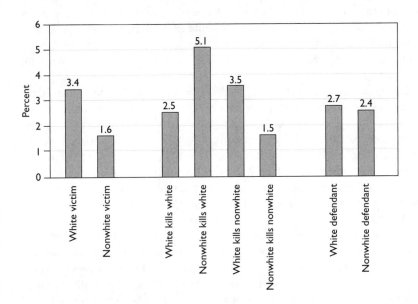

Figure 4.2 Percent of death sentences in North Carolina, 1993–1997 (all
homicides, weighted). Adapted from Unah (2011).

the victim's race is not considered. This finding is consistent with much of the post-*Gregg* literature.

Finally, I examine defendant/victim racial configurations. How do capital murder defendants fare in the justice system when judged in light of the color of their victim's skin? The most striking result is the treatment of victims killed by nonwhite defendants. When a nonwhite defendant kills a white victim, the death-sentencing rate is 5.1%. However, when a nonwhite defendant kills a nonwhite victim, the death-sentencing rate drops dramatically to only 1.5%. This difference is statistically significant using a difference of proportions test (p <0.01). The highest death-sentencing rate occurs where a nonwhite kills a white; the lowest occurs where a nonwhite kills another nonwhite. The sentencing of white defendants does not differ significantly in terms of their victim's race. However, as in the case of nonwhite defendants being significantly worse off when they commit interracial murders, white defendants who commit interracial murders also appear worse off, but the number of cases in that category is too small, rendering the ratio statistically meaningless.

Generally speaking, interracial homicides command higher death-sentencing rates than intra-racial homicides (see, e.g., Baldus, Woodworth, and Pulaski 1990; Paternoster *et al.* 2004). One explanation is that intra-racial homicides tend to involve primary relations such as relatives, acquaintances, or friends. These kinds of homicides are generally thought to carry lower levels of aggravation than interracial homicides, which typically involve strangers and thus presumably pack higher levels of aggravation. My data support that explanation. In cases where a nonwhite kills another nonwhite, 21% of those receiving death sentences involve strangers. But in cases where a nonwhite kills a white, the rate more than doubles: 44% of those receiving death involve strangers.

On the basis of this descriptive analysis, we can surmise that a discernible pattern exists. On account of race alone, death penalty sentencing in North Carolina is not evenhanded. Nonwhite killers of whites are overwhelmingly more likely to receive the death penalty than any other racial configuration. The case of Robert Bacon fits that pattern. The full percentages are reported in Table 4.1, including percentages for when death eligible cases alone are considered. My analysis thus far cannot fully account for the differential treatment of murder defendants and victims since I have not yet controlled for legal, socio-structural, and institutional factors.

Will the lack of evenhandedness displayed so far in my results disappear once I subject the data to more rigorous statistical testing that controls for other factors such as the law? I estimated a system of two equations using the Heckman probit method whereby the jury decision to impose death is contingent upon a prior decision to convict the defendant. The results are displayed in Table 4.2 and they pertain to the penalty phase only.

Table 4.1 Percentage of Death Sentences Imposed, Grouped by Racial Characteristics and Configuration (Weighted)

	All murder cases	Death eligible cases
Death sentences imposed	2.5% (99/3,958)	5.8% (99/1,717)
Defendant		
White defendant	2.7% (38/1,408)	5.9% (38/647)
Nonwhite defendant	2.4% (61/2,550)	5.7% (61/1,070)
Victim		
White victim	3.4% (67/1,945)***	7.1% (67/938)**
Nonwhite victim	1.6% (32/1,982)***	4.3% (32/747)**
Defendant/victim configuration		
White kills white	2.5% (34/1,333)	5.9% (34/572)
Nonwhite kills white	5.1% (33/644)***	9.0% (33/365)***
White kills nonwhite	3.5% (5/141)	11.0% (5/45)
Nonwhite kills nonwhite	1.5% (29/1,974)***	3.9% (29/738)***

Notes
Death eligible cases are first-degree murder cases where at least one statutory aggravating circumstance was found or the prosecutor seeks the death penalty, and the
defendant is more than 17 years of age. Adaped from Unah (2011).
**   p <0.05 (two-tailed test)
*** p <0.01 (two-tailed test).

What is in the Heckman?

For defendants and the relatives of murder victims, the most important part of criminal procedure is sentencing because it carries the most vivid material consequences for the crime. The multiple regression analysis I conducted through the Heckman probit method is based on 250 cases, about half of the full sample, because I am estimating a conditional model in which cases drop out of the justice system due to plea bargaining and acquittals. The findings suggest that the model is indeed plausible. Most of the key independent variables confirm my expectations. The analysis produced a chi-square value that is statistically significant, indicating that the data do fit the model well.

Socio-Structural Explanations of Death Sentencing

I find a connection between race and death sentencing in North Carolina during the 1990s. Consistent with the racial threat thesis, the configuration of nonwhite defendant and white victim is a fairly strong and statistically significant indicator of death sentencing. This authenticates the earlier reported finding in Figure 4.2. Nonwhite defendants who murder white victims fare particularly badly; they are 8% *more likely* to receive the death penalty than white defendants who murder white victims, even after controlling for 34

Table 4.2 Explaining Death Sentencing Outcomes in North Carolina, 1993–1997

Independent variable	Penalty phase: death/life		Marginal impact
	Coefficient	Standard error	
Socio-structural factors			
Nonwhite defendant/white victim	0.138***	(0.028)	0.08
Nonwhite defendant/nonwhite victim	−0.059***	(0.023)	0.03
Defendant age	0.039**	(0.018)	0.02
Defendant age^2	−0.0005**	(0.00002)	0.0003
Defendant education	−0.190**	(0.083)	0.11
Defendant sex	0.035	(0.184)	
Victim age	−0.014**	(0.006)	0.008
Victim age^2	0.0001***	(0.00003)	0.00006
Victim education	0.014	(0.031)	
Victim sex	−0.113**	(0.068)	0.07
Institutional factors			
Electoral proximity for prosecutor	−0.008	(0.031)	
County ideology x county nonwhite population	−2.542**	(1.371)	1.47
County ideology	0.015	(0.995)	
County nonwhite population	0.552	(0.875)	
Republican district attorney	−0.042**	(0.019)	0.02
Male district attorney	−0.401***	(0.103)	00.23
Public defender	−0.175	(0.161)	
Region			
North Carolina piedmont	0.082***	(0.012)	0.05
North Carolina coast	0.189***	(0.044)	0.11
Legal factors			
Murder element 2 (willful, deliberate, premeditated murder)	0.101***	(0.026)	0.06
Murder element 3 (murder and arson, rape, or robbery, etc.)	−0.023	(0.040)	
Statutory aggravating factors	0.183***	(0.014)	0.11
Statutory mitigating factors	−0.036***	(0.008)	0.02
Non-statutory mitigating factors (neglected as child; raised poor)	−0.008**	(0.003)	0.005
Prior homicide record	0.357***	(0.054)	0.21
Multiple victims	0.035***	(0.011)	0.02
Infliction of severe physical pain on victim	−0.007	(0.024)	
Non-statutory aggravating circumstance of the victim (e.g. supporting children)	−0.049**	(0.021)	0.03
Post-mortem abuse	0.049*	(0.031)	0.03
Offense heinousness index	−0.028**	(0.014)	0.02
Motives			
Sex	−0.007	(0.015)	
Money	−0.008	(0.010)	
Hatred	0.054**	(0.027)	0.03
Collateral crime	−0.003	(0.010)	

Table 4.2 Continued

Independent variable	Penalty phase: death/life		Marginal impact
	Coefficient	Standard error	
Heckman's Lambda (λ)	−0.351***	(0.006)	−
Constant	−10.602***	(2.090)	−
Number of observations		250	
Censored observations		17	
Uncensored observations		233	
Chi square		7.67***	

Note
** p <0.05; *** p <0.01 (one-tailed test). Adapted from Unah (2011).

other independent variables that include statutory aggravating and mitigating circumstances sanctioned by the North Carolina General Assembly.

The configuration of nonwhite defendants who murder nonwhite victims is also statistically significant. In this case, however, defendants are 3% *less likely* to receive a death penalty than white defendants who murder white victims. This result suggests that nonwhite victims undeservedly *suffer a race penalty* for being nonwhite, whereas nonwhite defendants undeservedly gain a race-based leniency for killing nonwhites. Putting these findings into proper perspective is the fact that in theory, race is not supposed to matter at all in death sentencing as the Supreme Court explained when justices affirmed structured sentencing in *Gregg v. Georgia* (1976). Insufficient cases in the white defendant/nonwhite victim configuration precluded inclusion of that variable in the model.

How do these findings compare with other major death-sentencing studies in the South? I can transform the probit coefficient of 0.138 for the nonwhite defendant/white victim configuration into a logistic estimate and then derive an odds ratio, which I can use to compare my findings to the Baldus study. Such a comparison is crude but useful because it allows us to obtain a sense of whether things have changed or remain the same across time and space in death sentencing. That transformation leads to an odds ratio of 1.28.[16] Thus, race effects on sentencing are slightly less pronounced in North Carolina during the 1990s than in Georgia during the 1970s where the Baldus study placed the odds of receiving death at 4.3 for black defendants convicted of killing whites. In Maryland, Paternoster *et al.* (2004) reported their findings in terms of probability rather than odds ratio. They find that the probability of a death sentence for black-on-white killings is 0.14, which is higher than the probability of 0.08 that I report for North Carolina. Note that both the Georgia and the Maryland studies are comparing black-on-white murders whereas I am comparing nonwhite-on-white murders. One can conclude that despite legal reforms designed to purge race from death sentencing, race continues to endure as an illegitimate silent aggravating factor in death sentencing in the 1990s.

A recurrent question regarding the death penalty is the extent to which outcomes in capital cases are explained by race versus class. One thesis is that "Race in the South, as in the nation, has always overwhelmed class" (Degler 1972, 102). Opponents of the racial impact thesis, however, insist that the linkage between race and capital punishment is preposterous, reasoning that insofar as there is any racial effect, such effect is actually social class bias masquerading as a racial effect (Kleck 1981). My test of this claim reveals no evidence that social class status of the victim as measured by educational attainment plays a statistically significant role in death sentencing. However, I do find strong evidence that the defendant's social class status plays a sizable role. More educated convicts are 11% less likely to be sentenced to death even after controlling for legal and institutional factors. Therefore, on the question of race versus class, both do matter in death sentencing up to a point. Race definitely matters in capital sentencing, especially in terms of victims. The defendant's social class also matters but the victim's does not.

I find that older defendants are more likely to receive a death sentence. However, very old and very young defendants are given the benefit of the doubt. Similarly, the killing of "helpless" victims who are either very young or very old is likely to result in a death sentence. I also find evidence for a gender gap in death sentencing with regard to victims. As I predicted, the killing of male victims is 7% less likely to result in a death sentence in North Carolina compared to the killing of female victims.

During the 1990s, intense media coverage of several notorious killings brought the issue of hate-motivated crime to the national agenda. The dragging death of a black man, James Byrd, Jr., by three white supremacists in Jasper, Texas in 1998 and the killing of a gay college student, Matthew Shepard, in Wyoming the same year are just two examples. To demonstrate society's revulsion toward such crimes, Congress and states such as North Carolina and Wisconsin responded by enacting punishment enhancement laws for hate-motivated crimes. I tested the importance of hatred and other criminal motives in death sentencing. Of the five motives examined, only hate-motivated killings evinced statistically significant impact, suggesting an expression of low tolerance among North Carolinians for hate-motivated killings during the 1990s.

Finally, I consider the importance of multiple homicide victims in death sentencing. A convict who kills multiple victims is 2% more likely to receive the death penalty than one who kills a single victim. But surprisingly, killing multiple victims is relatively less important than one might suspect. The analysis suggests that the effect on death sentencing for a convict who kills multiple victims is far less than that for a nonwhite who kills one white victim. In North Carolina, it appears that killing multiple victims is less important in capital sentencing than when a nonwhite kills one white person.

Institutional Explanations of Death Sentencing

Even though the decision to impose death is made by an unelected jury, it would be a mistake to think that the institutional factors do not play a role in death sentencing. I find that the interaction of county ideology with the proportion of nonwhites in the county is statistically significant. The interaction effect is the additional impact of county ideology for every 1% of nonwhite population in the county or the additional impact of county nonwhite population for every unit of county ideology. Thus for a conservative county, the probability of a death sentence will drop by 1.47% when the nonwhite population in the county increases by 1%. Moreover, Republican prosecutors are 2% less likely to persuade the jury to give a death sentence than Democratic prosecutors. In other words, during the sentencing phase, convicts are actually better off facing a Republican prosecutor than a Democratic one. Male prosecutors are even less successful compared to their female counterparts. Male prosecutors are 23% less likely to win a death sentence compared to female prosecutors who are, for whatever reason, far more convincing in their courtroom advocacy.

I created three variables to represent the mountain, piedmont, and coastal regions of North Carolina to test for differences in political attitude toward death sentencing across the state. The mountain region serves as the comparison category. It appears that V.O. Key was correct when he posited significant cultural variation within different sections of North Carolina. Region does make an important difference in the sentencing phase. Convicts in the piedmont, the most urbanized region of the state, including large cities such as Charlotte, Durham, and Raleigh are 5% more likely to receive the death penalty compared to convicts in the mountain region. Importantly, the effects more than double in the coastal sand hills, traditionally the most conservative region of the state.

The Effects of Legal Factors on Death Sentencing

Is the capital sentencing system functioning as intended? Ideally, homicide prosecution and sentencing should follow exacting standards prescribed by statute. Therefore, only legal factors associated with the case should matter in the disposition of capital cases. Unfortunately, the empirical literature and the results here suggest otherwise; the system is far from ideal. Nevertheless, I do highlight several legal factors that emerge as important correlates of death sentencing.

By law, statutory aggravating and mitigating circumstances constitute the cornerstone of death sentencing in North Carolina. Therefore, it comes as no surprise that statutory aggravating factors such as the killing of a police officer increase the probability of a death sentence by 11% after controlling for other conditions. I included two murder elements in the model and find that the second murder element dealing with willful, deliberate, and premeditated killing is 6% more likely to result in a death sentence compared to the first murder element, which deals with poisoning, lying-in-wait, starvation, or torture, etc. Felony murders, the third element, which typically lack premeditation fail to achieve statistical significance. The defendant's prior homicide record turns out to be the most important legally-relevant factor. Defendants such as parolees or fugitives who commit another murder are 21% more likely to receive the death penalty. I also find the killing of multiple victims in a single transaction is important in death sentencing. Statutory mitigating circumstances decrease a defendant's criminal culpability and the risk of a death sentence. I find that the effect of statutory mitigating factors is also consistent with my theoretical expectation. But mitigating factors are not nearly as effective in decreasing the chances of a death sentence as aggravating factors are in increasing the chances of a death sentence. I conclude that legal factors are a strong component of the application of capital punishment.

Conclusions

Justice Anthony Kennedy and other members of the Supreme Court agree that racial bias undermines the integrity of the U.S. justice system. Under the U.S. Constitution and under several state statutes, only legal factors associated with a crime should influence capital prosecution and sentencing. After analyzing a rich set of death sentencing data from North Carolina, I conclude that this ideal is far from reality. Beyond legitimate aggravating and mitigating circumstances, several illegitimate factors *do* indeed influence the decision to sentence defendants to death. Among these illegitimate factors is race, just as we discovered with the case of Robert Bacon.

My central question was to examine the extent to which race *still* matters in death sentencing in North Carolina, a state that prides itself as a "progressive plutocracy" according to V.O. Key. I formulated a theoretical model encompassing legal, structural (including racial threat), and institutional conditions. In focusing on the jury's decision at the penalty phase, I find evidence of continuity in that race remains essentially a silent statutory aggravating factor in death sentencing. The impact of race is present and nontrivial. In particular, the race of the victim *still* exerts a significant amount of influence in determining whether a homicide defendant lives or dies. Legal reforms instituted in *Furman* as well as legislative reforms such as the Voting Rights Act which improves the representation of minorities in politics and government have been significant in changing official behavior and policies toward minorities. However, attitudes are hard to change at the individual level. The problem of racial disparity in death sentencing remains acute at the sentencing stage, where ordinary citizens are the key deciders. Thus judicial officials must be proactive in educating jurors about hidden sources of bias in their decision-making.

Appendix A: Data Sources and Measurements

In Appendices A and B, I provide detailed information about my research design and measurements for purposes of future replication. I will also make the data available to all interested parties.

The data came from numerous sources. I list these sources below, along with the variable coding scheme. For most variables, I relied on multiple sources to gather the information. This allowed me to cross-check the validity of official records. For example, I used briefs filed by defendants and prosecutors to construct case facts. But I also relied on the medical examiner's autopsy notes to verify crime facts for consistency. I reconciled any differences through police reports of the offense.

Legally-Relevant Factors

North Carolina criminal statutes list both aggravating and mitigating circumstances, which I coded as follows:

Statutory aggravating factors = count of statutory aggravating factors found by jury

Statutory mitigating factors = count of statutory mitigating factors found by jury

Murder Element 1 (Poisoning, lying-in-wait, imprisonment, torture, starvation) = 1 if present; 0 otherwise

Murder Element 2 (Willful, deliberate, and premeditated killing) = 1 if present; 0 otherwise

Murder Element 3, i.e., Felony murder = (homicide accompanied by another felony) = 1 if present; 0 otherwise

Multiple victims = 1 if 2 or more victims; 0 if 1 victim.

Motives

I used trial briefs, police reports, arrest warrants, and interviews with prosecutors and defense attorneys to determine criminal motive. Each motive: hatred, financial, sexual, rage, and motive "related to other crimes" was measured as follows:

0 = no evidence of this item exists
1 = some evidence this item exists
2 = evidence of this item exists beyond reasonable doubt
3 = strong evidence of this item exists.

Hatred involves long-term hatred of the victim; retaliation or revenge for prior harm done to the defendant or another; avenging the role played by a judicial officer in the exercise of his/her duty; avenging the role played by a police officer; racial animosity; animosity toward the victim based on sexual orientation. *Money* involves killing to obtain money or item of monetary value; contract killing for money; collecting insurance proceeds; obtaining inheritance or property transfer as a result of the victim's death. *Rage* involves immediate rage or frustration (e.g. over victim's conduct during an illegal activity); killing to experience gratification or thrill; demonstrating physical or psychological prowess; no rage apparent indicating complete indifference to value of human life. *Sex* involves desire for sexual gratification, retaliation for sexual refusal, and retaliation for sexual rivalry (jealousy). *Collateral and other crimes* involve facilitating commission of another crime; panic (e.g. defendant became frightened when surprised by the crime victim in the course of a burglary); shootout with the crime victim; crime victim resisted (e.g. pushed silent alarm); silencing a witness to another crime; escaping apprehension, trial or punishment; retaliation for unpaid drug debt or dispute related to drug trade.

Victim and Defendant Socio-Structural Factors

Sources include: North Carolina Office of the Chief Medical Examiner (OCME). Files from these offices contain useful information about the victim, including race, sex, age, and information about probable cause of death and a narrative summary of the circumstances surrounding the death and the nature of the wounds sustained by the victim. Each victim has an OCME case number, which makes tracking information easier throughout the data collection process. The Department of Corrections website was used to verify defendant demographic characteristics and prior criminal record.

> *Race:* 1 = white; 0 = nonwhite
> *Age:* actual chronological age
> *Sex:* 1 = male; 0 = female
> *Education:* 0 = high school dropout or currently in grade school
>   1 = high school graduate or some higher education
>   2 = college graduate or higher
> *Stranger* = 1; 0 otherwise
> *Post-mortem abuse* = 1; 0 otherwise.

Defendant's Criminal History

I examined court records, including indictments sheets; records on appeal; superior court files; jury instructions and verdict sheets for both guilt and penalty phases; defendants' briefs; state's briefs; trial court issues and recommendations forms; and opinions from the North Carolina Court of Appeals and the North Carolina Supreme Court. I also examined police information network records of previous arrests and convictions; newspaper/journalistic accounts of the homicide; and North Carolina Department of Corrections' website. Finally, I interviewed prosecuting and defense attorneys to obtain more information about their cases.

Prior criminal record = number of prior felony convictions

Institutional Factors

Electoral proximity: 0 = four years before prosecutor's next election
1 = three years before prosecutor's next election
2 = two years before prosecutor's next election
3 = one year before prosecutor's next election.

County ideology: percent vote for Republican candidate for Senate in 1992 and 1996

Prosecutor's party affiliation: 1 = Republican; 0 = Democrat

Prosecutor's race: 1 = black; 0 = white

Prosecutor's sex: 1 = male; 0 = female

Public defender: 1 = if public defender or court appointed attorney; 0 = privately retained attorney

County nonwhite population: = proportion of county of offense that is nonwhite

Location: dummy variables representing Mountain, Piedmont, and Coastal regions of the state.

Appendix B: Multi-Stage Statistical Sampling

Stage 1: Selecting Judicial Districts

There are 44 judicial districts in North Carolina representing a total of 100 counties. Each judicial district is headed by one district attorney who manages the prosecution of cases in the counties within that district. This explains why I selected cases by judicial districts. In order to obtain a broad geographic representation of the state, I randomly selected 26 judicial districts.

Stage 2: Selecting Cases from Selected Districts

Overall, 3,990 known defendants were charged with homicide from January 1, 1993 to December 31, 1997. Cases from unselected districts were removed to meet budgetary constraints, leaving 2,504 cases from which I generated my analytical sample. In it, 99 defendants were sentenced to death and 303 were sentenced to life in prison based upon a first-degree murder conviction. Defendants in 181 second-degree murder cases also received life sentences. I randomly selected 10% of these for analysis (18 cases) because prosecutors have been known to undercharge otherwise death eligible offenses (see note 12). Similarly, I randomly selected an additional 100 cases (5.2%) from the remaining 1,921 cases with acquittals and term sentences of less than life in prison. My core analysis is therefore based upon 520 cases, representing 520 individual defendants who form the units of analysis. Overall, the cases represent 80 of the 100 counties of North Carolina. I created sampling weights to reflect the differing sampling probabilities in the two sampling stages and was able to map the sample back to the population.

Notes

1 I thank Jack Boger for his advice and eight UNC Law students for coding the data. I appreciate helpful comments on this project from Virginia Gray, Richard Lempert, Ken Meier, Richard Pacelle, Stuart Macdonald, George Rabinowitz, Susan Welch, Chris Zorn and colloquium participants at the National Science Foundation, American Politics Research Group, and the Law and Policy seminar at UNC-Chapel Hill. The Common Sense Foundation, UNC-Chapel Hill Research Council, and the Center for the Study of the American South provided funding. Chris Fitzsimon provided logistic support.

2 The case facts are detailed in: *North Carolina v. Bacon*, 326 N.C.404 (1990); *North Carolina v. Bacon*, 337 N.C. 66, 446 S.E.2d 542 (1994); *North Carolina v. Clark*, 324 N.C.146 (1989); Clemency petition filed by Gretchen M. Engels (available from author). Robert and Bonnie were living together when the murder occurred.

3 N.C. General Statute, Section 15A-2000. See also Thornburg (1995).

4 Pamela Bloom Smith was about 20 years old when she served as juror in the case of *North Carolina v. Bacon* (1991). She was 29 years old when she signed her affidavit, which is available upon request from the author. The affidavit was brought to the author's attention by Robert Bacon's senior defense counsel, Ms. Gretchen M. Engel of the Center for Death Penalty Litigation in Durham, NC.

5 This authority is stated in Art. III, Section 5(6) of the North Carolina Constitution. There are two different models of clemency adopted by states around the country: executive and administrative. Under executive clemency, the governor is either vested with the full authority to make the decision or to do so after a recommendation from a clemency board. Under the administrative model, the board has sole power to make the decision (Heise 2003, 258).

6 408 U.S. 238 (1972) (per curiam); see, e.g., ibid. at 249–257 (Douglas, J., concurring) (expressing concern that race may be playing an impermissible role in capital sentencing); ibid. at 293–295 (Brennan, J., concurring) (same); ibid. at 364–366, 388 (Marshall, J., concurring) (same).

7 See *Gregg v. Georgia*, 428 U.S. 123, 255 (White, J., concurring).

8 Social science evidence is indeed having an effect at the local level. My study was cited by the clemency petition in the Robert Bacon case. Also, my study has been the basis for a significant push by a coalition of concerned groups and citizens that led to the passage in 2009 of the Racial Justice Act. Among the first of its kind in the nation, the new law permits death row inmates (of all races) to use statistical evidence of racial discrimination in their county, judicial districts, or the state to seek judicial review of their own cases to determine if evidence of racial discrimination exists. If a judge finds such evidence, the law permits that judge to reduce the inmate's death sentence to life in prison. Virtually all inmates on North Carolina death row have filed such claims. The outcomes are not yet known.

9 The other mitigating factors include murder committed when the defendant was under the influence of mental or emotional disturbance; where the defendant was an accomplice in or accessory to the capital felony by another person and his participation was relatively minor; age of the defendant at the time of the crime; and

where the defendant aided in the apprehension or prosecution of another capital felon. N.C. General Statute Section 15A-2000.

10 North Carolina and many other states exempted from capital punishment criminal defendants under 18, well before the Supreme Court outlawed the execution of individuals under 18 in *Roper v. Simmons*, 2005.

11 This categorization was suggested by Professor Thad Beyle of the UNC-Chapel Hill Political Science Department, recognized nationally as an expert on North Carolina politics.

12 In North Carolina, homicides are charged as murder, first-degree murder, second-degree murder, and manslaughter. An all-inclusive category of "murder" is used if the prosecutor has insufficient evidence to classify the homicide as first- or second-degree murder or manslaughter. It further gives the prosecutor flexibility should a plea negotiation become necessary.

13 Because North Carolina counties are grouped into judicial districts with each being controlled by a single prosecutor, I first selected a random sample of judicial districts; I then derived the randomly selected cases from these judicial districts. My sampling weight, calculated to be 31.7, reflects these two sampling stages. To check the accuracy of this weight, I mapped the 520 cases back to the entire population of 3,990 and received a 99% accuracy rate (N = 3,956). Due to rounding of decimal fractions, such mapping hardly ever yields the exact population figure. But I think the sample weight is almost perfect.

14 For a more extensive discussion of Heckman probit models, see Achen (1986).

15 I define nonwhites to include blacks, Hispanics, Asians and other racial minorities, but most individuals in this category are black.

16 The Heckman probit coefficient of 0.138 can be easily transformed into a logistic coefficient by simply multiplying it by a normalization factor of 1.8138 (see Aldrich and Nelson 1984, 44). The result is a logistic coefficient of 0.250. The odds ratio of this logistic coefficient is simply its exponent, i.e., $e^{.250} = 1.28$.

Chapter 5

Under-Estimating and Over-Estimating Litigation

How Activist Plaintiffs may Advance their Causes Even as they Lose their Cases

William Haltom and Michael McCann

For more than three decades scholars and other analysts have debated whether the benefits of resorting to courts to pursue social change outweighed the costs of litigation to litigants, litigators, the economy, and society. Critics have questioned the net benefits of litigating as opposed to changing policies or practices through markets or in legislative, bureaucratic, electoral, or other non-judicial arenas (Horowitz 1977; Melnick 1983; Rosenberg 1991; Sandler and Schoenbrod 2003). Some of these criticisms have been general, system-wide if not always systematic, and even cultural (Glendon 1993; Kagan 2001). Other critiques have focused on specific cases or issues and have assessed concrete benefits and, especially, demonstrable costs (Derthick 2010a; Schuck 1986). Of course, legal scholars and practitioners have answered such questions and such questioning vigorously, especially by emphasizing advances and setbacks beyond winning or losing trials and other calculable, concrete outcomes (Bogus 2001; Feeley and Rubin 1998; Koenig and Rustad 2001; McCann 1994; Mather 1998; Rubin and Feeley 2003; Scheingold 1974; Wagner 2007).

Points and counterpoints regarding appropriate uses and inappropriate abuses of courts, lawsuits, or threats of courtrooms and lawsuits have each and all enhanced our understanding of adjudication as a strategy and tactic for reform, regulation, and change as well as arenas and venues within which changes and continuities in policies and practices might be contested. These dialogues and debates, however, promote at least two temptations. The first temptation is "Scorekeeping"—a tendency to tote proximate, direct costs and benefits of verdicts, judgments, and settlements but to overlook both longer-term, more indirect ramifications of litigation and the cultural consequences of alternatives to ordinary politicking. A second temptation is "Overgeneralization"—a tendency to exaggerate the facility or capacity of litigation to re-frame issues and contests and to overlook obstacles to successful re-framing.

In this chapter we review news coverage of litigation over tobacco, firearms, implants, and food to show that diminishing the responsibility of consumers by attacking the alleged irresponsibility or duplicity[1] of companies is a strategy or tactic the utility of which varies with cultural, legal, ideological, and political contexts. Our narrower objective is to urge analysts and activists alike to attend to costs and benefits both immediate and eventual, both straightforward and roundabout, and, maybe most important, both monetary and symbolic when striving to understand the culture and practice of litigation for social change. Our broader objective in this chapter is to deepen and complexify appreciation of the impacts and ramifications of litigation as tool, tactic, and strategy so that scholarly dialogue might be more complete and productive.

Broadening and Diversifying Scorekeeping

Some recent contributions to the many-sided discussions of adjudication and litigation have directed attention to case studies or specific sorts of litigation and to demonstrable, calculable outcomes. Gordon Silverstein (2009) has advanced interesting explanations of victories and defeats premised on narrow presumptions about what counts as winning and what as losing in litigating the regulation of abortions, environmental issues, campaign finance, presidential powers in wartime, and tobacco (Silverstein 2009). Likewise, in their recent, rigorous assessment of the strategic contexts of regulation by means of litigation, Wayne V. McIntosh and Cynthia L. Cates (2010) ended their chapters on tobacco, firearms, and foods with sections entitled "Winners and Losers" and defined winning and losing largely, albeit not entirely, by proximate, direct, calculable outcomes. In his even more recent study of attempts to regulate or reform tobacco and lead-pigment industries by means of lawsuits, Donald Gifford ranged beyond outcomes of trials and settlements on his scorecard but not far enough to include some political and cultural gains that tobacco and lead-pigment litigation may have yielded in the broader culture and polity (Gifford 2010, 215–229).

These assessments of litigative attempts to remedy or to regulate powerful concerns achieve considerable clarity at some costs to breadth of understanding of victories and defeats beyond verdicts, judgments, and money. In addition to particular, tangible results, lawsuits may result in symbolic and cultural consequences that, while less immediate, less direct, and less quantifiable, may matter greatly for politics and policies and for those who would alter some status quo (Haltom and McCann 2004). While lawsuits anticipated, threatened, or filed may focus issues, test arguments, and alter the short-run calculations of reformers and defenders alike, over longer runs and across political and cultural contexts such suits may also acquaint attentive publics with reformers' and defenders' alarums and calumnies, with claims and contentions, and muckraking narratives in settings in which powerful entities and their spokespeople may be more forthcoming than in legislative or electoral politicking. Changes in public awareness, in mass media's attention to and coverage of social causes as well as legal cases, and in attitudes toward novel claims and innovative issues are important examples of the consequences of lawsuits that develop and ramify long after verdicts, judgments, and awards have faded from political consciousness. Indeed, activists and advocates often aim to advance indirectly through such "radiating effects" of litigation or the threat of litigation what they have less expectation of achieving directly in courtrooms or in settlement offers.[2] Whatever their direct, case-specific aims, reformers may settle for or count on informing the public, challenging prevalent presumptions, and redefining responsibility on issues of great moment to consumers and citizens. Litigation is a venue replete with rhetorical flourishes, image-politicking, and contests to frame issues, problems, and policies, all of which may evolve gradually but persist long after piecemeal results have faded.

If reformers' litigative tactics and strategies are to yield consequences that radiate outward from resolutions of lawsuits, cases must publicize causes. Here, the tendencies of mass media coverage and commonplaces of reporters' and editors' understandings shape what would-be reformers might amplify and disseminate to wide audiences. Class-action and public-interest litigation that is deemed newsworthy may be reduced by the routine over-reporting of plaintiffs' payouts and win-rates and under-reporting of factual and legal predicates that studies of civil-justice disputes have uncovered (Bailis and MacCoun 1996; Garber and Bower 1999; Haltom and McCann 2004; MacCoun 2006).[3] This is the journalistic form of "scorekeeping." Simplistic, sensationalized, and succinct reporting may filter out the novel, complex, substantive contentions that reformers aim to publicize and may emphasize instead outlandish claims or derelictions of traditional assignments of responsibility. Claims that depart from common sense and causes that flout individual responsibility in favor of blaming government or corporations may introduce new ways of seeing familiar problems in ways that virtually guarantee that most readers will settle for familiar perspectives. In sum, what news media propagate, they tend to overstate and to understate in keeping with news values and common sense and not with the novel views or uncommon sensibilities needful to make readers and viewers aware or to change readers' and viewers' attitudes and beliefs.

If reports of reform efforts disparage attempts to change minds or to reconceive policies through themes friendly (or at least friendlier) to reformers, then reform-oriented lawsuits may boomerang in disadvantageous publicization. Cases sometimes serve causes poorly. If publicized litigation makes reformers and their causes look ridiculous, then news media may over time radiate assessments as harmful to reform messengers as to reform messages. Some activists might endure caricature or personal attacks in return for advances in their causes, but reformers and reforms portrayed as mutually reinforcing promotions of irresponsibility may make lawsuits counterproductive to their own causes.

In contrast, reform-minded legal activists may elicit coverage that supplants stereotypic villains (for examples, frivolous, ambulance-chasing lawyers, self-styled victims who pour coffee on themselves then sue, and judges who seek punitive damages for pants lost at the cleaners) and some customary perspectives (for example, that individuals bear responsibility for their own choices) with characterizations and frames more advantageous to their causes. With beneficial coverage reformers seeking to induce or coerce governments or corporations to share responsibility with the citizenry might fare better than in other litigation or in lobbying, electioneering, or other alternatives to litigation.

The strategic and tactical advantages of plaintiffs and the strategic and tactical liabilities and vulnerabilities of defendants look very different if we take seriously the capacity and potential of plaintiffs to change the minds of citizens and leaders about the makers and marketers of products that plaintiffs want regulated. Through litigation and discovery, plaintiffs have documented reckless indifference to the welfare of customers, deceits, and willful subordination of health and lives to profits. Reformers have shown how and how often makers and marketers of suspect products have engaged in duplicity, misrepresentations, and frauds to advertise their wares, to camouflage their misdeeds, and to promote images as solid corporate citizens that belie their conduct and orientations. Whistle-blowers and troves of secreted documents have enabled accusers to move beyond negligence and recklessness to actions and practices that resemble or constitute crimes. Litigants who establish the responsibility or even culpability of manufacturers, marketers, and other usual targets of civil suits before judges and juries may achieve public relations victories that survive courtroom defeats. Activists who long have waged publicity campaigns to "criminalize" industries (Kagan 2001) have often relished opportunities to deploy almost prosecutorial tactics against civil defendants that the activists view as malefactors. Often such legal actions have combined elements of civil and criminal litigation ordinarily deployed to pursue and punish white-collar defendants deemed criminals (Koenig and Rustad 1998, 2004; Simons 2008; Youngdale 2008). Whether lawsuits invoke innovative uses of "public nuisance" doctrines or basic principles of criminal fraud, litigants may through such tactics transcend their losing records in courts with much greater success in mainstream media.

If plaintiffs and plaintiffs' attorneys have wielded "game-changers" that often enable victories outside, beyond, or after trials in which activists and attorneys were soundly beaten, then causes may secure widespread cultural advances, if not flat-out victories, even from lawsuits that those causes routinely lose. The instant, obvious outcome may be defeat. Among the eventual, subtler consequences may be changes in definitions, perspectives, interpretations, symbolizations, and minds. That's the problem with "keeping score" too narrowly.

How Criminalization Changed Tobacco and Firearms Reform

If plaintiffs, activists, and reformers have some capacity to change coverage to reflect themes more advantageous to their causes and very disadvantageous to defendants and companies, has such capacity been realized to any extent in recent litigation? We answer that rhetorical question in the affirmative and now adduce two exemplary deployments of lawsuits to "prosecute" culprits.[4]

Our paper "Criminalizing Big Tobacco: Legal Mobilization and the Politics of Responsibility for Health Risks in the United States" showed how tobacco plaintiffs changed characterizations of tobacco suits in the *New York Times* and challenged Big Tobacco despite Big Tobacco being virtually unbeatable in court (McCann, Haltom, and Fisher 2009). Allegations that manufacturers and marketers of tobacco products had behaved irresponsibly and duplicitously crept upward despite an absence of overt vilification or imbalanced characterizations of defendants in the pages of the *New York Times* 1984–2005. Criminalization of tobacco defendants proceeded despite plaintiffs losing hundreds of lawsuits against tobacco companies. Themes that had long assisted tobacco defendants, especially the "Individual Responsibility" of those who elected to use tobacco products, slowly declined. Themes much more to the liking of tobacco plaintiffs ticked upward as suits revealed evidence of the responsibility of corporations for addicting consumers at early ages and the duplicity of corporations in covering up the carcinogenic effects of tobacco use. Themes piled up *against* tobacco companies and *in favor of* Big Tobacco's detractors despite very balanced descriptions of corporations, defense lawyers, and allies in *New York Times* reports.[5]

Did such sullying of Big Tobacco through media cued by and reliant on the *New York Times* in turn affect regulation of tobacco makers and marketers? Evidence and inference indicate that indirect effects of coverage and imagery matched the ramifications of largely losing litigation to force new policies and practices on the Industry (Center for Responsive Politics 2010, 2011; Derthick 2010b).[6] Beyond the Master Settlement Agreement of 1998, litigation, reportage, and imagery appear to have influenced the defection by Philip Morris, the largest seller and historically the manufacturer most concerned about its public image, which split the tobacco industry. A compelling study of internal documents disclosed in compliance with the Master Settlement Agreement reveals that Philip Morris began in 1999 to explore the option of supporting regulation by the Food and Drug Administration (FDA) in part because its polls and focus group studies showed that its corporate image had plunged among the citizenry (McDaniel and Malone 2005), a stark departure from the company's attitude toward FDA regulation (Kessler 2002). In 2009, Philip Morris spent more than $4 million lobbying for the FDA authorization bill that became law (Layton 2009). Internal communications from Philip Morris commented on the corporation's concerns about the lawsuits highlighting "the deceptive practices of the industry" and allegations of racketeering, conspiracy, and fraud. Moreover, Philip Morris supported governmental regulation of tobacco as

> part of a broader effort to address its negative public image, which has a damaging impact on the company's stock price, political influence, and employee morale. Through regulation, the company seeks to enhance its legitimacy, redefine itself as socially responsible, and alter the litigation environment.
>
> (McDaniel and Malone 2005)

Criminalization in the legal mobilization effort seemed to play a huge role in leveraging support for the regulatory authority over Big Tobacco. Both the increasing stakes and substantive re-framing of litigation arguably contributed to a "tipping point" recalibrating the equilibrium in tobacco policy (Wood 2006).

Reformers who organized lawsuits to reform policies regarding firearms provide a second example of how criminalization or near-prosecution can succeed in newspapers beyond apparent successes in courtrooms. As a result of charges, filings, discoveries, and other accumulations of arguments and information, manufacturers and marketers of firearms took many hits over their dishonesty or irresponsibility in various newspapers in 1984–2005 despite the absence of overt vilification of particular defendants in coverage and despite the victories of firearms makers in courts and in other venues.[7] Firearms lawsuits, like tobacco lawsuits, drew greater attention to and coverage of corporate responsibility for some gun-related problems and revealed examples of corporate duplicity even as attention to and invocation of themes of individual responsibility dipped in coverage in several major newspapers.

Perhaps the re-framing in newspapers and other media mattered little in the contest to regulate firearms. Perhaps firearms companies—far less well heeled than tobacco companies—tired of extensive fees for legal defenses or poor public relations. Nonetheless, the National Rifle Association and other defenders of the manufacturers, marketers, and owners of firearms moved quickly to induce legislatures to ban lawsuits against firearms interests. Scorekeepers who deem firearms suits to be failures owing to the few victories and many defeats of proponents of greater regulation of firearms should at least consider whether intangible, indirect advances by firearms plaintiffs might explain or justify closing the courthouse to such lawsuits; tangible, direct outcomes of such suits would seem to have threatened the makers and marketers of firearms at most minimally.

What Narrow Scorekeeping May Miss

In tobacco and firearms lawsuits alike "Individual Responsibility" frames—presumptions, expectations, or demands that consumers bearing the costs of their decisions to consume products or those who misuse legal products bearing blame for deaths, injuries, and crimes from those products—tended for decades to be features of producers' defenses against attempts to ban or regulate products via lawsuits. In newspapers from 1984 to 2005, these "Individual Responsibility" frames declined relative to frames emphasizing the responsibilities and sometimes even the criminal culpability of those who manufactured or marketed tobacco or firearms. Those who sought greater control of tobacco or of firearms circumvented disadvantageous "Individual Responsibility" frames through dramatic attributions of the collective responsibility to manufacturers and marketers—that is, "Corporate Responsibility" frames—and the collective culpability of manufacturers and marketers in misleading opponents and officials in courtrooms as in public relations—that is, the frames we call "Corporate Duplicity"—as we shall see in detail later in this chapter. Combinations of responsibilizing and criminalizing rhetorics often failed in courtrooms but made major headway in mass media, so those who would "score" litigation strategies or tactics ignore perhaps wider and more resonant changes in coverage and focus instead on narrower and perhaps highly technical results in courtrooms. Moreover, in the studies of tobacco and firearms coverage that we synopsized above, responsibilizing and criminalizing rhetorics dominated newspapers and other popular media more when lawsuits were involved prominently than when tobacco or firearms control was discussed with little or no mention of lawsuits. Articles that extensively or intensively reported lawsuits demonstrated the promulgation of "Corporate Responsibility" and "Corporate Duplicity" frames far beyond articles that featured little or no attention to litigation.

 Our studies of tobacco and firearms cases, in sum, revealed that even though plaintiffs almost always lost particular cases they secured coverage that publicized charges of corporate irresponsibility and corporate deceit or mendacity. Hundreds of newspaper articles in which coders could find little overt or direct vilification of producers and little or no detectable sympathy for consumers teemed with frames that plaintiffs preferred, so the shifting of frames and themes appeared to follow less from reportorial or editorial bias than from the structure and process of litigation. Civil litigation involves filings in which plaintiffs assert defendants' negligence, recklessness, or culpability as part of the cause of action. The more that reform-minded civil litigants deploy tools usually used to prosecute white-collar defendants, the more those litigants exacerbate charges and accusations. If activist plaintiffs appeared to have "criminalized"[8] tobacco and firearms companies in news media even when suits failed in courtrooms, this change of corporate image should be counted among the ramifications of regulating or reforming through lawsuits.

Avoiding Overgeneralization

If the use of lawsuits and litigative campaigns against Big Tobacco and against far smaller makers and marketers of firearms changed perceptions and perspectives that informed mainstream reporting, analysts and activists who would apply lessons from suits against tobacco and firearms concerns to other issues should resist the temptation to presume that the extended, indirect successes in those two issue-domains will be reproduced in other issue-domains. When we compare press coverage of suits against tobacco and firearms with coverage of lawsuits against silicone breast implants and against fast foods, fatty foods, or junk food, re-framing strategies and tactics plainly vary with contexts and contingencies (McCann and Haltom 2004). Some features of litigation on implants and on food augured ill for deployment of criminalization or other arts of besmirching that seemed to have succeeded against tobacco and firearms. Tactics derived from suits against Big Tobacco did not work all that well against fast food outlets or against fatty foods. In litigation against silicone implants the responsibility or duplicity of manufacturers was not easily established and emerging epidemiological evidence undermined conventional liability strategies. In short, that lawsuits sometimes re-frame responsibility or even establish culpability scarcely means that lawsuits routinely re-frame responsibility or establish culpability.

Narrow as we have argued their purview to be, McIntosh and Cates (2010, 143–147) have defined some contexts and contingencies that may qualify or obviate "success" in litigation. We formed our Table 5.1 from their Table 5.1 (p. 145).

Readers might disagree with McIntosh and Cates regarding this or that judgment.[9] Such disagreements lie to the side of our point in reproducing their pithy scheme. McIntosh and Cates posit some similarities and some differences among cases (barely about causes) that may condition the short-term, instrumental, direct results of litigation for social change. Similarities include that defendant manufacturers and marketers will pursue aggressive

Table 5.1 McIntosh and Cates' "Comparison of Multi-Party Litigation Characteristics in Tobacco, Gun, and Food Cases"

Litigation issue	Tobacco	Guns	Fast food
Potential plaintiffs perceived universal or sympathetic	No	No	Yes
Large plaintiff attorney payoffs	Yes	No	No
Public–private litigation partnership	Yes	Yes	No
Aggressive defendant legal strategy	Yes	Yes	Yes
Aggressive defendant legislative strategy	Yes	Yes	Yes
International implications	Yes	No	Yes

Note
Derived from Table 5.1 in McIntosh and Cates (2010).

legal and legislative strategies and hardball tactics. Beyond those invariants, sympathetic victims will sometimes advantage plaintiffs and make litigation more promising and will at other times make litigation more challenging. According to this schematic, the cause lawyer must align proper victims to proper villains to enhance the odds of success either in the instant suit or in the eventual crusade. McIntosh and Cates also note that firearms and food plaintiffs reduced or eliminated attorneys' fees[10] as an issue by undertaking cases without direct, immediate, mercenary interests evident. The ability of advocates to fend off distractions and defamation, then, may also condition the degree to which one set of cases is like another set and thus that one cause may emulate another cause. A third difference between causes identified by McIntosh and Cates is the degree of partnership between governmental and private plaintiffs, partnerships present in tobacco and firearms suits to a far greater extent than in food suits.[11] This difference, too, may qualify the expected returns from emulation.

In keeping with our interest in broad, symbolic, and cultural impacts of litigation, we now extend McIntosh and Cates' strategic analyses of cases to include some less direct outcomes sought by tobacco, firearms, and food causes. (We also consider coverage of silicone implants, an issue not taken up by McIntosh and Cates.) In Table 5.2 we add contingencies that make emulation of tobacco and firearms strategies and tactics even more problematic in food and implants litigation. We proceed below from tobacco to firearms to implants to food causes, the order from top to bottom of Table 5.2.

Tobacco Lawsuits

Scorekeepers' accounts of tobacco litigation do not detract from tobacco's example for follow-on cases and campaigns. That attorneys and advocates in each of the other issues expressly patterned their efforts after tobacco suggests some satisfaction with the accomplishments of tobacco plaintiffs and cases. What advantages did emulators espy? Let us proceed from left to right column in the "Tobacco" row of Table 5.2.

The left column of that row reveals a three-part re-framing that seemed to work in suits against Big Tobacco. First, anti-tobacco activists found a way to overcome or mitigate "Individual Responsibility" framings. If smokers and chewers elected to smoke or to chew, their consent was compromised by Big Tobacco's marketing to consumers under the age of consent, by non-smokers' non-consent to second-hand smoke, and by states' expenditures on health problems attendant on consumption. Jurors might not sympathize with smokers or chewers who took their pleasures from tobacco and now had remorse (as McIntosh and Cates presume in Table 5.1) yet might sympathize more with addicts, juveniles, and service workers whose choices were circumscribed. Next, plaintiffs played up "Corporate Responsibility" for advertising to minors, manipulation of levels of nicotine to keep smokers addicted, and denial that tobacco was carcinogenic (among other perils of tobacco consumption) especially through pseudo-science and public relations. Third, whistle-blowers, documents, and discovery as part of suing adduced ample evidence of "Corporate Duplicity," mendacity and manipulation of information and of those who held it. Diminishing consumers' responsibility or assumption of risk while augmenting the responsibility or venality of corporations through framings and re-framings unified various political forces around a common cause, so plaintiffs were able to contest the hegemony of Big Tobacco outside courtrooms if not so much inside them.

Those who would copy this three-part re-framing might not have apprehended, however, the unity and coherence of the forces arrayed against Big Tobacco (the middle column of the Tobacco row in Table 5.2). Big Tobacco defendants shared interests, resources, and information, forcing successful challengers to coalesce and coordinate to compete in courts and in media. Chronic adversaries of nicotine and tobacco incorporated emergent, powerful allies such as states' attorneys generals in cooperative fronts against Big Tobacco. The unity and coherence of those who challenged and nearly prosecuted tobacco companies must not be overlooked: such unity and coherence would be daunting and fleeting for those who would take on the firearms, silicone, and food industries.

We also note in Table 5.2 (the rightmost column in the Tobacco row) novels and films that spread the anti-tobacco cause through popular culture. Although we analyze newspaper coverage later in this chapter, we stress that whatever films, television programs, periodical articles, or books contributed to coordinated coalitions' efforts to re-frame was likely quantitatively and qualitatively unmatched by efforts against breast implants or fast or fatty foods.

Firearms Lawsuits

Litigators who sought to regulate or restrict firearms explicitly adapted strategies and tactics that had worked in tobacco lawsuits. Yet, even before the U.S. Supreme Court constitutionalized an individual's right to keep and bear arms, forces battling firearms and rights to keep and bear arms faced daunting obstacles (Sugarman 2006, 196–222).[12] We sketch those obstacles in the "Firearms" row of Table 5.2. Like tobacco causes, regulation or eradication of firearms depended on getting around "Individual Responsibility" by way of corporate liability, responsibility, or criminality. Cause lawyers produced sympathetic victims (for example, innocents, especially children, shot) and universal victims (for example, taxpayers who footed the bill for victims of gun violence and accidents) to increase the arguable responsibility of defendants. The makers of firearms accommodated activists by marketing practices and policy pronouncements easily characterized as irresponsible or reprehensible. Corporate misdeeds, cover-ups, and corruption furthered the re-framing

Table 5.2 Political and Cultural Characteristics of Tobacco, Firearms, Implants, and Food Causes and Cases

	Framing	Litigants' unity/coherence	Popular culture
Tobacco	*Reduce* "Individual Responsibility" by non-consent: nicotine addiction; choices made underage; involuntary second-hand smoke; and public health expenses borne by taxpayers. *Increase* "Corporate Responsibility" by how products made/marketed: manipulating levels of nicotine; advertising to minors; and denying carcinogens and other harms. *Increase* "Corporate Duplicity" by documenting dishonesty: phony science; perjury; confidentiality agreements and intimidation of whistle-blowers.	Enduring moral/policy cooperation: Big Tobacco's chronic challengers [health experts, scientists, and private lawyers] share cause with novel challengers [kids' advocates, public officials, and states' AGs]. vs. Enduring monetary/policy confluence of interests: Big Tobacco's defenders share interests in profits, campaign contributions, legal fees, state and U.S. taxes, and jobs in factories or on farms.	Christopher Buckley's novel *Thank You for Smoking* (1995) and the movie *Thank You for Smoking* (2006) John Grisham's novel *The Runaway Jury* (1999) The movie *The Insider* (1999)
Firearms	*Reduce* "Individual Responsibility" by focusing on victims: innocents shot; accidents, especially involving children; and public health expenses borne by taxpayers. *Increase* "Corporate Responsibility" via corporate misdeeds: misleading marketing; large-volume sales; inadequate background checks; willingness to get firearms to convicts; unsafe design of weapons; and willfully inadequate policing of distribution. *Increase* "Corporate Duplicity" by cover-ups and corruption: straw purchases; dealings with corrupt dealers and accommodations of illegal markets; and punishing whistle-blowers and hiding tracing data.	Temporary alliance around issues: police chiefs, kids' groups, city attorneys, and NAACP support specific suits by long-standing opponents of firearms practices or firearms rights [e.g. the Brady Center]. vs. Enduring alliance around rights: NRA, longtime allies, and makers and marketers of firearms mutually commit to rights and liberties of ownership and use of firearms.	Christopher Buckley's novel *Thank You for Smoking* (1995) The movies *Thank You for Smoking* (2006), *Runaway Jury* (2003), *Bowling for Columbine* (2002) John Lott's nonfiction *More Guns, Less Crime* (2000)

Silicone breast implants	*Reduce* "Individual Responsibility" by refocusing attention: non-cosmetic implants; limited information limited patients' consent; autoimmune and other side-effects not known or acknowledged. *Increase* "Corporate Responsibility" by shifting burdens to makers or marketers: manufacturers incurious about "concerns" failed to prove implants safe. *Increase* "Corporate Duplicity" by attacking secrecy: makers/marketers fail to warn MDs about nearly inevitable ruptures and leakage.	Trial lawyers and hopeful plaintiffs but not much of a "movement." Science/expert opinion divided. FDA moratorium and House subcommittee [Ted Weiss] hearings. FDA processes attacked. Plastic surgeons energetically lobby to keep implants on market.	Marcia Angell's nonfiction *Science on Trial* (1997) and John A. Byrne's nonfiction *Informed Consent* (1997) HBO's film *Breast Men* (1997) Connie Chung CBS broadcast (1990)
Fast/fatty foods	*Reduce* "Individual Responsibility" by defects in consumers' choices: unawareness of calories; marketing to children; evidence of addictiveness of fast/fatty foods. *Increase* "Corporate Responsibility" by negligence/recklessness of vendors: failures to warn or disclose nature of products; negligence in hawking foods high in fat, cholesterol, sugar, salt, and other unhealthful ingredients, which promote obesity; and profiting from "attractive nuisances" that lure children and product placements on children's programming. *Increase* "Corporate Duplicity" by mendacity: deceptive marketing, false advertising, or fraud [including McDonald's cooking "vegetarian" fries in beef tallow].	Ad hoc amalgam of litigators: Cross-cutting interests among health experts concerned about obesity, nutritionists opposed to fast food; exercise gurus, moralists, anti-corporate reformers.	Eric Schlosser's nonfiction *Fast Food Nation* (2005) The movies *Super Size Me* (2004), *Fast Food Nation* (2006), *Food Inc.* (2008)

efforts of plaintiffs, as had been the case with tobacco suits. Unlike tobacco reformers, firearms activists faced the formidable National Rifle Association and other long-time defenders of firearms and of rights with a makeshift, often case-specific, alliance desperate to contest in courtrooms what they seldom could contest effectively in legislatures or elections (see the middle column for the Firearms row). This meant that the unity, coherence, and breadth of anti-firearms forces was less, in our judgment, than those of anti-tobacco forces even when municipalities and other governmental entities entered the fray on the side of firearms plaintiffs. Firearms companies were neither as intimidating nor as well financed as Big Tobacco, but the NRA proved more than a match for the plaintiffs when it induced state legislatures to disallow suits against firearms manufacturers. Firearms reformers enjoyed considerable support from popular culture, just as crusaders against tobacco had, but confronted a very popular culture of gun enthusiasts and fans of the right to keep and bear arms (Kohn 2005).[13]

Implants Lawsuits

The obstacles that litigation over silicone breast implants had to surmount were more imposing than those overcome by tobacco and firearms activists, so emulation of "successful" litigation would demand overlooking disadvantages that burdened opponents of implants. Defendants could fend off "Corporate Responsibility" and "Corporate Duplicity" frames even without asserting "Individual Responsibility." For example, plaintiffs could point out that perhaps a fifth of implants were not "merely cosmetic," but such a showing might call to mind the motives behind the other 80%. This made breast augmentation easier for defenders and defendants to characterize as a personal choice for which patients bore some responsibility. Evidence of irresponsible manufacture or marketing was slim even before epidemiological findings began to undermine any defects or shortcomings in implants, making claims of corporate irresponsibility or duplicity harder to sustain. Making matters more difficult, plaintiffs sometimes hid a variety of positions and interests behind a loosely unified front (see the middle column of Table 5.2), juggling interests and issues in a manner more of ad hoc agitation than of a movement. In the realm of popular culture, opponents of implants enjoyed no advantages comparable to the fiction and nonfiction books and the compelling and much watched movies that assisted tobacco lawyers in vilifying Big Tobacco.

Lawsuits Concerning Fast, Fatty, or Junk Foods

Food causes, too, sought to follow the tobacco model, but each of the strategies on which we focus in the left column of the Food row in Table 5.2 was deeply problematic. However defective that advocates might make consumers' choices seem, judges, jurors, and citizens in general likely would hold consumers responsible for what they ate, so "Individual Responsibility" was nearly an immovable object against which food fighters could seldom marshal irresistible force or argument. Marketers zealously hawked junk food, fast food, and fatty foods, but lawyers could not easily portray iconic chains and popular restaurants as reckless or negligent in a society suffused with advertising and commercialism. "Corporate Responsibility" frames fashioned along the lines of efforts against tobacco ran into "consumer sovereignty." "Corporate Duplicity" frames could make little headway by emphasizing that marketing was deceptive, advertising exaggerated, or corporate public relations less than candid, so Ronald McDonald was far more resistant to denunciation than Joe Camel. Moreover, as the middle column of Table 5.2 notes, mobilizations against fast food, fat in foods, and so-called junk foods in no way approached the coordination or message coherence of crusades against tobacco or firearms. Indeed, that we must lump together causes and cases against fast food, fatty foods, and junk food to amalgamate a category should signify how diverse and scattered actions against various sorts of food were. What films and books supported food reform were similarly disparate and less likely to find audiences than popular culture that bolstered efforts against tobacco and firearms.

Framing, Coordination, and Popular Culture

Our sketch of similarities in strategies and differences in circumstances across tobacco, firearms, implant, and food issues illustrates perils of analogizing or generalizing across issues, especially when cultural, symbolic, and other intangible stakes of causes and cases are acknowledged. Litigators crusading against firearms, implants, or defective foods patterned their efforts after what they regarded as successes that brought Big Tobacco to the bargaining table if not "the bar of Justice." But lawyers and strategists for the firearms industry could not compete against the lobbying and electoral clout of the NRA, which effectively deprived litigators of their venues, nor the popular resonance of gun rights and culture (Kahan, Braman, and Gastil 2006, 105–126; Kohn 2005).[14] Lawyers and strategists for opponents of implants could not marshal science against the silicone makers because science repeatedly and emphatically supported defendants rather then plaintiffs. Persuading jurors and citizens that nicotine was habit-forming corresponded to experiences or observations of tens of millions over decades; analogizing to addictions to fast food, fats, salts, and similar products contradicted the experiences and observations of tens of millions over decades.

In sum, the tobacco lawyers blazed trails that other litigators found difficult to traverse. Emulation of what litigators (but perhaps not scorekeepers) regarded as triumphs over Big Tobacco was at best tricky and at worst tantalizing. Anti-firearms actions may have enjoyed some successes while municipalities and other governments could be mobilized on behalf of complainants, and such actions had some resonance in movies and books, albeit that in nonfiction at least intellectually respectable cases could be marshaled on the side of firearms and the rights of owners (Lott 2010).[15] Legal and political mobilization against silicone implants encountered grave difficulties vilifying makers and manufacturers, especially when heart-wrenching anecdotes and medical conjecture collided with monolithic epidemiological studies. Science stood against implants plaintiffs every bit as imposingly as science backed tobacco plaintiffs (Angell 1997).[16] Legal and political actions against purveyors of fast food had going for them almost no resources that opponents of Big Tobacco enjoyed: an addiction argument that might be true to some extent but contradicts to a great extent the experience of most consumers; a consumer culture suffused with fast, fatty, salty, and yummy treats against which the arrayed lawyers and nutritionists seem to be spoilsports and scolds; and cultural productions too limited in appeal or awareness to overcome frequent household guests, corporate icons, and royalty such as the Burger King and the Dairy Queen.

The factors arrayed by McIntosh and Cates in Table 5.1 may account for the inability of other causes to emulate efforts to regulate or restrict tobacco. The factors adduced by us in Table 5.2 may complement McIntosh and Cates' account. Either or both sets of factors, in our view, stand as admonitions against facile emulation of strategies and tactics at least somewhat successful against Big Tobacco and, perhaps, firearms.

Re-Scoring Tobacco, Firearms, Implants, and Food Litigation[17]

We now marshal data that reinforce the two oversimplifications against which we have inveighed above. First, newspaper coverage of mobilizations against the four "causes" we have been considering (Big Tobacco, firearms, silicone implants, and foods) show that threatening and filing lawsuits consistently accentuates negative frames that impugn defendants who make and market products even when lawsuits are conspicuously unsuccessful in courtrooms and in settlement negotiations. This finding, of course, undermines oversimplified "Scorekeeping," for it shows that litigation yields cultural and political dividends if mass media publicize charges and discoveries, even when plaintiffs lose verdicts and judgments. Second, press coverage also bears out differences among lawsuits regarding tobacco, firearms, implants, or foods that we sketched in Table 5.2. The re-framing that opponents or critics of tobacco practices and policies were able to work has proved at least more complicated if not counterproductive in other issue-areas.

Sampling Litigation-Heavy and Litigation-Light Reportage

We sampled articles from the *New York Times* (for tobacco issues) or from "major newspapers" as grouped by LexisNexis Academic (for firearms, implants, and food issues) according to protocols available online.[18] Our sample was targeted at articles that most and least emphasized specific litigation, the better to discern differences between coverage of broad causes (articles attending to one of our four issue-areas with little or no attention to particular lawsuits) and coverage of specific cases in which more comprehensive issues may be lost amid dramatic details and adversarial brio.

Litigation-Heavy and Litigation-Light Scorecards

Roughly to approximate the difference that lawsuits make for coverage of the four causes we selected, we constructed Table 5.3. Table 5.3 presents six frames of greatest relevance for this chapter, ordered from themes advantageous to plaintiffs (ordered, we presume, from "Corporate Duplicity" as the most damaging to defendants' images if not their cases to "Corporate Responsibility" to "Public Costs") to those advantageous to defendants ("Individual Responsibility" and "Attorneys' Fees") with "Governmental Responsibility"—the duty of governments at the national or state level to protect consumers from corporations or corporations from frivolous lawsuits or, at the least, do something about the product at issue—in between.[19] Frames most welcomed by plaintiffs appear on the left of Table 5.3; frames most welcomed by defendants appear on the right.

Overall, Table 5.3 suggests that reports of or comments on litigation tended to emphasize "Corporate Responsibility" and "Corporate Duplicity" frames far more and "Individual Responsibility" frames far less than reports of causes without a focus on lawsuits. Looking at the table in detail, we see that

1   The left-most columns in Table 5.3 reveal that frames that highlight the duplicity, irresponsibility, or liability of makers or marketers of products were detected far more often in litigation-heavy articles than in articles that discussed causes without mention of specific cases. Coverage of causes with few or no lawsuits worked far less vilification or criminalization than did coverage of lawsuits, we see from the upper-most rows for each issue-area. "Corporate Duplicity" frames increased impressively in coverage of tobacco and firearms cases over levels in reports of causes without cases and increase noticeably in coverage of implants and food cases over levels of coverage that does not concern specific suits. "Corporate Responsibility" frames made up one-third or more of frames detected in coverage that relayed specific cases.[20]

Table 5.3 Frames in Articles Regarding Tobacco, Firearms, Implants, and Food Causes and Cases Split by Minimal Attention to Specific Suits Versus Maximal Attention to Specific Suits

Subject of Litigation	Advantageous to Plaintiffs/Damaging to Defendants								Advantageous to Defendants/Damaging to Plaintiffs				Total	
	Corporate Duplicity		Corporate Responsibility		Public Costs		Government Responsibility		Attorneys' Fees		Individual Responsibility			
	Row%	(n)	Row%	(n)	Row%	(n)	Row%	(n)	Row%	(n)	Row%	(n)	Row%	(n)
Tobacco														
Litigation-Light Sample	16	(86)	19	(101)	19	(103)	31	(167)	0	(0)	16	(85)	101	(542)
Litigation-Heavy Sample	31	(364)	32	(379)	9	(108)	6	(68)	7	(81)	16	(186)	101	(1186)
Both Samples	26	(450)	28	(480)	12	(211)	14	(235)	5	(81)	16	(271)	101	(1728)
Firearms														
Litigation-Light Sample	10	(49)	29	(143)	12	(61)	30	(152)	0	(1)	19	(93)	100	(499)
Litigation-Heavy Sample	26	(446)	32	(540)	16	(273)	7	(112)	5	(78)	15	(252)	101	(1701)
Both Samples	23	(495)	31	(683)	15	(334)	12	(264)	4	(79)	16	(345)	101	(2200)
Silicone Breast Implants														
Litigation-Light Sample	25	(61)	21	(51)	7	(18)	12	(30)	6	(14)	30	(73)	101	(247)
Litigation-Heavy Sample	31	(142)	44	(203)	2	(8)	0	(1)	18	(82)	5	(25)	100	(461)
Both Samples	29	(203)	36	(254)	4	(26)	4	(31)	14	(96)	14	(98)	101	(708)
Fast, Fatty, Junk Foods														
Litigation-Light Sample	5	(93)	28	(475)	4	(69)	17	(288)	0	(1)	45	(767)	99	(1693)
Litigation-Heavy Sample	14	(193)	33	(463)	1	(17)	4	(62)	7	(98)	41	(588)	100	(1421)
Both Samples	9	(286)	30	(938)	3	(86)	11	(350)	3	(99)	44	(1355)	100	(3114)

2   Attention to Public Costs—expenses of consumption borne by governments and taxpayers—was minimal and declined in litigation-heavy coverage, so litigation, far from having increased attention to "Public Costs," seems to have elicited from newspapers more attention to "Corporate Responsibility" and "Corporate Duplicity."

3   Invocations of "Governmental Responsibility" frames consistently figure more in articles that do not concern or contain lawsuits than in articles concerned with or containing lawsuits, albeit that "Governmental Responsibility" is a theme far more prominent in coverage of tobacco and firearms causes than in coverage of implants and food causes. Public entities' interventions in tobacco and firearms cases somewhat ironically seem to have led to a decline in attention to "Governmental Responsibility" framings.

4   By contrast, "Attorneys' Fees" frames—the belief or suspicion that monetary gain rather than public good motivated plaintiffs' attorneys to sue— were far more common in litigation-heavy reports than in litigation-light reports but made up such small portions of framings in either litigation-heavy reports and litigation-light reports that they conferred a seemingly modest advantage on corporate defendants.[21]

5   "Individual Responsibility" framings—detection of the frame that consistently avails defendants in assigning choices and consequences to plaintiffs—overall factored into coverage that featured specific cases less than in reports about causes that did not focus on specific cases.[22] In food causes, the decline in such framings was minimal for case-centered coverage and in each sample made up more than 40% of all frames detected; this key advantage to makers or marketers of fast or fatty foods will interest us more as an indicator of differences across causes than it does regarding differences between suit-intensive coverage and other reportage.

Our Table 5.3 "scorecard" indicates that the frames most advantageous to makers or marketers—"Individual Responsibility" and "Attorneys' Fees"— manifest at most modest and occasional gains in coverage of cases relative to coverage of causes. By contrast, the frames most advantageous to advocates— "Corporate Responsibility" and "Corporate Duplicity"—were often more common and usually substantially more common in articles concerned with specific suits than in articles about causes but not cases. "Government Responsibility," more prominent when specific cases were not involved, was not very prominent when articles mentioned or profiled specific suits.

Gains in advantageous frames, we concede, only roughly indicate cultural, symbolic, and political gains from litigation in pursuit of product-related reforms, but those gains suggest why advocates of reform went after those who manufacture and those who market firearms, implants, and fast foods via tactics and strategies similar to those that had worked (in the view of the reformers if not that of socio-legal scholars) against Big Tobacco.[23] We now scrutinize gains and losses in litigating for regulation of consumer goods and services. Subtler, closer scrutiny will reveal many similarities but many differences between tobacco and firearms litigation and the other two sorts of causes.

Tobacco—Figure 5.1 reviews framing in coverage of tobacco causes and cases in the *New York Times* between 1984 and 2005 so that the causes and cases most emulated by the other sets of causes and cases may be inspected. In coverage of causes without cases (the Litigation-Light Sample) we find that "Science" frames dominated articles and that "Government Responsibility" frames outpaced pro-defense or pro-plaintiff frames.[24] When causes were covered amid detailed reporting of cases—the Litigation-Heavy Sample— "Science" and "Government Responsibility" frames were far less common, and "Corporate Responsibility" and "Corporate Duplicity" dominated other frames

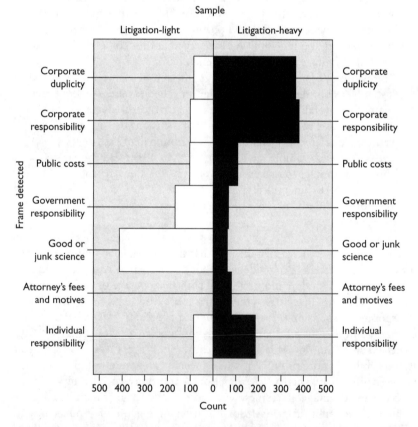

Figure 5.1 Use of selected frames in *New York Times* reportage of *tobacco* causes and cases, split by minimal attention to specific suits versus maximal attention to specific suits.

(as we saw in Table 5.3). Indeed, the three frames that plaintiffs preferred and sought—"Corporate Responsibility," "Corporate Duplicity," and "Public Costs"—make up almost 70% of the frames detected in the Litigation-Heavy Sample. "Individual Responsibility" frames also were found far more frequently in coverage laced with specific suits, which may indicate that tobacco defendants were successful at focusing on consumers who chose years or decades of tobacco enjoyment and now dared to sue companies for providing what consumers wanted. Still, the defendant-friendly frames "Individual Responsibility" and "Attorneys' Fees" constitute less than one-third of the frames detected in Litigation-Heavy articles, so coverage of specific suits seems to have favored reformers and their causes. In sum, invocations of defendant-welcomed themes were *absolutely* more frequent in case-heavy reports than in reports on issues and causes with minimal attention to cases but much less frequent *relative* to plaintiff-sought framings in case-heavy reports. Litigation appears from these data to have yielded plaintiffs great gains.

Firearms—Coverage of causes and cases concerned with manufacture, marketing, and uses of firearms differed from coverage of tobacco to some degree but resembled coverage of tobacco in enough respects that we see why firearms reformers and plaintiffs might follows tobacco reformers' lead. Litigation-Heavy articles in Figure 5.2 assume a profile much like the profile for tobacco in Figure 5.1:

1   "Government Responsibility" frames bulge to the left (Litigation-Light articles) far more than they appear in articles on the right side (Litigation-Heavy articles).
2   Coders detected "Individual Responsibility" frames more often in case-centric reports than in cause-centered reports.
3   "Corporate Responsibility" and "Corporate Duplicity" frames are much more common amid case-specific articles than among cause-related articles.

Taken together, the three frames preferred by firearms plaintiffs make up almost 70% of all frames in Figure 5.2, approximately the same as for tobacco articles in Figure 5.1. The two frames most advantageous to firearms companies again hover at around one-fifth of all frames as they did for tobacco.[25] Like tobacco causes and cases, "Governmental Responsibility" is more common when specific suits are not being covered than when specific suits elicit articles.

Implants—Coverage of implants differed from coverage of the first two sorts of policies and practices, as Figure 5.3 discloses. In implants causes and cases alike, frames related to science dominate coverage (albeit that science frames make up about 60% of Litigation-Light frames but about 40% of Litigation-Heavy frames). The role of epidemiological studies was such in silicone implants causes and cases that coverage seems to follow the science, a

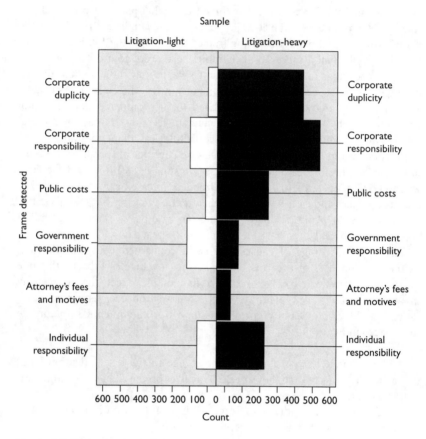

Figure 5.2 Use of selected frames in reportage of *firearms* causes and cases in "major newspapers" split by minimal attention to specific suits versus maximal attention to specific suits.

marked difference from tobacco articles and one indication why implant cases differed from tobacco cases. Still, implants reveal some advantages to litigation. "Corporate Responsibility" and "Corporate Duplicity" frames are far more common when suits are foci of articles than when suits are not the foci, much as was the case with tobacco and firearms disputes. Unlike the data for tobacco and firearms disputes, "Individual Responsibility" themes nearly disappeared in Litigation-Heavy coverage. Balancing those advantages to plaintiffs in coverage of suits to an extent were "Bankruptcy" frames, which were more common in Litigation-Heavy coverage than in Litigation-Light coverage, and "Attorneys' Fees" frames, which were three times more common in Litigation-Heavy coverage than in Litigation-Light coverage if only one in seven frames overall. "Individual Responsibility," "Attorneys' Fees," and "Bankruptcy" frames across both samples amount to about one-fifth of frames detected, which is not much

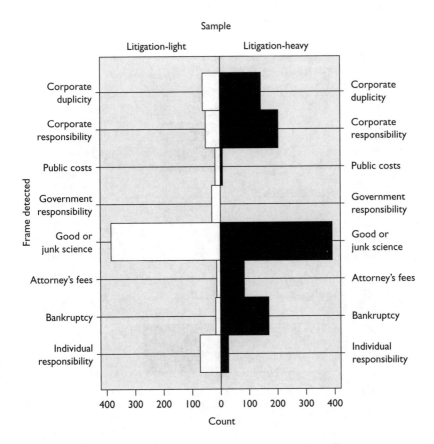

Figure 5.3 Use of selected frames in reportage of *silicone implants* causes and cases in "major newspapers" split by minimal attention to specific suits versus maximal attention to specific suits.

less than the one in four frames devoted to "Corporate Responsibility," "Corporate Duplicity," and "Public Costs." In sum, plaintiffs' advantages in framing issues were decidedly less for causes and for cases relating to silicone implants relative to reportage of tobacco and firearms.

Food—Coverage of fatty, junk, and fast foods deviated from tobacco and firearms coverage even more than implants. Figure 5.4 figuratively shouts the persistence of "Individual Responsibility," a favored frame of corporate defendants. The choices of individual consumers and citizens made up negligibly less of Litigation-Heavy articles than of Litigation-Light (see Table 5.3), yet accounted for more than 40% of all frames detected. Defendant-friendly frames ("Individual Responsibility" and "Attorneys' Fees") outnumbered plaintiff-friendly frames and, if "Government Responsibility" frames are omitted, constitute a majority of frames found in food articles. Beyond

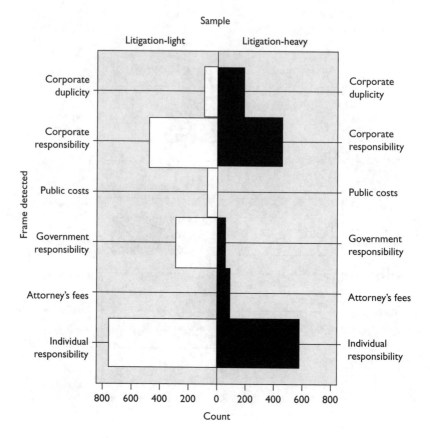

Figure 5.4 Use of selected frames in reportage of *food* causes and cases in "major newspapers" split by minimal attention to specific suits versus maximal attention to specific suits.

that stark difference and perhaps owing to the predominance of "Individual Responsibility" framings, "Corporate Responsibility" frames were about the same in coverage of causes without cases as in coverage of causes with cases, and "Corporate Duplicity" frames, three times more frequent in coverage of cases than in coverage of causes, made up only one frame in seven on the Litigation-Heavy side of Figure 5.4.

Considered together, the four diagrams permit us an overview of each over-statement examined in this chapter. Each diagram shows some gains in press coverage from litigation or settlement activities, so scorekeeping inside court-rooms or boardrooms seems to neglect some payoffs to causes that might jus-tify even losing lawsuits. These results reinforce our earlier arguments and findings regarding "Oversimplified Scorekeeping," the first temptation we identified. Regarding the second temptation, "Overgeneralization," the diagrams are if anything more compelling. We have found that plaintiffs and clients in silicone and food contests collided with scientific findings that undermined their cases and perhaps causes about as much as science aided tobacco plaintiffs and clients and statistics (on sales and distribution, for example) favored firearms plaintiffs and clients. We have found as well that food plaintiffs and clients did not overcome the "Individual Responsibility" of consumers for selecting fast foods, junk foods, and fatty foods and could not much criminalize the marketing or distribution practices of companies that make such offerings convenient and ubiquitous.

Summary and Discussion

We have reviewed newspaper coverage of four sorts of causes and cases to reinforce our concerns about facile scorekeeping and overgeneralization, the two foci of this chapter. We have uncovered evidence that struggles and suits elicit coverage in newspapers that advantages plaintiffs, victims, and crusaders against consumer ills and, perhaps more important, denigrates producers and vendors for practices proclaimed to be irresponsible or even criminal. Moreover, we find that litigation garners coverage more favorable to activists for and advocates of reforms and regulation than coverage of issues and policies alone. Lawsuits re-frame reform contests both in newspapers and in other news media that rely on leading newspapers. Exclusive or nearly exclusive attention to tangible or calculable consequences of litigation, it follows, underestimates the ramifications of litigating for social changes. Scorekeepers should expand their focus or foci to take into account the intangible, incalculable, but nonetheless actual effects of litigation.

In addition, we have uncovered evidence that the intangible, incalculable, but nonetheless actual contexts of litigation condition the effects of litigation and especially the benefits that activists and plaintiffs may wring from litigation for social changes. We have not in Table 5.2 exhausted the differences in strategic contexts among the four sorts of policy-issues or the disparities in cultural and political changes to be expected from tobacco and firearms litigation on the one side and silicone and food litigation on the other side. We have nevertheless charted a promising path for further research.

We hope that scholars will explore more deeply and fully the four sorts of contests over policy and reform on which we have concentrated above. We hope as well that scholars will test our findings "backward" against coverage of asbestos litigation and other causes and cases that predate much of the litigation against tobacco. We also hope that socio-legal analysts will apply our findings to coverage of simultaneous or subsequent coverage of policy contests and reform litigation.

In sum, we intend this chapter to counsel improved scorekeeping and contextualized generalizations. If we have succeeded in that intention, we reckon our efforts worthwhile.

104 William Haltom and Michael McCann

Notes

1 Throughout this chapter we refer to various deceptions, misrepresentations, or prevarications by marketers or makers of products. Some deceptions sank to the level of perjury or mendacity. Other deceptions partook more of spin or euphemisms common in public relations or advertising. Rather than sort through such strategies or tactics, we use "duplicity" to subsume the tricks of these trades. We remind readers that duplicity is alleged more often than it can be verified or proved, so we do not presume the nature or gravity of duplicity in any instance.

2 On such cultural, often indirect and complex, ramifications, see generally Scheingold (1974), Brigham (1996), Sarat and Scheingold (1998), Handler, Hollingsworth, and Erlanger (1998).

3 In noting these tendencies of news media, we intend to criticize neither media nor litigators. Our focus instead is on how litigation strategies and tactics tend to appear in published accounts.

4 We do not here mean to state that the corporate defendants in such actions are culprits or culpable. Nor do we use "exemplary" to endorse these tactics as in any sense ideal. Rather we raise these instances to illustrate that causes have achieved some lasting, demonstrable gains from defeats.

5 Professor Mather (1998) demonstrated the transformation of themes through periodicals, so these results are not limited to the *New York Times*.

6 Derthick (2010b); Center for Responsive Politics (2010, 2011).

7 Please note well that we studied tobacco coverage only in the *New York Times* and firearms coverage in "major newspapers" as designated by LexisNexis Academic.

8 Please recall that we mean by "criminalize" allegations or charges beyond negligence or even recklessness, wrongs that reflect intentions or acts that, if proved, might justify conviction and severe punishments beyond compensating some plaintiff or victim.

9 For example, McIntosh and Cates' summary characterizations of the universality or sympathy of plaintiffs lack nuance and seem to overlook the degree to which universality or sympathy of plaintiffs and defendants alike is socially, politically, and jurally constructed. Many actual, let alone potential, plaintiffs in food cases are far from sympathetic or "universal," as McIntosh and Cates themselves demonstrate (2010); many survivors of the carnage wrought by tobacco or firearms could not be more sympathetic and, alas, too often seem quite ordinary in their suffering.

10 Attacks on plaintiffs' attorneys for profiting from suing corporations were common from the mid-1990s on and may be a form of vilification of victims' causes and cases without directly attacking the victims themselves.

11 McIntosh and Cates demonstrate governmental interventions in their discussion of regulation of food via litigation, so they must realize that their "no" in the row associated with public–private partnership may mislead those who have not been reading McIntosh and Cates carefully.

12 Sugarman (2006, 196–222).

13 See Kohn (2005).

14 Kohn (2005); Kahan, Braman, and Gastil (2006, 105–126).

15 Lott (2010).

16 Angell (1997).

17 The authors thank the National Science Foundation for Award #0451207, which supported gathering and coding of data.

18 See "Appendices for McGuire Chapter" at www.pugetsound.edu/faculty-sites/bill-haltom/ (accessed May 14, 2011).

19 The entire array of frames detected in each of the four sorts of causes may be found

in Appendix D at "Appendices for McGuire Chapter" at www.pugetsound.edu/ faculty-sites/bill-haltom/ (accessed May 14, 2011).

20 For articles regarding tobacco or implants, case-focused coverage featured substantially greater "Corporate Responsibility" than coverage related to causes but not cases. Articles regarding food or firearms displayed no substantial differences—corporate responsibility accounted for approximately one in three frames detected in either sample.

21 Although coders had "Attorneys' Fees" frames available for coding for every article, attacks on contingency fees and lawyers profiting from suits against tobacco companies proliferated in the mid-1990s and faded thereafter.

22 We note that "Individual Responsibility" held steady at 16% in each sample of coverage of tobacco causes.

23 We have rehearsed earlier in this chapter and in previous papers considerable evidence of the efficacy of litigation against Big Tobacco and against other companies.

24 Coders were provided "Junk Science" and "Good Science" as frames. We combine the categories herein because each term tended to be assigned too often in ambiguous or subtle ways that did not admit of reliable categorizations.

25 Table 5.3, of course, provides specific percentages.

Part III

Appellate Courts

Chapter 6

Patterns of Policy Making across State Supreme Courts

Scott A. Comparato, Scott D. McClurg, and Shane A. Gleason

In recent years, a number of state supreme courts have explicitly declined to follow decisions of the United States Supreme Court. In a 1998 opinion,[1] the Supreme Court of Georgia struck down a state law criminalizing sodomy and expressly rejected the Supreme Court's decision in *Bowers v. Hardwick*.[2] Likewise, several states have rebuffed a major decision of the Court on the free exercise of religion[3], while a number of its criminal rights rulings have met with outright defiance from state supreme courts.[4] In one particularly egregious example, the Connecticut Supreme Court made clear its displeasure with the standard to be used in search and seizure cases established by the Supreme Court in *Illinois v. Gates*:[5]

> We eschew the amorphous standard of *Gates* in passing upon article first, § 7, interpretation and apply the more specific standards of the *Aguilar-Spinelli* test … The *Aguilar-Spinelli* test, with its two prongs of "veracity" or "reliability" and "basis of knowledge," offers a practical and independent test under our constitution that predictably guides the conduct of all concerned, including magistrates and law enforcement officials, in the determination of probable cause.[6]

This example suggests that lower courts may ignore, resist, or blatantly defy the standards established by the Supreme Court. Consequently, the substantive application of law may vary widely across jurisdictions. Variation across circuits, districts, or states can create uncertainty about the proper application of rules among trial court judges, legal professionals, police, and the public. Defiance or noncompliance with precedent in lower courts may also lead to possible equal protection issues under the Fourteenth Amendment, as individuals in different jurisdictions are subject to different standards of behavior.

The seriousness of this issue stimulates considerable interest in the nature of judicial conflict. How frequently do lower courts deviate? Do they defy these decisions outright or do they engage in more subtle forms of resistance such as accepting the doctrine's validity but finding reasons not to apply it consistently across cases? What political, institutional, cultural, and legal factors lead to defiant behavior by a lower court?

Understanding the Judicial Hierarchy

In order to understand the differences in how state supreme courts apply precedent from the United States Supreme Court, it is first necessary to discuss the institutional structure of the court system. The hierarchical nature of the court system in the United States suggests that lower courts are bound to follow the dictates of those courts above them. The doctrine of *stare decisis* should provide some authority over the decisions of judges sitting on the same court over time, but it also requires that the decisions of higher courts be binding on those inferior courts in the system (but see Brenner and Spaeth 1995; Segal and Spaeth 1996, 1999, 2002). The question that arises in a system of this kind is whether, and under what conditions, lower courts make decisions that are inconsistent with the precedent of higher courts.

As the highest court in the nation, the Supreme Court makes decisions that are binding on all lower courts, both federal and state. But, unlike Congress and the president, who are able to influence the behavior of agencies through the allocation of funds and personnel changes, the Supreme Court's ability to "control" lower courts is substantially limited. The primary power available to the Court to enforce its decisions is the ability to review, and overturn, aberrant decisions of lower courts. Compounding the inherent difficulty in using such a blunt instrument to induce compliance among lower courts, the docket of the Supreme Court has shrunk to fewer than 100 cases a year, reducing the likelihood of review of aberrant lower court decisions. When viewed together, this implies that these lower courts may be able to determine legal standards that are the product, not of Supreme Court precedent, but of their own preferences. This is particularly true for state supreme courts.

State supreme courts serve a dual role in interpreting both the United States Constitution as well as their own state constitutions, and taking primary responsibility for reconciling the two. Despite the fact that the Judiciary Act of 1789 gives the Supreme Court the right to review decisions of state supreme courts, justices on those courts do entertain a level of flexibility unknown to judges on the federal courts of appeals. State supreme courts generate, in absolute terms, far more decisions than do courts of appeals, making it more difficult for the Supreme Court to identify rulings that deviate from precedent. And lastly, one of the Supreme Court's primary responsibilities is to review and maintain consistency among the federal courts, suggesting that they will be more attentive to the product of courts of appeals.[7]

Explaining State Supreme Court Responses

Although there has been some attention given to the relationship between federal courts of appeals and the Supreme Court (Cameron, Segal, and Songer 2000; Johnson 1979; Songer 1987; Songer, Segal, and Cameron 1994), it is by no means clear how state supreme courts comport with decisions of the Supreme Court.[8] This is a glaring shortcoming, given the evolving role of state supreme courts in recent years. Some of the changes are clearly the result of forces internal to the state or institution itself, while others are potentially traceable to the actions of the Supreme Court. State supreme courts have become more professionalized, with increased support staff and other resources to assist in processing cases. Additionally, judicial elections have become more costly and competitive with greater fundraising efforts required by judicial candidates. At the same time, the Supreme Court struck state-level restrictions on campaign speech by judicial candidates, opening the door for candidates to air their views on potentially salient and controversial issues.[9]

The Court may have further contributed to the autonomy of state supreme courts, particularly in the area of civil liberties, through decisions in a pair of *Miranda* rights cases, suggesting that if state supreme courts relied on their own precedent, the Supreme Court could not review them.[10] While all of these may have contributed to greater independence of state supreme courts, we know little about whether in fact that is the case.

The Role of Precedent

Supporters of the legal model of decision-making assume that judges base their decisions on the facts of the case, using one or more of a number of accepted modes of adjudication, such as original intent, textualism, or precedent. One argument for such an approach is that it is value neutral—the judge does not invest any of her own prejudices or personal beliefs in determining the outcome. Proponents also point out that such an approach provides stability and continuity in the law; if judges are basing their decisions on precedent, they cannot deviate far from accepted and well-settled areas of law in deciding the case before them. Only through repeated decisions over time do we get incremental changes in the law.

This legal approach, long espoused by law professors, is not without some support in the field of judicial politics, at least insofar as one tenet of the legal approach is concerned—the role of case facts. There are numerous examples of empirical research finding that case facts play an important role in cases before the Supreme Court (George and Epstein 1992; Schubert 1965, 1974; Segal 1984; Segal and Spaeth 2002), courts of appeals (Songer and Haire 1992), and state supreme courts (Brace and Hall 1995, 1997; Emmert 1992; Emmert and Traut 1994). Clearly, the specific fact situation plays some role in determining the outcome of cases decided by courts at all levels.

More controversial is the role played by precedent generally. Supporters of the attitudinal approach suggest that precedent is hardly binding and serves only to disguise the unfiltered assertion of judicial preferences through the opinion writing process (see Segal and Spaeth 1996, 1999, 2002). Few would quibble with the idea that precedent is not determinative, dictating specific and clear outcomes based on previous cases. Yet even were we to assume that justices are single-minded seekers of policy, we should not assume that precedent is unimportant (see Epstein and Knight 1998; Knight and Epstein 1996a; Landes and Posner 1976; Spriggs and Hansford 2000, 2001, 2002; Wahlbeck 1997). In part, this is true because precedent guides decision-making in cases with similar fact situations.

More important from our perspective is that precedent can also be seen as a normative constraint on the behavior of judicial decision-makers. For example, Knight and Epstein write that

> justices have a preferred rule that they would like to establish in the case before them, but they strategically modify their position to take account of a normative constraint in order to produce a decision as close as is possible to their preferred outcome.
>
> (Epstein and Knight 1996a, 1021)

This suggests that acknowledging and using precedent is important for understanding the decisions of even politically-oriented actors in courts. Equally as important, it implies that we should pay careful attention to how precedent is used and treated by these actors.

The New Judicial Federalism and the Place of States in the Judicial Hierarchy

Though the Supreme Court can at least partly constrain the behavior of lower federal courts, it is not clear that it can have similar success in the states. This is true because the relationship between state courts and the Supreme Court is not strictly hierarchical. That is, not all decisions handed down by the Supreme Court—even in issue areas that overlap with its jurisdiction—are open to Supreme Court review. This means that, in addition to factors that may allow *all* lower courts to avoid implementing decisions of the Supreme Court, state supreme courts can also rely on their own state constitutions and laws to determine the outcome of cases.

Ironically, the foundation for this independence is based on precedent. The Supreme Court decided in 1875 that it would not accept cases from states for review unless federal law was somehow implicated in the state supreme court's decision.[11] Essentially, this allows states to interpret their own constitutions and statutes free from review by the Supreme Court, unless that interpretation concerns a matter on which the United States Constitution has spoken. Supportive of the independence of state courts, the Supreme Court established, in 1875 in the *Murdock* case, the "adequate and independent state grounds test" as a guide for lower courts.

The Court's decision in *Murdock* and the idea of "adequate and independent state grounds" has taken on a renewed vigor in recent years. Responding to an increasing conservatism on the Supreme Court, Justice Brennan, in a dissenting opinion in *Michigan v. Mosley*, called on states that wanted to avoid Supreme Court review to rely on their own law and constitutions in reaching liberal decisions in civil liberties cases.[12] He would later expand on this reasoning in *Mosley*, arguing that "decisions of the [Supreme] Court are not, and should not be, dispositive of questions regarding rights guaranteed by counterpart provisions of state law ... such decisions are not mechanically applicable to state law issues."[13]

At first blush, this implies that the impact of Supreme Court precedent on state court decisions should be limited. But this is not necessarily the case. First, Supreme Court precedent can be a useful strategic tool for state judicial actors. Since a large majority of state supreme court justices are *not* lifetime appointees and are therefore subordinates in local state political hierarchies, they may seek opportunities to use their specialized knowledge of Supreme Court precedent in order to "shirk" locally. The Supreme Court itself has an interest in maintaining its own latitude for reviewing state decisions and using that to affect policy change on a broader scale. For instance, Justice O'Connor, writing for the majority in *Michigan v. Long*, largely in response to Brennan's call to the states, argued that the Court would assume that decisions of state supreme courts did not rest on adequate and independent state grounds unless explicitly stated in the opinion.[14]

Reinforcing the call for a "new judicial federalism" are two types of political factors that encourage state court independence. As noted earlier, the ability of the Supreme Court to monitor and check lower courts is minimal. The sheer number of cases decided in both federal and state lower courts makes it impossible to recognize all instances where precedent is not followed or, even if this is recognized, to alter those decisions. Even more germane for the study of state courts is the fact that they *are* clearly embedded in local political hierarchies. In other words, state judges typically face political pressures from either voters or the political elite who influence their ability to retain office. Under some circumstances, these pressures may encourage the states to make decisions that are inconsistent with the policies outlined in Supreme Court decisions.

Evidence of Judicial Impact and Unanswered Questions

While these arguments are persuasive, it is not entirely clear that state supreme courts ignore relevant Supreme Court precedent. Most simply, the ability of states to deviate from Supreme Court precedent on civil liberties issues is clearly truncated at one end of the political spectrum. Although they can offer *more* freedoms to individuals than are provided in the Court's interpretations of the Constitution, they technically are not allowed to make decisions that provide for *less* individual protection. One implication of this for understanding the impact of precedent in the states is that *noncompliance* in search and seizure can only occur when state supreme courts limit freedoms and expand state power. This indicates that lower court latitude is restricted to one side of the political scale.

Measuring State Court Behavior

From a theoretical standpoint, the lines of debate in judicial impact research are clearly drawn. On one side are scholars, primarily from law schools, who emphasize the importance of legal factors. To simplify the argument considerably, proponents of this perspective suggest that higher and lower courts seek to coordinate their behavior in such a manner that it produces coherent application of the law. The primary mechanism for implementing this coordination is the standards and guidelines embedded in precedent, particularly that issued by the United States Supreme Court. The idea here is not that lower courts are unthinking automatons that always make decisions that mimic the Supreme Court's, but that lower courts try to behave in a manner consistent with those decisions. Consequently, state supreme court justices look to precedent to guide their decision-making. And the clearer, more applicable precedent is to the cases they decide, the more impact it will have on their decisions. Based on such assumptions, there is a clear emphasis in this work on legal understandings and explanations of compliance.

On the other side are those scholars who see political factors underlying judicial compliance. While this side does not believe legal factors lack in importance, the assumption underlying this perspective is that political preferences and institutional context are fundamentally important to understanding judicial behavior. Thus this perspective sees the compliance with judicial precedent as being constrained by political conflict and enhanced by political agreement. Further enriching this perspective is an emphasis on the political institutions that can influence decision-makers. Therefore, some scholars investigate the ability of the Supreme Court to encourage lower courts to take their precedent seriously through review of their cases (Songer, Segal, and Cameron 1994). At the state level, others have sought to determine the extent to which mechanisms for selecting judges influence their responsiveness to the Supreme Court's precedent (Brace and Hall 1993, 1995, 1997).

Though proponents of both positions would accept that the other side has merit, they would also argue that the variables favored by their theoretical perspective have primacy. Is compliance driven mostly by legal factors, such as understandings of the law and applicability to new situations? Or, is it a decision driven principally by the ideological interests of legal actors operating in political context? Obviously, answers to these questions depend upon empirical evidence.

One method of evaluating impact used by scholars is to pick a specific case, or small set of landmark cases, in a specific issue area decided by the Supreme

Court, identify relevant lower court cases following that decision in the same issue area, and conduct in-depth analyses of those cases. Usually, this means that the researcher reads those lower court decisions and makes qualitative judgments about the applicability of the precedent, and how the lower court responded to the precedent. This method can be quite useful in understanding how specific cases in highly salient areas are interpreted and applied by lower courts. It provides us with rich descriptions of the interpretation and application of the Court's precedent by specific courts at a specific time. We are often able to learn much about the legal, political, and social forces that shape the lower courts' behavior, but we are not able to extrapolate beyond that case to understand whether the conditions that led to the response by those lower courts in that instance are generalizable to other cases, issue areas, and contexts.

A different approach to understanding compliance evaluates responses to Supreme Court decisions by gathering data on legal, political, and institutional variables and assessing impact across a large number of lower court cases. These studies complement the case study approach by providing theoretical and methodological approaches that can be applied to the study of judicial impact in other issue areas (Benesh and Reddick 2002; Brace and Hall 1997; Johnson 1987; Songer 1987; Songer and Sheehan 1990; Songer, Segal, and Cameron 1994).

These studies suffer from a different problem than that of the case studies—it is difficult to generalize about the effect of a Supreme Court decision to the hundreds and thousands of progeny generated by that decision without a tremendous loss in information that is specific to those cases. Legal issues are often quite complex and even with the inclusion of variables to capture the status of the litigants, the institutional environment, and the case facts, much information is lost that might be crucial to understanding the decision of the lower court judges.

Answers to substantive questions about judicial compliance depend deeply on methodological assumptions. Yet, that does not provide clear ground for moving the empirical discussion forward. As each side has different methodological predilections that can be justified on different epistemological grounds, there is the temptation to dismiss or downgrade evidence presented by the other side as unscientific (in the case of legal scholars) or de-contextualized (in the case of political scientists). Consequently, the methodological divide between the two arguments makes it difficult to make progress in understanding the substance of compliance. In short, resolution of debates about the factors that underlie compliance cannot be accomplished by looking solely at the empirical record as both sides can marshal considerable empirical support for their arguments.

Defining Compliance

Existing definitions of compliance treat it as a two-dimensional concept with a legal dimension centered on the treatment of precedent, and a policy dimension focused on winners and losers (Benesh and Reddick 2002; Dickson 1994; Gruhl 1980). We advocate a definition that further refines this concept into four dimensions, each of which is grounded in existing research: the treatment of legal principle; the application of precedent by lower courts according to fact patterns; the relationship between precedent and policy change; and the extent to which the lower court relies on either federal or state law in making its decision. A graphical representation of the concept, along with the definitional elements that can be used to assess compliance for each, is shown in Figure 6.1. As a methodological matter, the four conceptual dimensions displayed in this graph may be considered as different types of compliance or as different elements of the same concept.[15]

The Treatment of Legal Principle

One way to understand compliance is to assess the degree to which a lower court accepts the Supreme Court's interpretation of a statute or the Constitution (e.g. Spriggs and Hanford 2000). We restrict our definition of this dimension so that it only refers to lower court reactions to the *nature* of precedent, but not its *applicability* to the facts of the cited case. Such a distinction allows for the possibility of a greater range of behaviors in judicial compliance, giving us more leverage over understanding variation in the application of the law across jurisdictions. A lower court can react in three ways to the legal principle set by the Court. First, it may comply fully. Full compliance would

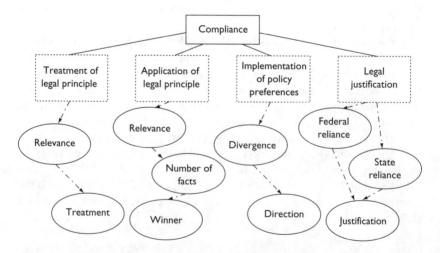

Figure 6.1 Dimensions of compliance and their attributes.

be characterized by the state supreme court embracing the legal reasoning of the Court. Second, it may signal its noncompliance openly. This would include some outright criticism of the legal standard's validity, applicability, or breadth of interpretation. Finally, a lower court could remain neutral, refusing to discuss the merits of the legal principle outlined in the precedent and remaining silent on the legal principles involved.

This definition focuses our attention on two attributes of a cited precedent in a lower court decision. The first is what we label the *legal relevance* of the standard outlined in the precedent; does the state supreme court discuss the validity of the legal standard enunciated in the precedent? Assuming that the standard is discussed, the second step is to determine how that standard is *legally treated*. Using *Shepard's Citation Service* rules, usage of key words like "controlling" and "followed" implies a compliant treatment, while a narrow interpretation of the statute or outright criticism suggests noncompliance.

The Application of a Legal Principle

One definition of compliance relates to how precedent is applied to a particular set of case facts (Cameron, Segal, and Songer 2000; Segal 1984; Songer, Segal, and Cameron 1994). This view of compliance does not focus on a lower court's discussion of a particular legal principle's validity, but instead focuses on how similar the case before a lower court is to the case decided in the precedent. Thus this is a distinct, but nevertheless important, way in which lower courts can treat precedent based on the facts of the case. Such a definition has a clear basis in legal reasoning, where precedent is seen as a guide applied to varying fact patterns. In this context, compliance implies that a greater overlap in fact patterns between the case under consideration and the precedent-setting case should result in a higher probability that the lower court will make the same decisions as found in the precedent.

There are again three possible relationships between a higher court's decision and the behavior of the lower court relevant to this dimension of compliance. A compliant lower court decision would favor the same party as the higher court in the presence of the same facts whereas noncompliance occurs when the lower court favors a different party. The third situation is one of neutrality, where the facts highlighted by the higher court are not central to the primary legal controversy discussed in the lower court decision.

To determine which outcome applies to a particular case, we examine two attributes of state supreme court decisions. The first is *factual relevance* (which is different than *legal relevance*), which requires that the facts relevant to the lower court's decision at least be a subset of those highlighted by the Supreme Court precedent. For example, if a lower court is deciding on the legality of a search (a Fourth Amendment question), the presence or absence of *Miranda* warnings (a Fifth Amendment question) would not be appropriate for assessing this form of compliance. The second attribute is the extent to which the facts in the lower case are congruent with those in the precedent, which we label *factual overlap*. As overlap increases, we assess compliance by comparing the outcome of the lower and higher court decisions.

Using the Supreme Court's decision in *Illinois v. Gates*—a Fourth Amendment case that established that search warrants could be issued based upon "the totality of the circumstances"—we coded for the following facts:

1   the presence of an informant;
2   if an informant existed, whether s/he was anonymous;
3   the presence of a warrant; and
4   a trial court finding of sufficient police corroboration of the informant's tip.

Finally, we judge compliance by examining the degree of factual overlap between the lower court case and the Supreme Court precedent and by comparing the identity of the winner in both cases. When most of these facts exist, compliance occurs when the lower court favors the state and upholds the search; when most of these facts do not occur we should see the state court more favorable to defendants, which is also compliant.

The Implementation of Policy Preferences

Another crucial element of compliance revolves around the central question of politics—who wins and who loses? This is motivated by the belief that judicial actors are driven as much by their policy preferences as they are by legal considerations and political pressures. By treating this as a distinct form of compliance, we are implying that lower courts can engage in behavior that is *politically* noncompliant though it may be *legally* compliant.

Our definition takes advantage of the fact that qualitative examinations can go a step further. Generally, we begin by asking whether the lower court substantively changed the policy position set forth in the precedent (*policy divergence*) and evaluate it by examining the practical consequences of the state supreme court decision. In the context of *Gates*, this means asking whether the decision made the job of police easier or more difficult for establishing probable cause than in the standard set forth in *Gates*. Having established whether significant divergence exists, we also code the direction of that policy shift as being favorable to the police or favorable to defendants (*policy direction*).

The Legal Justifications for Lower Court Decisions

The final form of compliance seeks to allow for varying behavior on the basis of how decisions are justified by different bodies of law. This is particularly important for the study of state courts because they can justify their decisions on state constitutions and statutes, potentially insulating themselves from reversal. In order to properly conceptualize compliance, we must therefore consider what we call the legal justification for decisions.

The key consideration here is whether a lower court relies on federal law in its decision and, if it does not, whether there is reason to believe that the federal standard *should* have been considered. Even if a state court were to make a decision consistent with both the legal and policy principles of the Supreme Court, a decision to ignore the Court's standard is an assertion of independence and thus a form of noncompliance that can reflect variance in judicial behavior. Along these lines, there are three possible types of outcomes for this dimension. Compliance occurs when federal law applies to the controversy being addressed and the lower court justifies its decision in those terms. In this instance, using state law as part of the justification is not in and of itself inconsistent with compliance as long as the appropriate federal law is used in the decision. Conversely, a lower court is noncompliant when federal law appears to apply but is not the basis for the state supreme court's decision. If there is no reason for the federal statute to be controlling given the specific legal controversy before the lower court, then there is a neutral outcome.

To measure this dimension of compliance, we consider first whether both federal and state legal standards are applicable to the citing case (*federal applicability, state applicability*). We ask whether, according to the opinion writer in the citing case, federal law or the federal Constitution applies, and whether the state constitution or statutes apply. If federal law is considered to be applicable, we then examine the decision to establish whether the primary justification for the lower court's decision uses the standards established in the applicable federal statute or Constitution (*federal reliance*).

Explaining State Court Behavior

The use of Supreme Court precedent by state supreme courts is complicated by the difficulty state judges have in reconciling state and federal law. While the Supreme Court has substantial power to review state courts, the relationship is not strictly hierarchical for reasons discussed above. Second, unlike judges on lower federal courts, state supreme courts are embedded in state political environments that include other actors with the ability to influence their decisions. Governors, state legislatures, and the public have means at their disposal to alter policy in response to the written decisions of state supreme courts. In that respect, state supreme courts are not much different than their federal counterparts. But unlike federal judges, the vast majority of state supreme court judges must stand for re-election or retention on a regular basis. Thus, there is an electoral component that may operate to constrain the decision-making process of state supreme court justices, further complicating their relationship with the Supreme Court.

We think that a more accurate representation would be what we call "an agent with two principals," though even that understates the independence and responsibility of state supreme courts. State supreme court justices are likely to be mindful of the importance of Supreme Court precedent, but they will also consider the implications of their decisions on the state level and the potential political consequences that may follow from these decisions. This is not to suggest that state supreme court justices are simply instruments of those at the state level with the power to retain those judges, but it does have profound implications for understanding how state supreme courts make use of Supreme Court precedent.

Consistent with theories of judicial behavior, we believe that state supreme court justices are driven by policy goals. However, we note that their ability to affect policy depends on their ability to remain on the court. As a result, state supreme court justices, most of whom do not enjoy life tenure, are driven by electoral as well as policy goals. We consider it axiomatic that state supreme court justices do not wish to be overturned by the Supreme Court. Further, we contend that they will respond differently to both state political forces and the Supreme Court as a result of how it relates to the probability of retaining their seat. Altogether this suggests that the decision-making of state supreme court justices is a function of three factors:

1   monitoring in the state political system;
2   monitoring by the Supreme Court; and
3   their own political preferences.

Our baseline expectation is that, in the absence of monitoring by any external actor, the decisions of state supreme court justices are largely a function of ideology, and Supreme Court precedent would have little, if any, impact. However, state supreme court justices are embedded in both legal and political environments. And for state supreme court justices the more relevant, and potentially harmful, monitoring comes from the state political system. Moreover, we argue that there is a key distinction in monitoring based upon whether judges must face some form of retention election. Because political elites are more likely to be interested in, and informed about, the actions of the state supreme court we expect them to exercise closer scrutiny of justices than will state electorates.

Although the state justices' retention motives and the Supreme Court's limited control over state courts should limit the impact of Supreme Court precedent on state decisions, we argue that monitoring by the Supreme Court still matters. What differs from the Court's monitoring of federal courts is that its impact depends upon the political position of the state court. When ignoring the Supreme Court benefits the ability of lower courts to signal their quality to the appropriate decision-makers at the state level, we wholly expect them to ignore precedent. However, there may be situations where conflict with the Court draws unwanted attention and hurts the chances of state judges retaining their seats, thus creating a situation where judges may be more willing to follow precedent. The question, of course, is when monitoring by the Supreme Court interacts with local monitoring to create a situation in which they follow precedent.

Figure 6.2 shows how the probability of a pro-government decision changes with frequency of reversal. We compute probabilities for courts that are relatively liberal, moderate, and conservative and engage in this exercise for Supreme Court precedent that is both pro-individual (labeled as "Liberal" in the graph) and pro-government (labeled as "Conservative"). (These probabilities are derived from a set of statistical models, which for reasons of brevity we do not discuss here. Interested readers, however, may consult these models in the Appendix at the end of this chapter.)

The graph shows that in elite selection systems—regardless of whether the original Supreme Court decision favors the individual (Liberal) or the state (Conservative)—the frequency of reversal by the Supreme Court results in a decrease in the probability that the state will win. On its face, this result is somewhat surprising, though it might be understood as an indication that state supreme courts in states where the justices do not face the voters may believe that elite actors will be more aware of instances where they are in conflict with the Supreme Court, and therefore more likely to sanction them as a result for such deviance. Moreover, there is little evidence that the ideology of the state supreme courts is a factor, as the lines for liberal, moderate, and conservative courts are all quite similar.

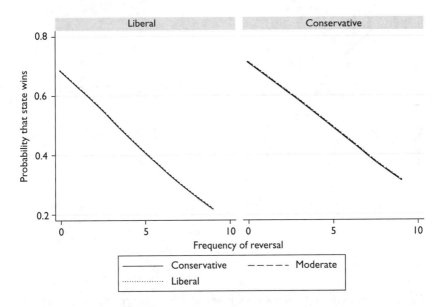

Figure 6.2 Impact of frequency of reversal, state court ideology, and the direction of Supreme Court precedent in elite selection systems.

Figure 6.3 shows the results for states that use competitive election systems to retain state supreme court justices. Here, there is a substantial difference in responses depending on the direction of the original Supreme Court precedent. When the precedent is liberal, the effect of increasing reversals is stark, as the probability of the state winning declines from a high of over 80%, regardless of the state court ideology, when there are no reversals, to less than 50% for states that have been overturned five or more times, and less than 30% for those reversed eight or more times. The picture is quite different for conservative precedent, as increased reversal has only a small impact on the probability of the state winning. The results suggest that there is more resistance to conservative precedent in these states, which is consistent with the idea that the Constitution sets a floor for individual rights and that states are free to grant greater protections to individuals.

Conclusion

Our results have important implications for the understanding of Supreme Court–state supreme court interactions. The findings suggest that state supreme courts do often operate quite independently of the Supreme Court and that they use precedent of the Supreme Court instrumentally—generally in circumstances to further their own policy preferences or to improve their electoral fortunes. But the relationship is even more complicated. Though

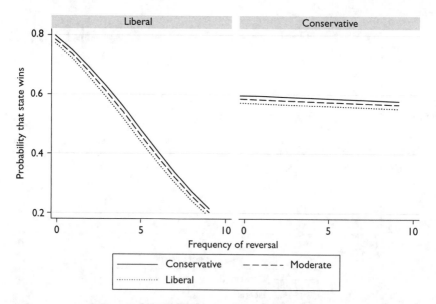

Figure 6.3 Impact of frequency of reversal, state court ideology, and the direction of Supreme Court precedent in competitive electoral systems.

states are bound by the Court's decisions in the area of search and seizure, they do often "shirk" from applying that precedent, suggesting that the application of Supreme Court precedent is not uniformly applied across the states, and that the reason for such variation is the result of institutional differences. The salience of a case to the Supreme Court and the degree of conflict that a state supreme court has experienced with the Supreme Court in the recent past condition the response by the state supreme court, though not always in the manner expected. Our research sheds light on the role of state institutional mechanisms as intervening factors in the application and use of Supreme Court precedent. Hopefully, this will lead to further research on the application of precedent in the states in other issue areas, taking account of further institutional differences among the states.

Appendix

Table 6A.1 Models of State Judicial Decision-Making across Institutional Contexts

Independent variables	Elite selection		Competitive election		Merit retention election	
	β	Std. error	β	Std. error	β	Std. error
Search and seizure case facts	0.62	0.17***	0.28	0.15**	0.40	0.18**
Median state court ideology	0.00	0.01	-0.01	0.01	-0.02	0.01**
Supreme court decision direction	0.14	0.33	-1.20	0.41***	-0.91	0.61
Salience	0.04	0.03	0.01	0.01	0.02	0.02
Frequency of reversal	-0.23	0.06***	-0.31	0.09***	-0.61	0.25**
Reversal * supreme court decision direction	0.04	0.09	0.30	0.10***	0.72	0.25***
Constant	-1.54	0.65**	0.90	0.50*	0.35	0.81
N	186		389		179	
Pseudo-R^2	0.10		0.04		0.06	
Likelihood χ^2	89.24***		22.74**		140.39***	
Log likelihood	-111.47		-252.82		115.30	

Notes

These logit coefficients show the effect of political and legal variables on state judicial decisions across the three types of selection systems used in American states.

*** p <0.01, two-tailed test. ** p <0.05, two-tailed test. * p <0.10, two-tailed test.

Notes

1 *Powell v. State of Georgia*, 510 S.E. 2d 18 (1998).
2 *Bowers v. Hardwick*, 478 U.S. 186 (1986).
3 *Employment Division, Department of Human Resources of Oregon v. Smith*, 494 U.S. 872 (1990).
4 See *Commonwealth of Pennsylvania v. Labron*, 690 A. 2d. 228 (1997), *Commonwealth of Pennsylvania v. Matos*, 749 A. 2d. 468 (1996), *Florida v. White*, 664 So. 2d. 442 (1995), *Montana v. Bullock*, 901 P. 2d. 61 (1995), and *Sitz v. Michigan Department of State Police*, 506 N.W. 2d. 209 (1993).
5 *Illinois v. Gates*, 462 U.S. 213 (1983).
6 *State of Connecticut v. Kimbro*, 496 A. 2d. 498 (1985), 507–508.
7 Rule 10 suggests that criteria for granting writs of certiorari include decisions of courts of appeals that are incongruent with federal law and Supreme Court precedent, and inconsistency among courts of appeals in applying that precedent.
8 Beiser (1968) focused on responses to a single reapportionment case by state and federal courts, though his study was limited to a very narrow time frame (1962–1964).
9 *Republican Party of Minnesota v. White*, 536 US 765 (2002).
10 See *Michigan v. Mosley*, 423 US 96 (1975) and *Michigan v. Long*, 463 US 1032 (1983).
11 *Murdock v. City of Memphis*, 20 Wall. 590 (1875).
12 *Michigan v. Moseley*, 423 US 96 (1975).
13 Ibid., p. 502.
14 *Michigan v. Long*, 463 US 1032 (1983).
15 See Collier and Mahon (1993) for a discussion of different ways that concepts can be related.

Chapter 7

Decision Making in the U.S. Courts of Appeals

The Determinants of Reversal on Appeal

Virginia A. Hettinger and Stefanie A. Lindquist

The United States courts of appeals serve as the intermediate appellate courts in the federal judicial system. Organized geographically by circuit, the federal appeals courts (or "circuit courts," as they are commonly called) were created by Congress to provide the first level of appellate review over decisions rendered in the federal district courts and by most federal administrative agencies. Cases appealed to the circuit courts are subject to mandatory review: that is, unless the appeal presents arguments that are legally frivolous, parties who lose at the trial or agency level have the right to appeal to the appropriate circuit court. As a result, the circuit courts resolve many thousands of appeals each year. In 2010, for example, circuit judges decided more than 60,000 appeals from federal district courts and administrative agencies.

In contrast to circuit courts' obligation to hear most appeals, the U.S. Supreme Court has broad discretion to choose the cases it will hear via the writ of certiorari, subject only to the rule that four justices must agree to hear an appeal.[1] In recent years, the Supreme Court has exercised its discretion to hear only about 100 cases per year. For the vast majority of cases, therefore, the federal courts of appeals offer litigants their last opportunity to ensure that the initial district court or agency decision was legally and factually correct. Federal circuit courts thus "serve as the instrument[s] of accountability for those who make the basic decisions in trial courts and administrative agencies" (Carrington, Meador, and Rosenberg 1976, 2).

In this chapter, we explore how the federal appellate courts perform this important supervisory role by evaluating the factors that influence circuit judges' decisions to reverse decisions made by district judges and federal agencies. We begin by briefly explaining the structure and function of the federal circuit courts, as well as the relationship between the key functions served by appellate courts and the power to reverse the decision below. We then consider general trends in circuit court reversal rates over the last several decades to explore different norms across the circuits and to consider the potential relationship between reversal rates and caseload. Finally, we consider what factors shape individual circuit judges' votes to reverse by modeling those votes as a function of judges' experiences, ideology, case factors, institutional roles, and circuit characteristics.

The U.S. Courts of Appeals in the Federal System

Although critical to the functioning of the federal judicial system, the U.S. courts of appeals are not mandated or created by the U.S. Constitution. According to Article III of the Constitution, federal power resides "in one supreme Court, and in such inferior Courts as the Congress may from time to time ordain and establish." In accordance with its power granted under Article III, Congress enacted the first Judiciary Act in 1789, which established two tiers to the federal judiciary in addition to the Supreme Court. Later, in the Circuit Court of Appeals Act of 1891, Congress created the basic contours of the modern federal court structure by establishing nine courts of appeals organized geographically along state lines. The 1891 Act also enhanced the Supreme Court's discretion over its own docket by expanding its power to shape its docket via the writ of certiorari, which was further expanded in 1925 to give the Supreme Court almost complete control over the cases it chooses to hear. This gradual narrowing of the Supreme Court's mandatory docket left most appeals to the circuit courts for resolution. Under the current regime, the idea that litigants will "take their case all the way to the U.S. Supreme Court!" is largely empty rhetoric. Most cases will receive appellate review only in the federal circuit courts.

Figure 7.1 Geographic boundaries of the United States courts of appeals and United States district courts (source: Administrative Office of the United States Courts).

Today, the number of circuit courts has expanded to 12, organized geographically (11 numbered circuits and the District of Columbia circuit), as well as one circuit (the "Federal Circuit") created in 1982 to handle appeals involving claims against the federal government, patents and trademarks, and veterans' appeals (see Figure 7.1). The number of appellate judges in each circuit differs depending on the circuit's caseload; in 2011, the size of each circuit court varied from 29 judges in the Ninth Circuit (covering nine western states, including California and Alaska) to six in the First Circuit (covering six states in New England and Puerto Rico). Circuit judges generally hear cases in panels of three judges randomly assigned to appeals as they arise, with the full contingent of circuit judges sitting together only in rare instances in which the court hears cases *en banc*, a process reserved only for the most important cases on the circuit's docket or to preserve uniform decision making across three-judge panels.[2]

Like justices on the U.S. Supreme Court, federal appeals court judges are nominated by the president and confirmed by the Senate. They receive lifetime appointments pursuant to Article III's mandate that they "shall hold their offices during good behavior." Circuit judges' independence is further protected by the constitutional prohibition against reduction of their compensation while in office. And because they enjoy life tenure and serve such an important role in the federal judiciary, appointments to the circuit bench are often highly politicized. During the George W. Bush administration, for example, the Senate reached a deadlock over the nomination of several conservative judges to the circuit courts, with Democrats threatening to filibuster President Bush's nominees over concern that those judges would render decisions that were antithetical to Democratic senators' policy preferences. Ultimately, the deadlock was broken when 14 Democratic and Republican senators negotiated a compromise that involved the withdrawal of some of the nominations and the confirmation of others. More recently, Republican senators defeated via filibuster the nomination of one of President Obama's nominees to the Ninth Circuit (*New York Times* 2011; see also Binder and Maltzman 2002).

Political battles over nominees to the federal circuit courts reflect the importance of the legal and policy stakes at issue and the power of the federal appellate bench. The federal appeals courts serve two primary functions that have critical implications for the development of federal law. First, the circuit courts provide an important check on the decisions of individual judges in trial courts or administrative agencies through the process of *error correction*. Because the circuit courts typically decide appeals in panels of three judges, the review process ensures that decisions of individual judges are reviewed by multiple judges and that errors are corrected through reversal on appeal. In addition to error correction, circuit judges are responsible for ensuring that federal law is applied uniformly by trial judges and administrative agencies within the circuit's geographic region. In the context of deciding individual appeals, then, circuit court panels must often announce, clarify, or harmonize federal law as applied within the circuit (Carrington, Meador, and Rosenberg 1976, 3). Circuit court judges thus engage in *law making* in some cases, especially when legal issues are new or evolving or when existing rules are incomplete. To be sure, many cases presented to the circuit courts are less likely to provide appellate judges with the opportunity to make law because they involve repetitive or well-developed legal issues. Nevertheless, in a substantial number of cases, circuit judges engage in the process of shaping or creating new legal rules (Klein 2002). It comes as no surprise, therefore, that presidents and senators appreciate the significant potential for circuit judges to determine federal legal policy and thus expend substantial energy to ensure that appointed judges share these politicians' policy preferences.

Federal circuit judges therefore engage in two central functions—error correction and law making. How do they ensure that lower courts and agencies make correct decisions or apply the proper legal rules? The procedural mechanism that judges use to ensure the uniform application of federal law within the circuit, to correct legal errors below, and to refine and even create new legal doctrine, is reversal. As the name implies, an appellate court can change the outcome of a case by issuing a ruling in favor of the losing party.[3] Understanding the role and function of appellate courts therefore requires a clear understanding of their decisions to reverse or affirm.

The Decision to Reverse: Patterns across the Circuits

The foregoing discussion demonstrates that judges on the U.S. courts of appeals hold key positions in the federal judicial hierarchy because they ensure correct outcomes and announce and refine federal legal policies, and that the power to reverse the lower court or agency constitutes the principal mechanism circuit judges use to perform these functions on appeal. But how often do circuit panels actually reverse? And does the likelihood of reversal vary geographically by circuit? Figure 7.2 presents data on reversal rates for each circuit over the period 1983 to 2009. Although the data suggest that reversal happens in a minority of cases (generally less than 15% per year), these data also reflect significant variation in reversal rates both over time and across circuits. In terms of trends over time, reversal rates in a number of circuits appear to have decreased over the period presented in the graphs (1983 to 2009), with a particularly pronounced downward trend in the First, Fourth, Eighth, and Tenth Circuits. In contrast to the low reversal rate in the circuit courts, the U.S. Supreme Court reverses about 60% of the decisions it chooses to review. These dramatically different reversal rates likely reflect several factors, including the influence of a mandatory docket (which produces fewer close cases for review), the deferential standard applied to district court decisions (particularly with respect to factual findings), and the heavier caseload burden faced by circuit court judges. Since the decision to reverse requires careful assessment of the record below, workload pressures may compromise the time judges have to consider each appeal. Reversing the lower court takes time and expends judicial resources both at the circuit and district courts, since a reversal might be accompanied by remand (that is, an order that returns the case) for a new trial or reconsideration by the agency below.

Indeed, the graphs suggest a possible relationship between caseload growth and reversal rates in the Second, Fourth, Fifth, and Eleventh Circuits. In those circuits, caseload per judge steadily increased over time while reversal rates steadily declined, suggesting the possibility of an inverse relationship between workload pressures and reversal rates.

Moreover, the extent to which workload pressures exist may vary by circuit, with some circuits experiencing faster caseload growth than others. Sometimes the circuit's geographic region shapes its caseload in unique ways; the Ninth Circuit—including states along the U.S.–Mexico border—has a caseload with a greater proportion of immigration matters than other circuits. In contrast, the DC Circuit, given its location in Washington, DC, experiences a docket with a greater proportion of appeals from federal administrative agencies. Variation in workload burdens across the circuits is often exacerbated by judicial vacancies that sometimes persist for months or even years because of delays in the White House nominations or in the Senate confirmation process.[4] Individual circuits have addressed these caseload burdens differently, with some limiting the percentage of cases in which oral argument is granted or reducing the percentage of cases in which the judges write published opinions (Cohen 2002; Lindquist 2007).

Although Figure 7.2 suggests some significant variation across the circuits in terms of their propensity to reverse, Figure 7.3 presents a clear visual representation of this circuit level variation in reversal rates. The dark center point for each circuit represents the average reversal rate per year over the 26-year period, hovering at about 12% for most circuits, with the Seventh and the DC Circuits having the highest reversal rates, and the Second and the Fourth Circuits having the lowest reversal rates. The "width" of the vertical lines reflects one standard deviation on either side of the mean; the dotted lines represent two standard deviations from the mean. These lines indicate that the Third, Eighth, and DC Circuits do not vary much in their reversal rates over time, while the First and Second clearly do.

These figures demonstrate that the circuits differ in their propensity to reverse the lower court or agency; significant variation clearly exists *at the circuit level*, suggesting the impact of varying institutional features and caseload pressures on circuit judge decision making. While these statistics provide some insight into judicial behavior in the circuits, they nevertheless reflect the aggregated decisions of *individual circuit judges*. To understand why judges vote to reverse, it is preferable to explore explanations of the choices made by individual judges in individual cases.[5] For that reason, we turn our attention

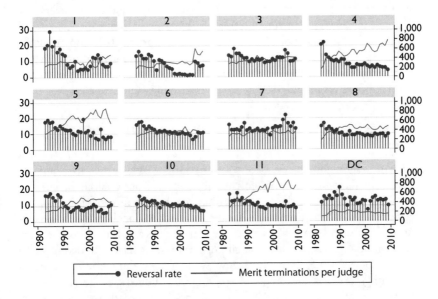

Figure 7.2 Relationship between circuit caseload and reversal rates, 1983–2009.

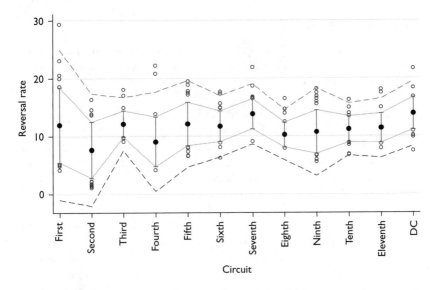

Figure 7.3 Distribution of reversal rate data across years and circuits, 1983–2009.

Note
Graph represents mean reversal rate, inner and outer fences in distribution across years.

now to factors that might influence individual circuit judges to reverse or affirm the lower court. In constructing our hypotheses and statistical model, we rely on an integrated or New Institutionalist approach (Clayton and Gillman 1999). This approach draws on attitudinal, legal, and institutional factors to explain decision making in the courts of appeals—thus allowing us to test multiple influences on judges' votes to reverse in the same statistical model.

The Decision to Reverse: The Votes of Individual Judges

A circuit judge's vote to reverse the lower court is likely related to a number of different factors associated with the judge's own personal characteristics and policy preferences, the nature of the legal claims raised on appeal, the characteristics of the other judges on the three-judge panel on which the circuit judge sits, the types of parties involved in the case, the procedures followed in the court below, and the circuit-level norms related to deference to the trial court. In the discussion below, we identify a number of hypotheses concerning variables that might shape a circuit judge's vote to reverse the lower court. We then specify a statistical model to test these relationships using data on judicial votes to affirm or reverse on the U.S. courts of appeals from 1983 to 2002.

Ideological Influences

In describing the work of the circuit courts of appeals, we noted the critical role these appeals court judges play in the development of legal policy. Circuit judges' policy-making authority is not lost on the president or senators, who seek to ensure that judges who share these politicians' own policy preferences are appointed to the federal appellate bench. The ideological valence to federal judicial selection is manifested in decision making as well. Scholars who study the influence of ideology on judges' behavior have developed an "attitudinal model" of judicial decision making. Even though its strongest advocates stress that the model works best at the Supreme Court level—because there is no higher court that supervises the life-tenured justices (see Segal and Spaeth 1993, 2002)—many scholars have extended the argument to the lower courts. Decades of social scientific research have now clearly demonstrated the influence of judges' policy preferences and ideological predispositions on their voting behavior at the circuit courts (Hettinger, Lindquist, and Martinek 2004, 2006; Songer, Sheehan, and Haire 2000). Because there is no clear liberal or conservative expectation for reversing versus affirming, however, the ideology of the voting circuit judge must be compared to some other reference point in order to derive an expectation about the likelihood of a vote to reverse. One effort in this area compared the ideology of the median member of the panel to the ideology of the district court judge, expecting, but not finding, that the greater the distance, the more likely a reversal in the courts of appeals (Hettinger, Lindquist, and Martinek 2006). On the other hand, later research compared the ideology of the median judge on the panel to the position advocated by the appellant (Collins and Martinek 2010). This approach was more successful, finding a significant and substantial relationship between ideological congruence and reversals.

We follow a similar approach based on the degree of "ideological incongruence" between the lower decision and voting judge's ideological preferences. Quite simply, we expect that a conservative judge will be more likely to reverse a liberal outcome below, and vice versa. To create a variable reflecting ideological incongruence between the reviewing judge and the judgment below, we need measures of both judge ideology and the ideological direction of the decision in the court or agency below. For the former component, we rely on a measure of judge ideology known as the GHP scores based on the initials of the score's creators—Professors Giles, Hettinger, and Peppers (2001, 2002). These scores are created to reflect the ideology of the appointing president, while taking the ideology of a home-state senator into account.[6] To code the ideological direction of the lower court outcome, we relied on the case direction variable in the U.S. Courts of Appeals Database produced by Professor Donald Songer and his colleagues.[7] When combined with the variable reflecting whether the circuit panel affirmed or reversed, we created a variable measuring the ideological outcome at the lower court or agency. We multiplied that variable by the voting judge's GHP score to produce a continuous variable with greater values reflecting increasing *incongruence* between the circuit judges' preferences and the outcome below.

We add an additional ideological measure to our model of circuit judge votes to reverse. In particular, we expect that *ideological variation* on the reviewing circuit might affect the likelihood of a vote to reverse. This expectation is based on the perspective of the lower court judge or agency rendering the decision below. Where the lower court faces a circuit staffed by judges with widely varying policy preferences, it is more difficult for that judge to make precise calculations about how a randomly selected reviewing panel will apply or interpret governing law. In that sense, the lower court is faced with greater *uncertainty* about decision making at the appellate court and may therefore be more prone to error. For that reason, we hypothesize that variation in circuit court preferences—measured as the range of GHP scores for that circuit each year—will be positively associated with an individual circuit judge's vote to reverse.

 ## Judicial Background Characteristics

In addition to a judge's ideological predisposition, other characteristics of judges on the panel may affect the willingness of individual judges to vote to reverse the lower court. Previous research has also examined the role of the chief judge on the decision to reverse. For example, co-authors Hettinger, Lindquist, and Martinek (2003) considered whether a chief judge, with an eye toward preserving collegiality between the levels of judicial hierarchy, would be less likely to reverse, or whether chief judges would have a greater interest in error correction and be more likely to reverse. In the end they found no relationship between the chief judge as majority opinion writer and the decision to reverse. On the other hand, the mere presence of the chief judge on a panel *was* associated with the decision to reverse. Because of these mixed results, we concluded that it would be productive to pursue the effect of chief judge status when the dependent variable is the individual vote to reverse (as in this study), rather than the panel's decision to reverse (as in earlier studies). We therefore included a variable in our model reflecting whether, at the time the vote was cast, the voting judge was serving as chief circuit court judge.

We also chose to evaluate whether first-hand experience at the district court level would influence the decision to reverse. Sometimes district court judges sit "by designation" on circuit court panels, both to alleviate caseload pressures caused by vacancies on the appellate bench and to provide district court judges with some experience deciding appeals. A district court judge in a temporary capacity may experience divided loyalties between her role as a district court judge and her temporary position on the federal panels on the circuit court, or she may simply be more sensitive to the demands on lower court judges. Whatever the motivation a district court judge sitting by desig-nation may be less willing to reverse district court decisions. The latter logic can also be applied to circuit court judges who served on a district court prior to appointment to the circuit court. Greater understanding of the conditions, constraints, or pressures facing lower court judges could influence the level of deference a circuit judge may be willing to show the lower courts. Thus, we expect any judge with experience in the district courts to be less likely to vote to reverse a lower court decision. For that reason, we include a variable in our model reflecting whether the judge is a designated district court judge or a court of appeals judge with prior district experience, coded 1 if the judge had such experience and 0 otherwise.

Parties in the Courts of Appeals

Much of the earliest systematic research on the courts of appeals focused on testing Marc Galanter's now famous arguments about differential success of parties in court (Songer and Sheehan 1992; Songer, Sheehan, and Haire 1999). This body of research focused on winners and losers in court, rather than on reversals. The key independent variable of interest compared the resource differences between the parties, arguing that higher resource parties will have greater success in the courts. The consistent finding emerging from this line of research was that parties with higher resources, especially those that fall into the category of repeat players, have greater success than their lower resource opponents. Repeat players that enjoy the higher resource differential include the U.S. government against all other litigants, state governments against businesses and individuals, and businesses against individuals. In terms of reversal, this research suggests that when repeat players are seeking reversal on appeal, they may be more likely to succeed as appellants than are non-repeat players. We test this hypothesis empirically by including a variable in our model of reversal voting that measures whether the most powerful repeat player—the federal government—is the appellant, coded 1 if the federal government is appealing the lower court judgment, and 0 otherwise.

Resources are not the only thing that matters in terms of party success, however. Law Professors Clermont and Eisenberg studied the success of parties in civil cases with an explicit focus on whether the original plaintiff or defendant has greater success in gaining reversals (Clermont and Eisenberg 2000, 2002; Scott and Eisenberg 2002). Clermont and Eisenberg (2002) found that defendants who lose below are far more likely to win on appeal than are plaintiffs who lose at trial: "defendants appealing their losses after trial by jury obtain reversals at a rate of 31 percent, while losing plaintiffs succeed in only 13 percent of their appeals from jury trials" (p. 949). They attribute the differences to "appellate judges' misperceptions regarding the trial level treatment of plaintiffs," with appellate judges seemingly acting "on their perceptions of the trial courts being pro-plaintiff" (p. 949). It is also possible that defendants are more successful on appeal because of the different burdens of proof faced by plaintiffs and defendants. Civil plaintiffs must demonstrate their case by at least the preponderance of evidence; defendants have no burden of proof. To prevail on appeal, therefore, plaintiffs likely face a greater uphill battle. Based on Clermont and Eisenberg's research, therefore, we hypothesize that civil defendants will have greater success on appeal than civil plaintiffs. We test this hypothesis by incorporating a variable into our model reflecting whether the appellant in a civil case was the defendant below (coded 1 if the appellant was the original defendant below, and 0 otherwise). We expect that appellate judges will be more likely to vote to reverse in cases involving the defendant (rather than the plaintiff) as appellant.

Finally, the influence of party resources in appellate courts may be altered by assistance from outside groups. For example, in their study of three state supreme courts rather than the courts of appeals, Songer, Kuersten, and Kaheny (2000) found that disadvantaged groups, when supported by amicus curiae, were able to overcome the resource disadvantage they would otherwise face. Similarly, Collins and Martinek (2010) found that amicus briefs filed on behalf of the appellant, regardless of appellant status, were related to higher likelihood of reversal. Based on these studies, we expect that cases accompanied by amicus filings are more likely to result in a vote to reverse.

Legal Issues

The issues in the case presented on appeal are also important. Various authors have proposed that litigants in certain types of cases are more or less likely to win on appeal. Criminal appeals brought by the recently convicted represent the category of cases likely to be described as without merit and, thus, less likely to be successful on appeal (Songer, Sheehan, and Haire 2000). Prisoner civil rights claims and habeas corpus claims are also less likely to be reversed on appeal than other civil rights claims (Clermont and Eisenberg 2002; Lindquist 2007). On the other hand, non-habeas cases involving civil rights and civil liberties are among the most politically salient and important cases that appeals court judges review. For that reason, they may produce a greater level of scrutiny by the appellate panel and thus be accompanied by a higher likelihood of reversal. For these reasons, we include two variables in our model indicating whether the case involved criminal or prisoner appeals, and whether the case involved issues associated with civil rights and liberties. These variables are dichotomous dummy variables coded as 1 if the case falls in the relevant category, and 0 otherwise.

Legal considerations are not limited solely to the substantive law underpinning a particular case. The procedural posture of a case, or its institutional source, might also matter. Consider the difference between a case appealed from a jury verdict after trial and a case appealed on the basis of a preliminary motion to dismiss before trial. The conventional wisdom holds that appellate judges will be loathe to overturn decisions made following a trial because of the deference they hold for the jury (in the case of a jury trial) or because they are sensitive to the expenditure of institutional and litigant resources required by a trial (whether a jury or bench trial). Current research suggests that this reluctance to reverse a trial verdict may not exist when controls are introduced for the appellant's status as defendant below (Clermont and Eisenberg 2001). To further evaluate this hypothesis, we include a variable in our model that measures whether a trial (either bench or jury) was held below.[8] We expect this variable to be negatively related to a vote to reverse.

We add one additional variable related to the source of the case on review. Most of our discussion thus far has focused on the district court as the originating institution from which appeals emerge for review. But as we noted earlier, circuit court judges also review appeals from administrative agencies (Humphries and Songer 1999). Although some of these agency appeals involve high-profile challenges to controversial administrative regulations or other agency actions, many involve more routine review of individual adjudications, as in the case of Social Security disability appeals. Administrative action is also typically subject to deferential standards of review under the federal Administrative Procedure Act, whereby agency action may be reversed only if it is found "arbitrary and capricious" or without grounding in "substantial evidence." Because we suspect that this deferential standard of review likely results in a reduced probability of reversal—in combination with the routine nature of many of these appeals—we include a variable reflecting whether the case under review originated in a federal administrative agency, coded 1 if it did, and 0 otherwise.

Institutional Norms and Variations

Institutional norms vary across circuits. While all the circuits operate under federal rules regarding appellate procedure, they also can supplement those rules. Some of these norms involve collegial relations among the judges on the panels. The courts of appeals demonstrate a high level of collegiality in that most decisions are decided unanimously. Prior research has explored when and why individual judges choose to violate the norm of consensus by publishing a dissent (disagreement with the outcome and reasoning) or concurrence (usually agreement with the outcome but not the reasoning). In particular, some circuits have a greater tendency to publish separate opinions than others, even after controlling for other case, ideological, and institutional factors, which suggests that some circuits may operate under different informal rules about expressing disagreement (Hettinger, Lindquist, and Martinek 2006; Lindquist 2007). From the perspective of the district court judge or administrative agency, high levels of disagreement on a particular circuit may complicate the lower tribunal's task. Appellate court decisions that generate dissents or concurrences suggest that the circuit's judges are divided on the appropriate legal standard governing certain appeals. Where the law is in flux, the district court or administrative agency may have a more difficult time applying the correct legal standard. For that reason, we expect that reversal will be more prevalent in circuits with higher separate opinion rates. Previous research has borne out that result (Lindquist 2007). To control for this effect, we incorporate a variable in our model that measures the circuit court's separate opinion rate in the previous year; these rates were calculated based on a search in Westlaw to identify the number of separate opinions written in each circuit per year, divided by the number of reported opinions written in that same year.

Finally, Figure 7.2 indicated a potential relationship between judicial caseload and reversal rates. Although the data included in the figure are measured at the aggregate level, the influence of caseload pressures are clearly implicated in decisions of individual judges to vote to reverse. Accordingly, we added a variable to our model that reflects the number of decisions rendered by circuit court judges in each circuit in the year of decision.

Data and Methods

Because our dependent variable is dichotomous (with a vote to reverse coded 1, and to affirm coded 0), a logit model properly captures the non-linear nature of the dependent variable. The majority of the data are drawn from the

United States Courts of Appeals Database and the Update to the United States Courts of Appeals Database. The original database includes a sample of cases by circuit by year from 1928 until 1996. The update extends the database through 2002. Cases decided with signed opinions from the years 1983 to 2002 were included in the analysis. We restricted our database in three additional ways. First, we only included decisions involving three-judge panels; *en banc* decisions were excluded. In addition, we also included only the cases in which the outcome clearly favored either the appellant or the appellee. Thus, decisions that affirmed in part and reversed in part were excluded from our analysis. Finally we limited the analysis to cases that were decided with signed majority opinions.

Model Results

The results of the statistical model are presented in Table 7.1. In this table, statistically significant variables are indicated by the probability variables in

Table 7.1 Logit Regression Model of Vote to Reverse by Judges on U.S. Courts of Appeals, 1983–2002

Variable	Coefficient	Robust standard error	P-value
Ideology			
Compatibility of judge ideology and lower court outcome	0.590	0.054	0.000
Ideological variation on circuit	−0.407	0.344	0.237
Institutional roles			
Prior district court experience	−0.065	0.039	0.043
Chief judge	−0.076	0.074	0.304
Litigant characteristics			
Federal government appellant	1.417	0.124	0.000
Defendant as appellant	0.168	0.072	0.010
Presence of amicus filings	0.393	0.125	0.001
Case characteristics			
Criminal appeal or prisoner petition	−0.441	0.077	0.000
Civil liberties or civil rights claim	0.021	0.085	0.797
Administrative appeal	−0.367	0.136	0.004
Trial below	−0.121	0.080	0.065
Circuit characteristics			
Caseload per judge	0.0001	0.0003	0.642
Separate opinion rate	−0.005	0.009	0.584

Notes
N = 13878; log-likelihood = −8,059.36; Wald Chi-Square = 432.77. Robust standard error clustered on citation, circuit dummy variables omitted from table; p-values reflect one-tailed tests in hypothesized direction.

the final column in the table: where those values are less than 0.05, they reflect conventional levels of statistical significance. Values less than 0.10 are close to that conventional level and thus also worthy of careful consideration.

These results indicate that a number of our hypotheses were supported, while others were not. First, it seems clear that ideological factors affect the decision to reverse, but only with respect to the degree to which the ideological direction of the district court decision is inconsistent with the reviewing judge's policy preferences. The impact of the variable reflecting "ideological incongruence" between the decision below and the reviewing judge's preferences is demonstrated graphically in Figure 7.4. The figure demonstrates that as the value of the ideological incongruence variable increases from its lowest to its highest value, the probability of a judge voting to reverse increases about 20 percentage points, from 0.3 to about 0.5. Thus the degree of ideological inconsistency between the decision below and the reviewing judge's preferences has a substantial impact on the reviewing judge's propensity to reverse. Like Supreme Court justices, circuit court judges vote to reverse lower court outcomes with which they disagree on policy grounds.

We also hypothesized that ideological variation on the circuit court might affect the likelihood of reversal. In their analysis of district judges' affirmance rates, Choi, Gulati, and Posner (n.d.) conclude that ideological diversity at the circuit level is associated with an increased probability of reversal rates, and their data support this hypothesis to some degree. Yet our study of individual

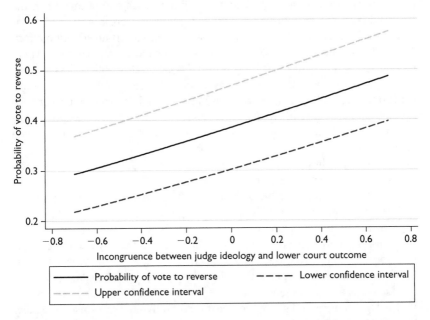

Figure 7.4 Impact of ideological incongruence on probability of reversal vote.

votes (as opposed to affirmance rates) fails to confirm this hypothesis. We are able to draw no firm conclusions regarding the relationship between variation in ideological predispositions at the circuit level and the likelihood of a vote to reverse by circuit judges in individual cases.

Our test of other judicial background characteristics produced mixed results. Having district court decision making experience is statistically significant and also has a powerful substantive impact. Calculations of the predicted probabilities of a vote to reverse in the presence or absence of district court experience demonstrate a 27% decrease in the probability of a vote to reverse when the voting judge has experience as a district court judge. This represents a substantial change in the judge's willingness to reverse the lower court and may be attributable to some enhanced deference to the lower court promoted by an understanding of the constraints on lower court judges. On the other hand, chief judges are neither more nor less likely to vote to reverse the lower court. Note that this result differs somewhat from our earlier findings in previous research indicating that chief judges are less likely to reverse when they draft the majority opinion, perhaps because they are less likely to choose to write an opinion when the result is a reversal (Hettinger, Lindquist, and Martinek 2003). In terms of their general voting behavior on the panel, however, this result does not hold.

We also find that litigant characteristics have an important impact on circuit judges' propensity to reverse. A decision by the federal government to appeal a loss below is strongly associated with reversal on appeal. When the United States appeals, the probability of reversal increases from 0.28 to 0.71—a 43% increase! This result is probably due to a certain selection effect: attorneys representing the U.S. government may choose to appeal cases where the facts or law are most likely to produce a reversal. In other, less sympathetic cases, this powerful repeat player may choose to abide by the lower court or agency ruling. Similarly, when the original defendants appeal, circuit court judges are more likely to vote to reverse, a finding that comports with existing research describing a certain "plaintiphobia" in the federal appellate courts.

We also hypothesized that the presence of amicus filings would be associated with a vote to reverse on grounds that amicus filings in the circuit courts most often accompany highly salient cases that circuit judges may be more inclined to scrutinize for errors below or might use to clarify legal standards. Indeed, the presence of one or more amicus briefs—regardless of whether those briefs support the appellant or appellee—is significantly related to a vote to reverse on appeal, although the substantive impact of this variable is less impressive. When an amicus brief is present, the probability of a vote to reverse increases by a modest 5%.

The legal context and procedural posture of individual cases also influences the propensity of circuit judges to reverse. As we expected, in criminal and administrative agency appeals, as well as in cases appealed after trial, the likelihood of a vote to reverse is reduced. Criminal appeals are 43% less likely to produce a vote to reverse than are non-criminal appeals, administrative agency appeals are 39% less likely to do so, and appeals from trial verdicts are 29% less likely to produce a vote to reverse. On the other hand, cases raising civil rights or liberties claims are no different than other cases with respect to the likelihood of a vote to reverse on appeal.

Finally, we tested whether circuit norms and workload shape judges' individual choices to reverse, but we find no significant relationship between separate opinion rates at the circuit court and the dependent variable, or between workload and the choice to reverse.

Discussion: An Integrated Model of Reversal

When a court of appeals judge votes to reverse a lower court decision, the decision to issue that vote is complex. Traditional explanations of the decision making process suggest that appellate judges consider only legal factors in this decision. Clearly the analysis presented above shows that many other factors play a systematic and significant role in the reversal decision. Ideological differences are very important in this decision, but other factors, institutional, case specific, and litigant specific, are also important. Even after controlling for ideology, judges are less likely to rule in favor of criminal appellants. They are more likely to support appellants who were defendants at the trial level. They are even less likely to upset lower court decisions when they have experience as lower court judges. These systematic differences may occur because of legal training, personal experiences, bias, or informal norms, and we have offered a few possible explanations for these patterns in the discussion above.

Confirmation battles over judicial nominees have increased in number and degree and the role of ideology in the decision making process highlights why this has happened. At the same time there are many other factors at work in the vote to reverse that may get lost in the pitched battles over judicial ideology. The courts of appeals decision making environment is complex. Unlike Supreme Court justices, circuit judges must supervise every outcome in the lower courts and agencies when appeals from those decisions are brought to the circuit in order to ensure that no error was made below. In addition, circuit judges must attend to the development of legal policies and sometimes engage in law making in the context of individual decisions. Given this broad mandate and their varied caseloads, it is not surprising that their decisions cannot be explained on the basis of ideology alone. The model we presented here indicates that, in addition to their interests in policy outcomes, circuit judges respond to a variety of different pressures and constraints in determining the outcome on appeal.

The diversity of these factors stresses the importance of understanding courts of appeals decision making through an integrated or New Institutional approach, especially given the multifaceted role of the federal courts of appeals in correcting errors below, developing legal policy, and serving as the court of last resort. New Institutionalism suggests that the institutions within which judges decide cases—including the rules governing those institutions and other systemic constraints on judges' behavior—shape judicial behavior. New Institutionalism does not ignore the role of judicial ideology, but simply acknowledges that the influence of ideology may be tempered or constrained by other institutional forces. In this study of reversal votes, we find that, indeed, institutional structures and characteristics do influence how judges vote: the kinds of cases judges hear, the types of litigants that bring those cases, the processes that give rise to appeals, and the influence of interest groups in the litigation process through amicus filings, all affect the individual choice to reverse. At the same time, judges' own preferences and backgrounds play an important role in the choice to reverse as well, further supporting Professor James Gibson's recognition decades ago that judges' decisions are "a function of what they prefer to do, tempered by what they think they ought to do, but constrained by what they perceive as feasible to do" (Gibson 1983, 9).

Notes

1 Some cases may be filed directly in the U.S. Supreme Court as a matter of that court's "original jurisdiction" under Article III. See U.S. Constitution, Article III, Section 2 ("In all cases affecting ambassadors, other public ministers and consuls, and those in which a state shall be party, the Supreme Court shall have original jurisdiction"). Theoretically, when the Supreme Court hears a case on the basis of its original jurisdiction, it could sit as a trial court; as a practical matter, however, the Court typically refers these matters to a special master to hold a trial. In a small number of other cases in which a special three-judge district court is required, the U.S. Supreme Court also has mandatory jurisdiction in the sense that appeals from those district courts come directly to the Supreme Court. These cases typically involve voting rights issues and legislative reapportionment.

2 Cases can be heard or panel decisions reheard *en banc* if a majority of the judges in the circuit vote to do so; in circuits with more than 15 judges, the circuit may adopt procedures for *en banc* review by some smaller number of judges on the circuit. In the Ninth Circuit, for example, an *en banc* court consists of 11 judges.

3 An appellate court can also "vacate" a judgment, a decision that does not reverse a lower court decision but rather nullifies it, as if it never took place, so that the case may be returned (or "remanded") for a retrial. Whether a decision is vacated (and remanded) or reversed, it typically signifies a victory for the appealing party.

4 For a tally of current federal judicial vacancies, see the table of vacancies maintained by the Administrative Office of the United States Courts at: www.uscourts.gov/JudgesAndJudgeships/JudicialVacancies/CurrentJudicialVacancies.aspx.

5 Many social scientists adhere to the principle of "methodological individualism"—or the idea that our theories of social or political behavior must be grounded in an understanding of choices made by individuals.

6   In light of the presidential prerogatives in the appointment process, Giles and his colleagues assign each judge appointed to the circuit bench in the absence of senatorial courtesy the Poole ideology score corresponding to his or her

appointing president. However, for those judges appointed when there was one home-state senator of the president's party, Giles, Hettinger, and Peppers give those judges the Poole ideology score corresponding to the home-state senator. When both home-state senators were of the president's party, the corresponding ideology score for the judge is equal to the average Poole score of the two senators.

(Hettinger, Lindquist, and Martinek 2006, 50–51)

7 For further information about this database and its later updates, see www.wmich. edu/nsf-coa/.

8 The Songer Database does not distinguish between bench or jury trials.

Chapter 8

Supreme Court Agenda Setting
Policy Uncertainty and Legal Considerations

Ryan C. Black and Ryan J. Owens

On November 2, 1992, the National Organization for Women (NOW) requested that the U.S. Supreme Court exercise its discretionary agenda-setting powers and review the lower court's decision in *NOW v. Scheidler* (No. 92–780). NOW asked the Court to apply the Racketeer Influenced and Corrupt Organizations Act (RICO) against a group of abortion protestors who allegedly combined to drive them out of business. The issue was important for a host of financial and symbolic reasons. Racketeering, generally, is a form of organized crime that extorts money from businesses through means of intimidation or physical violence. If the courts allowed abortion protestors to be prosecuted under RICO, the symbolic effect would be negative for the pro-life cause. Just as importantly, if RICO was applied to pro-life groups, those groups would have to dip further into their finances to defend themselves against additional causes of action. Simply put, determining whether to apply RICO to pro-life groups had significant policy implications, and the Court's decision to hear the case would therefore have profound consequences.

When the justices met during their private conference to decide if they would hear the case, each of them faced significant uncertainty. If they voted to hear it, would they be a part of the Court majority that created precedent? Would the result reached by the Court generate a policy more favorable to them than the status quo? And what did the legal considerations involved in the case suggest? Before voting to grant review to this politically charged abortion case, justices needed to answer these questions.

Our goal here is not to examine the Court's abortion jurisprudence, nor is it to analyze how outside interests such as NOW influence the Court. These are topics that could, themselves, fill up numerous books. Instead, our goal is to explain the conditions under which justices set the Court's agenda. We make three inter-related arguments. First, we argue that justices make probabilistic decisions when setting the Court's agenda. They will cast their agenda votes based on the probability that the Court's eventual decision will result in a more favorable policy than currently exists. Second, we argue that legal considerations, such as lower court conflict, judicial review, and legal importance influence justices' agenda votes. Finally, and perhaps most importantly, we argue that policy and legal considerations *interactively* influence justices' agenda votes. When legal considerations and policy considerations point toward the same ends, a justice is freed up to follow her policy goals. But when the law points toward an outcome that the justice dislikes on policy grounds, she will often follow the law despite her policy misgivings. In short, we argue that policy and law jointly influence how justices set the Court's agenda with policy sometimes giving way to law.

Our results support our hypotheses. We find, first, that justices make predictions about likely policy outcomes and vote to grant review, in part, based on these predictions. More specifically, as a justice's probability of being made better off by the Court's merits decision increases, the justice becomes increasingly likely to vote to review the case. Second, we observe that legal considerations also influence whether justices review cases. The presence of important legal cues strongly drive up the probability that a justice votes to review a case. And, finally, we find that policy and law interact, with law oftentimes conditioning justices' policy behavior. Even justices who disagree entirely with the expected policy outcome of a case will vote to review it. These findings, of course, shed light on the Court's agenda-setting process, but they also highlight a broader aspect of judicial decision-making, something we discuss more fully in the conclusion.

In what follows, we begin with a brief overview of the Court's agenda setting, with the aim to let readers "look under the hood" of the process. We then provide a more detailed description of our theoretical argument and the hypotheses we derive from it. We next explain our data and results, and conclude with a discussion about Supreme Court agenda setting and judicial behavior more broadly.

The Nuts and Bolts of Supreme Court Agenda Setting

Modern Supreme Court justices have the discretion to determine which cases the Court will hear. Through a number of bills passed over the years, Congress has altered the Supreme Court's jurisdiction, changing the Court from one which was largely required to hear most of its cases (via mandatory jurisdiction) to one that could set its own agenda (via discretionary jurisdiction). When Congress passed the Judiciary Act of 1891, it eased the Court's workload burden by, first, creating the United States courts of appeals to hear all cases appealed from federal district courts and, second, carving out a small discretionary docket for the Supreme Court. As a result, with circuit courts hearing all appeals, justices had more power to select the cases they wanted to hear. Thirty-four years later, Congress passed the Judiciary Act of 1925 which removed much of the Court's remaining mandatory jurisdiction, leaving justices with even more power to set their own agenda. Finally, in 1988, Congress largely finished the job when it passed legislation that removed virtually *all* the Court's mandatory jurisdiction. Accordingly, today's justices can choose the cases they wish to hear, with little to no direction as to the types—or numbers—of cases before the Court (Owens, Stras, and Simon, n.d.).

In a moment, we will address the factors that lead justices to grant review to cases, but for now, we begin by providing background on how the Supreme Court sets its agenda. The process begins when a litigant asks the Court to hear its case, which most frequently means filing a petition for a "writ of certiorari" with the Court (i.e., a "cert petition"). Each year, the Court receives thousands of cases seeking its review, but elects to hear fewer than 100. For example, during the Court's 2009–2010 session, justices received 8,159 requests to review lower court decisions, but opted to hear only 82 of them (Roberts 2010, 9–10).

Given the large number of review requests, justices have been forced to rely heavily upon their law clerks to help them study and review cert petitions. Starting in 1972, a group of justices created the "cert pool" by combining the collective efforts of their law clerks (Ward and Weiden 2006).[1] Each clerk in the pool reviews a cert petition and reports back to the other justices and their clerks in the pool. That is, once the Court receives a petition, it is randomly assigned to one of the law clerks in the cert pool, who writes a preliminary memorandum (the "pool memo") to the justices in the pool. The pool memo summarizes the proceedings in the lower courts and all legal claims made in the petition and response. It concludes with a recommendation for how the Court should treat the petition (e.g. grant, deny, or some other measure).

Relying on the pool memo and other materials, the chief justice then circulates a list of the petitions he thinks deserve further consideration from the Court at its next weekly conference. This list is called the "discuss list." (We provide an example of a discuss list below in Figure 8.1.) Associate justices can add petitions to the discuss list that they think deserve a discussion, but they cannot remove from the list a petition that a colleague added.[2] Importantly, the Court summarily (i.e., without a vote) denies all petitions that do not make the discuss list.

Each Friday, the Court holds a conference in which the justices discuss the cert petitions and vote on them. During this conference, the justice who placed the case on the discuss list (usually the Chief) leads off discussion of the petition. After presenting his or her views, the justice then casts an agenda vote. In order of seniority, the remaining justices state their positions and cast their votes. If four or more justices vote to grant review, the case proceeds to the merits stage.[3] Figure 8.2 illustrates, using the vote in *Lucas v. South Carolina Coastal Council*, how the justices record their votes during these conferences. As this figure shows, the Court held two rounds of voting. Chief Justice Rehnquist and Justices White, O'Connor, and Scalia voted to grant review in both rounds. Justice Blackmun voted to "Join-3" (that is, to provide the necessary fourth vote if there were three justices who supported review) in the first round and then to reverse summarily in the second round. Justices Stevens, Kennedy,

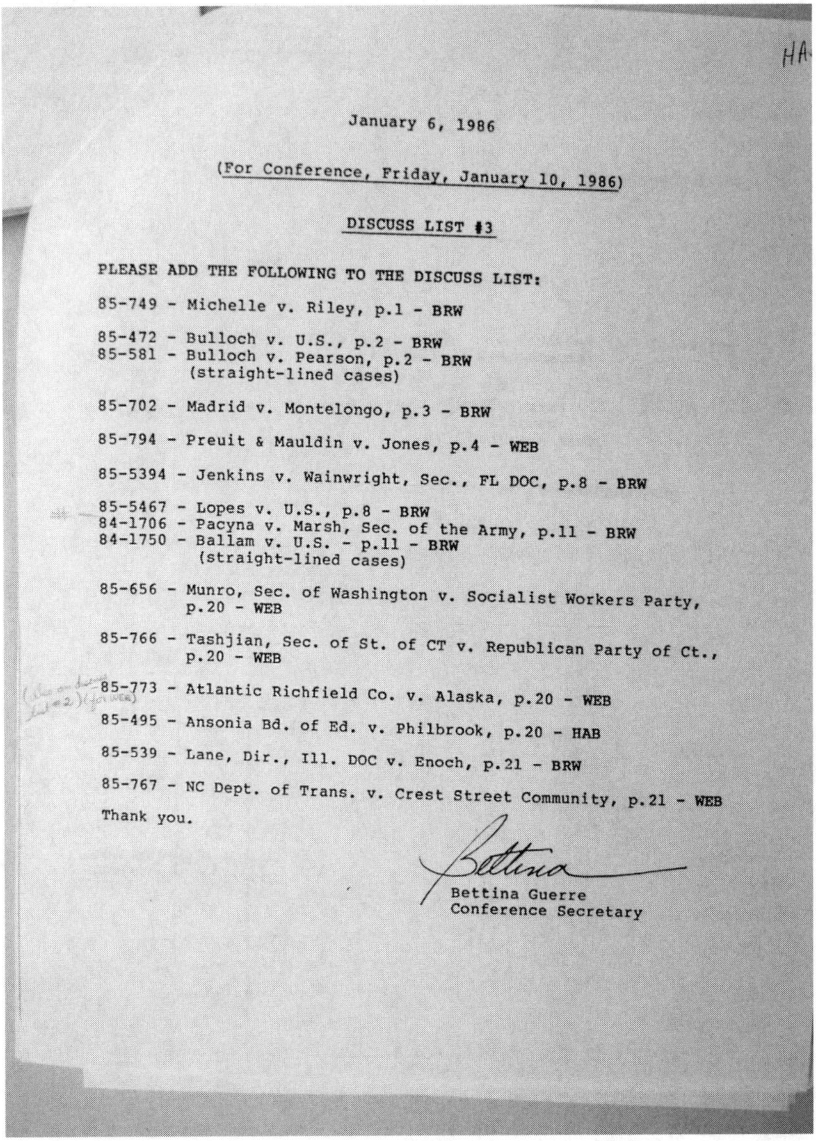

January 6, 1986

(For Conference, Friday, January 10, 1986)

DISCUSS LIST #3

PLEASE ADD THE FOLLOWING TO THE DISCUSS LIST:

85-749 - Michelle v. Riley, p.1 - BRW

85-472 - Bulloch v. U.S., p.2 - BRW
85-581 - Bulloch v. Pearson, p.2 - BRW
         (straight-lined cases)

85-702 - Madrid v. Montelongo, p.3 - BRW

85-794 - Preuit & Mauldin v. Jones, p.4 - WEB

85-5394 - Jenkins v. Wainwright, Sec., FL DOC, p.8 - BRW

85-5467 - Lopes v. U.S., p.8 - BRW
84-1706 - Pacyna v. Marsh, Sec. of the Army, p.11 - BRW
84-1750 - Ballam v. U.S. - p.11 - BRW
          (straight-lined cases)

85-656 - Munro, Sec. of Washington v. Socialist Workers Party,
         p.20 - WEB

85-766 - Tashjian, Sec. of St. of CT v. Republican Party of Ct.,
         p.20 - WEB

85-773 - Atlantic Richfield Co. v. Alaska, p.20 - WEB

85-495 - Ansonia Bd. of Ed. v. Philbrook, p.20 - HAB

85-539 - Lane, Dir., Ill. DOC v. Enoch, p.21 - BRW

85-767 - NC Dept. of Trans. v. Crest Street Community, p.21 - WEB

Thank you.

Bettina Guerre
Conference Secretary

Figure 8.1 Discuss list for Court's Conference on January 10, 1986. Initials next to each case correspond to the justice who put the case on the discuss list. We obtained this document from the Papers of Justice Harry A. Blackmun, which are housed in the Library of Congress, Washington, DC.

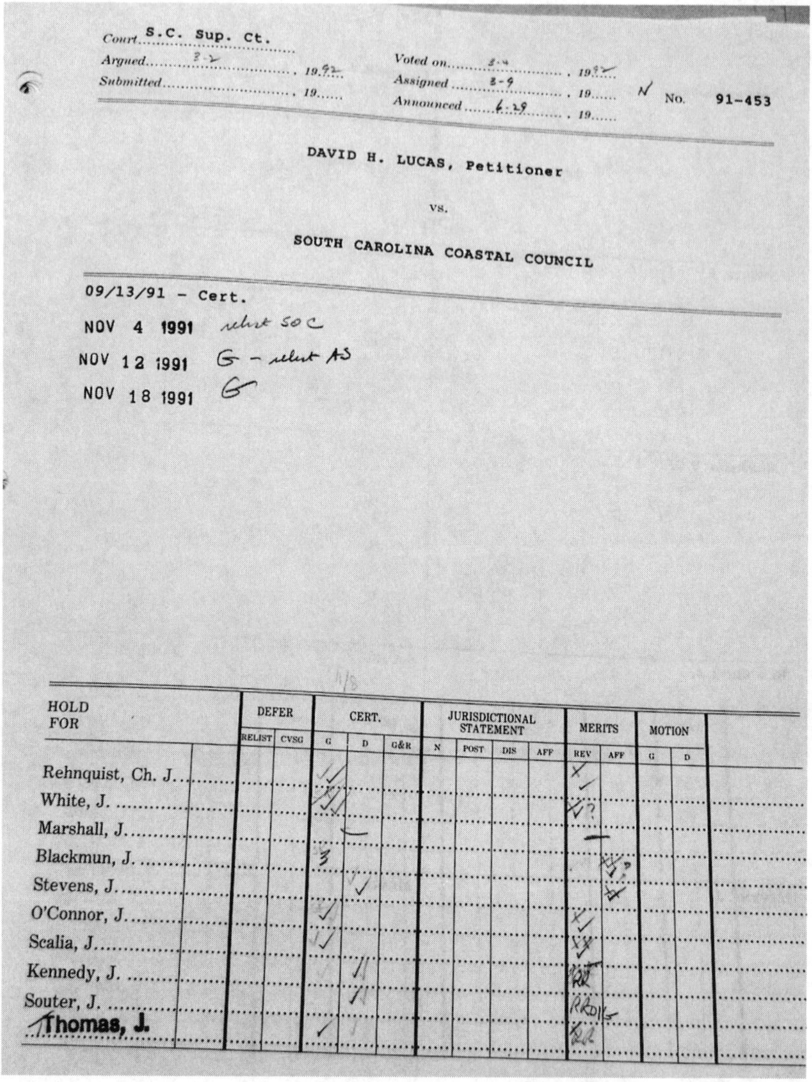

Court S.C. Sup. Ct.

Argued.......... 3 ν ...., 19.9ι.
Submitted......................., 19.....

Voted on......... 3·ιι ...., 19.9ι.
Assigned .... 3-9 ...., 19...... N   No.   91-453
Announced ...... 6·29 ...., 19......

DAVID H. LUCAS, Petitioner

vs.

SOUTH CAROLINA COASTAL COUNCIL

09/13/91 - Cert.

NOV 4 1991   relist SoC

NOV 12 1991   G - relist AS

NOV 18 1991   G

HOLD FOR	DEFER		CERT.			JURISDICTIONAL STATEMENT				MERITS		MOTION		
	RELIST	CVSG	G	D	G&R	N	POST	DIS	AFF	REV	AFF	G	D		
Rehnquist, Ch. J.			✓							✓					
White, J.			✓							✓?					
Marshall, J.				✓											
Blackmun, J.			3												
Stevens, J.				✓						✓?					
O'Connor, J.			✓							✓					
Scalia, J.			✓							✓					
Kennedy, J.				✓						RR					
Souter, J.				✓						RRDIG					
Thomas, J.				✓						RR					

Figure 8.2 Justice Blackmun's docket sheet in *Lucas v. South Carolina Coastal Council*, 505 U.S. 1003 (1992). Docket sheet comes from Epstein, Segal, and Spaeth (2007). Case granted review with four votes to grant (Rehnquist, White, O'Connor, and Scalia). Justice Blackmun voted for summary reversal. Justices Stevens, Kennedy, Souter, and Thomas voted to deny review.

and Souter voted to deny review in both rounds. Interestingly, we can see that Justice Thomas originally voted to grant review to the case but, in the second round of voting, switched his vote to deny. At any rate, because four justices cast grant votes, the Court granted review to the case and proceeded to the merits stage.

Certiorari votes are entirely discretionary and, unless divulged by the personal papers of a deceased or retired justice, are completely secret. Neither the Court staff nor the justices' own law clerks are allowed in the conference room during these deliberations. This secrecy, plus the Court's lack of formal requirements for taking cases, leads us to our central question: under what conditions will justices vote to review a case?

A Theory of Supreme Court Agenda Setting

We argue that three broad considerations influence how justices set the Court's agenda. We believe that justices vote to grant review to cases when they expect policy gains from hearing the case. We also believe that they will vote to grant review to a case when certain legal factors counsel toward hearing it. And, finally, we believe that policy and legal considerations interact with each other and jointly explain Supreme Court agenda setting. We address each of these factors below.

Policy Considerations

Like many before us, we argue that justices are seekers of policy who want to etch their preferences into law (Epstein and Knight 1998). "Most justices, in most cases, pursue policy; that is, they want to move the substantive content of law as close as possible to their preferred position" (p. 23). A number of influential studies highlight the role of policy in judicial decision-making. For example, Maltzman, Spriggs, and Wahlbeck (2000) show that a justice's decision to respond to a majority opinion draft—and to accommodate colleagues' suggestions in those drafts—stem from ideological motivations. Martin and Quinn (2002), Bailey (2007), and Epstein et al. (2007a) provide sophisticated empirical models to show that justices can be located spatially according to their revealed policy preferences. Of course, Segal and Spaeth (2002) win the prize for making the most forceful argument about the role of policy, stating that "the legal model and its components serve only to rationalize the Court's decisions and to cloak the reality of the Court's decision-making process" (p. 53). Even scholars who are sympathetic to the potentially constraining effect of law on justices concede that policy is the predominant motivation that drives justices (see, for example, Richards and Kritzer 2002).

Yet, justices must pursue their policy goals in an interdependent environment in which their decisions are also a function of the preferences of those with whom they must interact. Most important for our purposes, justices must interact with their *colleagues* on the Court. This requirement (to acquire a majority to make binding precedent) influences justices' behavior throughout the decision-making process (Bonneau *et al.* 2007; Maltzman, Spriggs, and Wahlbeck 2000). Chief justices and Senior Associate justices who assign majority opinions do so to make favorable policy, but they also must keep the majority coalition together. Opinion writers must also make sure that their opinions reflect the preferences of their colleagues, lest they lose their support and find themselves writing in dissent. This means pre-emptively accommodating their colleagues and, when necessary, making changes to opinion drafts. In order to make binding precedent, justices must engage in such practices (Hansford and Spriggs 2006). They must predict how their colleagues will act throughout the decision-making process. These and other studies, then, show that policy matters dearly to justices, but that they must also—at all times—consider how their colleagues' responses will affect their eventual policy success.

We believe that at the agenda stage, justices will engage in similar behavior: they will seek their policy goals but will also look to the behavior of their colleagues to determine whether they will be in the majority or in the minority in a case. That is, when deciding whether to grant review to a case, justices must consider and predict the likely behavior of their colleagues at the merits stage. To win on the merits, a justice must be able to join with at least four of her colleagues. In short, they must *predict* the behavior of their colleagues when they set the Court's agenda, and determine whether their colleagues' predicted behavior at the merits stage will improve policy for them, or make worse policy than the status quo.

Numerous comments from justices and their clerks provide strong evidence to support the argument that justices are forward-looking agenda setters. Consider the following statement taken from H.W. Perry's (1991) seminal text on agenda setting: "I might think the Nebraska Supreme Court made a horrible decision, but I wouldn't want to take the case, for if we take the case and affirm it, then it would become a precedent" (H.W. Perry 1991, 200). Clearly, this quote suggests that justices base their agenda decisions, at least in part, on the existing status quo and the expectations about their colleagues' behavior. Similar types of comments can be found throughout the papers of former Justice Harry A. Blackmun. Consider the following in *Dupnik v. Cooper* (No. 92–210), in which Blackmun's clerk advised him: "This is a defensive deny if nothing else." Or, look at *Freeman v. Pitts* (No. 89–1290) in which Blackmun's clerk stated: "[G]iven the current mood of the Court, I am not eager to see the petition granted." Indeed, consider the following quintessential quote from Blackmun's clerk in *Thornburgh v. Abbott* (No. 87–1344):

> I think it pretty much comes down to whether you want to reverse the judgment below (the likely outcome of a grant). If you are pretty sure you do, you should vote to grant now. Otherwise, it's better to wait.
>
> (Epstein, Segal, and Spaeth 2007)

Empirical evidence confirms the reliability of these comments, supporting the notion that justices are forward-looking agenda setters who, we believe, make predictions about the likely behavior of their colleagues at later stages of the decision-making process (Benesh, Brenner, and Spaeth 2002; Boucher and Segal 1995; Brenner 1979; Palmer 1982). Caldeira, Wright, and Zorn (1999) find that justices will be more likely to vote to grant review as they become increasingly similar ideologically to the majority on the Court. Black and Owens (2009a) find, among other things, that justices who prefer the predicted merits outcome in a case to the status quo are roughly 75% more likely to grant review than those who are closer ideologically to the status quo.

We seek to build on these and other works by showing that justices make *probabilistic* forward-looking agenda-setting decisions. We examine how justices behave when they predict a *range* of possible merits outcomes rather than one specific outcome. In other words, rather than assuming that the Court's merits outcome can be reflected by the ideal point of, say, one justice (see, for example, Black and Owens 2009a), we argue that justices predict the Court's merits outcome will fall within a certain range of probable outcomes. To be sure, it may be defensible to assert that actors know the policy location of the status quo and the preferences of colleagues with whom they must frequently interact. It is problematic, however, to assume that actors have complete and perfect information about the final result of the policy they will make—especially when that policy must undergo treatment from other actors (such as their colleagues). Predictions will seldom be perfectly accurate, particularly when making decisions in multi-stage settings. What is needed is an approach that examines how justices make probabilistic predictions under conditions of uncertainty.

We argue that when the probability increases that the Court's expected merits decision will be better for a justice than the status quo, the justice will be more likely to vote to grant review to the case. Conversely, when that probability decreases, the justice will be less likely to vote to grant review to the case. The logic is obvious: justices will seek to open the gates and allow cases to proceed when their probability of winning at the merits increases, and they will be less likely to open those gates when the probability of winning on the merits decreases. This gives rise to the following hypothesis:

Probabilistic Policy Hypothesis: a justice will become increasingly likely to vote to grant review to a petition as the probability increases that the Court's merits decision will be better policy for that justice than the status quo.

Legal Considerations

While policy considerations clearly are important for justices, so too are legal considerations. After all, justices are trained in the law and taught, like all lawyers, that the law is sacrosanct and must be followed. At the same time, other actors such as Congress, the president, the public, and the bar expect justices to respect the law. Since justices rely on these institutions to execute the Court's decisions and sustain its legitimacy, they must behave in a manner consistent with those expectations. So, justices wanting to make efficacious decisions must largely comply with predominant beliefs about proper legal behavior (Lindquist and Klein 2006).

What are these legal considerations that influence justices at the agenda stage? To answer this question, we reviewed two well-known studies on Supreme Court agenda setting—H.W. Perry (1991) and Stern et al. (2002). Both of these works illuminate the legal factors that influence justices' agenda votes. H.W. Perry (1991) gained insight into the Court's agenda behavior through a number of extensive interviews with justices and their clerks, while Stern et al. (2002) rely on years of experience within the Court and litigating before it. Perry argues that legal conflict and legal importance constitute two (empirically testable) legal variables, while Stern and his co-authors argue that judicial review exercised in the lower court is an important legal factor driving the Court's agenda. The importance of these factors has been verified by a number of studies (see, for example, Black and Owens 2009a). We consider each of them more extensively.

One of the Supreme Court's most important duties is to resolve legal conflict among the lower courts. When lower courts disagree on the proper interpretation of federal law, the Court is expected to wade into the conflict and declare the correct interpretation of the law. Both the Court's own rules (see Supreme Court Rule 10) and statements by the justices themselves suggest that the presence of legal conflict drives up the likelihood that they will vote to grant review. Consider the following quote from an anonymous justice:

> I would say that [cert votes] are sometimes tentative votes on the merits. Now I would say that there are certain cases that I would vote for, for example, if there was a clear split in circuits, *I would vote for cert. without even looking at the merits.* But there are other cases I would have more of a notion of what the merits were.
>
> (H.W. Perry 1991, 269; emphasis supplied)

Empirical scholarship confirms the point. Lindquist and Klein (2006) argue: "[E]ven a cursory examination" of the Court's docket shows that policy implications alone do not explain Supreme Court agenda setting. "Justices [may] choose to hear [cases] not because they care so much about the policies involved but in order to clarify federal law" (p. 139). Other studies also show that the Court is more likely to grant review to cases that observe legal conflict than those that do not (Caldeira and Wright 1988). Thus, we expect that a justice will be more likely to vote to grant review when the lower courts conflict with each other over how to interpret federal law:

> Legal Conflict Hypothesis: a justice will be more likely to vote to grant review to a petition when the lower courts conflict over the proper interpretation of federal law.

At the same time, when a lower federal court exercises judicial review over a federal statute, the Supreme Court is expected to weigh in. When a lower federal court strikes down a federal law as unconstitutional, legal norms suggest the Supreme Court should review the decision (Stern et al. 2002, 244). Justices themselves have claimed that they owe Congress the duty to review whether, as the lower court determined, the statute is indeed unconstitutional. Thus, we expect the following:

> Judicial Review Hypothesis: a justice will be more likely to vote to grant review to a petition when the lower court struck down a federal law as unconstitutional.

Case importance is a third legal consideration that can drive agenda setting. Perry's (1991) interviews show that justices believe they should review cases that are legally important. There are simply some issues that the broader public demands the Court resolve. Stated one justice: "Sometimes the people just demand that the Supreme Court resolve an issue whether we really ought to or not. That does affect us sometimes. We just feel that the Supreme Court has to decide" (H.W. Perry 1991, 259).

We expect that, all else equal, justices will be more likely to vote to grant review in these legally important cases:

> Legal Importance Hypothesis: a justice will be more likely to vote to grant review to a legally important petition.

The Conditional Influence of Law on Policy

To be sure, we believe that the independent effects of policy and law are influential and can explain much agenda-setting behavior. Yet, it is likely that the interaction of the two considerations jointly explain agenda setting (and, likely, judicial behavior more broadly). Scholars are just beginning to examine how law and policy interact. Consider, for example, Johnson, Wahlbeck, and Spriggs (2006), who show that ideology and an attorney's quality of oral argumentation conditionally influence whether a party wins before the Court. Justices pursue their policy goals, of course, but are influenced by the legal argumentation proffered by the attorneys in a case. At the same time, Hansford and Spriggs (2006) show that precedent vitality (i.e., how strong a precedent is) can influence how justices go about seeking their policy goals when interpreting precedent. These studies suggest quite strongly that policy behavior can be conditioned by the legal considerations in a case—and we have every reason to believe that such a dynamic occurs at the agenda stage.

Indeed, perhaps the key contribution made by Black and Owens (2009a) in their examination of agenda votes was the finding that policy and legal considerations *do* interact, and that legal factors sometimes force justices to behave contrary to their policy goals. Simply put, as judges, there are a number of legal considerations that must enter their decision calculus, considerations which can either trump their policy goals or aid them as they seek their policy goals. The conditioning effect can be positive or negative, depending on whether law and policy point toward the same or different ends. We apply the logic of this argument to our approach.

On the one hand, justices may wish to pursue their policy goals but find themselves *constrained* by legal considerations. Imagine a justice who wants to cast a defensive deny vote to protect the status quo policy: the justice knows that if she votes to grant review to the case, the full Court on the merits would be highly likely to make worse policy (from her standpoint) than the status quo. As such, for policy reasons, she would want to vote to deny review. Yet, consider what happens when she observes a considerable amount of conflict among the lower courts over the correct interpretation of the federal law. Will that same justice cling to her policy goals and vote to deny review to the case? We think not. Instead, her probability of voting to grant review will increase. That is, when justices want to deny review for policy reasons, legal considerations (such as legal conflict, judicial review exercised below, and legal importance) can drive up their likelihood of voting to grant review.

On the other hand, if justices' policy goals *accord* with what legal norms countenance, the law will *aid* and provide cover for their policy-seeking behavior. If there is a large probability that the Court's policy decision at the merits stage will improve the status quo, the law will actually enhance the justice's desire to grant review to the case. Consider a justice who wants to grant review because she expects the Court's merits decision will make better policy for her than the status quo. Now consider what happens if the lower court that heard the case struck down a federal statute. The justice should become even more likely to vote to grant review than she otherwise would have been. She can, in short, vote to grant review to pursue her policy goals but claim to be following the law. Legal considerations can free her up to pursue her policy goals. This gives rise to the following hypothesis:

> *The Conditional Influence of Law Hypothesis*: a justice with a small (or no) probability of being made better off by the Court's merits decision will nevertheless be more likely to vote to grant review to a petition when

legal factors point toward review. Conversely, a justice with a large probability of being made better off by the Court's merits decision will be even more likely to vote to grant review to a petition when legal factors point toward review.

Data and Measures

To test our theory, we examined the private, archival records of former Justice Harry A. Blackmun.[4] While certiorari outcomes (i.e., grant or deny) are publicly available for all cases, the votes of individual justices and knowledge of which cases made the discuss list are not. As a result, we needed to utilize archival data to obtain such information. We obtained these raw data from Epstein, Segal, and Spaeth (2007). Accordingly, we analyzed a random sample of petitions that made the Supreme Court's discuss list. Our unit of analysis is the justice vote. Our dependent variable is each justice's cert vote, which we code as 1 for grant and 0 for deny.[5]

Policy measures. Our policy-based explanation for agenda setting examines the probability that a justice will be made better off by the Court's merits decision than the status quo. To quantify this variable, we measured four attributes:

1   each justice's policy preferences;
2   the status quo in each case;
3   the set of likely outcomes resulting from a predicted Court decision on the merits; and
4   the probability that the set of likely merits outcomes would be better for the justice (policy-wise) than the status quo.

We measured each justice's policy preferences by referring to the Judicial Common Space (JCS) and finding the justice's JCS score for the term in question (Epstein *et al.* 2007a). The Judicial Common Space is a collection of scores used to measure the preferences of Supreme Court justices, Members of Congress, and lower federal court judges. It provides an estimate of each justice's revealed preferences and allows scholars to estimate how liberal or conservative a justice behaved each year. By using the justice's JCS score for the term in question, we can quantify how liberal or conservative the justice was at the time of the agenda vote.

To measure the status quo in each case, we followed Black and Owens (2009a) and analyzed the JCS scores of the judges who sat on the lower federal court panel that heard the case. In particular, we coded the status quo as the JCS score of the median judge on the three-judge circuit court panel that heard the case below. In cases where a lower court judge filed a dissent or special concurrence, we coded the status quo as the midpoint between the two circuit judges in the majority. And, if the lower court reviewed the case *en banc*—as a full collection of the circuit judges rather than the standard three-judge panels—we coded the status quo as the median judge in the *en banc* majority.

Measuring the set of likely outcomes resulting from a predicted Court decision on the merits was more tricky. Unlike existing studies, which largely claim that justices know precisely where in policy space the Court's merits decision will be (see, for example, Black and Owens 2009a; Owens 2010), we argue that justices make probabilistic predictions about the location of that policy outcome. That is, we believe justices can predict a range of likely outcomes and base their decisions to grant or deny on that range. But how do they determine that range of possible outcomes? We assume that to predict *future* case outcomes, justices look backwards at *previous* Court rulings on similar issues. To predict how the Court today will rule in a case, they will look at the Court's past track record dealing with similar cases.

To capture this set of likely outcomes, we began by reading the cert pool memos written in every petition so as to determine the issue in the case. Then, we used the Supreme Court Database to identify the last 10 cases the Supreme Court decided on that same issue (our results are similar if we use values other than 10). Once we identified the Court's previous cases in that issue area, we needed to determine the ideological content of those cases. To do so, we looked to the members of the majority coalition in each of those cases. Carrubba *et al.* (2007) show that the policy generated in each case is determined by the preferences of the median member of the majority coalition (see also Clark and Lauderdale 2010). We adopted their approach and identified the JCS score of the median justice of the majority coalition for each of these previous cases.

Having located the medians of majority coalitions in similar previous cases, we then used a data-smoothing procedure to back out the underlying distribution that was most likely to have given rise to these past outcomes. That is, using JCS values from the Court's previous cases as an input, we estimated the underlying policy distribution that generated those specific values. Then (finally!), to calculate the probability that the set of possible outcomes in the case would be better for the justices than the status quo we integrated across all values of the possible merits outcome where a voting justice would prefer that outcome over the status quo.

We appreciate the complexity of this approach and, to make it clearer to the reader, illustrate it in Figure 8.3. Each panel shows the policy continuum, where values on the far left are most liberal and values on the far right are most conservative. Within each of the three panels, we show *SQ*, which is the status quo, the current state of legal policy related to the case. If the Court decided not to grant review in a case, this is what legal policy would look like. J_i represents a specific justice's most preferred policy outcome, which is often referred to as her "ideal point." J' represents the justice's indifference point—the point in policy space the justices likes equally to the status quo. The region between *SQ* and J' represent the range of policy outcomes that the justice

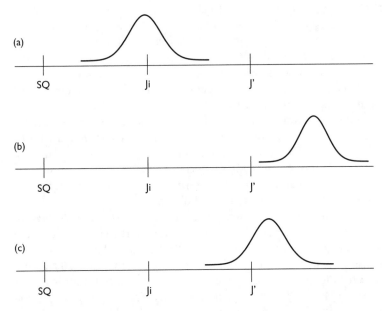

Figure 8.3 Justice preferences relative to the staus quo and hypothetical merits outcomes.

would prefer to the status quo. Thus, when a potential policy outcome falls between *SQ* and *J'*, the justice prefers that policy to the status quo. Finally, the thick lines that form bell-shaped curves represent a justice's belief about what type of legal policy the Court would create if it were to grant cert the petition seeking review. Recall that the inputs for this distribution come from the location of the Court's previous decisions in cases with a similar issue.

Justice$_i$ will prefer the merits outcome over the status quo for any Court-made policy that falls between *SQ* and *J'*, since that policy will be closer to her estimated ideal point than is the status quo. As such, panel (a) of Figure 8.3 implies that our hypothetical justice would prefer all likely merits outcomes to the status quo. Her value of *Policy Improvement Probability* would therefore equal 1. (The entire area under the curve falls between *SQ* and *J'*.) In panel (b), since none of the curve falls between *SQ* and *J'*, *none* of the possible merits outcomes would improve policy for J$_i$. Accordingly, she would receive a value of 0 for *Policy Improvement Probability* (and would be quite unlikely to vote to grant review to the case). Finally, if the merits range took on the location presented in panel (c), J$_i$ would prefer some values of the possible merits outcome distribution over the status quo. Under this configuration, the value of *Policy Improvement Probability* for the justice would equal the area under the curve between *SQ* and *J'*. As that value of *Policy Improvement Probability* increases, so too will the likelihood that the justice will vote to grant review to the petition.

Legal Measures. To operationalize legal conflict, we include three variables: *Legal Conflict Alleged, Weak Legal Conflict,* and *Strong Legal Conflict.* We coded each of these variables by reading the law clerks' discussions in the cert pool memos. We coded *Legal Conflict Alleged* as 1 if the petitioner alleged the existence of conflict, but the law clerk found that assertion without merit. *Weak Legal Conflict* is coded as 1 if the petitioner alleged the existence of legal conflict but the law clerk tamped down the allegation and claimed instead that the conflict was minor and tolerable (it is coded as 0 otherwise). (Also called "shallow conflict," this occurs when the conflict includes few circuits or revolves around a conflict that the circuits themselves appear to be clarifying on their own.) We code *Strong Legal Conflict* as 1 (0 otherwise) when the petitioner alleges a conflict and the pool memo writer concurs in its presence and notes that the conflict is neither minor nor tolerable.

To measure judicial review, we created *Lower Court Exercises Judicial Review,* which takes on a value of 1 if the circuit court that heard the case below struck down a federal statute as unconstitutional; 0 otherwise.

To measure legal importance, we followed Black and Owens (2009a) and relied on three different measures, the first of which comes from the circuit court's opinion type. We code *Unpublished Lower Court Opinion* as 1 if the intermediate court's opinion was unpublished and 0 if published. Our second measure of legal importance comes from the pages of the *U.S. Law Week,* a legal periodical that seeks to "[alert] the legal profession to the most important cases and why they are important" (LexisNexis Source Information). We expect that, on average, legally important cases will generate summaries in *U.S. Law Week* while legally mundane cases will not. We code *Case Media Salience* as 1 if there was a story written about the circuit court opinion; 0 otherwise. Finally, our third measure of legal importance turns on the number of amicus curiae briefs filed in a case. When organized interests involve themselves in the agenda-setting process, they send a signal to the Court that the case is important, especially since the cost of filing such briefs is high (Caldeira and Wright 1988). We suggest that as the number of groups filing amicus briefs increases, the perceived legal importance of the case should also increase. Accordingly, we coded *Outside Interest Participation* as the total number of amicus curiae briefs filed both in support of and in opposition to the petition. We explain below how we measured the interactive relationship between policy and law.

Finally, we also controlled for a variety of additional factors, such as whether the lower court decision was *en banc,* whether the United States supported or opposed review in the case, whether the circuit court of appeals reversed the court below it, and whether the circuit court decision observed a dissent by one of its judges in the case. As a statistical matter, it was important that we include these potential alternative explanations that might be related to the hypotheses we wish to test. Further, including these variables was important to maintaining consistency with a long line of existing studies on

Supreme Court agenda setting (e.g. Caldeira and Wright 1988; Caldeira, Wright, and Zorn 1999; Tanenhaus *et al.* 1963). Measurement details for these additional variables can be found in Table 8A.1 in the Appendix.

Methods and Results

Because our dependent variable is binary (i.e., takes on a value of yes or no for whether a justice voted to grant review) we estimate a logistic regression model. As the raw model results are difficult to interpret, we relegate the table of results to the Appendix and turn directly to summarizing what our data say about our hypotheses. Recall that we proposed three basic arguments: first, we argued that justices cast their agenda votes based on the probability that the Court's eventual merits decision will result in a more favorable policy than the status quo. Second, we asserted that justices weigh legal factors when making their agenda-setting decisions. Third, we claimed that policy and legal considerations interact with one another, with policy goals sometimes taking a back seat to legal considerations. We evaluate each in turn.

The Importance of Policy Considerations

Our initial argument was that, while casting their agenda votes, justices ask themselves: "How likely is it that this case will result in a policy improvement for me versus what currently exists?" When the justice believes there is a high probability of being made better off policy-wise, she will be more likely to vote to grant review. Our data confirm this hypothesis. Figure 8.4 illustrates. The horizontal axis represents the probability that the Court's merits decision in the case would result in a favorable policy gain for the justice. The vertical axis represents the probability that a justice will vote to grant review to the case.

The slope of the line is positive, which indicates that as the predicted improvement in policy increases in probability, so too does the likelihood that a justice will vote to grant review to the case. This is exactly what our policy hypothesis suggested. More specifically, we estimate only an 8% chance that a justice votes to grant review when there is no chance that the case will result in a policy improvement for her. By contrast, when a justice is very confident that the case will improve policy, the probability the justice votes to grant review doubles.

The Importance of Legal Considerations

While we believe policy considerations are important, we also argued that legal considerations matter. We hypothesized that when positive legal cues were present—such as legal conflict, judicial review, and case importance— justices would be more likely to vote to grant review. Conversely, when the case was legally unimportant—such as when its lower court opinion was

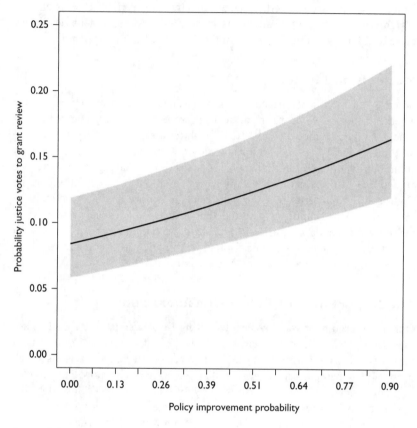

Figure 8.4 Impact of policy improvement on a justice's vote to grant review.

unpublished—justices would be less likely to vote to grant review. Figure 8.5 illustrates our results for these variables.

In Figure 8.5, we reverse the horizontal and vertical axes from the previous figure and display a justice's probability of voting to grant review on the horizontal axis. Each of our legal factors is labeled on the vertical axis and identified in the plot with a square point. This figure also includes (as a dashed vertical line) the "Baseline Probability" of a justice voting to grant. This value simply reflects the probability a justice would vote to grant review in an "average" case. (Such a case has a low value of legal importance, which helps explain why the estimate is relatively low—only about 12%.) Starting first with our legal conflict variables, we argued that when justices are confronted with a case in which the circuits are split as to the proper interpretation of law, they will need to intervene and clear up the conflict. Our results support this hypothesis. We predict an 18% chance that justices vote to grant review when "weak" conflict is present and a 38% chance when "strong" conflict is present.

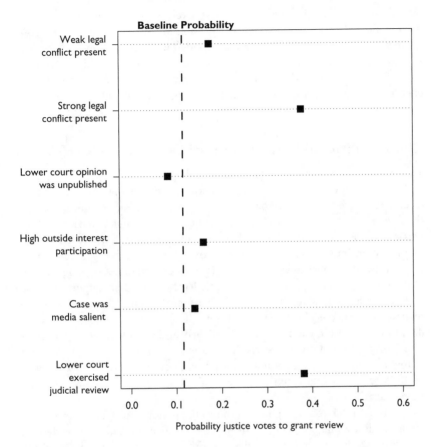

Figure 8.5 Impact of legal factors on a justice's vote to grant review.

These are, of course, significant increases over the baseline probability of voting to grant, especially in those cases with strong conflict.

We also find a significant increase in the probability of voting to review a case when the lower court exercised judicial review and declared a federal law unconstitutional. We suspected that the Court would have an institutional incentive to make sure the lower court judges decided the case correctly. Our findings bear this out. We estimate a 38% chance that a justice will vote to grant review when judicial review has been exercised in the court below, which is more than triple the initial baseline probability.

Our measures of legal importance also perform as expected, though they are not nearly as strong as the other legal considerations. Recall that the non-publication of a lower court opinion suggests that a particular case is *unim-portant*. As such, we argued that justices would be less likely to vote to grant review to lower court decisions that were unpublished. Consistent with our hypothesis, we find that justices are less likely to vote to grant review to unpublished decisions than the baseline opinion, which is published. We estimate only an 8% chance that a case decided with an unpublished opinion will convince a justice to support granting review. We find similarly modest effect sizes for our outside interests and media salience variables, whose presence increase the likelihood of a justice voting to grant review to 16% and 14%, respectively.

The Conditional Relationship of Law and Policy

Thus far, our results have focused on the independent role played by policy and legal considerations in affecting justices' agenda-setting votes. Yet, as we discussed above, we believe that these two factors interact to influence justices' votes. To test this account, we modified our initial statistical model. In particular, instead of treating each legal variable separately, we combined them into an index that summarizes the overall number of legal factors that might push the Court toward granting (versus denying) review. High values of the index mean the presence of multiple legal factors that support granting review, while low values indicate a lack of legal justifications for granting review. More specifically, we summed the values of weak conflict, strong conflict, lower court judicial review, case salience, and outside interest participation (converted to a dummy variable for any level of participation). We then estimated a statistical model that allowed us to evaluate how justices' policy behavior changes as a result of these legal considerations.[6] Figure 8.6 illustrates our results.

The horizontal axis in Figure 8.6 shows the policy improvement probability on the horizontal axis and the likelihood a justice votes to grant review on the vertical axis. Figure 8.6 provides two different scenarios for comparison. More specifically, the figure shows how policy considerations affect the probability of voting to grant review (a) when the law suggests the justice should deny review, and (b) when the law suggests a grant is warranted. The solid line shows the effect of predicted policy improvement on a justice's vote when the legal factors in the case tend to suggest that the Court should *deny* review. For example, assume there is no legal conflict in a case, the lower court did not exercise judicial review, and the various indicators of case importance suggest the case is not legally important. As the flat slope of the line indicates, there is no appreciable effect for the policy improvement variable when legal factors suggest the justice should deny review. In other words, no amount of policy improvement can persuade a justice to hear the case when the law suggests it is not cert-worthy. That is, regardless of the value of policy improvement we estimate only an 8% chance that a justice will vote to grant review.

By contrast, the dashed line shows the effect of predicted policy improvement when the case presents the Court with a series of important legal cues such as conflict and overall case importance. In such cases, we observe a

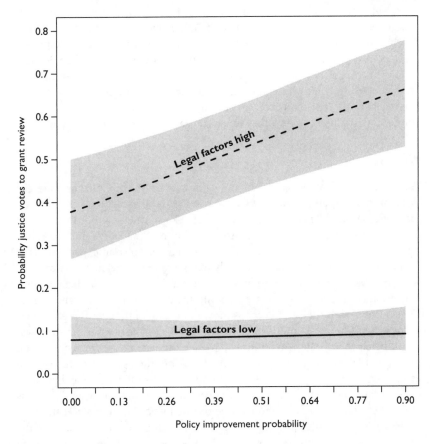

Figure 8.6 Impact of policy improvement and legal factors on a justice's vote to grant review.

strong positive relationship between the policy improvement probability variable and the likelihood a justice votes to grant review. More specifically, when legal cues suggest a justice should grant review—*but the probability the Court will improve policy for the justice is zero*—the justice votes to grant 38% of the time. When, however, legal cues suggest a grant and *the probability is quite high* that the Court will improve policy for the justice, she is 66% likely to vote to grant review, a relative increase of nearly 75%.

Perhaps just as important, compare the behavior of a justice who will be made better off by the Court's decision when there are no legal cues to grant, with a justice who will be made worse off in a case where legal cues suggest she should grant review. In the former case, the justice votes to grant with an 8% probability. In the latter case, she votes to grant review with a 38% probability!

Put plainly, when looking at the law and policy jointly, it is apparent that legal considerations matter to justices at the agenda stage, and they matter dearly. When law and policy work together, justices can more freely pursue their policy goals. Yet, policy goals are often not enough. When justices should, from a policy perspective, seek to kill the petition, they nevertheless vote to open the gates in a significant number of instances. They do so, we believe, because legal considerations weigh heavily on their minds. For justices, then, to achieve policy, they must also garner support from the law.

Discussion

What do these findings tell us about agenda setting on the Court and judicial decision-making more broadly? In a narrow sense, they tell us about the factors that matter to justices when they set the Court's agenda. Both policy and legal considerations influence the cases they put on the Court's docket. When a justice stands to be made better off in a policy sense by an expected merits decision, that justice will be more likely to vote to grant review to the case. At the same time, when legal considerations such as legal conflict, judicial review, and broader case importance are present, justices become much more likely to grant review to the case. Perhaps most importantly, though, these findings suggest that law can condition justices' policy goals. Justices, to be sure, will seek to etch their policy preferences into law, but when their behavior would be defined by nothing other than policy seeking, they give way. Justices, in essence, must be able to attach legal motivations to their policy behavior in order to proceed. Why this is the case, we cannot be sure, but what is clear is that policy alone cannot be enough to motivate justices at the agenda stage.

More broadly, these findings suggest that scholars should look for the influence of law on justices' decisions in other areas of the decision-making process. We do not quarrel with the notion, long confirmed in the literature, that justices are seekers of legal policy. Hundreds of articles and books show quite convincingly that policy goals fill justices' minds. Yet, we do believe that our results suggest that policy goals do not *exclusively* motivate justices. Why, after all, would justices care about legal factors at the agenda stage—so much so that they would vote to hear a case knowing that it would likely result in a policy loss for them—but then disregard such factors at later stages? To ask the question is to answer it: they would not. Instead, it is much more likely that legal factors motivate justices in manners heretofore unstudied. Perhaps legal considerations force justices to decide cases using different legal grounds than they otherwise would prefer. Perhaps the models social scientists have employed to examine the influence of law are simply too blunt to detect its role. These and other aspects of political jurisprudence must be studied further. For now, at least, it seems quite clear that policy considerations and legal considerations jointly influence justices' agenda votes.

Appendix

Table 8A.1 Control Variable Names and Coding Rules

Variable name	Coding
En banc lower court opinion	Was decision seeking the Court's review decided by a full complement of circuit judges (coded as 1) or a more common three-judge panel (coded as 0)?
U.S. supports review	Did the U.S. seek review of the petition either as the petitioning party or as amicus curiae? 0 = no; 1 = yes.
U.S. opposes review	Did the U.S. oppose review of the petition either as the responding party or as amicus curiae? 0 = no; 1 = yes.
Lower court reverse trial court	Did the lower court reverse the initial decision of the trial court? 0 = no; 1 = yes.
Dissent in lower court	Was there a dissenting opinion present in the decision seeking review from the lower court? 0 = no; 1 = yes.

Table 8A.2 Logistic Regression Model of whether a Justice Votes to Grant (Coded as 1) or Deny Review (Coded as 0) in a Cert Petition

	Coefficient	Robust S.E.
Policy improvement probability	0.848*	0.165
Legal conflict alleged	0.154	0.228
Weak legal conflict	0.484*	0.186
Strong legal conflict	1.534*	0.188
Lower court exercises judicial review	1.548*	0.398
Case media salience	0.225	0.172
Unpublished lower court opinion	−0.361	0.418
Outside interest participation	0.188*	0.078
En banc lower court opinion	0.107	0.371
U.S. supports review	0.884*	0.226
U.S. opposes review	−0.184	0.198
Lower court reverse trial court	0.375*	0.159
Dissent in lower court	0.279	0.193
Constant	−2.545	0.229
Observations	3,024	
Log likelihood	−1,577.189	

Notes
Standard errors are clustered on each of the unique 3,024 dockets in our data.
* denotes $p < 0.05$ (two-tailed test).

Table 8A.3 Logistic Regression Model of whether a Justice Votes to Grant (Coded as 1) or Deny Review (Coded as 0) in a Cert Petition

	Coefficient	Robust S.E.
Policy improvement probability	0.437	0.301
Net legal factors	0.486*	0.113
Policy improvement probability x net legal factors	0.288	0.191
Legal conflict alleged	0.354	0.199
U.S. supports review	1.020*	0.220
U.S. opposes review	−0.221	0.197
Lower court reverse trial court	0.270	0.162
Dissent in lower court	0.273	0.202
En banc lower court opinion	−0.011	0.354
Constant	−2.317*	0.242
Observations	3,024	
Log likelihood	−1,643.631	

Notes
Standard errors are clustered on each of the unique 3,024 dockets in our data.
* denotes p <0.05 (two-tailed test).

Notes

1 Each justice makes her own decision as to whether she wants to participate in the cert pool. As of the Court's 2010 term, Justice Samuel Alito was the only justice known not to participate in it.

2 It is worth pointing out that until 1950, the Court's default position was that all petitions would be discussed and voted upon unless a justice put that specific petition on a list of petitions *not* to be discussed—the "dead list." Any justice could revive a dead petition and remove it from this list. As the number of requests to the Court increased, though, such a scenario became increasingly untenable, leading the Court to reverse the default position (Ward and Weiden 2006, 115). Thus, whereas the default used to be that every petition was discussed unless shifted to the dead list, today the default is that every petition will be denied summarily unless put on the discuss list.

3 Technically, the Court will grant review to a petition upon three grant votes plus one Join-3 vote (Black and Owens 2009b). A Join-3 vote is like a conditional grant vote: If at least three other justices vote to grant review to the case, the Join-3 vote is the equivalent of a grant vote. If fewer than three other justices vote to grant review, the Join-3 is treated as a denial.

4 Black and Owens (2009c) show that Blackmun's papers are highly reliable.

5 See Black and Owens (2009a) for additional details on how we constructed our sample and coded our dependent variable.

6 We treated an unpublished opinion as a value of −1. Our re-estimated model excludes these specific variables in lieu of an index, which is interacted with our policy probability variable. Table 8A.2 in the Appendix presents parameter results.

Chapter 9

The Origin and Development of Stare Decisis at the U.S. Supreme Court

Timothy R. Johnson, James F. Spriggs, II, and Paul J. Wahlbeck

In the past few decades there has been a wealth of scholarship aimed at understanding the origin and development of institutional rules as agents of political, economic, and social change. In the eyes of many scholars, the questions of where institutions originate and how they develop are two of the most important puzzles confronting social science. Indeed, social scientists have spent a great deal of time trying to understand why institutional rules emerge, when and where they emerge, and the effects of their emergence on society. Existing literature examines the development of such political institutions as constitutions (Riker 1988; Tsebelis 1990), legislative rules (Bach and Smith 1988; Binder 1997; Jenkins, Crespin, and Carson 2005; McCubbins, Noll, and Weingast 1987; Shepsle 1986; Shipan 1995, 1996, 1997), and voting rules (Duverger 1954).

This scholarly interest in institutional rules stems from a general recognition that they can have pronounced effects on social outcomes—that is, they are not neutral but serve to allocate resources in society (Knight 1992; North 1990). Simply put, rules determine opportunities by defining choice sets and by giving strategic advantage to some actors over others. For instance, the rules of legislative debate in the U.S. House of Representatives often advantage one political party over the other and thus influence legislative outcomes (Binder 1996). More generally, rules provide the structure within which both government and nongovernmental actors make choices and, as a result, affect the distribution of political, social, and economic benefits. As North (1990, 30) argues, "Institutions are the rules of the game in society, or more formally, are the humanly devised constraints that shape human interaction."

Our interest lies with understanding the quintessential institutional rule in the American judiciary—*stare decisis*. This informal norm directs judges to follow legal rulings from prior cases that are factually similar to ones being decided.[1] It is the defining feature of American courts, and lawyers, judges, and scholars recognize it represents the most critical piece of American judicial infrastructure (Knight and Epstein 1996a; Powell 1990; Schauer 1987). Additionally, the transfer of the common law framework from England to the United States, and the role *stare decisis* plays within it, is the "central theme of early American legal history" (Flaherty 1969, 5). Indeed, put into place in the mid-eighteenth and nineteenth centuries, the creation and development of this institutional structure represents a significant part of the American nation-building experience and serves as the most important transformational change in U.S. legal history (Friedman 1985; Hall 1989).

Despite the recognized centrality of *stare decisis* in the American judiciary, no social scientific study to date has endeavored to explain systematically why and when it developed. Instead, scholars generally discuss the purported advantages of *stare decisis* (e.g., stability, fairness, legitimacy, and efficiency) without reference to whether these factors were the motivating reasons for its adoption in the first place (Healy 2001; Knight and Epstein 1996a; Lee 1999; Schauer 1987). Additionally, while social scientists try to understand why judges follow precedent (e.g. Bueno de Mesquita and Stephenson 2002; Hansford and Spriggs 2006; Rasmusen 1994), they tend not to explain the origin of this rule (but see Heiner 1986; Shapiro 1972). Finally, most of the discussions of its origin and development come from legal historians (e.g. Allen 1964, 220–230; Friedman 1985, 124–126; Karsten 1997; Kempin 1959), who have not subjected their various conjectures to rigorous empirical tests.

Beyond the lack of a generalizable explanation for why it arose, scholars do not even agree on when the norm respecting precedent became institutionalized in the United States. Legal historians generally agree that the idea of past cases being binding did not exist prior to the late eighteenth century, but there is no consensus concerning when this norm became a routine part of legal decision-making. Some suggest that it was "firmly established" by the time of the American Revolution (*Anastasoff v. United States* 2000; Holdsworth 1934; Jones 1975, 452; Lee 1999; Price 2000). As Justice Story argued in his *Commentaries on the Constitution of the United States*, stare decisis was "in full view of the framers of the constitution" and "was required, and enforced in every state in the Union" (1833, § 378). Other legal historians, however, contend that the principle, at least as we know it today, did not develop until later in the nineteenth century. These scholars suggest during the pre-revolutionary period "the whole theory and practice of precedent was in a highly fluctuating condition" (Allen 1964, 209), and prior to somewhere between 1800 and 1850 American courts "had no firm doctrine of *stare decisis*" (Berman and Greiner 1966, 491–494; Caminker 1994; Healy 2001; Kempin 1959, 50).

This discussion leads to our central question: how, when, and why did the rule of treating prior cases as binding precedent emerge and develop in the United States? To answer this vitally important question, we argue that judges, desirous of increasing their policy-making authority, fostered *stare decisis* as a way to legitimize the judiciary and to insulate it from outside political attack. By doing so and by promoting the idea that judging is driven by neutral, legal considerations, rather than by politics, the judiciary gained a strengthened presence in the American political system. This argument is consistent with McGuire's (2004) analysis, which indicates that as the Court institutionalized itself within the system of federal policy-making justices were better able to achieve their legal and policy objectives. It is also consistent with some historical work on the Marshall Court era, which contends that Chief Justice Marshall emphasized the rule of law as a way to bolster the Court's authority (Knight and Epstein 1996b; Newmyer 1985).

To test our theoretical argument, the chapter proceeds as follows. In the next section we build the case that the U.S. Supreme Court began to base its decisions on its own precedents by the early 1800s and that such a norm was entrenched by 1815. We do so with two separate datasets. The first compares the Court's use of English common law (that is, law developed through the decisions of England's judges) to its citation of its own precedents and other American legal authorities (including lower court decisions and statutes) from 1791 to 1815. This initial analysis demonstrates the movement away from what had been the controlling legal rules in the form of English common law to the new rules set by American courts. From there we analyze the way in which the Court cites and interprets its own precedents from 1791 to 2005. By focusing on how the Court utilizes its own case law we can begin to pinpoint when the Court began to clearly invoke its own precedents to justify its decisions.

The Shift from Common Law to Supreme Court Precedent

To come to terms with how the United States institutionalized the use of, and respect for, American precedent, we analyze all Supreme Court cases decided between 1791 and 1815. The sample includes 706 cases, 275 of which include references to legal citations. Thus, our initial analysis focuses on these cases. Specifically, we read each opinion and coded all references to English common law, citations to federal and state statutes, citations to legal books, citations to Supreme Court precedents, citations to state and U.S. constitutional provisions, and citations to precedents from other courts in the United States. The key comparison for us is the movement of the Court toward its own precedents and rules and away from a reliance on English common law.

To give a sense of how the Court justified its decisions during its early years, Table 9.1 presents data on the types of legal citations the justices utilized in their decisions over our sample time period. Certainly, the justices of this era relied mostly on English common law (51.8% of citations), and little on their own precedents (4.3% of citations to authority). This is unsurprising given how few cases the Court decided in its early years. However, when we break down these citations between the early and later years of the sample, a different picture emerges.

As evident in Table 9.2, the Court's use of English common law drops precipitously after 1800. Between the founding and 1800, nearly three-quarters of all citations were to the common law, but beginning in 1801 the balance shifts

Table 9.1 Types of Citations used by the U.S. Supreme Court, 1791–1815

Reference	Number (percent of total)
English common law	729 (51.8%)
U.S. Supreme Court precedent	60 (4.3%)
Other U.S. court precedent (including lower federal courts, state supreme courts, and lower state courts)	283 (20.1%)
U.S. Constitution	29 (2.1%)
Federal statute	103 (7.3%)
State constitution	7 (0.5%)
State statute	104 (7.4%)
Other U.S. statute (e.g. local statutes)	69 (4.9%)
Legal book (not common law texts)	23 (1.6%)
Total	1,407 (100.0%)

Table 9.2 Comparison of Legal Citations by U.S. Supreme Court, 1791–1815

Years	Common law	Supreme Court precedent	All citations excluding references to common law
1791–1800	667 (75.8%)	8 (0.9%)	213 (24.2%)
1801–1805	17 (14.8%)	9 (7.8%)	98 (85.2%)
1806–1815	45 (10.9%)	43 (10.4%)	367 (89.1%)
Total	729 (51.8%)	60 (4.3%)	678 (48.2%)

Note
The percentages in parentheses are based on citations within a period of time (or across rows).

to sources other than the common law, which comprise about 85% of the cites. At that same time there is a sharp increase in the Court's use of its own precedents, especially after 1806; more specifically, there was a 33% increase from 1801–1805 to 1806–1815. In fact, between 1806 and 1815 the Court makes almost as many references to its own precedents (43) as it does to common law (45). The other noteworthy aspect of Table 9.2 is that the Court cites U.S. legal authorities quite often in each time period. Whereas citations to English common law and Supreme Court decisions fluctuate from one period to the next, citations to other U.S. authorities never dip much below a quarter of the citations. Additionally, by the time the United States is about 20 years old the vast majority of citations are made to precedents set by American courts, to the federal and state constitutions, and to federal and state statutes.

At the case level, the results are similar. On average, the Court makes almost three references to English common law per case (with a standard deviation [S.D.] of 9.61). However, prior to 1800, this number stood at over five references per case (S.D. = 13.37), while after 1805 it fell to 0.32 references per case (S.D. = 1.98). In comparison, the Court referenced only 0.22 of its own precedents per case on average (S.D. = 0.66), but this number more than doubles to 0.46 references per case after 1805 (S.D. = 1.03). Finally, note that the Court makes almost two and a half references to all U.S. legal citations combined over the entire period of 1791 to 1815 (S.D. = 4.22), but the rate increased nearly 66% from the earliest period (1791–1800) to the latest period (1806–1815). This evidence, while not complete, highlights a movement away from reliance on English common law and toward a reliance on American law.

To further compare the change in the Court's use of its own opinions and other American legal authorities to English common law, we examine the average number of such references per opinion across time. Specifically, we conduct difference of means tests to compare the average number of references to English common law with the average number of references to the Supreme Court's own precedent, as well as a comparison of citations to English common law and the average number of citations to all other U.S. legal references. As reported in Table 9.3, there is a significant difference in citations of English common law, compared to Supreme Court precedent, in the earliest period, but thereafter the citation patterns are similar. In contrast, the citations to English common law, compared to all American authorities, changes even more substantially, with English common law constituting a considerably larger share of cites in the early period and American law constituting a larger share in the latter period.

Overall, these preliminary data indicate that, for the U.S. Supreme Court, English common law became less important over the first quarter century of its existence, while its own precedent, and precedent and legal authorities

Table 9.3 Comparisons of Mean Number of Citations to Supreme Court Precedent, 1791–1815

Years of comparison	Mean references to common law	Mean references to Supreme Court precedent	t-statistic
Full sample	2.65	0.22	4.18*
1791–1800	5.09	0.06	4.30*
1801–1805	0.43	0.23	0.59
1806–1815	0.32	0.46	0.90

Years of comparison	Mean references to common law	Mean references to all U.S. authorities	t-statistic
Full sample	2.65	2.47	0.30
1791–1800	5.09	1.63	3.01*
1801–1805	0.43	2.45	3.82*
1806–1815	0.32	2.73	6.53*

Note
* Difference significant at p <0.05.

from within the United States (the state and federal constitutions, for example) became more important. While we do not show a complete picture here, our results suggest American precedent became a more relevant source of legal authority for the Supreme Court than English common law as the nation moved into the nineteenth century. This piece of the puzzle is key to understanding the development of the norm that Supreme Court justices should respect precedent.

The Court's Use of Its Own Precedents

We next turn to an analysis of how the Supreme Court cited and interpreted its own precedents over time. Using *Shepard's Citations*, we collected data on each time one of the Supreme Court's majority opinions cited one of its earlier decided majority opinions. We relied on a comprehensive list of 26,751 orally argued signed or per curiam majority opinions of the Court released between 1791 and 2005, as identified by Fowler *et al.* (2007) and Black and Spriggs (2008). We then "shepardized" each of these cases to locate all subsequent citations to them in other majority opinions of the Court. Figure 9.1 displays the average number of Supreme Court opinions cited in the Court's majority opinions released in each year. What we observe is a roughly linear

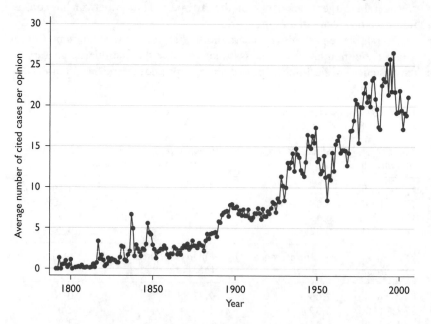

Figure 9.1 The average number of Supreme Court precedents cited in majority opinions of the Court, 1791–2005.

Note
The authors collected these data from *Shepard's Citations*.

increase in the number of citations to Court precedents, from an average of 1.1 cites in the first 50 years to an average of 18.7 citations in the last 50 years. This increase is one observable trait for the institutionalization of the norm of precedent at the Court over time.

In addition to examining citations to precedent, we also focus on the Court's interpretation of its precedents. A legal interpretation is a reference to a case that goes beyond a mere legal citation and includes language in the opinion that has a potential legal effect on the cited case. While one can consider a legal citation as a latent judgment about the continuing relevance of the cited case, a legal interpretation goes further and subjects the cited case to legal analysis (see Hansford and Spriggs 2006). To gather these data we rely on *Shepard's Citations*, which provide an "editorial analysis" for the potential legal effect each citing case has on each cited case.

Broadly speaking, legal interpretation takes two well-known forms. The Court can positively interpret a precedent by relying on the case as legal authority for the outcome of the citing case. Positive interpretation thus reinforces the legal vitality of a cited case and possibly expands its scope. Negative interpretation, by contrast, casts some doubt on the legal authority of a cited case by, at a minimum, indicating that it is inapplicable to the legal question at issue and, at the maximum, declaring that the precedent is no longer good law.

Our focus on legal interpretation follows from the norm of *stare decisis* itself, which proceeds through the use of analogical reasoning. The norm instructs judges to compare the factual circumstances of the precedent to those in the case being decided and, reasoning by analogy, to first determine if the precedent-setting case is applicable to the legal dispute. Its applicability, of course, turns on the degree to which the precedent-setting case and the case under consideration have similar factual circumstances. Second, the judge then chooses whether and how to apply the legal rules from the precedent-setting cases based on the factual similarities of the two cases. This process leads to two dominant forms of legal interpretation. When judges determine that the example of the precedent is on point for the legal dispute they are deciding to "follow" the precedent and thus interpret it positively. When they find a case as inapposite for a dispute they subject the precedent to negative interpretation, ordinarily by distinguishing the case and noting that it is not sufficiently similar to be relied on as precedent.

To examine empirically the Court's interpretation of precedent over time, we present data in Figures 9.2, 9.3, and 9.4. Figure 9.2 shows that the Court manifests a pronounced increase over time in its tendency to legally interpret its own precedents.[2] One of the most telling pieces of evidence for the development of the norm of precedent is the steep rise in the Court's following of its own cases, as evident in Figure 9.3. For example, prior to 1850 the Court positively interpreted only 0.06 precedents per majority opinion. Within the next decade, however, the Court increased this number to nearly 0.3 followed

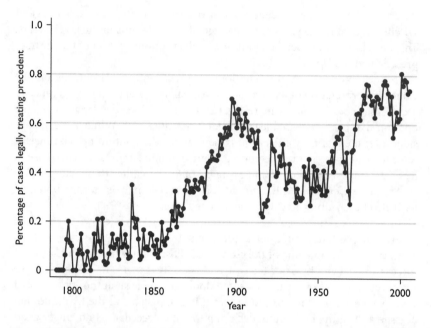

Figure 9.2 The percentage of Supreme Court majority opinions legally treating precedent, 1791–2005.

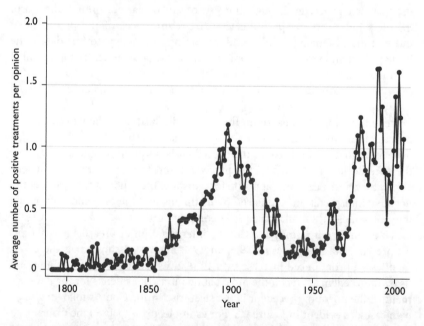

Figure 9.3 The average number of Supreme Court precedents followed in majority opinions of the Court, 1791–2005.

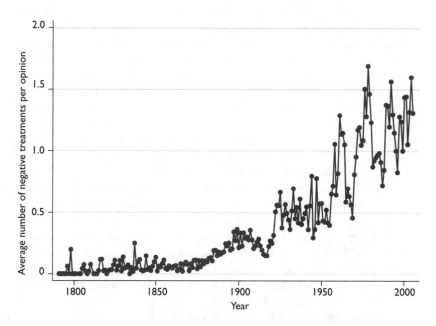

Figure 9.4 The average number of Supreme Court precedents negatively treated in majority opinions of the Court, 1791–2005.

precedents per case. While this may seem a small number in absolute terms, two features of the data suggest this is a substantively meaningful increase. Indeed, in relative terms this represents a 400% increase in the number of followed precedents per case. Further, Figure 9.3 shows that within another decade or two the Court's propensity to follow precedent reached modern levels.

For reasons we have yet to explore, the Court's negative treatment of precedent, as seen in Figure 9.4, developed more slowly. It may be, for example, that since the norm of *stare decisis* explicitly tells judges to follow legally relevant precedent that it took longer for them to institutionalize the tendency to explain explicitly when they chose not to do so by, for instance, distinguishing a precedent. Whatever the reason, this figure, along with Figures 9.2 and 9.3, indicates a clear adherence to precedent in our nation's Court of last resort.

Why Did the Court Begin to Rely on *Stare Decisis*?

The data in the previous section certainly indicate that as the eighteenth century moved to the nineteenth, and the nineteenth century became the mid-nineteenth century, the Supreme Court built up a cache of precedents that it could use to protect itself from attack by other institutions. In this section we build this theoretical argument and provide testable hypotheses based on this theory.

Our argument rests on two premises—first, judges are policy-oriented actors who decide legal disputes in ways that will yield the distributional consequences they desire; and, second, courts need institutional legitimacy in order to make effective decisions. Scholars have focused on these premises to explain how the modern Supreme Court makes decisions (Epstein and Knight 1998; Hansford and Spriggs 2006), and we contend they can also help explain the origin of respect for *stare decisis.* Specifically, we argue judges encouraged *stare decisis* to foster the judiciary's legitimacy so they could gain greater independence from the political branches and, as a result, enhanced policymaking authority. This rule thus stems in part from forward-thinking judges developing it to increase the power of the judiciary.

The first premise posits that judges are policy-oriented decision-makers who wish to set law that will structure social, economic, and political outcomes in ways consistent with their preferences. This idea stands as the centerpiece of most theories of modern Supreme Court decision-making (Epstein and Knight 1998; Hansford and Spriggs 2006; Maltzman, Spriggs, and Wahlbeck 2000; Segal and Spaeth 2002), and we, like others (Knight and Epstein 1996b), contend that judges early in American history were likewise motivated. In short, judges decide cases and adopt rules in ways that will foster the judiciary's authority and result in social changes they desire.

Our second premise is that a necessary condition for the efficacy of judicial policy choices is the perception that the judiciary is legitimate. Because courts lack the power to implement their own opinions (see Federalist 78), they must, in the words of Justice Ginsburg (2004, 199), rely on their "prestige to persuade." The basic idea is that the judiciary must rely on third parties to implement its policies, and a central way to promote compliance is through institutional legitimacy. Indeed, if the judiciary is not perceived as legitimate then the prospects for compliance with its decisions are likely to be low. The majority in *Planned Parenthood v. Casey* (1992, 865–866) makes this point evident:

> The Court's power lies, rather, in its legitimacy, a product of substance and perception that shows itself in the people's acceptance of the Judiciary as fit to determine what the Nation's law means and to declare what it demands ... Thus, the Court's legitimacy depends on making legally principled decisions under circumstances in which their principled character is sufficiently plausible to be accepted by the Nation.

Scholars (Friedman *et al.* 1981; Hansford and Spriggs 2006; Knight and Epstein 1996a; Schauer 1987) and judges (*Bush v. Vera* 1996; Powell 1990; Stevens 1983; *Vasquez v. Hillery* 1986; Wald 1995) commonly recognize that *stare decisis* serves to legitimize the judiciary.

Today, many scholars, politicians, and judges take the judiciary's legitimacy for granted, but during the Founding era judges faced significant obstacles to becoming decision-makers capable of wielding significant influence over policy. One must recall that, prior to the Revolution, state judiciaries were not independent but rather generally subordinate to the legislature. While new state constitutions—starting with Virginia in 1776—began to place the judiciary on a more coequal status with the legislative and executive branches, it took considerable time before the judiciary emerged as a player on par with the other branches of government (Hall 1989, 62–64).

Federal judges' authority was even more precarious. This was mainly due to a lack of institutional prestige, a dearth of legitimacy, and the presence of competitors for the power to be the ultimate interpreter of the Constitution (most notably the states). Indeed, one of the burning issues of the Founding era and beyond was how much authority the federal judiciary would possess, especially vis-à-vis the states (Friedman 1985; Haskins and Johnson 1981, ch. 5; Newmyer 1985). At the time, state courts were the more important policy-makers, and Federalist judges, especially on the U.S. Supreme Court, worked to expand federal courts' authority.

Two separate attacks on the federal judiciary are notable. The first occurred when the Jeffersonian Republicans, who perceived federal judges as politically motivated actors who were "partial, vindictive, and cruel" (qtd. in Friedman 1985, 127), attempted to restrict the federal courts' power (see Hall 1989, 78–82; Haskins and Johnson 1981, ch. 5; Newmyer 1985, 152–209). Their tactics for doing so are now legendary, including the attempt to impeach Justice Samuel Chase and Judge John Pickering, the Repeal Act of 1802 (which led to *Marbury v. Madison* [1803]), the cancellation of the Court's 1802 term, and the Aaron Burr treason trial (Haskins and Johnson 1981, chs. 5–10). Each of these events serves as an example of the Republicans acting on their fear that the federal judiciary was at odds with American democracy. Albert Beveridge referred to this attack on the federal judiciary as "one of the few really great crises in American history" (qtd. in Friedman 1985, 131).

The second major assault on federal judges occurred between 1815 and the early 1830s, with "a no-holds-barred debate over the nature of the Court, the Constitution, and the federal union" (Newmyer 1985, 299).[3] This period saw the emergence of Jacksonian Democrats and a radical states' rights move-ment, especially in the South. The Supreme Court's rulings regarding the Necessary and Proper Clause, the Commerce Clause, and the power of the federal courts (nearly all of which were Nationalist in orientation) spurred advocates of states' rights to launch a concerted attack on the federal judici-ary, the scope of which was unprecedented in American history. For instance, states like Georgia and Ohio presented a direct challenge to the Court's authority by openly defying its ruling in *McCulloch v. Maryland* (1819). The Virginia Court of Appeals, in *Martin v. Hunter's Lessee* (1816), even denied the Supreme Court's authority, under Section 25 of the Judiciary Act of 1789, to exercise appellate jurisdiction over state court decisions. States, not federal judges, the Virginia Court concluded, were the appropriate decision-makers to decide the constitutionality of state actions (Newmyer 1985, 299–302, 357).

Overall, during this period, federal courts were under open attack for allegedly usurping powers that rightly belonged to the states, and state courts had not yet attained a level of power independent of the elected branches of government. As a result, and based on our two premises—that judges have preferences over substantive outcomes and recognize the need for judicial legitimacy—we submit that judges in the early to mid-1800s pushed the norm of *stare decisis* to insulate themselves from political attack and to ensure their independence. That is, judges made calculated choices about how to develop the policy-making role of the federal judiciary, and they recognized that institutional legitimacy was a necessary condition for federal courts to flourish. More specifically, we argue that the rule of *stare decisis* developed largely because judges recognized that it could legitimize the judiciary and help increase the overall policy-making authority of judges in both state and federal courts.

Friedman (1985, 132) insinuates this dynamic when he suggests that after the failed attempt to impeach Samuel Chase judges determined to "take refuge in professional decorum." He suggests judges chose, at least ostensibly, to base decisions on neutral legal principles rather than on partisan politics in order to bolster their independence from elected officials and cement their institutional legitimacy (see Haskins and Johnson 1981, 397). Chief Justice Marshall is an exemplar of the tendency of judges during this era to emphasize the rule of law and to characterize judging as nonpolitical. His greatest legacy is arguably that he helped forge the idea that law is "free from overt political considerations" (Hall 1989, 82) and thus helped the Court protect itself from "political vulnerabilities most effectively by projecting itself as a legal institution" (Newmyer 1985, 378). Interestingly, Congress discussed similar decision-making criteria for judges. Indeed, Haines (1944, 507) argued in a discussion during 1826, "The ideal of the 'just judge' acting as a judicial automaton was beginning to find its way into the popular imagination."

Based on our argument and on what historians have delineated about attacks on the Court, we posit several hypotheses about how external threats led the Supreme Court to entrench its decisions in precedent. The two key hypotheses focus on threats from the elected branches of the federal government. As Haines (1944, 515–516) asserted, President Jefferson wanted to enact a constitutional amendment that would

> be a joint protestation of both houses of Congress that the doctrines expressed in such a case are contrary to the Constitution. An avowal such as this, he thought, would effectively prevent the execution of the judgment within the states.

These attacks on the courts are somewhat episodic, but one attempt to manipulate the courts is manifest when Congress and the president enact judgeship bills. When facing a judiciary that is overtly hostile to the elected branches' will, those branches have the ability to change the courts' composition. Rather than rely on time and retirements to displace hostile judges, especially given the strategic nature of retirements (see Spriggs and Wahlbeck 1995), judicial opponents can effect widespread change by expanding the number of judges. This, of course, explains why President Jimmy Carter and the Democratic Congress were able to increase the Democrats' share of appellate judgeships from about 43% to more than 60%. While only five Republican judges retired during Carter's tenure, he was able to fill 35 new appellate judgeships. The use of judgeship bills to effect change on a reluctant judiciary by expanding the number of authorized judgeships leads us to hypothesize:

> *Hypothesis 1*: the Court is more likely to increase its reliance on precedent when facing a threat from the elected branches as evidenced by an increased number of authorized judgeships.

Although threats like this are not entirely uncommon, when would such threats be most likely? One release valve on tensions between the Court and the elected branches is the appointment of a new justice. On average, every two years the president has the opportunity to appoint a new member to the Court (see Dahl 1957). Not only do appointments give the president and Congress a chance to render the Court a part of the dominant governing coalition, appointments have the capacity to relieve pressure between the branches. For instance, Caldeira recounts that the retirement of Justice Willis Van Devanter "sent the enemies of the Supreme Court into a tailspin" (1987, 1148) with its resulting diminished support for Franklin Roosevelt's Court-packing plan. This link between the opportunity to appoint new justices and the level of threat posed by the elected branches leads us to hypothesize:

> *Hypothesis 2*: the Court is more likely to increase its reliance on precedent due to a threat from the elected branches when more time has elapsed since the last vacancy on the Supreme Court.

Beyond Congress and the president the Court also fought resistance from the states and other implementers of its decisions. As Horwitz (1977, 2) argued, judges also worried about the effects of their decisions on the public: "[B]y 1820 ... judges began to conceive of common law adjudication as a process of making and not merely discovering legal rules, they were led to frame general doctrines based on a self-conscious consideration of social and economic policies." If the Court would like to influence legal policy, it is dependent on agents, lower court judges, to faithfully implement its decisions (Songer, Segal, and Cameron 1994). Although the Court can minimize shirking by regularly monitoring lower court decisions, another tack is to be more explicit in the directions that it gives to its agents. This can be done by increasing its reliance on precedent and more full treatment of those cases. This leads us to hypothesize:

Hypothesis 3: the Court is more likely to increase its reliance on precedent due to opposition from lower court judges.

These arguments, that judges act strategically to foster the legitimacy and independence of the judiciary, contrast with the factors legal historians generally point to as precipitating the development of *stare decisis*. Most of these studies offer functionalist explanations, arguing that the norm of *stare decisis* developed due to particular legal and political needs of the times. As Lawrence Friedman (1985, 114) put it:

> In short, law had to suit the needs of its customers; it had to be at least in a form that lawyers, as brokers of legal information could use. What happened to American law in the 19th century, basically, was that it underwent tremendous changes, to conform to the vast increase in numbers of consumers.

These scholars suggest, for example, that the need to stabilize property rights and foster economic development led judges to follow precedent and more generally create law (Friedman 1985; Hall 1989; Price 2000). They further contend that one of the main causes of *stare decisis* was the creation of reliable law reporters, which disseminated court opinions to judges and other decision-makers. Other commonly discussed causes include the professionalization of legal education, the increasing volume of litigation, the codification debates, and changes in conception of law (such as a move from a natural law perspective to an instrumental, positivist approach) (see Friedman 1985; Goodhart 1930; Healy 2001; Kempin 1959; Price 2000). While we do not disagree that some of these factors may matter, we see many of them as necessary, but not sufficient, conditions for the development of this norm. Law reporters, for example, certainly played a role in fostering *stare decisis* but can just as easily be a response to the development of the norm as a cause of it. At the same time, the development of the legal profession may have facilitated the emergence of the norm. This leads us to hypothesize:

> *Hypothesis 4*: the Court is more likely to increase its reliance on precedent due to the development of the legal reporter system.
> *Hypothesis 5*: the Court is more likely to increase its reliance on precedent as the Court becomes more professionalized.

In the end, our theoretical argument, and the hypotheses set out here, are consistent with the most prominent contemporary approach to institutional emergence and change, which holds that decision-makers create rules in order to structure outcomes in ways they prefer (see Knight 1992; North 1990). The literature on the emergence and change in legislative rules, for example, contends that legislators create rules of procedure to advantage themselves in the making of policy (Binder 1996; Shepsle and Weingast 1987), its implementation by bureaucratic agencies (McCubbins, Noll, and Weingast 1987), and its review by courts (Shipan 1997). In the area of judicial decision-making Knight and Epstein (1996b) apply this approach to the origin of federal judicial supremacy in *Marbury v. Madison* (1803). They argue that the decision in this case was driven by Justice Marshall's preference to enhance the judiciary's power with judicial review while simultaneously minimizing the possibility of political reprisal for that choice. Further, McGuire (2004) demonstrates how the institutionalization of the Court helped it gain power within the federal government. Political decision-makers, in short, recognize that rules can affect outcomes, and they attempt to structure rules to promote their preferences over outcomes.

Data

As we did with our descriptive data, here we examine the degree to which the Court interprets precedents in its majority opinions. Our assumption is that the institutionalization of *stare decisis* will be manifested in a more pronounced tendency of the Court to interpret its own prior cases, and that the degree to which the justices interpret precedent will vary by the perceived political threats to the Court. We constructed the dependent variable in this section by first "shepardizing" each of the 26,715 majority opinions of the Court released from 1791 through 2005.[4] We then calculated the average number of positive or negative treatments per majority opinion in each year from 1791–2005.[5] As such, the dependent variable represents the change in the number of legal interpretations in majority opinions released in year t+1 as compared to majority opinions released in year t. For instance, in 1997 the Court legally treated an average of 2.0 precedents per majority opinion, while in 1996 it interpreted an average of 1.61 prior cases, for a difference of 0.39 from 1996 to 1997. The observation for 1997 in our data set therefore equals 0.39. Our objective is to explain the variation in changes in the average propensity of the Court to legally interpret precedents in its majority opinions.[6]

To measure *Change In The Number Of Authorized Judgeships*, we utilized data from the Administrative Office of the U.S. Courts on the number of authorized judgeships from 1789 to 2002.[7] In particular, the data include the number of authorized positions on the courts of appeals and the district courts. We take the difference in authorized judgeships in one year from the number of authorized positions in the prior year.[8] Then, to account for the changing size of the judiciary, we calculate the percentage change. For example, in 1978, the number of judgeships increased by 151 positions over the number authorized in 1977; this represented an increase of 30.8% over that year. The mean percent change in authorized positions was 2.5% (0.025) with a standard deviation of 0.083.

To measure the number of years since the last appointment to the Supreme Court, we used data from Epstein, Segal, Spaeth, and Walker (1996, Table 5–2). These data provide the date on which each natural court began and ended. A natural court is a period of time over which a stable set of justices preside on the Court—it begins with an appointment of a justice and ends when a justice leaves the bench. For instance, one of the longest natural courts began when Stephen Breyer was appointed to the Court on August 3, 1994; it lasted until William Rehnquist died on September 3, 2005. This variable, *Time Since Last Supreme Court Nomination*, is the number of years since the last appointment. The average number of years since the last Supreme Court appointment was 1.5 with a standard deviation of 1.9 (and a range of 0 to 11).

Our measure of *District Court Composition* captures the proportion of district court judges who shared the partisan affiliation of a majority of Supreme Court justices. To calculate this measure, we needed two pieces of information: first, the party affiliation of a majority of Supreme Court justices and, second, the partisan composition of the district courts. We used Epstein *et al.* (2007c) to identify the partisan affiliation of Supreme Court justices.[9] To code the partisan affiliation of district court judges, we used Gryski, Zuk, and Goldman (n.d.), which contains the partisan affiliation of every district court judge. We calculated the percentage of district court judges who shared the exact partisan affiliation of the Supreme Court majority for every year. A low number, thus, represents a district court judiciary that does not share the Supreme Court's dominant partisanship, while a high number represents a district court bench that shares the Supreme Court's partisan views. The average is 64.6, while *District Court Composition* ranges from a low of 29.6 (1833 and 1834) to a high of 94.7 (1796).

To measure the development of the legal reporter system, we relied upon changes in the number of volumes published by reporters over time. Surrency (1981, 65) reports a study by legal historian Charles Warren (1911) that discusses the development of legal reporters. In short, courts were not originally required to publish their decisions in any form. When legislatures passed laws mandating the publication of decisions, private reporters were hired although they proved to be unreliable. Eventually, however, by the mid-1850s, courts hired their own reporters for these tasks. Following Warren's census of legal reports in the United States (see Surrency 1981, 65 n66), we measure *Legal Reporter Development* as equal to 0 before 1804, 1 from 1804 to 1809, 2 from 1810 to 1835, 3 from 1836 to 1847, 4 from 1848 to 1881, 5 from 1882 to 1884, 6 from 1885 to 1909, and 7 from 1910 to the present.

The *Supreme Court Law Clerk* variable captures the changing role of law clerks and support staff on the Supreme Court (Peppers 2006), and thus it taps the level of professionalization on the Court. The first formal employee hired by the Court was the reporter of decisions in 1816, which was followed in the 1860s by the hiring of a Court Marshal and messengers. Following the appointment of the first clerk in 1886, clerks served as stenographers until

1919. From 1920 to 1952 law clerks took on duties associated with an assistant with delegation of some tasks. Since 1953, clerks have moved from assistants to a role similar to a law firm associate. The *Supreme Court Law Clerk* variable takes the value of 0 until 1816, 1 from 1817 to 1860, 2 from 1861 to 1885, 3 from 1886 to 1919, 4 from 1920 to 1952, and 5 for years after 1953.

To measure the *Number of Opinions*, we counted the number of orally argued signed or per curiam opinions released in each year using the Fowler *et al.* (2007) list (as updated by Black and Spriggs 2008). We then counted the total number of opinions released in each year, and our variable assigns to every year the sum of opinions from the prior 20 years.[10] We counted opinions in the last 20 years to account for the well-known propensity of the Court to cite and treat younger cases (see Black and Spriggs 2008; Fowler *et al.* 2007).

Results

The model in Table 9.4 explains variance in the rate at which the Supreme Court treats precedent over time. The F-statistic allows us to reject the null hypothesis that the coefficients are jointly equal to zero. Moreover, three of

Table 9.4 Prais–Winsten Regression of Annual Number of Precedential Treatments, 1792–2002

Variable	Coefficient (standard error)	Probability
Change in the number of authorized judgeships	0.082 (0.176)	0.320
Time since last Supreme Court nomination	0.019 (0.010)	0.032
District court composition	0.002 (0.004)	0.272
Legal reporter development	0.128 (0.071)	0.037
Supreme Court law clerks	0.152 (0.083)	0.034
Number of opinions announced in previous 20 years	−0.00003 (0.0001)	0.402
Constant	−0.330 (0.341)	0.168
Rho	0.882	
Durbin–Watson statistic (original)	0.397	
Durbin–Watson statistic (transformed)	2.235	
Number of observations	209	
R-squared	0.096	
F-statistic (6, 202 d.f.)	3.58	0.002

Note
The probability is based on a one-tail test.

our hypotheses are supported by the data analysis: the Court's treatment of precedent varies with the development of the legal profession (as seen in the *Legal Reporter Development* variable and the *Supreme Court Law Clerk* variable) and the political threat variable (the *Time Since Last Supreme Court Nomination* variable).

The coefficient for *Time Since Last Supreme Court Nomination* is positive and significant. This suggests that as more time has elapsed since the last vacancy on the high bench, the Court, which may face increasing hostility from the elected branches, will rely on its precedents more often by explicitly treating them. A Court that is out of tune with the elected branches may need the added boost in legitimacy that is provided by grounding decisions in legal precedent. When an appointment has occurred in the past year (and this variable takes the value of 0), the average number of treatments per case was 0.83. In contrast, when it has been five years since the last vacancy, the average number of treatments rises almost 50% to 1.24. It nearly doubles to 1.66 treatments per case when a decade has passed without a new nomination.

The coefficients for *Legal Reporter Development* and *Supreme Court Law Clerks* give support to the legal historians' account of the rise of *stare decisis*. As the legal reporter system grew over the 1800s, the Court grew more likely to treat its precedents. In 1800, before the advent of the systematic reporter system, the average number of treatments was about 0.20 per case. By the 1850s, this number had more than tripled to 0.71 per case. With the hiring of the first law clerk in the 1880s, the average number of treatments swelled to 0.87. This number increased to 1.02 and 1.17 as the role of law clerks grew over the 1900s.

Conclusion

In this chapter we have explored the development of the norm of *stare decisis* on the Supreme Court. The descriptive data we present at the outset suggest the Court began to rely on its own precedents as it moved into the nineteenth century. Specifically, this entrenchment of its own body of law makes it clear that, by the 1810s, precedent became an important criterion for the justices. More generally it suggests the law, and specifically the Court's interpretation of it, is vitally important for how they make decisions.

On the other hand, we also provide some evidence that the norm of *stare decisis* developed as the Court sought to enhance its legitimacy. That is, the justices began to use their cache of cases to protect the Court as an institution from outside actors including the coordinate branches of government. The point is that, as the justices moved precedent into a pre-eminent role as they decided cases, they did so for both legal and political reasons. As such, we believe scholars, lawyers, and Court watchers should understand the justices' invocation of precedent through both lenses.

Notes

1 It is an informal norm in that, rather than being a formal rule created by a single political act (such as a single legislative vote), it developed over time as lawyers, judges, and the public accepted its dictates.

2 Positive interpretation includes the Shepard's categories of "Follow" and "Parallel," while negative interpretation includes "Distinguish," "Limit," "Criticize," "Question," "Overrule in part," and "Overrule." See Hansford and Spriggs (2006) for a discussion of the validity and reliability of *Shepard's Citations*.

3 One specific action Thomas Jefferson took both demonstrates his desire to curb the Court's power and his recognition that institutional rules can influence power and legitimacy. Chief Justice Marshall fostered the practice of the Court issuing a single majority opinion for the Court, rather than each justice issuing his own individual opinion, in part to bolster the Court's authority (Friedman 1985, 134; Haskins and Johnson 1981, 382–383). In recognition of this rule's effect, Jefferson asked Justice William Johnson to reintroduce seriatim opinions and dissents "as a way of undercutting Marshall's dominance" on the Court and thus reducing the Court's power. Justice Johnson did make this attempt, though the use of majority opinions continued to flourish on the Court (Newmyer 1985, 381).

4 We used the list of orally argued signed and per curiam Supreme Court opinions from Fowler *et al.* (2007) and updated by Black and Spriggs (2008).

5 See note 2 for an explanation of positive and negative citations.

6 We estimate our model, given that our dependent variable is a time series, using Prais–Winsten regression. This method estimates the coefficient when the data have errors that are serially correlated. In particular, we estimate the model using the prais command in Stata 9.2.

7 These data were obtained at www.uscourts.gov/history/tablek.pdf (last accessed on March 20, 2008).

8 We exclude from our calculations temporary positions that were created.

9 On a few occasions, parties were tied in support by Supreme Court justices. This usually happened as the Court was undergoing a transition from dominance by one party to another party. We coded the Court's majority partisanship as the party that had held sway until it was surpassed.

10 For the first 20 years of the Court's existence, this variable takes the sum of opinions published in all prior years.

Chapter 10

Bargaining and Opinion Writing on the U.S. Supreme Court

Tom S. Clark

One of the most widely studied phenomena in judicial politics is the process of bargaining and opinion writing at the U.S. Supreme Court. This research is often concerned with how the institutional structures of the Supreme Court give rise to different patterns of interaction among the justices. For example, how does the rule that an opinion only has precedential value if endorsed by a majority of the justices affect the way in which different justices bargain with each other? How does the requirement that only four justices must agree to hear a case shape the way justices can pursue their policy goals? Does this affect their decisions about which cases they will agree to hear? It is on these types of dynamics that scholarship on collegiality has focused most intensely.

This chapter outlines the terms of the literature as it currently stands and then suggests a few avenues for future research. I begin by outlining a basic description of the bargaining process on the Supreme Court. While I do not give each step a complete treatment, I do focus in particular on what I consider critical steps in the bargaining process. Next, I provide a critical overview of the various theories that dominate the literature; then I describe the empirical approaches that have been developed for evaluating those theories and the support for each of the various models. In the final section of this chapter, I offer my own thoughts about how the study of collegiality and bargaining on the Supreme Court can, and should, move forward.

Bargaining on the Supreme Court

The Supreme Court's internal decision-making process is characterized by a number of interesting institutions; the goal of the research on bargaining and opinion writing is to understand how those institutions affect the types of decisions the Court makes. In this section, I briefly summarize the institutions that are most critically connected to bargaining and interactions among the justices while crafting opinions. When reviewing and evaluating the various theoretical models from the literature, this overview of the institutional features will serve to highlight what the theoretical models do and do not

capture, and what abstractions may or may not distort the strategic environment in which the justices operate.

Bringing Cases to the Court

The first crucial feature of the Court is one that is often overlooked in the
literature on collegiality. The Court is a passive institution; its function is to
resolve disputes that have been brought to it by litigants. What is more, the
Court almost uniformly requires that every other potential means of resolution be exhausted before a case can be brought to the Court. This feature—in
general, a defining one of courts—sets the judiciary apart from other institutions, especially legislatures. Whereas a legislature can take up any issue it
wishes—subject to its powers—a court must wait for a dispute to be brought
to it.

Deciding to Decide

In 1991, H.W. Perry published a landmark book entitled *Deciding to Decide.*
The book marked a watershed moment in the study of Supreme Court
decision-making. In that book, using evidence from interviews he conducted
with justices and clerks, Perry provided a thorough description of the factors
and criteria by which the justices operate when deciding which cases to hear.
The Supreme Court, unlike most other courts in the United States, has virtually unlimited discretion in choosing which of the cases brought to its door-
step it will hear. The lower federal courts and nearly all lower state courts have
essentially mandatory jurisdiction over cases brought by litigants—they must
decide the cases they are asked to hear. Indeed, even most state high courts
have much less discretion over their dockets than does the U.S. Supreme
Court. The Supreme Court, though, only hears so-called discretionary cases if
four of the nine justices agree (this is the so-called Rule of Four). Because the
specifics of the vote about whether to hear the case are not public (we only
observe whether the Court hears the case or not) and the Court has no firmly-
established criteria according to which it must act, Perry's book represented
an important insight into the workings of the Rule of Four.

Political scientists have examined the process of granting certiorari from a
variety of perspectives. There have been theoretical treatments and empirical
treatments of its origins and stability as well as of its consequences for collegiality. Most well known, perhaps, is the observation that justices may engage in
"aggressive grants" and "defensive denials." Aggressive grants occur when a
justice votes to hear a case to force it on the Court's docket in expectation of a
favorable outcome (from that justice's perspective). Importantly, this can
occur even when a justice likes the decision reached by the lower court; she
wants to hear the case not to reverse it but to impose the case as a Supreme
Court precedent. A defensive denial occurs when a justice would otherwise

prefer to hear a case but votes not to in anticipation of an adverse outcome in the case. Importantly, this can occur even when a justice does not agree with the decision below. She might otherwise prefer to hear the case and reverse it, but votes not to because she fears she will lose the case, making what was a lower court (and therefore geographically limited) precedent a national, Supreme Court precedent.

Defensive denials and aggressive grants implicate collegiality, because they are choices justices make in anticipation of the ultimate outcome from the process of bargaining. More directly, though, these decisions are made in a collegial setting—they are collective choices made by multiple judges deciding together. The Court operates in an unusual minority rule in this case, but the decision is still a collective one and involves the interdependent choices of the justices acting together. As a consequence, these types of behaviors are straightforward in a world where the justices are forward-looking.

Opinion Assignment

The next critical feature of the collegial process at the U.S. Supreme Court is the rules by which the majority opinion writer is assigned. Regularly, usually after oral arguments, the justices meet together "in conference." In this meeting, which is closed to everyone except the justices themselves, the justices discuss cases and cast their initial votes on the disposition, though those votes are not binding commitments. The justices thus divide themselves into a majority and minority bloc (unless all the justices are in agreement) regarding the disposition of the case; that is, whether to affirm or reverse the lower court. This decision defines who wins and who loses the case. By convention (again, as with most of its internal institutions, the Supreme Court operates by unwritten rules), if the chief justice is in the initial majority, he chooses which justice will be responsible for writing the Opinion of the Court.[1] If the chief justice is not in the majority disposition coalition, the most senior justice in the majority coalition gets to assign the opinion.

Bargaining Over Opinion Content

There is no reason why an opinion written by the opinion assignee must become the Opinion of the Court or even an opinion representing the majority disposition vote. Once assigned an opinion, a writer must prepare a first draft. Maltzman, Spriggs, and Wahlbeck report figures from the Burger Court indicating the initial draft of an opinion takes on average 48 days to be completed. Clearly, an opinion writer must take into account the anticipated reactions of the other justices—especially those whose support is critical for the opinion to carry the majority—when crafting the first draft of the opinion. However, this is not to say the justices can perfectly anticipate each other's reactions; we find in the justices' personal papers extensive records of bargaining among the justices over the content of opinions. Fortunately for scholars, this bargaining usually takes place in writing, in the form of memoranda among the justices proposing and negotiating over changes to opinions. Epstein and Knight report that in 57.4% of cases at least one such "bargaining statement" is made. The paper record of these negotiations has shed considerable light on the ways in which bargaining over opinion content has played out in past cases.

Examination of those papers reveals that the primary source of leverage a justice can exercise over an opinion writer is his or her vote; opinion writers often work hard to garner as much of their colleagues' support (votes) as they can. In his 1968 landmark study, J. Woodford Howard examined "vote fluidity"—the rate at which justices' dispositional votes change during the process of opinion writing.[2] As opinions are drafted and amended during the negotiation process, the justices may become convinced of alternative arguments which imply a different disposition than the one for which they initially voted. This risk implies that an assigned majority opinion writer potentially may have to balance his or her interest in writing an opinion with which he or she agrees against a desire to keep a majority of the Court. Would a justice prefer to cede doctrinal ground in her opinion and etch that opinion into law by commanding a majority or instead to write an opinion she fully endorses at the risk of that view remaining a minority view? As we will see below, most (if not all) of the models of bargaining in the literature assume a justice would prefer any opinion she would write and command a majority to losing a case. However, it is not entirely clear, at least to me, why this must be. Indeed, this strikes me as a potentially interesting avenue for future research by scholars of bargaining and opinion writing.

Final Votes

The final step of the bargaining and opinion writing process is the final votes the justices cast. They cast two distinct, though related, votes. The first vote is which disposition to endorse—whether the lower court should be affirmed or reversed. The second vote is which opinion to endorse, or, more accurately, which *opinions* to endorse. Critically, if the Opinion of the Court is to carry the weight of law and constitute a binding, authoritative precedent, it must receive the endorsement of at least a majority of the participating justices (usually, five of the nine justices). The justices can choose from among, essentially, four different opinion strategies. If in the minority, they can write a dissenting opinion or join another justice's dissenting opinion. This opinion states that the justices disagree with the disposition (who won) and what are the legal standards that led them to that conclusion. If in the majority, they have three options from among which they can choose. First, a justice can join the majority opinion (constituting one of the votes endorsing the opinion). In this strategy, the justice does not write anything herself but instead simply agrees with the majority opinion. Second, a justice may join the majority opinion but also write a regular concurrence (again, constituting one of the votes endorsing the majority opinion). In this case, the justice agrees with the majority opinion but wishes to write something supplemental on her own. That "something supplemental" constitutes a "concurring opinion." Finally, the justice may write a special concurrence without joining the majority opinion (in this case, the justice is not counted as endorsing the majority opinion). In this case, the justice does not agree with the majority opinion but does agree with the disposition reached by the majority opinion. The justice writes a separate opinion to say what she thinks is the correct legal opinion. Thus, because each justice is entitled to write her own opinion, on whichever side of the disposition she finds herself, it is entirely possible to have a unanimous disposition with nine separate opinions, each with no more than one justice endorsing it. In the event where a majority opinion fails to receive the support of five or more justices, the opinion is said to be a "plurality" opinion and does not constitute binding precedent.

Just as with vote fluidity, though, there can be considerable fluidity in the status of opinions written by the justices. If an opinion written by someone other than the majority opinion assignee ultimately commands more support than the original assignee's opinion, that alternative opinion is the Opinion of the Court. An example of this comes from *Planned Parenthood v. Casey*. In that case, Chief Justice Rehnquist prepared the initial majority opinion draft; in response, Justices O'Connor and Souter instead prepared their own opinion, which was ultimately supported by Justice Kennedy. They joined with Justices Stevens and Blackmun on the disposition and therefore constituted the plurality opinion for the majority. Thus, while Chief Justice Rehnquist initially had the support of seven of the nine justices after the Conference, in reaction to his draft opinion three justices decided to write their own opinion which garnered the minority's support and led to a different disposition and considerably different doctrinal holding.

Clearly, the rules and procedures of bargaining have important implications for the process of bargaining and opinion writing. For example, if a justice places any value in the status of his or her opinion (i.e., if a majority opinion assignee values garnering five votes in support of her opinion), then we will want to know how the status of an opinion affects the ways the justices interact with each other. To this end, when scholars develop theories, they should consider how these different rules (institutions) interact with each other. How do a justice's expectations about bargaining affect the way she will vote on the case disposition? In other words, it is important to remember that each of these steps along the way to a decision is interdependent with the other steps.

In the next section, I review some of the dominant models of bargaining on the Supreme Court. The goals in this review are, first, to highlight how these various institutional features have been incorporated into the theoretical literature and, second, to motivate the review of empirical analyses that follows.

Theories of Bargaining

How can we understand the ways these various institutional structures interact with the justices' individual goals to explain the choices the justices make in the process of opinion writing? A variety of theoretical models have been proposed. These various approaches to bargaining on the Supreme Court come in many flavors; to ease exposition of these theories, I divide them into two categories: monopoly and influence models.[3] The typology is, of course, rough but it is useful. The primary distinction between the two groups of theories is whether one particular justice strictly controls the content of an opinion (monopoly models) or instead whether multiple justices exert some influence (potentially simultaneously) over the content of an opinion (influence models). We now turn to the particular models to be evaluated.

Monopoly Models

Median Justice Model

Perhaps the most widely-known, applied, and accepted model of Supreme Court bargaining is the median justice model. This model predicts that all opinions will directly reflect the preferences of the median member of the Court, regardless of who authors the opinion or which party wins. That is, the only equilibrium opinion that will gain a majority's support is one written at precisely the median justice's ideal point. This model is essentially an application of the median voter theorem to the Supreme Court. The importing of the median voter theorem to the Supreme Court rests on a reasonable interpretation of the Supreme Court's decision-making process. As noted above, in order to become the Opinion of the Court—and thereby constitute binding precedent—an opinion must attract the endorsement of a majority of the justices hearing a case. Assuming the justices have spatial preferences and vote on opinions according to their preferences, this implies that an opinion must gain the assent of the median justice, plus four justices to one side or the other.

The median justice model is attractive for its simplicity; it is also attractive because it seems a reasonable approximation of the relatively unconstrained environment in which bargaining over Supreme Court opinions takes place. What is more, and as we will see below, the median justice model has been widely accepted in the literature and essentially dominates the empirical and theoretical work in which the bargaining process is collapsed into a "black box." Nevertheless, there are several institutional features missing from the model—features we may think have real, tangible implications for the bargaining process. For example, it does not matter in this model who writes an opinion; however, conventional wisdom and expert opinion often suggest that authorship does influence opinion content. Costless proposals and delay may account for this feature of the median justice model. Similarly, it is possible that an opinion writer's first-mover advantage increases his influence over an opinion that could produce non-median outcomes.

Author Monopoly Model

Another model of bargaining that is found in the literature is the so-called author monopoly model. This argument has not, to my knowledge, been formally represented but is instead an informal conjecture often advanced in studies of doctrine and jurisprudence. The essence of the argument is that the opinion author will be able to write an opinion at her own ideal point—that is, the opinion will perfectly reflect the author's preferences. While the model has not been formally derived as such, the prediction can be derived as a special case of several of the models we describe here.

One significant limitation of the author monopoly model is that it is not micro-founded. That is, the model does not rest on a specific theory about the bargaining process and how individual justices act when interacting with each other. The institutional rules outlined above suggest plenty of reasons why an opinion author might not be able to control the content of an opinion, chief among them the opportunity for other justices to write any opinion they want and potentially create a new Opinion of the Court that has the support of a majority of the justices. In addition, the processes of strategic litigation (which cases come to the Court) and certiorari imply that the agenda of items before the Court is influenced by other actors.

Median of the Majority Coalition Model

A final model that falls within the "monopoly" model category is the median of the majority coalition model. This model has been presented both formally and informally. The basic intuition behind this model is that as long as the justices care enough about the disposition of a case—who wins and who loses—the justices not in the majority coalition will be irrelevant for the bargaining process. As a consequence, the decision-making process is modeled as a two-step process; the justices first divide themselves into dispositional coalitions and then bargain over opinion content. Bargaining yields an opinion located at the ideal point of the median member of the majority coalition, following the logic of the median voter theorem.

This model, it should be apparent, abstracts away many of the institutional features that characterize the decision-making process outlined in the above sections. Most notably, the model cannot handle vote fluidity; the justices are assumed to always (or almost always) place disposition above any policy considerations. However, the structure of the bargaining process—straw poll, policy negotiations, and then final binding vote—seems to place an institutional emphasis on the policy dimension of the process.

Influence Models

Opinion Authors and Opinion Strength

Among the class of "influence" models, Schwartz's (1992) model is perhaps the first to formally incorporate the role that an opinion author plays in shaping a Supreme Court opinion. In Schwartz's model, an opinion author must choose between two exogenously determined policies. Schwartz does not specify from where those policies are derived but one plausible idea is that they come from an agenda of potential policies set by lower court proceedings or the litigants.[4] The opinion author then must decide how much "precedential value" to instill in an opinion. Schwartz assumes that opinion authors always prefer to endow an opinion with higher precedential value. Presumably, this is because opinions with higher precedential value more strongly affect future policy outcomes.

Of course, the most glaring limitation of this model is that it assumes all the bargaining process does is to endow a legal rule with some varying level of precedential strength. However, we know that the justices do not behave this way and that the bulk of bargaining is on doctrinal content rather than on precedential strength. While the justices bargain over the breadth of a rule or the clarity of the rule, they do so in the context of endogenously creating and crafting rules. The Schwartz model assumes the policies come to the Court exogenously (the Court does not pick the policy contained in the opinion; it is just handed to the Court and cannot be changed) and so places the emphasis on the wrong part of the bargaining process. As a consequence, it cannot yield predictions about how the doctrinal, policy content of an opinion is influenced by the institutional rules and composition of the Court. Indeed, Schwartz assumes the Supreme Court cannot affect an opinion's policy content.

Romer–Rosenthal Meets the Court

Another "author influence" model that has come to attract considerable attention in the literature is essentially a direct application of the Romer–Rosenthal model to Supreme Court opinion writing. As generally developed,[5] this model involves a proposer (the opinion author) and a chooser (the median justice, whose vote is critical for maintaining the "majority" status of an opinion). The strategic tension in the model is as follows. The median justice is assumed to be constrained either to endorse the opinion written by the opinion author or instead to endorse an exogenously determined status quo. That is, opinion writing is modeled as a "closed rule" process.[6] While less restrictive than the

Schwartz (1992) model in some sense—the opinion author is able to select policy content in this model—the Romer–Rosenthal model, as applied to the Supreme Court, misrepresents a series of critical features of how the Supreme Court decides cases.

Perhaps most critically, the Romer–Rosenthal model presumes a "closed rule" bargaining process whereby the chooser must select either the option offered by the proposer or some exogenous reversion point, the status quo. In the context of the Supreme Court, these assumptions are not empirically tenable, though they entirely drive the model's predictions. On the Supreme Court, there is no closed-rule procedure. Any justice is free at any time to propose anything he or she may like. Indeed, tomes of research in political science have been devoted to studying the process of bargaining and negotiation that takes place in the opinion-writing process.[7] The example from *Planned Parenthood* described above is a case in point. Thus, by artificially limiting the set of options available to the chooser—the median justice—the Romer–Rosenthal model forces the chooser to select an option that in practice may likely not be the equilibrium choice made. This artificial constraining of the options available to the median justice endows the opinion author with additional agenda-setting power and influence over the Court opinion that would be absent in a model of the Supreme Court's actual bargaining process.

The closed rule bargaining process captured by the Romer–Rosenthal model assumes there exists an exogenous status quo which the median justice compares against the opinion written by the opinion author. That is, a median justice only has the option of selecting between the exogenous status quo and a new potential majority opinion. The modeling choice here is critical—there are assumed to be no dissenting opinions that may compete for the median justice's vote. Rather, there is simply a predetermined status quo that is presumably represented by the lower court opinion; the median justice is forced to compare that status quo to the new majority opinion. There are several significant limitations that bear mentioning here. First, the model seems to assume that all Supreme Court opinions reverse the lower court. If not, then it is not clear what the exogenous status quo is. Suppose an initial majority votes to affirm the lower court; what is the minority position that the median justice compares to the initial majority's position? Second, the model also assumes that if the Supreme Court wants to reverse the lower court and the median justice prefers to uphold the lower court, then the only policy option available to the median justice is to simply say "ditto" to the lower court's opinion. However, this is not how the judicial process works; rather the Court always writes a new opinion, and rarely does either side entirely endorse a lower court ruling. Both the majority and minority sides generally propose their own preferred legal rules and standards. That is, the status quo is largely irrelevant, because given the justices have decided to hear a case, they will inevitably *do something*.[8] It is hard to imagine why the Supreme Court would review a case when it agrees entirely with the lower court's opinion.

Multidimensional Opinion Writing

A final class of models that is coming to attract attention in the literature involves "multidimensional" opinion writing. As was noted above, Schwartz's model assumes that opinions exist in two dimensions—they have both policy and precedential values—but his model only allows a dichotomous choice over policy (the Court can only choose policy A or policy B). Lax and Cameron endogenize the policy component of the Schwartz model, by allowing a justice to simultaneously choose the policy content of an opinion as well as its "quality." Higher quality opinions yield subsequent applications that are more closely aligned with the opinion's policy than do lower quality opinions. The emphasis in the Lax–Cameron model is on negotiation between the initial majority and the initial minority. The two sides compete to attract the median justice. The majority side has a sort of first-mover advantage. The initial majority opinion assignee writes an opinion, which is a combination of policy content and quality that is chosen to prevent the minority from writing an opinion that could "peel" the median justice away. That is, the opinion author writes an opinion such that the minority would rather lose the case than write an opinion that the median would prefer. Again, opinions are defined in terms of content and quality, so the opinion that the minority would have to write to "beat" the majority could be either too costly in terms of giving up policy ground or too costly in terms of the effort needed to write an opinion of sufficiently high quality. The critical prediction from this model (for our purposes) is that the policy content of an opinion will be a compromise of the opinion author's preferences and the median justice's preferences. As the policy content approaches the author's preferred position, the opinion quality will rise.

The Lax–Cameron model represents an important advance and yields several nice intuitions. The model brings together multiple features of the Court's collegial institutions, including bargaining, opinion-assignment, vote fluidity, and potentially even certiorari. However, as the other models, it abstracts away from the collegial process enough that it cannot explain some remaining phenomena. Primarily, while the model is one of bargaining between the two sides, it cannot predict whether high-quality dissenting opinions will ever be written. (Lax and Cameron assume an author may write a low-quality dissenting opinion with no cost. However, we often see dissenting justices produce high-quality dissenting opinions.) In addition, the model in its starkest form cannot explain vote fluidity, though we do see that happen as well. It is likely, though, that introducing uncertainty about the justices' preferences might give rise to both failed bargaining (i.e., the production of high-quality dissenting opinions) and vote fluidity.

Empirical Approaches

These various theories all yield empirical implications about the bargaining process and, perhaps most important, the content of Supreme Court opinions. For scholars interested in the bargaining and opinion-writing process, presumably the motivation for their interest is that the opinions the Court writes constitute binding rules that affect daily life. Thus, while the bargaining process is interesting, it is interesting insofar as it provides a systematic framework for understanding how those rules come about. A theory of bargaining, to the extent it is an empirically supported theory, is a useful tool for understanding how various institutional rules and features of the Court (such as *who* is on the Court) affect the Court's output. Thus, in order to most fully realize the impact of research on opinion writing, we must subject our theories to empirical scrutiny. Several such approaches have been proposed. Here, I review some of the past approaches and describe a current empirical strategy on which I have worked.

Case Studies

Historically, empirical approaches to evaluating the various theories of bargaining on the Supreme Court were severely limited by political scientists' lack of systematic measures of the subject of their theories—the content of Supreme Court opinions. Early investigations of the process of bargaining on the Supreme Court often relied on case studies of specific cases. More recently, scholars have made use of records from the justices' private papers—many of which have been donated to the Library of Congress and so are available to the public—which contain records of bargaining among the justices. For example, in their landmark study of bargaining on the Court, Maltzman, Spriggs, and Wahlbeck use the justices' private papers—specifically, the number of draft opinions, the amount of time each justice took to join the opinion, and the extent of bargaining efforts—to assess how myriad incentives predict bargaining behavior.

Votes as Indicators of Opinion Content

Unfortunately, while these studies can investigate empirical patterns that characterize the process of bargaining, none of these approaches can tell us much about the *content* of the final opinion. The various theories described above all make predictions about the spatial location of an opinion, relative to the justices on the Court. To this end, scholars have adopted what we may call an "inferential" approach. In this approach, one assumes that justices sign on to whichever opinion is closest to their ideal points. The investigator then examines voting and agreement patterns; from those patterns, one infers *where an opinion must have been, conditional on the assumption about how the justices vote*. This approach has been adopted in a variety of studies and is potentially very useful. Indeed, knowing which opinions a justice endorses and refuses to endorse seems very informative about what those opinions say. I suspect this approach will continue to yield empirical insights well into the future.

Perhaps the most significant limitation of the approach, though, is that it rests on assumptions about the bargaining and voting process. However, estimates of opinion content are most useful if they can be employed to evaluate theories of bargaining and voting on the Supreme Court. Indeed, this chapter highlights the centrality of that substantive question to our discipline. In this spirit, two additional approaches, which attempt to measure the opinion itself, have been recently advanced.

Measuring Opinion Content—Textual Analysis

The first of these two approaches has employed technology from computer science and artificial intelligence to conduct textual analysis. Modern computing power and increasingly sophisticated algorithms for textual analysis have made software programs such as Worsdcores widely available. These techniques allow textual documents, such as party platforms or Supreme Court opinions, to be scaled relative to each other; the scale can capture, at least in theory, the policy content of the opinions. Application of the technology presents a number of challenges to the researcher, mostly involving identification and interpretation of the latent dimension that emerges from the scaling procedures. Perhaps for these reasons, this approach has not yet gained much ground in the applied research.

Measuring Opinion Content—Doctrine Space

The second approach to measuring opinion content was developed by Benjamin Lauderdale and me.[9] The basic argument underlying our approach is the following. Opinion writing involves an inherently difficult task of communication.[10] The justices, in writing their opinions, seek to communicate their interpretation of the law to lower courts and external actors. Part of their mechanism for communicating is to analogize the current opinion and its interpretation to (and contrast them with) previous cases. To do this, the opinions' authors cite previous cases, usually either showing how the cases are similar or dissimilar. In essence, we claim that citations provide information about an opinion's legal policy content. Because judges justify and explain their rules by associating it with existing precedents, an opinion author uses citations to communicate the meaning of a new opinion's legal interpretations. By citing the appropriate precedents, an opinion can most fully illuminate the standard to be applied and justify its reasoning.

Thus, by identifying which previous cases (precedents) are invoked favorably and which ones are invoked negatively, we can assess the extent to which the various opinions stand for similar or dissimilar legal propositions. Note, critically, this information is *a consequence of the bargaining process*. Thus, if we want to assess the outcome of bargaining, we can potentially use this information.

To take advantage of this insight, we collect data on each citation from each opinion to each precedent. We limit the scope of our study to two areas of the law—search and seizure and freedom of religion. We impose this limitation only because of the difficulty of collecting the data. However, recent developments in automated text coding have enabled much more efficient collection of these data, and at least one recent application has successfully extended this technology to cover all areas of the law.[11]

We then develop a statistical model that lines up all of the opinions relative to each other according to how favorably or negatively they cite each other. Opinions that cite each other favorably are close together while opinions that cite each other negatively are further away from each other. This type of statistical model has been widely used in political science (and other disciplines) and is known as a latent variable model. This model yields a location for each opinion in an underlying, unobserved dimension, which we call "doctrine space."[12]

The first task in any such enterprise, of course, is to interpret the latent dimension that emerges from the estimation. That is, while we have assumed a dimension exists and that it is correlated with citations, it remains to be seen that the latent dimension is substantively interpretable as "doctrine" as we claim it is.[13] To do this, we begin by comparing our estimates to another, exogenous indicator—the disposition the opinion endorsed. That is, as noted above, judicial decisions announce legal rules that then imply dispositions. While part of the motivation for this project was that there may be a variety of legal rules that could lead to any one disposition (evidence obtained from a very intrusive search could be excluded under liberal interpretations of the Fourth Amendment as well as many conservative interpretations of the Fourth Amendment), it should nevertheless be the case that more liberal rules lead to more liberal dispositions and vice versa.

Thus, I begin by comparing the estimates of the doctrinal content of opinions to the dispositions the opinions endorsed. Figure 10.1 shows the distribution of these estimates of opinion location, divided by the disposition (was it a liberal or conservative disposition). As the figure makes clear, opinions that lead to a liberal disposition tend to come from one end of the dimension, while opinions that endorse a conservative disposition tend to come from the other end. Nevertheless, and critically, there is considerable overlap between the two sets of opinions—that is, there is a significant range wherein opinions might lead to either type of disposition.

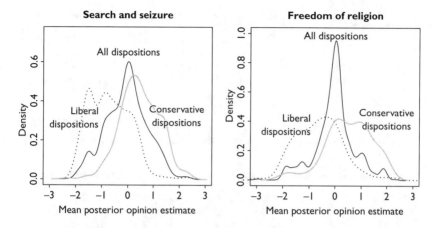

Figure 10.1 Doctrine space estimates of opinions in search and seizure and freedom of religion cases (solid black lines show all dispositions; dashed line shows liberal disposition opinions only; gray line shows conservative disposition opinions only).

Evaluating Models of Bargaining

Using these data, one can compare these opinion estimates to a series of critical actors in the bargaining process. First, one can compare the estimates of opinion location to the individuals implicated by the three monopoly models—the bench median, the opinion author, and the median of the majority coalition. By assuming that dissenting opinions are sincere reflections of their authors' ideal points, I am able to place the justices and the opinions in a common space (as above, details of the estimation are provided elsewhere). Thus, in Figure 10.2, I directly compare the estimated location of each opinion in doctrine space to the estimated ideal point of each justice in doctrine space. The top row shows each of the three comparisons using the search and seizure data; the bottom row shows the comparisons using the freedom of religion data. Because each of the monopoly models predicts a one-to-one correspondence between the relevant justice and the opinion, all opinions should fall on the 45-degree line in any given panel.

As this figure makes clear, there is a notable difference across the three comparisons in each set of cases. First, the median justice is in fact positively correlated with the opinion location; however, the dominant source of variation does not seem to follow the median justice's ideal point. Many points are very far away from the 45-degree line. By contrast, with respect to the opinion author, there is essentially no correlation between the author's ideal point and the opinion location; again, this is true in both sets of cases. Not only do the opinions not correlate well with the 45-degree line, but the

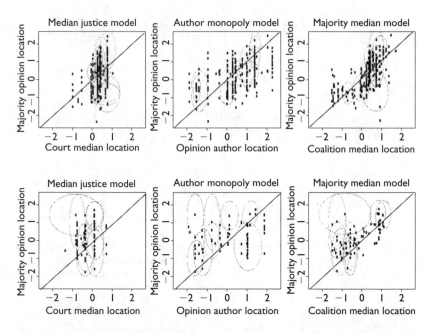

Figure 10.2 Comparison of estimated opinion locations to estimated justice ideal points (top row shows search and seizure cases; bottom row shows freedom of religion cases. Ellipses show uncertainty in estimates for a random subset of cases).

45-degree line is a worse fit to the data than a flat line predicting all opinions will have the same location. Finally, when one considers the median of the majority coalition, one finds the best fit among the three models. The primary dimension along which the opinion location estimates vary appears to be the 45-degree line. Obviously, not all opinions are statistically indistinguishable from the line, though most are. Indeed, estimating simple predictive models confirms that the median-of-the-majority-coalition model outperforms the other two.

However, it remains to be seen how the various influence models perform. The various author influence models are more difficult to test, because they require one to measure additional complicated concepts, such as opinion quality. Each of the influence models surveyed above implicates features of the opinion beyond their doctrinal or policy content. The Schwartz model implicates "precedential value"; the Romer–Rosenthal model implicates the "status quo"; while the Lax–Cameron model implicates "opinion quality." Measuring these quantities varies from very difficult (as in the case of the Lax–Cameron model) to most surely impossible (what does the status quo even represent). Thus, absent measures of those features, we are left without point predictions about where an opinion will be located but instead a potential range of locations (in the Romer–Rosenthal and Lax–Cameron models). This challenge poses an opportunity for future empirical research on bargaining.

Where Now?

There are several areas where the literature on collegiality can and should develop. Here, I briefly chart a course for some potential avenues for advancing both the theoretical and empirical scholarship.

Moving the Theoretical Scholarship Forward

As the above discussion of institutions and theories demonstrates, none of the models to date can adequately explain Supreme Court decision-making. Each of the various models contributes in some respect to our understanding of how judges and judicial institutions interact to produce judge-made law. Moreover, the various models build upon and complement each other nicely. However, while all models are "wrong" and all models make simplifying assumptions that may not be "correct," the usefulness of a model is determined primarily by what we can learn from it and how many of its implications are driven by bad assumptions. Thus, for example, the Romer–Rosenthal model is based on fundamentally inaccurate assumptions about the opinion-writing process and choices the justices face. This is not problematic in and of itself. However, those assumptions turn out to drive all of the predictions derived from the model. By contrast, other models such as the Lax–Cameron model involve potentially tenuous assumptions about the information environment in which the justices operate and the costs of writing dissenting opinions. Nevertheless, those assumptions are not responsible for the primary insights gleaned from the model.

Future research on Supreme Court bargaining and opinion writing should build from models that prove most useful for understanding the incentives and structure in judicial bargaining. Such research can follow one of two directions. First, it may relax various modeling assumptions to more correctly capture the strategic environment. This avenue may involve introducing incomplete information on the part of the justices about each other's preferences. Alternatively, one may relax the various assumptions about the costs of writing and publishing dissenting opinions. For example, if bargaining takes place sequentially in a written process, as it does, then perhaps dissenting opinions are simply the by-product of a bargaining process.

Another avenue for research, and one which I think more likely to be fruitful, involves not necessarily relaxing simplifying assumptions but instead extending the scope of our models. How does the strategic environment in which the Supreme Court interacts with lower courts affect the bargaining and opinion-writing processes? Does the Court's interest in maintaining coherent precedent and effectively communicating its doctrine to lower courts affect the ways in which the justices interact? How does the bargaining process interact with strategic litigation? As noted above, the certiorari process is an important institutional feature of the Supreme Court opinion-writing process; however it is rarely incorporated into models of Supreme Court policy-making.

Moving the Empirical Scholarship Forward

From the empirical end of things, I also see two avenues for potentially fruitful future research. First, scholars should push further forward in their efforts to measure the doctrinal content of Supreme Court opinions. The doctrine space method that Ben Lauderdale and I have developed is but one step in that direction. There are other sources of information about opinion content that the model does not use. For example, the variation in votes across opinions by different justices can tell us something about how the various opinions in any given case are related to each other. In addition, opinions often contain explicit connections to other opinions, allowing us to impose substantive restrictions on the way specific opinions are related to each other.

Second, and following from the above discussion, scholars need to focus their empirical tools on non-ideological features of the judicial decision-making process. In recent years, the judicial politics literature has demonstrated a renewed interest in "law." Theoretical models of judicial decision-making as well as empirical approaches to law and courts have all made an effort to incorporate the distinctive features of law that distinguish it from other forms of policy for which most social science tools were developed. The "case space model" is perhaps the most important example of how our theoretical approaches to studying judicial decision-making have evolved.[14] However, the political science of law nevertheless retains ideology and policy as the primary locus of interest. I am hopeful that our empirical tools will be brought to bear on non-policy features of judicial decisions, such as a decision's breadth or scope, its quality (à la Lax–Cameron), its substantive connections to other cases, and many other characteristics to which legal scholars often pay attention.

Conclusion

Bargaining and opinion writing on the Supreme Court constitute one of the most widely studied activities of the American court system. The literature has developed sophisticated models of bargaining that allow scholars to systematically evaluate the consequences of various institutional rules for the content of the opinions the Supreme Court produces. Recently, more advanced methods have been brought to bear on the empirical evaluation of those models, though considerable work remains to be done. In this chapter, I have outlined the existing theoretical and empirical frameworks and identified several avenues for future research that I expect will prove fruitful.

As a closing note, though, I would like to underscore the importance of this topic. While collegiality and opinion writing are but one aspect of the judicial process, they have significant and direct implications for almost every other area of study in judicial politics. Indeed, many of the other chapters in this volume highlight the centrality of opinion writing to the scholarly treatment of judicial decision-making. The importance of Supreme Court nominations and confirmations (see Chapters 1 and 2) is predicated on having a theory about how a new justice will alter the Court's output (through some model of internal collegiality). How strategic litigants frame their arguments and advance their causes (see Chapters 11 and 12) is shaped by their own calculations about the Court's decision-making process. And, surely, the justices' internal decision-making is inextricably linked with their expectations about how external actors and lower courts respond to and implement those decisions (see Chapters 13 and 14). In my own research outside of this volume, I have explored how lower courts decide cases in anticipation of what the internal decision-making process at the Supreme Court will yield. Thus, no matter what one wants to study in judicial politics, it is important to have a clear view of how the Court's internal decision-making process takes place. For this reason, if for no other, I hope this already impressive body of scholarship continues to grow and develop.

Notes

1 During its early years, the justices each wrote their own opinion in each case—a practice known as seriatim opinion writing. That process ended during the early 1800s, under the leadership of Chief Justice John Marshall.
2 Howard (1968).
3 I owe this framework for thinking about theories of bargaining to Jeff Lax. See, for example, Lax (2011).
4 Critically, though, the policy options cannot be influenced by internal bargaining; otherwise, the model results in disequilibrium. Of course, it seems likely that those policy options are in fact the product of internal bargaining.
5 Hammond, Bonneau, and Sheehan (2005).
6 In legislative politics, a distinction is often made between "closed rule" and "open rule" proposals. Closed rule proposals are bills that come to the floor for a final vote and cannot be amended; open rule proposals are bills that are subject to amendment.
7 See, for example, the various theories of bargaining described here. For purely empirical work, see Maltzman, Spriggs, and Wahlbeck (2000); Clark and Lauderdale (2010).
8 It does bear mentioning, though, that in the event the Supreme Court cannot agree on a new opinion, its decision does not have precedential value. In this instance, the legal status quo remains. However, that legal status quo is not the lower court's opinion; rather it is existing Supreme Court doctrine. Thus, to the extent the status quo matters, it can only be as a reservation value for the breakdown of bargaining on the Supreme Court.
9 Clark and Lauderdale (2010).
10 Staton and Vanberg (2008); Bueno de Mesquita and Stephenson (2002).

11 Sulam (2011).
12 Details of the estimation are provided in Clark and Lauderdale (2010).
13 We demonstrate in Clark and Lauderdale (2010) that the latent dimension is a useful predictor of citations.
14 See, for example, Kornhauser (1992); Cameron (1993); Lax (2007); Carrubba and Clark (2010).

Part IV

Courts and Their Political Environments

Chapter 11

Goldilocks and the Supreme Court

Understanding the Relationship between the Supreme Court, the President, and the Congress

Michael A. Bailey and Forrest Maltzman

The relationship of the Supreme Court to the president and Congress reflects a fundamental tension inherent in the judicial branch. On the one hand, the Court needs to be independent; disputes need to be resolved on their merits and not on the basis of political or economic power. Otherwise, those in power may be tempted to act above the law and, among other misdeeds, may perpetuate their control even when they do not have popular support. On the other hand, the Supreme Court cannot be too independent. If it is, justices may be imposing the views of nine individuals about law and policy on a nation of hundreds of millions of people. In short, the Court is a Goldilocks institution: it must be independent enough to protect democracy, but not *too* independent lest it threaten the ability of people to govern themselves.

As the highest court in the land, the United States Supreme Court frequently finds itself pulled in both directions. The Court gets the most complicated, politically sensitive and high-profile cases and these are precisely the cases where justices should be independent. Nonetheless, we worry that justices may become disconnected from the will of the people and prevent democratic institutions from deciding important policy issues of the day.

We focus on how the Court navigates its relationship with the elected branches. There are four mechanisms for elected branches to influence the Court: appointments, judicial deference, overrides, and expertise. We will consider each in turn. In contrast to those who believe justices are completely independent, we argue that there are layers of constraints on the Court and that each allows the national will to influence what the Court does. None is overwhelming and each mechanism has its own subtleties, but taken together it is clear the Court must be understood as it operates within a broader political and normative system.

The Appointment Process

The appointment process is a focal element of the relationship between the Court and the public for a good reason. This is the most obvious and direct chance for the president and Senate to affect the composition of the Court

(Devins and Fisher 2004, 46). Certainly the rituals of the process—the thrilled nominee standing next to the president in the Rose Garden, the press scrums and camera flashes of the confirmation hearings—have become a part of the political fabric of this country.

Appointments only occur, however, when there are vacancies and these vacancies only occur when a justice leaves. If justices left randomly or at fixed terms, the timing of vacancies would not be that interesting. However, justices' departures are *endogenous*; they are potentially the result of political calculations by justices.

Therefore we begin with departures. No one doubts that justices are aware of the political implications of their retirements. Conservative Chief Justice Taft delayed retiring from the Court in the late 1920s because he thought President Hoover was "a Progressive just as [Justice] Stone is, and just as [Justice] Brandeis is and just as [Justice] Holmes is" (Ward 2003, 120–121). Liberal Chief Justice Earl Warren retired in the last months of the Johnson presidency because he believed that Richard Nixon would win the 1968 presidential election (Whittington 2009). On election night in 2000, Justice O'Connor's husband revealed that his wife wanted to retire, but not under a Democratic president (Toobin 2007, 168) and most observers believed it was not a coincidence that liberal Justice Stevens retired under President Obama.

If justices are politically savvy, it is conceivable that they could time their retirements so as to maximize the chances that they are replaced by similar justices (Spriggs and Wahlbeck 1995). Liberal justices would delay retiring under Republican presidents and retire more readily under Democrats; conservative justices would do the opposite. As a consequence, we would expect to see justices leaving voluntarily under presidents of their own party and holding out, and when this went on too long, dying under presidents of the other party. In fact, this is what we have seen: from 1789 to 2006, 35 of the 54 justices who resigned voluntarily did so under a president of the same party as appointed them while 29 of the 49 justices who died while on the bench did so under a president from the opposing party (Calabresi and Lindgren 2006, 805).

If this happened a lot, the appointment process, for all the attention it generates, would give departing justices the ability to help craft the Court. This has led some legal scholars to propose 18-year fixed terms for each justice; this would ensure a new appointee every two years so that every president elected to a full term would get at least two nominations (avoiding the situation of President Carter who did not make a single appointment to the Supreme Court in his four years in office). While this situation would defuse the kind of manipulation discussed above, it would also dramatically increase Court turnover, a potentially destabilizing development. And, Bailey and Yoon (2011) show in simulations that even if justices do try to time their retirements for political reasons, liberal and conservative justices more or less offset each other, meaning that the net effect of politically-timed retirements on the Court is modest.

Once a seat opens up, the Court is at the center of one of its most public phases: the appointment process. Earlier chapters in this volume have gone into great detail on this process, so we focus largely on what the process means for the ability of elected branches to influence the Court. Political scientists Bryon Moraski and Charles Shipan (1999) offer a widely-used and incredibly useful framework for thinking about the process. They build on the observation of one of the great scholars of the appointment process, Henry Abraham, who concluded that "political and ideological compatibility has arguably been the controlling factor" behind nominations (1999, 3). Following standard models of the Supreme Court, they characterize the ideology of justices in terms of "ideal points" in policy space, which are numeric characterizations of the political preferences of justices. Some justices, such as Justices Breyer or Sotomayor, are liberal and have ideal points that are negative numbers (on the left if you draw them on a line); other justices, such as Justices Scalia and Thomas, are conservative and have ideal points that are positive numbers (on the right if you draw them on a line). The median justice can dominate the Court and get outcomes he or she wants because he or she can be the decisive vote for either the liberal or conservative outcome. In this view, if either side wants to win it must do what the median justice wants lest the other side gets there first.

From this perspective, what is most important when a vacancy opens up is what happens to the Court median. Will it move to the right? Or the left? Or stay the same? Moraski and Shipan (1999) note that if the president and Senate are both liberal and if the vacancy that has occurred is either at or to the right of the Court median, then the president can nominate and the Senate confirm a new justice who is on the left such that the new Supreme Court median is the justice who had been the fourth most liberal justice before the departure. If the president and Senate are both conservative, then the president can nominate and the Senate confirm a new justice who is on the right such that the new Supreme Court median is the justice who had been the sixth most liberal justice before the departure (the justice just to the right of the median). If the president and Senate are on opposite sides of the ideological spectrum, then the only nominee who will be confirmed is one who maintains the status quo: the model predicts that a liberal president will not nominate a justice who moves the Court median to the right and a conservative Senate will not confirm a justice who moves the Court median to the left.

Under this model, the Court can be controlled, slowly, perhaps, but clearly by the elected branches. As the public moves right, it is more likely to elect conservative presidents and senators and hence to create the conditions to move the Court right. As the public moves left, it is more likely to elect liberal presidents and senators and hence to create the conditions to move the Court left. This is more or less the pattern that Yale political scientist Robert Dahl observed in 1957 and the pattern that persists today.

However, at least three factors make the process unpredictable. First, elections may be decided on matters unrelated to the Court, so even if, for example, the public thinks the Court is too liberal, they may elect liberal senators for other reasons. Second, presidents may be able to use their ability to nominate justices who have non-ideological attributes that make them politically appealing. This can enable presidents to nominate someone who may not be ideologically compatible with the Senate but whom the Senate confirms nonetheless. For example, in 1991 the Republican President George H.W. Bush faced off against a Democratic Senate over the replacement of liberal Justice Thurgood Marshall who had retired due to declining health. In normal circumstances, the Moraski and Shipan model would predict a liberal replacement, as such a justice would not move the Court median. In this case, however, Bush tapped Clarence Thomas, who was very conservative, but also African American. Senators who may have been turned off by Thomas' ideology were attracted to the idea of making sure that there was at least one African American on the nation's highest court and hence Thomas likely garnered more support than he would otherwise have received (although accusations of sexual harassment against him worked to reduce his support as well). Third, presidents and senators work in a world of imperfect information; strategic individuals who seek a position (including a seat on the bench) may not accurately portray how they will perform once in office.

Judicial Deference

Does political influence on the Court end with the confirmation vote? Many think it does; justices are not bound to stick to the political or legal views they expressed in the confirmation hearings and the political preferences of a number of justices (based on their votes on the Court) have moved considerably over time (Bailey 2007; Bailey and Maltzman 2011). The most prominent scholars who reject the idea that there are constraints on justices are Segal and Spaeth (1993, 2002) who have written a number of seminal works arguing that justices are best understood as unfettered political actors.

However, not everyone agrees. Justices may be bound to respect or accommodate public preferences by internal norms about the appropriate role of the Court in the political system. There is a long scholarly tradition of arguing that the lack of democratic accountability for the Court implies that justices should not overturn laws unless the laws clearly conflict with constitutional provisions (Thayer 1893; Wechsler 1959). Chief Justice John Roberts characterized this view as follows:

> Judges and justices are servants of the law, not the other way around. Judges are like umpires. Umpires don't make the rules; they apply them.

The role of an umpire and a judge is critical. They make sure everybody plays by the rules. But it is a limited role. Nobody ever went to a ball game to see the umpire. Judges have to have the humility to recognize that they operate within a system of precedent, shaped by other judges equally striving to live up to the judicial oath.

(Roberts 2003)

Such views have been widespread on the bench. Justice Oliver Wendell Holmes quipped, "if my fellow citizens want to go to hell I will help them. It's my job" (1920, cited in Howe 1953). Justice Stone noted "the truth is that I feel obliged to uphold some laws which turn my stomach" (Dunne 1977, 199). Justice John Marshall Harlan II stated

the constitution is not a panacea for every blot upon the public welfare, nor should this Court, ordained as a judicial body, be thought of as a general haven for reform movements. This Court, limited in function in accordance with that premise, does not serve its high purpose when it exceeds its authority, even to satisfy justified impatience with the slow workings of the political process.

(Harlan 1964, 624–625)

Where do such sentiments come from? One place is Congress itself. For all the controversy that can accompany the nomination process, there is one point that unifies members of Congress: they want justices who will subjugate their personal views and defer to Congress and the Constitution whenever possible. Justice Sonia Sotomayor learned this the hard way. In 2001, well before she was nominated, she had said "I would hope that a wise Latina woman with the richness of her experiences would more often than not reach a better conclusion than a white male who hasn't lived that life" (Savage 2009). Senators honed in on this comment and Sotomayor had to repudiate her earlier speech and state her judicial philosophy as

fidelity to the law. The task of a judge is not to make law, it is to apply the law. And it is clear, I believe, that my record ... reflects my rigorous commitment to interpreting the Constitution according to its terms, interpreting statutes according to their terms and Congress's intent and hewing faithfully to precedents established by the Supreme Court and by my Circuit Court.

(Sotomayor 2009)

Her statement put her closer in line to the Roberts statement earlier, even as many, if not most, observers of the Court would agree with conservative judge and scholar Richard Posner when he wrote "it is rarely possible to say with a straight face of a Supreme Court constitutional decision that it was decided correctly or incorrectly" (2005, 40). Instead, for the complicated cases facing the Supreme Court, most believe that personal views of some sort will often enter, despite the taboo against admitting this in the confirmation process.

Judicial sentiment for deferring to elected branches can also come from justices and their place in the legal system. Justices are educated in a legal system and operate in a rather closed legal environment in which normative theories about good law and the respect of one's peers are valuable (Baum 2006). The strong intellectual foundations of ideas of judicial restraint and backlash against perceived Court overreaching that began during the Warren Court make the sentiment of deferring to elected branches when possible a highly attractive legal doctrine for many justices.

But are these sentiments for judicial restraint real? Do they really affect what justices decide, or are they window-dressing to dupe a naïve public into believing the Court is apolitical? In other work we have examined this question in considerable detail (Bailey and Maltzman 2008, 2011). The challenge is that it is very hard to distinguish between ideological behavior on the Court and non-ideological deference by justices.

For example, how should we characterize Justice Thomas' opinion on the 2003 privacy case, *Lawrence v. Texas*. The issue in this case was whether a Texas law against homosexual sodomy (and not against heterosexual sodomy) violated the Constitution. Thomas said that although he found the law "uncommonly silly" it did not violate the Constitution and that it was up to the Texas state legislature to undo the law, not the courts. Was this an admirable case of judicial deference to elected officials? Or was this an example of Thomas using the norm of judicial deference to justify a politically conservative decision with which he may well have sympathized? Each view has its logic, and this single case makes sense in either framework. And many cases have this characteristic, as justices make elaborate use of a legal norm such as deference while cynics focus on an underlying political story.

What if we could isolate the political aspect of a case? That is, what if we could find a group of people who view things only through a political lens and see what they say about a given case? If a justice acts like those people, it would be reasonable to treat the justice as a political actor. If the justice parts ways with those people in ways explicable by judicial norms, however, that would be evidence that the justice is truly influenced by those norms.

We conducted such research on Supreme Court justices from 1953 to 2008. We modeled justices as having "ideal points" which are simply the political preferences of justices on a liberal–conservative spectrum. For example, President Obama's ideal point is toward the left end and former President George W. Bush's ideal point is toward the right. We used justices' votes on Supreme Court cases to measure their ideal points. We used Members of Congress as our group of people who look at Supreme Court cases through a primarily political lens. There is considerable evidence that this is how things work: a former Republican member of the House Judiciary Committee told political scientist Mitchell Pickerill that "when I go home and talk to my constituents, they ask me to help solve problems in Congress. They don't ask if it's constitutional. They want common sense" (Pickerill 2004, 134; see also pp. 4, 20, 65, 115). Members of Congress often take positions on cases before the Court by filing amicus briefs ("friend of the court" briefs that argue for one side or the other on a case) or by speaking out publicly on cases.

We then assessed whether justices voted with ideologically similar members of Congress when ruling on the constitutionality of congressional statutes. If conservative justices voted conservatively just like conservative Members of Congress and liberal justices voted liberally just like liberal Members of Congress, we would say that the oft-cited norm of judicial deference did not really affect behavior. If, on the other hand, conservative justices were more likely to accept liberal laws than their conservative counterparts in Congress and liberal justices were more likely to accept conservative laws than their liberal counterparts in Congress we would conclude that the deference was real.

We found that quite a few justices acted in the latter way: they really do appear to have followed a norm of deference. For five justices the evidence of truly deferential behavior was very strong; for another seven justices, there was evidence of deferential behavior at conventional statistical significance levels. In all, 12 of 32 justices included in our study exhibited deferential behavior, leading us to conclude that the deference is a real phenomenon, but hardly a straitjacket on the Court.

And the pattern of who showed signs of deference is interesting. Almost all of the justices who showed deference served in the 1950s or 1960s. Among more contemporary justices, only Justice Stevens exhibited deferential behavior; all the rest show little sign of deferring to Congress when ruling on congressional statutes. How can we explain this? Probably the best explanation is to think about the changes in the "judicial regime," the shifting pattern of political, normative, and functional relationships within and beyond the Court (Barnes 2007). The justices who showed signs of deference mostly came to the Court during the New Deal era. In this era, the Court was viewed with suspicion and outright hostility by those who wanted a more active government, because that Court had for decades made a sport of knocking back expansions of government, be they income taxes, limits on work weeks, minimum wage laws, or bans on child labor. A very common and relevant opinion of the time was that the Court needed to step back and let democratically elected leaders make policies demanded by voters.

Justice Felix Frankfurter exemplified this view. He was an outspoken liberal with ties to many of the leading intellectual and political leaders of the time. Once on the Court, however, he acted like a conservative as he very often found ways to allow Congress or a state legislature to do whatever it was trying to do, efforts that often impinged on civil liberties or other rights liberals sought to protect. This happened because Frankfurter believed that "the role of the Court was to accept the verdict of democratically elected legislative majorities" (Levinson 1977, 83). Frankfurter particularly respected Justice Holmes who took a famously restrained view of what the Court should do. Just before joining the Court, Frankfurter (1938, 22) wrote approvingly of Holmes that

> it was not for him to prescribe for society or to deny it the right of experimentation with very wide limits. That was to be left for contest by the political forces in the state. The duty of the Court was to keep the ring free.

Not all liberals in Frankfurter's era shared Frankfurter's approach. Justices Black, Jackson, Reed, Douglas, and Frankfurter had all "originally been regarded as New Dealers, expected to take almost similar political philosophies to the Court" (Katcher 1967, 312) but Black and Douglas in particular showed little interest in judicial deference (Friedman 2009, 239). These presumably liberal justices clashed repeatedly, often with a great deal of animosity, making it clear that judicial values were not fully determined by ideology and historical context (Yalof 1999, 27).

The internal norm of deferring to elected branches has been a real source of constraint on the Court, but it is precarious and decaying. It has always depended on individual justices making a choice to respect this norm, and modern justices are dramatically less likely to make this choice. Are there other ways in which voters can influence the Court? We turn in the next section to ways in which constraints may possibly be imposed on the Court by external actors.

Threats from External Actors

If justices do not take on the task of accommodating public views, then perhaps Congress and the President can somehow force the Court's hand. This is most plausible in statutory cases. These are cases where the Court is interpreting statutory language, and if Congress does not like the Court's interpretation it can, in theory at least, simply pass new legislation clarifying the law in the manner it desires. Ferejohn and Shipan (1990) and Ferejohn and Weingast (1992) formalized this line of thought with a series of models in which the Court first makes a decision and then the House, Senate, and president come together to legislate in the policy area of the case. If the Court chooses a position that is in between the outcomes desired by the president and the House, then there will be no overriding legislation as the president would veto any effort to move policy from the Court's decision toward the House's and the House would not pass any effort to move the policy from the Court's decision toward the president's. If the Court were to choose something extreme such that all of the elected branches agree on the direction of change (e.g., each of the president, House, and Senate wants to move policy to the left or each wants to move policy to the right) the Court's decision would not only be overridden, but policy could move far away from that desired by the Court. If the Court is forward-thinking, it will choose a policy that is desired by the closest of the elected branches; this actor (be it the president, House, or Senate) will protect the Court's decision and thereby prevent a move even further from the Court's policy ideal. The influence of elected branches is largely *pre-emptive*; it is the Court that accommodates the elected branches in order to make sure they do not unite to move further than the Court's pre-emption policy position.

It is not the case that the Court completely pre-empts congressional activity, however. It is not uncommon for the Court to strike a congressional statute and have Congress come back and pass a cleaned-up law; Pickerill (2004, 41) finds that Congress saved unconstitutional legislation 48% of the time (while repealing struck laws 14 percent of the time and doing nothing 38% of the time). For example, after the Court's landmark decision in *U.S. v. Lopez* (1995) that struck down part of the Gun-Free School Zones Act saying that the federal government did not have the authority to regulate gun possession on school property, Congress did a minor fix to the statute and re-passed it (Pickerill 2004, 51).

In constitutional cases, it is likely much harder for the elected branches to constrain the Court. If they want to directly override a Court decision, they face not a legislative process—which we know is hard enough to navigate—but a constitutional amendment process which requires support from a two-thirds majority in each house of Congress and ratification by three-fourths of the state legislatures (or an even less likely and more complicated constitutional convention process). There have been only 17 constitutional amendments after the Bill of Rights.

Therefore, external political constraints on the Court in constitutional cases likely need to operate through the threat of adverse outcomes other than direct overrides. These adverse outcomes do not include cuts to judicial salaries which are constitutionally prohibited and typically would not include removal of individual justices which faces steep hurdles and has only been attempted once. However, other arrows remain in the quiver. The Court famously lacks an army or even postal carriers and must, therefore, depend on the acquiescence of others in order to see its decisions implemented. Rosenberg (2008) documents, for example, how the Court's civil rights decisions went unenforced for at least a decade in many parts of the country. And crossing all three elected branches could de-legitimize the Court in a way that could erode the core of its power which is based on its perceived legitimacy and fairness.

Assessing whether the Court is in fact constrained by external actors is challenging. One challenge is that the effects are pre-emptive, so we cannot simply look at the number of congressional overrides of Court cases or the times when Congress and the president imposed some costs on the Court for decisions they did not approve of. Another challenge is that the theory crosses institutional boundaries; this means that we have to consider whether Members of Congress approved of Court decisions or whether the Court has moved to the left of the president and so forth.

In Bailey and Maltzman (2011) we tackled these challenges by assessing the possibility of elected branch influence on both statutory and constitutional cases. In statutory cases, the theory predicts that elected branches will only influence the Court when the Court is extreme relative to all three elected branches; if the Court is more liberal than at least one branch and more conservative than at least another then Court decisions will be protected from being overruled either to the left or right. Therefore, we used statistical techniques to identify when the Court is extreme and assess whether individual justices are more likely to moderate their views in those instances. We found that 12 of 32 justices exhibit some such behavior and, in contrast to the results described above on normative-based deference to Congress, there is no clear time pattern. Some modern justices (such as Souter, Thomas, and Kennedy) and some justices from the early postwar era (such as Warren, Brennan, and Stewart) acted in a way consistent with the view that justices pre-emptively moderate their views when the Court is extreme relative to the elected branches. While the deference described above could be considered a mechanism of respect (of the democratic process if not the actual presidents and representatives in Congress), this mechanism is one of fear: these justices are only moderating when the Court likely faces some retribution were it not to moderate.

We also investigated the possibility of pre-emptive movement by justices in constitutional cases. To do so, we looked at important elections where the partisan control of the presidency changed hands. These elections signal a shift in the preferences of elected officials, and if justices are taking into account these preferences there should be some observable shifts in preferences among justices. Of course, when a major election occurs, a lot of things change including the agenda, and it could be that the preferences of all political actors shift based simply on a change in the tenor of the times. Therefore, we looked for relative change as more convincing evidence of shifts in Court behavior: evidence of external influence would be justices moving relative to Members of Congress in the direction predicted by the theory. For example, if Justice X had an ideology close to Senator Y before one of these major electoral changes, then we would look to see if Justice X shifted away from Senator Y in the direction of the new president. If it is simply a case where both Justice X and Senator Y shifted toward the president, this would be attributed to the mood of the times, rather than external influence.

In virtually every election in which the presidency changed partisan hands, there were corresponding shifts in the preferences of justices. In some years, such as 1960, only a few justices moved, but they were the justices near the median of the Court and therefore the most influential. (In 1960 Justice Stewart was the median and he went from being estimated to have roughly the same preferences of Republican Minority Leader Everett Dirksen (R, IL) before the election to having approximately the preferences of Democratic Senator Thomas Dodd (D, CT)—the father of recent Connecticut Senator Christopher Dodd.) In other years, such as 1980, there was wholesale movement of Court members relative to Members of Congress in a conservative direction, as would be predicted if the justices were being influenced by the preferences of elected officials. In no year was there substantial movement against the direction predicted by the theory.

Another piece of evidence comes from looking at how often the Court strikes down congressional legislation. Harvey and Friedman (2006) show that congressional statutes are less likely to be struck down when the Court is more extreme than all the elected branches; in another article, Harvey and Friedman (2009) show that the Court takes this caution to the next level by not even considering some cases when they are in disagreement with Congress and the president. This point is important to remember because it means that some Court deference is hard to see: we might not even see the Court upholding a law if the Court doesn't even hear a case in which it is challenged.

And pressure on the Court may not be limited to periods when it is ideologically extreme. Members of Congress have long had complaints about something the Supreme Court has done, and they commonly express these complaints via "court-curbing legislation"; for example, legislators may propose limiting the Court's jurisdiction such that it cannot consider appeals to state anti-busing laws. These legislative proposals seldom pass or even have much chance of passing (although some have come close), but they are a public and measurable manifestation of public and political dissatisfaction with the Court. When these types of bills increase, the Court listens: political scientist Tom Clark (2009, 2010) shows that when Members of Congress offer a lot of court-curbing legislation, the Court strikes acts of Congress less frequently.

The constraint is real, but limited. Justices do seem to act differently when they are outside of the range of preferences of political branches or when there is a major shift in presidential preferences. The effects are neither universal nor overwhelming, but they are most relevant in periods when the constraint is most needed: periods in which the Court is extreme relative to the elected branches. Justices themselves agree; an anonymous justice told Clark (2009, 973) that "the Court is pretty good about knowing how far it can go ... Congress is better than we are, especially the House. They really have their finger on the pulse of the public" and that "we have to be careful not to reach too far."

Expertise

Another way in which elected branches can influence the Court is via expertise. The Court is a small institution with only nine justices and modest staff support. They all live in the Washington, DC area and typically operate in the relatively closed world of elite legal and policy-making communities. There is much that they do not know.

Elected officials, on the other hand, have larger staffs and represent all corners of the country. They have very strong incentives to learn the effects of legal cases and rulings on people throughout the nation. So the question is, is there evidence that the Court listens to other branches?

One way in which the Court seeks out the expertise of the Congress is to invite more legislation (Hausegger and Baum 1999). In roughly 7% of all majority decisions there is some kind of invitation from the Court to Congress to clarify matters with additional legislation (and an even greater proportion of dissents). A Court that cared nothing for the law or what Congress thought could simply write a decision that mandated the justices' desired outcome. One of the determinants of this behavior is that justices tended to invite congressional action when they do not like the policy implications of the outcome. That is, when liberal justices produce a conservative decision, the opinion is more likely to suggest that Congress should pass legislation to change the outcome. This implies that the justices are constrained by something other than policy preferences—some aspect of law, presumably—and that they leave it to Congress to get the policy more to their liking.

The president and executive branch, in particular, are well situated to learn about the effects of legal decisions as many top lawyers work in the executive branch cheek-to-jowl with political types who spend their time listening to and interacting with political interests and politically savvy people.

Another way that the Court might respond to information from elected branches is by taking seriously the information provided in amicus briefs. The actor who is most active in filing briefs is the Solicitor General, the top lawyer in the federal government and someone who focuses much of his or her energy on cases that make their way to the Supreme Court. The Supreme Court also regularly requests the Solicitor General's opinion on cases, as well (see Johnson 2003). If the Court defers to the expertise of the president, justices will be more likely to decide a case in a conservative direction when the Solicitor General files an amicus arguing for a conservative decision than when there is no brief or a liberal brief.

The Solicitor General does well before the Court (Kearney and Merrill, 2000). This success occurs at every stage of the process. The Supreme Court is more likely to grant certiorari in cases where the Solicitor General requests it (Caldeira and Wright 1988) and disproportionately sides with the Solicitor General's position when she represents a party to the case or files an amicus brief (Johnson 2003; McGuire 1998; Segal 1988). In addition, we know that the Court often incorporates into its opinions the arguments contained in the Solicitor General's amicus briefs (Spriggs and Wahlbeck 1997). Such success has given rise to the widely held view that the Solicitor General is the "Tenth Justice" (Caplan 1987).

Bailey and Maltzman (2011) and Bailey, Kamoie, and Maltzman (2005) use models of Supreme Court voting to assess whether justices are more likely to vote in the direction requested in Solicitor General amicus briefs. They found that more than half of the justices were significantly more likely to vote with the Solicitor General. They also found that the persuasiveness of the Solicitor General's briefs varied according to the ideological compatibility of the justice and the president under which the Solicitor General served. When the justice and the president were close ideologically, justices were even more likely to follow the recommendation of the Solicitor General. These results are consistent with "signaling theory" in which messages about political topics are more likely to be influential when they pass between like-minded individuals (Crawford and Sobel 1982).

The Solicitor General's success is commonly attributed to its ability to effectively articulate its case. This is largely the result of experience (Caldeira and Wright 1988; McGuire 1998; Spriggs and Wahlbeck 1997). As a "repeat player", the Solicitor General benefits from an established reputation in the legal profession. Perry discovered the importance of being a repeat player when a former clerk told him that the Solicitor General was successful because "the Solicitor General also knows all the catchwords, and they just know how to write them in a brief" (1991, 132).

Another explanation for the Solicitor General's success is that the Court may defer to the Solicitor General due to political factors. Thomas W. Merrill, deputy Solicitor General from 1987 to 1990, insisted the amicus brief was important because in high profile cases the justices "look to the Solicitor General for guidance ... for signals about the political atmosphere, 'for what's do-able'" (Greenhouse 2003). While one could conceive of "do-ability" as a legal concept, this is more likely a political concept. Justices may wish to avoid alienating the president in order to avoid having the president endorse legislation unappealing to the Court. Likewise, the Court may defer to the president to prevent him from unilaterally deciding not to enforce Supreme Court decisions.

Bailey, Kamoie, and Maltzman therefore develop a signaling model where justices appreciate both that the Solicitor General has potentially useful information and that the Solicitor General does not necessarily share the justices' ideological predispositions. In the model, justices assess the credibility of the Solicitor General's recommendation in light of what the justices know about the Solicitor General's ideology in general. If the justice and Solicitor General are very close ideologically, then the information from the Solicitor General is likely to be quite useful to a justice. But information can also be credibly transmitted if the Solicitor General is far from the justice ideologically, but goes against expectations. For example, if a liberal Solicitor General advocates a conservative position this will be credible, as the liberal Solicitor General's only incentive to mislead is to try to trick conservatives into voting liberally. Bailey, Kamoie, and Maltzman argue that what appears to be deference by the justices to the Solicitor General is in part conditioned upon the signals sent by the Solicitor General.

Certainly the Court is not under the thumb of the president. The executive branch is, however, part of the conversation. When it weighs in on a case, justices listen, particularly the justices who are ideologically sympathetic to the sitting president.

Conclusion

The Constitution created independent courts in order to enforce the Constitution and laws as they were written, not as some politically powerful interests wish them to be. Beneath this noble goal, however, lies an insidious threat: what if the courts impose their own preferences under the cloak of judicial independence? President Lincoln expressed exactly this concern in his 1861 inaugural speech, declaring that if policies can be "irrevocably fixed" by the Supreme Court, then "the people will have ceased to be their own rulers, having to that extent practically resigned their government into the hands of that eminent tribunal." Hence the theme of this chapter has been that the U.S. Supreme Court operates on a Goldilocks principle—it needs to be independent, but not too independent.

The institutional design features that provide for judicial independence are clear: lifetime tenure for justices and a high hurdle for amending the Constitution. The institutional design that constrains the Court is the appointment process. But is that all there is? After all, justices serve long (and increasing) periods on the Court, and many little resemble the man or woman confirmed by the Senate.

The other mechanisms for constraining the Court are real but are not strong. Justices take into account public sentiment out of respect, fear, and ignorance; respect via an internal norm of deference to legislative branches, fear via pre-emptive responsiveness to election outcomes, and ignorance via incorporation of information provided by knowledgeable political actors such as the Solicitor General. None of these mechanisms is completely reliable, however, and it is via the layering of these multiple constraints that the Court navigates its political boundaries while maintaining its independence.

Chapter 12

Interest Groups and Their Influence on Judicial Policy[1]

Paul M. Collins, Jr.

Interest groups participate in virtually all aspects of the American political and legal systems. In electoral politics, organizations regularly make campaign donations to candidates and many groups endorse individuals seeking political office. In the legislative sphere, interest groups draft legislation, testify in front of committees, and meet with legislators in hopes of having their preferred policies written into law. In the executive branch, organizations monitor the implementation of policies, testify before regulatory boards, and work with bureaucrats in an attempt to ensure that their prerogatives are reflected in policy implementation. More generally, interest groups mount grassroots lobbying campaigns, aimed at building public support for the groups' goals, in addition to engaging in orchestrated efforts to educate the public regarding their agendas and policy objectives. And, of course, groups are no strangers to the American judiciary. In recent years, interest groups have participated in more than 90% of cases decided by the U.S. Supreme Court (Collins 2008, 47).

The purpose of this chapter is to explore the role of interest groups in the United States Supreme Court, paying special attention to the primary means of interest group involvement in the judiciary: amicus curiae ("friend of the court") participation. This method of lobbying is a staple of interest group activity in the American legal system, as well as other legal systems throughout the world. First, the various methods of interest group litigation in the American courts are addressed. Next, I provide a treatment of interest group amicus curiae participation in the Supreme Court. It is illustrated that, in recent years, virtually all Supreme Court cases are accompanied by amicus curiae briefs and these briefs are filed across a wide spectrum of issue areas. Following this, I discuss the types of organizations that file amicus briefs in the Supreme Court. I provide evidence that a diverse array of interest groups actively participate, indicating that a host of organizations find a voice in the Court. Fourth, I provide an overview of extant scholarship on amicus influence on the Supreme Court. This chapter closes with a brief conclusion section suggesting directions for future research on amicus curiae participation in the Supreme Court, as well as interest group litigation in other judicial venues.

Interest Group Litigation in the American Legal System

In the U.S. courts, interest groups have four primary means of participation. First, interest groups can initiate test cases. Using this strategy, interest groups can either challenge a law or policy in their own name (provided they can secure standing), or, alternatively, orchestrate litigation on behalf of an individual (or individuals) who can demonstrate standing to sue.[2] An example of the former occurred in *Ysursa v. Pocatello Education Association* (2009), in which a coalition of labor unions unsuccessfully sued State of Idaho officials challenging a state law that prohibited payroll deductions for "political activities" on the grounds that it violated the First Amendment's freedom of speech clause. Perhaps the most famous example of the latter occurred in *Brown v. Board of Education* (1954). In that case, the NAACP (National Association for the Advancement of Colored People) Legal Defense and Education Fund recruited litigants in Topeka, Kansas, and other cities, to challenge the practice of racial segregation in public schools. This litigation campaign resulted in the Supreme Court's landmark desegregation decision, in which the Court declared that the "separate but equal" doctrine was unconstitutional in the field of public education.

A second method of interest group participation in the American legal system involves case sponsorship. Like test cases, under this strategy, an organization provides attorneys, staff, and other resources for a party in exchange for using the litigation to pursue its policy goals. This means of participation differs from test cases in that case sponsorship occurs after the initial litigation has already commenced. In this sense, groups look for "targets of opportunity" by taking over cases that individuals have begun once the litigation reaches the appellate courts. For example, *Moore v. Dempsey* (1923) began when 12 black sharecroppers were convicted of first-degree murder in Arkansas for allegedly killing five whites during a riot. At their trials, a veritable mob of heavily armed whites stood outside of the courtroom, demanding guilty verdicts and the death sentence for each defendant. Moreover, the crowd made it clear that, should the judge fail to return death sentences for the defendants, the mob would lynch them. The accused met their attorneys for the first time when the trail began, their lawyers failed to produce witnesses on their clients' behalves, and the defendants did not testify in their defense. The jury returned guilty verdicts for all of the defendants in less than 10 minutes and the judge subsequently sentenced the defendants to death. Upon becoming informed of the case, the NAACP sent a representative from the organization, Walter White, to investigate. Concluding that the trials were a sham, White convinced the NAACP to sponsor an appeal. The case ultimately reached the U.S. Supreme Court, which determined that the defendants' rights to due process of law were violated (Cortner 1988).

A third method of interest group involvement in the American legal system involves intervention, in which an organization becomes what is effectively a party to the litigation after the case has entered the legal system. Under Federal Rule of Civil Procedure 24(a), organizations, and other interested entities, have the opportunity to intervene in a case as a matter of right, while Rule 24(b) authorizes intervention, not as a matter of right, but when the prospective intervenor "has a claim or defense that shares with the main action a common question of law or fact." Rule 24(a) specifies that an organization seeking intervenor status must demonstrate either that it is authorized to intervene under federal statute or that it has "an interest relating to the property or transaction that is the subject of the action," such that the disposition of the litigation would impair the prospective intervenor's interests. Moreover, the would-be intervenor must illustrate that its interests would not be adequately represented by the direct parties to litigation. Should an organization successfully obtain intervenor status, the intervenor becomes, in effect, a full-blown participant in litigation, bound by the resulting judgment in the case, not only as a matter of precedent, but as a matter of res judicata (Hilliker 1981).[3] Attesting to the reality that intervenors in American law are effectively litigants, they are authorized to make motions, introduce new legal arguments, and, at the trial court level, present evidence and witnesses.

While Rule 24(a) seems to indicate that there are few procedural barriers to becoming an intervenor as a matter of right, in practice, the federal courts treat all requests to intervene as discretionary decisions (Hilliker 1981; Tobias 1991). That is, the U.S. Supreme Court has failed to articulate a bright line rule (that is, a rule subject to minimal interpretation) as to exactly what an applicant must show to intervene under Rule 24(a). This responsibility has been left to lower federal courts, which have applied myriad standards with regard to allowing intervention as a matter of right (Tobias 1991, 415). Because of the various standards utilized to determine whether an organization is authorized to intervene, and because many courts deny motions to intervene, concluding that the prospective intervenor was not able to demonstrate a clear interest in the litigation, a practical impairment, or inadequate representation by the parties, this method of interest group litigation is used rather sparingly. Instead, organizations most commonly advance their interests through the amicus curiae brief (Goepp 2002; Hilliker 1981, 23).

Amicus curiae briefs act as the primary method of interest group involvement in the U.S. courts (Collins 2008).[4] While the literal translation of amicus curiae, "friend of the court," implies neutrality, these briefs are, in fact, used as adversarial weapons, providing a means for organizations to pursue their interests in the adversarial system that is American law (Krislov 1963). Indeed, there was never a time in American jurisprudence that amici acted solely as neutral third parties (Banner 2003). As amici curiae, organizations pursue their policy goals by providing courts with information not addressed by the direct parties to litigation, presenting alternative or reframed legal arguments, and addressing the far-ranging policy implications of a court's decisions. In addition, because many amici are specialists in particular areas of economic, legal, or social policy, they frequently supply courts with social scientific information to further their policy agendas (Rustad and Koenig 1993).

The U.S. Supreme Court maintains an open-door policy with regard to the participation of organized interests (Collins 2008, 42; Kearney and Merrill 2000, 761). Under Supreme Court Rule 37, private amici must obtain written permission from the parties to litigation to file an amicus curiae brief.[5] However, representatives of state, local, and territorial governments, as well as the federal government, need not fulfill this procedural requirement. Practically speaking, the requirement of party consent is negligible, as virtually all litigants willingly comply with requests by amici. Should one (or both) of the litigants fail to provide consent to file, the prospective amicus may petition the Court for leave to file. This motion must be accompanied by the amicus brief. The Court's treatment of these motions—to almost always grant motions for consent to file, provided they are timely—further evidences its open-door policy. For example, during the 1994 term, the Court granted 99.1% of motions for leave to file amicus briefs, denying only a single motion (Epstein and Knight 1999, 225).

Under U.S. Supreme Court Rule 37, amici are directed to indicate the position taken in the brief (i.e., affirmance or reversal of the lower court) and are instructed to provide a statement of interest, outlining how the case affects their well-being. Rule 37 further specifies that the Court does not favor the input of third parties that merely repeat the arguments raised by the litigants:

> An *amicus curiae* brief that brings to the attention of the Court relevant matter not already brought to its attention by the parties may be of considerable help to the Court. An *amicus curiae* brief that does not serve this purpose burdens the Court, and its filing is not favored.

In what can appropriately be viewed as an effort to enhance the ability of amici to reduce the repetition of arguments raised by the litigants, in 2007, the U.S. Supreme Court amended its rule governing the due dates for amicus briefs filed in its decisions on the merits. Prior to this rule change, amicus briefs were due on the same date as the brief of the party the amici supported. This rule change extended this by a week, requiring that amici submit their briefs no later than seven days after the brief of the party they support is filed with the Court.[6]

A 1997 amendment to Rule 37 requires that amici divulge whether the attorneys for the parties to litigation authored the amicus briefs, in whole or in part, and additionally compels amici to indicate whether any entities, other than those listed as amici curiae, made monetary contributions to fund the preparation of the amicus brief. Although the U.S. Supreme Court provided no justification for this rule change, Kearney and Merrill (2000, 767) suggest that a possible explanation for the former points to the Court's concern that attorneys for the litigants were "ghostwriting" amicus briefs, enabling them to evade the Court's page limits for litigant briefs and present additional argumentation to support their positions. As to the latter, it is plausible that the justices' may have feared amicus briefs were being manipulated as a means of showing apparently broad support for a cause of interest.[7]

Amicus Curiae Participation in the U.S. Supreme Court

Organized interests have long used the U.S. Supreme Court to pursue their policy goals. The first amicus brief filed by a non-governmental interest group occurred in 1904 when the Chinese Charitable and Benevolent Association of New York acted as an amicus in *Ah How (alias Louie Ah How) v. United States* (1904), a case involving the deportation of Chinese immigrants in New York (Krislov 1963, 707). In the following decades, a wide range of organizations filed amicus briefs in the Court, including the American Civil Liberties Union, the American Farm Bureau Association, the League for Economic Equality, the NAACP, the National Consumers League, and the National Association of Cotton Manufacturers (Collins 2008, 41). By the post-World War II era, amicus participation was a regular occurrence in the Court.

Figure 12.1 plots the percentage of U.S. Supreme Court cases, decided with oral argument, in which at least one amicus curiae brief was filed during the Court's 1946–2007 terms.[8] As this figure makes clear, there has been a marked

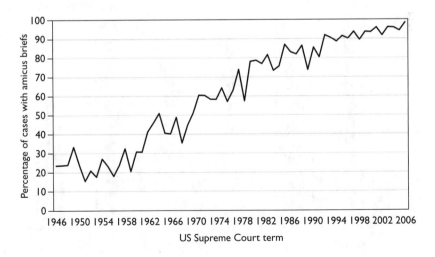

Figure 12.1 Percentage of U.S. Supreme Court cases with amicus curiae participation, 1946–2007 terms.

rise in the percentage of cases with amicus participation over the course of the last 60 years. From 1946–1960, the percentage of cases with amicus briefs was relatively stable, averaging 23%. A rather dramatic surge occurred during the 1960s, when the percentage of cases with amicus participation increased from 31% in 1961 to 44% in 1969. This swell in amicus participation is no doubt due in part to the striking increase in the number of interest groups operating in American politics during this period (Berry 1997). Following the explosion of amicus participation in the 1960s, later decades witnessed more stable increases. For example, the percentage of cases with amicus briefs in the 1970s was 60% and the 1980s saw this number increase to 80%. By the mid-1990s, the percentage of cases with amicus briefs effectively stabilized at over 90%, reaching a high of 98% in 2007. As such, these data make clear that it is a rare occurrence in the contemporary U.S. Supreme Court that a case is *not* accompanied by the participation of amici curiae.

While Figure 12.1 provides useful information regarding the overall percentage of cases in which amicus briefs are filed, it cannot speak to whether certain issue areas exhibit more or less amicus activity. Figure 12.2 provides this information by graphing the percentage of cases in which at least one amicus brief was filed in five issue areas during the chief justiceships of Vinson (1946–1952), Warren (1953–1969), Burger (1970–1985), Rehnquist (1986–2004), and Roberts (2005–2007). Civil rights cases include disputes involving criminal procedure, civil rights, the First Amendment (which

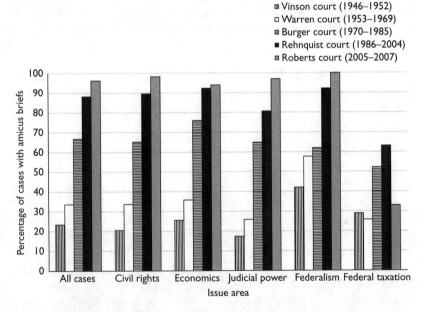

Figure 12.2 Amicus curiae participation by issue area and chief justice's court, 1946–2007 terms.

contains protections related to the freedoms of religion, speech, and the press, along with the rights to assembly and petition), due process of law, privacy, and attorneys' rights (which typically involve attorneys' commercial speech rights). Economics cases include issues related to economic and union activity, such as liability claims and union arbitration. Judicial power cases involve controversies surrounding the authority of the federal courts, such as federal court deference to the proceedings of state courts. Federalism disputes encompass the power of the federal government vis-à-vis that of state or local governments. Federal taxation cases include primarily issues related to the Internal Revenue Code.[9]

Several notable points emerge from this figure. First, it is evident that the percentage of cases with amicus participation rose over time for virtually all issue areas. Second, it is clear that amici participate in all of the issue areas presented in Figure 12.2, although some issue areas exhibit higher levels of participation. That is, amicus briefs are most commonly filed in cases involving civil rights, economics, federalism, and judicial power. Relatively few amicus briefs are filed in federal taxation cases.[10] Finally, this figure corroborates the reality that, with the exception of federal taxation cases, virtually all disputes in the contemporary Roberts Court witness the participation of organized interests, regardless of the substance of the litigation.

Figures 12.1 and 12.2 plainly indicate that amicus curiae participation is a staple of interest group activity in the U.S. Supreme Court. However, they do not evince how many amicus briefs are filed at the Court. Figure 12.3 contains this information by tracking the average number of amicus briefs, per case, filed during the 1946–2007 terms. From 1946–1969, the justices could expect

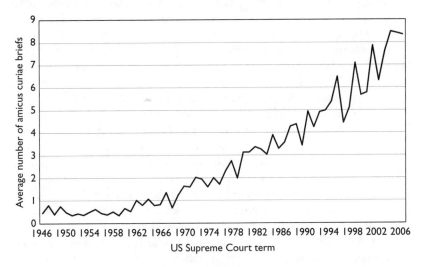

Figure 12.3 Average number of amicus curiae briefs, per case, filed in the U.S. Supreme Court, 1946–2007 terms.

a single amicus brief in any given case. This rose to two amicus briefs during the 1970s and increased more dramatically to four amicus briefs in the 1980s. During the 1990s, the justice could expect to see an average of five amicus briefs per case, while an average of eight amicus briefs were filed, per case, in the 2000s. As such, this figure makes it perspicuous that, not only has the percentage of cases with amicus briefs dramatically intensified over time, but the average number of amicus briefs filed per case has increased more than eightfold since the 1950s.

The Diversity of Organized Interests in the U.S. Supreme Court

Extant research indicates that a varied assortment of organizations find a voice in the U.S. Supreme Court (Caldeira and Wright 1990; Collins and Solowiej 2007). That is, moneyed interests, such as businesses and corporations, do not dominate amicus activity in the Supreme Court. Rather, a wide array of organizations participates in the Court's jurisprudence, including public advocacy organizations, public interest law firms, and ad hoc associations of individuals. This separates the U.S. Supreme Court from Washington lobbying more generally, in that there is substantial evidence of an upper-class bias in terms of the types of groups represented in the U.S. Capitol, with most lobbying activity conducted by institutional interests, such as corporations (Salisbury 1984; Schlozman 1984). In part, this distinction is likely due to the fact that all non-governmental organizations face the same procedural requirements to participate as amici, and none of these requirements is especially burdensome. Conversely, there is evidence that in the absence of a geographic tie to a member of Congress, access to legislators is governed by campaign donations (Langbein 1986; Wright 1989).

To provide some perspective on the diversity of interest groups participating as friends of the court, Table 12.1 presents a classification of amici curiae in *District of Columbia v. Heller* (2008). This case marked the first time in almost 70 years that the U.S. Supreme Court considered the meaning of the Second Amendment to the U.S. Constitution, which reads: "A well regulated Militia, being necessary to the security of a free State, the right of the people to keep and bear Arms, shall not be infringed." At issue in the case was the constitutionality of a District of Columbia law that, among other things, effectively outlawed the possession of handguns within the district.[11] The respondent, a security guard, argued that the handgun ban violated his right to keep and bear arms. In so doing, Heller asked the Court to embrace the position that the Second Amendment implied an individual right to gun ownership, irrespective of one's connection to a militia. The District of Columbia argued that the ban was fully within its power because the Second Amendment granted only a collective right to gun ownership, contingent on one's official connection to a governmental militia. In a 5–4 decision, the Supreme

Court endorsed the respondent's position, determining that the Second Amendment protects an individual's right to possess a firearm, regardless of that individual's connection with a militia, so long as the firearm is used for traditionally lawful purposes, such as self-defense.

The amicus effort in *Heller* was staggering. Sixty-seven amicus briefs were filed in the case: 20 supported the District of Columbia's handgun ban, while 47 sought to overturn the prohibition. Though this case is unusual with regard to the number of amicus briefs filed—it ranks third in terms of Supreme Court cases with the most amicus filings[12]—it nonetheless highlights the diversity of interests at the Court. The amici in Table 12.1 were coded into each typology based on a well-established methodology that focuses on their membership characteristics (Caldeira and Wright 1990; Collins 2008, 56–63; Collins and Solowiej 2007). The information used to classify organizations was taken from the "Statement of Interest" section of each amicus brief, a required component of amicus briefs under Supreme Court Rule 37.

Individuals include amicus briefs that were filed by ad hoc organizations of individuals, such as academics, police chiefs, and Members of Congress. Corporations, of which there were none in *Heller*, encompass businesses and corporations that are identified by their corporate monikers. Amicus briefs filed by the United States are most commonly submitted by the Solicitor General (as was the case in *Heller*), although they are occasionally filed by the Solicitor General and cosigned by another executive branch official or bureaucracy. Amici classified as state and territorial governments include the U.S. states, as well as territories and possessions. Local governments are made up of governments below the state level, such as cities, counties, school boards, and the like. Public advocacy amici are composed of groups whose membership is individuals, regardless of their occupational status, and who pursue primarily political, as opposed to economic goals, such as non-profit charities, community organizations, and groups who represent the interests of the disadvantaged. Public interest law firms are non-profit legal organizations who provide attorneys to represent individual litigants or initiate lawsuits themselves in pursuit of their interests. The distinguishing characteristic of a professional association is that its membership is based on occupation in a specific profession. In addition, professional associations tend to pursue economic, as well as political, benefits for their members. Amici are classified as unions if they identify themselves as a union representing the interests of its members who serve in a particular occupation. Peak associations are, in effect, organizations of organizations. That is, peak associations are organizations who do not have members in the ordinary sense; rather, their membership is comprised of other institutions, such as labor unions, businesses, and interest groups. Finally, organizations that do not fit into any of the categories previously discussed are identified as "other" organizations. In *Heller*, this included two political parties: the DC Statehood Green Party and the Libertarian National Committee.

The first column in Table 12.1 indicates the number of briefs on which each category of amici appeared. Because different categories of amici frequently cosign a single amicus brief, the percentages (indicated in parentheses) do not sum to 100. The second column provides information regarding the number of amici participating in the case, thus offering insight into how frequently the justices observe each category of amicus. Beginning with column one, it is evident that a wide assortment of interest groups participated as amici curiae. Public advocacy organizations appeared on the largest number of amicus briefs, almost 50%, followed by individuals (36%), public interest law firms (19%), and professional associations (16%). The categories of amici who appeared on the fewest number of amicus briefs were corporations (0%), the federal government (1.5%), unions (1.5%), and peak associations (1.5%).

Column two speaks to the overall number of amici participating in *Heller*, providing information regarding the coalitional activity of organized interests. Individuals made up the largest category of amici, representing 71% of all amici. This indicates that, on average, 28 individuals appeared together on the same amicus brief. However, it should be noted that a single amicus brief was filed by 306 Members of the U.S. Congress: 250 members of the House, 55 senators, and the vice president of the United States in his capacity as president of the Senate. Following individuals, 160 public advocacy organizations participated, comprising 17% of all amici. On average, a brief filed by a public advocacy organization was cosigned by four other public advocacy groups. Thirty-eight states and territorial governments appeared as amici on three briefs. Two of these briefs were filed in opposition to the District of Columbia's handgun ban, one of which was submitted by the State of Wisconsin, while the other was cosigned by 31 states. Supporting the District's prohibition, New York, Hawaii, Maryland, Massachusetts, New Jersey, and Puerto Rico filed a joint brief. The fourth largest category of amici in *Heller* was comprised of professional associations. Thirty-six trade associations appeared on 11 amicus briefs.

Table 12.1 speaks to three significant points. First, it is evident that a diverse assortment of interest groups utilized the amicus brief in *Heller* in pursuit of their policy goals. Moreover, moneyed interests, such as professional associations and corporations, far from dominated the amicus activity in this case. Rather, the Court heard perspectives on the Second Amendment from ad hoc associations of individuals, governmental entities, public advocacy organizations, and public interest law firms. Second, the amicus effort in *Heller* provides an excellent example of the reality that coalitional amicus participation is the norm in the Court. Indeed, 951 distinct amici participated, appearing on 67 briefs. This suggests that groups recognize the benefits of coalitional amicus strategies, whether to show broad support for a cause of interest or to reduce the costs of filing a brief by a single organization.[13] Finally, note the absence of corporate amici in *Heller*. To be sure, this is an

Table 12.1 Amicus Curiae Participation in District of Columbia v. Heller (2008)

Amicus curiae type	Number of briefs	Number of amici	Examples
Individuals	24 (35.8)	672 (70.7)	Academics, district attorneys, Members of Congress, military officers, police chiefs, state legislators
Corporations	0 (0)	0	None
United States	1 (1.5)	1 (0.1)	United States Solicitor General
State and territorial governments	3 (4.5)	38 (4.0)	Hawaii, New York, Puerto Rico, Texas, Wyoming
Local governments	3 (4.5)	26 (2.7)	Board of Education of the City of Chicago, City of San Francisco, Maricopa County Attorney's Office
Public advocacy groups	33 (49.3)	160 (16.8)	American Hunters and Shooters Association, Congress of Racial Equality, Heartland Institute, NAACP, Women Against Gun Violence
Public interest law firms	13 (19.4)	13 (1.4)	Legal Community Against Violence, Mountain States Legal Foundation, NAACP LDF, NRA Civil Rights Defense Fund, Rutherford Institute
Professional associations	11 (16.4)	36 (3.8)	Association of American Physicians and Surgeons, American Bar Association, American Public Health Association, United States Conference of Mayors
Unions	1 (1.5)	1 (0.1)	International Brotherhood of Police Officers
Peak associations	1 (1.5)	2 (0.2)	ACTION OHIO, National Network to End Domestic Violence
Other	2 (3.0)	2 (0.2)	DC Statehood Green Party, Libertarian National Committee
Totals	67	951	

Notes
Entries in parentheses indicate within column percentages. These were computed by dividing the total number of times each category of amicus curiae appeared on a brief by the total number of amicus curiae briefs filed (column one) or the total number of amici curiae participating in the case (column two). Because different categories of amici frequently cosign a single amicus brief, the percentages in column one do not sum to 100.

anomaly. For example, during the 1995 term, corporations appeared on 12% of amicus briefs, comprising 7% of all amici (Collins and Solowiej 2007, 967). Although one can only speculate, the absence of business interests, such as handgun manufacturers, may be a partial function of the fear that the Court might view them as motivated by economic self-interest, as opposed to being genuinely concerned with the sensitive legal and social policy issues implicated in the case.

The Impact of Amicus Curiae Briefs on the U.S. Supreme Court

There is a voluminous body of scholarship devoted to ascertaining the influence of amici curiae on the U.S. Supreme Court. While a complete review of this literature is beyond the purview of this chapter, it is nonetheless useful to engage a sample of this research.[14] My purpose here is two-fold. First, by discussing the conclusions drawn from extant research, I hope to provide the reader with a sense of whether or not amicus briefs influence Supreme Court decision-making. Second, in examining this scholarship, I intend to shed light on the diverse range of methodologies used to examine interest group effectiveness in the Supreme Court. Scholars studying the impact of amici curiae employ a range of research methods and analyze a variety of possible influences on the Court, and it is clear that no single methodological approach dominates the scholarly examination of friends of the court.

Prior to discussing the approaches taken by scholars analyzing amicus influence in the Supreme Court, it is useful to provide a brief treatment of the primary theoretical perspective shared by many of these studies. That is, scholars have generally approached the analysis of amici curiae by presenting a theory of amicus impact based on the informational value of amicus briefs (Caldeira and Wright 1988; Collins 2008; Epstein and Knight 1999; Hansford 2004; Kearney and Merrill 2000; Spriggs and Wahlbeck 1997). These scholars posit that amicus briefs are influential inasmuch as they provide the justices with new or reframed perspectives of the legal issues facing the Court, discuss the wide-ranging economic, legal, and social policy implications of the decision, in addition to presenting the justices with information regarding the preferences of outside actors, including the public, Congress, the executive branch, and state and local governments. Because American jurisprudence is based on the adversarial system—in which litigants and amici must marshal the language of the law in pursuit of their goals—the information supplied by amici is said to be capable of persuading the justices to endorse particular positions or legal rules, and, indeed, there is empirical evidence to support this perspective.

The most common method of analyzing amicus influence on the Supreme Court involves large-n statistical studies that tend to focus on a relatively long time frame. While these studies share a common methodological approach, they differ in terms of the phenomena (i.e., dependent variable) under examination. For example, Caldeira and Wright (1988) analyze the influence of amicus curiae briefs at the Supreme Court's agenda-setting stage. They uncover evidence that petitions for a writ of certiorari—the primary vehicle by which cases arrive at the Supreme Court—are far more likely to be granted when accompanied by one or more amicus briefs (see also McGuire and Caldeira 1993). They conclude that, because amicus briefs at the agenda-setting stage are so rare, the briefs provide information regarding the salience of the case for the justices, thus making review more likely.

A second quantitative approach to analyzing amicus influence focuses on examining litigation outcomes; that is, whether the Court ruled in favor of the petitioner or respondent (Collins 2008; Kearney and Merrill 2000; Songer and Sheehan 1993). These studies seek to determine if the party supported by the larger number of amicus briefs is more likely to prevail. For example, Collins (2008) scrutinizes litigation success from 1953 to 1985 and discovers that the litigant supported by the larger number of amicus briefs was more likely to win. Such is said to be the case because a relatively large number of amicus briefs filed in support of a litigant provide the justices with myriad legal arguments supporting that litigant's position.

More recently, Collins (2007, 2008) has posited that scholars studying the influence of amici curiae are better suited by examining the ideological direction (i.e., liberal or conservative) of the Court's decisions and that of the individual justice's votes, rather than focusing on litigation success. Collins argues this dependent variable is desirable because the primary goal of amici is not to ensure that a particular litigant wins or loses, but instead is to influence the ideological direction of the Court's policy outputs. In his book-length treatment of friends of the court, Collins (2008) reveals that amici are capable of shaping the ideological direction of the individual justice's votes. Moreover, the influence of amici is so strong that the justices' attitudes do not necessarily diminish the significance of the arguments raised by amici. That is, conservative amici are capable of persuading liberal justices to cast conservative votes, while liberal amici are capable of persuading conservative justices to cast liberal votes.

A fourth quantitative approach to studying amicus influence focuses on exploring the ability of amici to shape the language used by the justices in the Supreme Court's opinions. Frequently, this is accomplished by counting citations to amicus briefs in the justice's opinions. For example, Kearney and Merrill (2000) examine citations to amicus briefs in the Supreme Court's majority, concurring, and dissenting opinions from 1946 to 1995 (see also Owens and Epstein 2005). Their results indicate that amicus briefs were cited by the Court's majority in 28% of cases in which an amicus brief was filed. Moreover, they show that amicus briefs were directly quoted in 9% of cases accompanied by at least one amicus brief. Spriggs and Wahlbeck (1997) take an alternative approach by examining the justices' incorporation of the arguments of amici curiae into the Court's majority opinions. Those authors sought to determine whether the Court was more likely to adopt arguments forwarded by amici depending on whether the arguments reiterated the briefs of the litigants or presented novel information. Interestingly, they find that the Court was more likely to adopt the positions advanced by the amici if those arguments reiterated the points raised by the parties, suggesting amici influence may not be due to the original information presented in the briefs.

In addition to the aforementioned quantitative approaches to studying the influence of amicus curiae briefs on the U.S. Supreme Court, a number of scholars have utilized more qualitative methods to examine amicus impact. Through these approaches, scholars are enabled to provide a rich understanding of how amicus briefs shape the legal doctrines enunciated in the Court's opinions, in addition to offering insights into the views of, for example, the law clerks who work with the justices. Epstein and Kobylka (1992) examine the role of amici curiae in the Supreme Court's death penalty and abortion jurisprudence. These authors provide persuasive evidence as to the ability of amici to shape the justice's decision-making in these issue areas by illustrating how the arguments presented by the amici found their way into the Court's majority, concurring, and dissenting opinions. Using a similar research strategy, Samuels (2004) demonstrates how friends of the court shaped the nature of the Court's decision-making in privacy disputes, including abortion, assistance in dying, and protected relationships. In addition to providing evidence as to the Court's heavy reliance on citations to amicus briefs in its privacy opinions, Samuels illuminates how many of the arguments forwarded by the amici found their way into the Court's opinions without attribution.

Using a novel methodological approach to examine the influence of amicus briefs on the Supreme Court, Lynch (2004) conducted 70 interviews with former Supreme Court law clerks for the purpose of providing insight into how law clerks view amicus submissions.[15] Among other things, the clerks indicated that they read virtually all of the amicus briefs, that amicus briefs were most helpful in highly technical cases, and were given more attention if they presented social scientific data. The clerks also revealed that briefs filed by highly experienced advocates were considered more carefully than briefs filed by relatively inexperienced litigators and that they would overwhelmingly prefer to see more collaboration on amicus briefs and less repetition of the arguments advanced by the parties to litigation.

Conclusions

The purpose of this chapter was to shed light on public interest litigation in the U.S. Supreme Court. As the above discussion makes clear, interest group litigation is firmly ingrained in the Court's jurisprudence, particularly with regard to the amicus curiae brief. In fact, it is a rarity that a U.S. Supreme Court case is not accompanied by at least one amicus brief. In part, this is due to the Court's open-door policy toward the participation of organized interests. Inasmuch as the Court's rules present few real barriers to amicus participation, the amicus practice is allowed to proliferate. Insofar as the participation of interest groups may better enable judges to render efficacious decisions, this can be viewed as a desirable state of affairs. For example, U.S. Supreme Court Justice Stephen Breyer articulated his view of the utility of amicus briefs in no uncertain terms in noting that amicus "briefs play an important role in educating the judges on potentially relevant technical matters, helping make us not experts, but moderately educated lay persons, and that education helps to improve the quality of our decisions" (Breyer 1998, 26).[16]

In addition to providing a treatment of the amicus practice in the U.S. Supreme Court, this chapter also discussed extant research regarding the influence of organizational participation in the judicial arena. Although this literature has made a great deal of strides in enhancing our understanding of interest group litigation, there are still a variety of questions whose answers are less clear. For example, we have a very limited understanding of interest group intervention, including the success rates of applications for intervention, how intervenors shape the course of litigation, and how intervention relates to the development of legal and social change. With regard to amicus briefs, we know relatively little about the perspectives of interest groups regarding the effectiveness of amicus curiae briefs or how groups choose to target certain cases. Moreover, comparatively little is known regarding under what circumstances organizations choose to join together to form coalitions in pursuit of their interests. While quantitative studies can provide insight into these questions, so too can interviews with representatives from interest groups and in-depth analyses of particular cases or issue areas. There has likewise been limited attention to determining whether certain organizations are especially effective amici, a question with enormous normative significance since it speaks to possible biases in the administration of justice. Further, we know relatively little about how judges view the participation of outside interests.[17]

It is also important to note that, while interest group litigation is a major feature of the contemporary U.S. Supreme Court, there exist a variety of similar mechanisms for organizational input into American courts at the state and lower federal court levels, as well as in foreign and transnational judiciaries. In the U.S., organizations frequently file amicus curiae briefs in U.S. courts of appeals (Collins and Martinek 2010) and state high court litigation (Comparato 2003), recognizing the significant policy-making roles played by these institutions. Outside of the United States, through a process known as "intervention," interest groups can file analogues to the American amicus curiae brief in the Supreme Courts of Canada (Brodie 2002) and the United Kingdom (Fordham 2009). Similar mechanisms for organizational involvement exist in transnational judiciaries, including the European Court of Justice, the

Inter-American Court of Human Rights, the International Court of Justice, and the World Trade Organization (Cawley 2004; Shelton 1994). Despite these courts' openness to the participation of outside interests, relative to our knowledge of amicus participation in the U.S. Supreme Court, we know very little about group influence in these judiciaries. To be sure, the participation of organized interests is an important part of democracy, in the United States and beyond. While substantial gains have been made toward enhancing our understanding of the roles of interest groups in the courts, a host of questions still await scholarly analysis.

Notes

1 A previous version of this chapter was presented at the Symposium on the Role of Interveners in Public Interest Litigation at the David Asper Centre for Constitutional Rights, University of Toronto Faculty of Law
2 The doctrine of standing dictates that, in order to bring a suit, an individual or entity (such as an interest group) must demonstrate that an actual controversy exists that will significantly impair its interests (see, e.g., Stern *et al.* 2002, 810).
3 The doctrine of res judicata ("a matter adjudged") holds that the judgment of the court is conclusive and binding for both the litigants and intervenors in any future disputes involving the same cause of action.
4 In addition to filing amicus briefs, on rare occasions, amici may be granted the opportunity to participate in oral arguments in appellate courts. Attesting to the scarcity of this method of amicus participation, from 1953 to 1985, amici presented oral arguments to the U.S. Supreme Court in less than 6% of cases. An amicus participating in oral arguments must also file an amicus brief with the Court (Collins 2008, 38).
5 On rare occasions, the U.S. Supreme Court may invite the participation of an amicus curiae. These invitations are most commonly extended to the United States Solicitor General, the chief attorney for the executive branch in the Supreme Court, or to federal agencies, and are almost always accepted (see Nicholson and Collins 2008, 385).
6 This rule change applies to amicus briefs filed in the Court's decisions on the merits. Because the U.S. Supreme Court has discretionary jurisdiction over almost all appeals, its decision-making takes place in two stages. At the agenda-setting stage, the Court determines which cases will be fully briefed and orally argued. At the merits stage, the Court disposes of cases. Amicus curiae briefs may be filed at either stage of decision-making, although they are relatively rare at the agenda-setting stage (see Caldeira and Wright 1988).
7 In addition to these regulations, the U.S. Supreme Court has a variety of more mundane rules regarding amicus curiae participation. For example, Rule 9 specifies that amicus briefs must be filed by members of the Supreme Court Bar. Rule 33 contains the guidelines regarding the format of amicus briefs, including word limits (6,000 words at the agenda-setting stage and 9,000 words for decisions on the merits) and the color of the briefs' covers.
8 The data in Figures 12.1, 12.2, and 12.3 were obtained from Kearney and Merrill (2000) for the 1946–1995 terms; Collins (2008) for the 1996–2001 terms; and were collected by the author for the 2002–2007 terms. The U.S. Supreme Court's term opens on the first Monday in October and traditionally extends to July 1 of the following year.

9 The issue areas presented in Figure 12.2 were derived from Spaeth (2002, 2009).

10 During the time period under analysis, only 4% of the Court's docket dealt with federal taxation cases and the Roberts Court disposed of a mere three of these cases, one of which was accompanied by amicus curiae briefs: *Knight v. Commissioner of the Internal Revenue Service* (2008). As such, one should not make much of the relatively low level of amicus participation in federal taxation cases during the Roberts Court era since that Court has handled a very small number of such cases.

11 In addition to highlighting the diversity of amici, *District of Columbia v. Heller* provides a recent example of a test case. Seeking to have the Supreme Court clarify the meaning of the Second Amendment, Robert A. Levy, a senior fellow at the Cato Institute, a non-profit public policy research foundation, orchestrated and personally financed the litigation. Levy interviewed dozens of potential plaintiffs in the District of Columbia, settling on six plaintiffs from diverse backgrounds to challenge the handgun ban (see Liptak 2007).

12 More than 100 amicus briefs were filed in the University of Michigan affirmative action cases, *Gratz v. Bollinger* (2003) and *Grutter v. Bollinger* (2003), which centered on the use of racial preferences in college admissions. Seventy-eight amicus briefs were filed in *Webster v. Reproductive Health Services* (1989), a case involving restrictions on a woman's access to an abortion.

13 For a discussion of the effectiveness of coalitional amicus briefs, see Collins (2004).

14 For a concise review of the more than 40 published studies examining the influence of amicus briefs on the U.S. Supreme Court, see Collins (2008, 4–10).

15 At the U.S. Supreme Court, law clerks play a number of significant roles, including reviewing and making recommendations to the justices regarding certiorari petitions and drafting opinions (see Ward and Weiden 2006).

16 It should be noted that not all jurists subscribe to Breyer's view. In particular, Judge Richard Posner of the Seventh Circuit Court of Appeals has been rather vocal regarding his resistance to the amicus practice. For example, in *Voices for Choices v. Illinois Bell Telephone Company* (2003), Posner stated the following:

> The fact that powerful public officials or business or labor organizations support or oppose an appeal is a datum that is irrelevant to judicial decision making, except in a few cases, of which this is not one, in which the position of a nonparty has legal significance. And even in those cases the position can usually be conveyed by a letter or affidavit more concisely and authoritatively than by a brief.

(p. 545)

17 For an exception to this, see Simard (2008).

Chapter 13

Public Opinion, Religion, and Constraints on Judicial Behavior

Kevin T. McGuire

Religion is a powerful force in American politics. From the time of the American Revolution and the framing of the Constitution to the present day, religious faith has animated the public conversation about all manner of governmental policy (Lambert 2010). Nowhere have the questions about the role of religion in public life assumed greater prominence than in the debates about the meaning of the First Amendment's Establishment Clause. The constitutional prohibition against governmental endorsement of religion has influenced the consideration of any number of issues, including abortion and contraception, gay marriage, school vouchers, the teaching of evolution, and medical research on AIDS and stem cells.

Because courts are arbiters of the meaning of the First Amendment, judges are often at the center of these conflicts. Although the individual controversies vary a good deal, a basic conflict between majority rule and minority rights animates these cases. Many Americans believe that religion should be a more integral part of public life, and so elected officials often respond by enacting policies that have religious implications. Occasionally those actions may cross the boundary between incidental support for religion and impermissible endorsement of religious beliefs. When various interests believe that government has violated the constitutional separation of church and state, they turn to the courts for relief.

Resolving legal disputes is often problematic: the meaning of a law may be unclear; the intentions of lawmakers may be hard to discern; and prior rulings on an issue may be plausibly construed in different ways. Those problems are only exacerbated when those disputes involve emotionally charged issues, like religion, on which different segments of society have deep and conflicting convictions. How do judges make decisions in such an environment?

In this chapter, I analyze how such external pressures may affect judicial decision-making. Specifically, I examine cases in which judges on state supreme courts are called upon to interpret the First Amendment's Establishment Clause and to apply the precedents of the U.S. Supreme Court. To what extent do these state judges follow the legal rules put in place by their federal counterparts? The results reveal that these judges respond directly to a variety of pressures. Among other things, local political preferences, as well as the traditional values of the Christian Right in the South, shape how these judges interpret the rulings of the Supreme Court. Elected judges, in particular, find it difficult to follow the Court's commands, since doing so may harm their chances for re-election.

Religious Establishments and the U.S. Supreme Court

At least since the 1940s, cases raising issues related to government support of religion have occupied a prominent place on the docket of the U.S. Supreme Court. Many of those cases can be regarded as "accommodationist"; they have been decided in ways that favor the interests of religion. So, for example, the justices have permitted tax exemptions for tuition paid to parochial schools, public funding to provide interpreters for deaf children attending religious schools, access for religious groups to public facilities that are generally available to non-sectarian groups, and school vouchers that provide financial support for children attending religious schools.[1] More often than not, these decisions have been predicated on the idea that religious interests are not the exclusive beneficiaries. That is, while religious institutions may receive some public subsidy, they are just one of many different types of institutions that might benefit from a particular public policy.

A common thread running through a large number of these cases is that they involve challenges to fiscal policy. Taxing and spending can, and often does, provoke public discontent—"Taxes are too high," or "Government wastes too much money," are regular refrains—but because they typically turn on the mechanical details by which government raises and spends revenue, the Court's decisions in this area lack symbolic value.

By contrast, it has been the Supreme Court's "separationist" decisions— those striking down governmental support for religion—that have tapped into greater levels of civic symbolism. When the Court invalidated laws providing for prayer and moments of silence in the public schools, it trampled a venerated historical practice.[2] When it declared unconstitutional a state law requiring that Creationism be taught as an alternative theory to evolution, it defied the religious convictions of millions of Americans.[3] When it held that public schools could not permit members of the clergy to offer an invocation at graduation ceremonies nor students to lead prayer before athletic events, it barred practices common in countless schools across the country.[4]

Decisions such as these struck down culturally significant practices about which many Americans had strong feelings, and the depth of those feelings are borne out in one opinion poll after another. Virtually all Americans express a belief in God, and the vast majority say that their religious faith plays an important part in their lives. Anywhere from 30 to 40% believe that the Bible should be understood literally, and almost half of all Americans think that it is appropriate to teach the Bible in the public schools. No doubt many think that the Bible *should* be taught in public schools; roughly 50% say that religious values should receive greater emphasis in the curriculum. Another obvious way to provide that emphasis is through organized religious activity in the schools; in staggeringly high percentages—in some cases, as much as 90%—Americans favor a voluntary prayer or moment of silence during the school day.

These strong preferences notwithstanding, roughly half of all Americans perceive religion, and Christianity in particular, as under attack, and they lay much of the blame on the courthouse steps. When asked whether judges "have gone too far in taking religion out of public life," nearly 80% agree that they have.[5]

The intensity of these opinions is evident in the public reaction to the limits that courts have placed on religion in the public schools. In the 1960s, the Supreme Court's ban on school prayer provoked national criticism from civic and religious leaders, who labeled the decision "disappointing," "unfortunate," "frighten[ing]," and "positively shocking and scandalizing" (Clayton 1962). This decision gave rise to various proposals to reverse the Court by constitutional amendment, some of which gained serious ground in the 1980s under President Reagan (Goodman 1984). In 1997, after he issued an order blocking student-led prayer in the public schools, a federal judge in Alabama was condemned by the governor while students around the state launched "prayer protests." In one small town, dozens of students rallied outside their high school, chanting "We want prayer!" (Sack 1997). In recent years in the South, schools have sought to evade, or have simply defied, rulings banning prayer and the posting of the Ten Commandments in the classroom (Applebome 1994; Johnson 2000).

In light of such opinions and reactions, it is not difficult to see why judges would have a hard time coming to terms with the U.S. Supreme Court's rulings striking down such culturally significant practices. Like other lower court judges, members of state supreme courts must surely know that, when making decisions in church–state cases, they have the ability to anger large numbers of people. There are, it turns out, strong reasons why those judges would want to avoid doing so.

Political Pressures on State Supreme Courts

Individuals in public life are sensitive to religious preferences, both their own and those of the citizenry (see, for example, Cleary and Hertzke 2005; Kellstedt and Noll 1990; Oldmixon 2005; Wilcox and Robinson 2010). In a republic—a government in which decision-makers act on behalf of those whom they are chosen to represent—it should scarcely be surprising that elected officials would reflect the will of the voters as well as their own judgments about what constitutes the best course for public policy.

Judges, by contrast, are not obliged (at least not theoretically) to consider such factors when making decisions. After all, the textbook depiction of judging involves the application of the law to a specific set of facts. Absent discretion in evaluating the meaning of the law, judges simply make the decisions that the law demands, without regard to the parties or the practical implications. That a decision may adversely affect a large segment of society or prove unpopular with the electorate, under this model, is supposed to be irrelevant to the rulings that judges render.

Yet the evidence is quite strong that judges do consider such factors. Many judges seem to behave strategically, weighing how their decisions will be viewed by their colleagues, organized interests, elected officials, and elite and mass publics (see, for example, Bailey and Maltzman 2011; Baum 2006; Collins 2008; Epstein and Knight 1998; McGuire and Stimson 2004; Murphy 1964). So, decisions of both federal and state courts can depart from the personal preferences that might otherwise guide a judge's choices (Brace and Hall 1993; Hettinger, Lindquist, and Martinek 2006; Klein 2002).

For judges on state supreme courts, making decisions about religious establishments involves interpretation of the Constitution's First Amendment. Since the U.S. Supreme Court has the last word on that law's meaning, those judges are obliged to base their decisions on that court's precedents. Even with such legal guidance, making decisions about religion's permissible place under the law can be especially problematic for judges at the state level. It is one thing to believe, as an abstract matter, that a decision must be based upon the authoritative rulings of the U.S. Supreme Court. When actually doing so may provoke a backlash, it is quite another. The professional satisfaction of adhering to the doctrines of the justices—who may be located hundreds of miles away in Washington, DC—will be cold comfort to a judge who is stung by criticism when she upends a cherished local custom. What kinds of factors might affect how members of state supreme courts make decisions in cases that are of such symbolic importance?

Re-election

The vast majority of judges on state supreme courts are elected by the voters. To be sure, there is a good deal of variation in state judicial selection: some judges are elected, like other officials, in partisan contests; others run for election without regard to their partisanship; still others are retained in office by the voters only after having been selected through the combined efforts of an independent commission and a state governor; a few are chosen by their state legislature. Despite this variation, most of these judges obtain and retain their offices by appealing directly to the voters in competitive elections (Bonneau and Hall 2009). Elections, by design, create incentives for office-holders to come to terms with the preferences of the voters. Elected judges, therefore, have reason to consider what the consequences of a decision may be for their ability to retain their offices.

Many seem to do just that. Judges with prior experience in the electoral arena understand the need to maintain their standing in the eyes of the voters, and elections constrain them from straying too far from the political mainstream; in cases involving highly-charged issues, such as capital punishment, both liberal judges and judges who have previously served in some type of representational role seem to appreciate the need to hew closely to public sentiment and are more supportive of the death penalty than they might otherwise be (Brace and Hall 1993; Hall 1992).

Issues such as capital punishment and religion resonate strongly with voters. Judges on state supreme courts want to avoid being labeled as "soft on crime." So too do they wish to steer clear of being characterized as "hostile to God." Such accusations would constitute significant baggage in a re-election campaign, and therefore judges who must face the electorate have especially good reasons to find ways to avoid the Supreme Court's separationist precedents.

Regional Norms

Nowhere in the United States has religion been more integrated into public life than in the South. Religious faith has long been closely tied to that region's social structure (Harvey 2007; Mathews 1979). Even today, southerners have distinctive religious values, relative to the rest of the nation. They are more likely to read the Bible, to attribute the healing of an illness to prayer, and to believe in demonic possession. And when polled, "48 percent of southern respondents agreed with the statement, 'The U.S. is a Christian country and the government should make laws to keep it that way,' while 32 percent of non-southerners agreed" (Goldfield 2004, 11).

It is scarcely a wonder, then, that many of the U.S. Supreme Court's cases challenging religious practices have come from the South. More to the point, when the Court has struck down such religious practices as unconstitutional, the South has been more reluctant to obey the Court's rulings than other parts of the nation (Birkby 1966; McGuire 2009; Way 1968).

Southern judges—especially those who live amongst large numbers of conservative Christians—would naturally be socialized in the norm of support for religion. Imbued with these cultural values, they should find it easier to resist the Supreme Court's liberal impulses on questions of religious establishment. Even if supreme court judges in the South are not necessarily inclined to support a greater role for religion in public life, they would surely be aware of the strength of the convictions of their fellow citizens. Like most people, judges place a psychological value on their reputations (Baum 2006), and they should act in ways that enhance (or limit damage to) their standing in the community. In the 1950s, federal judges in the South who were charged with putting into effect the Supreme Court's desegregation policy learned this lesson quite painfully (Peltason 1961). Faced with similarly unpopular rulings on religious practices, the supreme court judges in southern states should look for ways to avoid following the liberal rulings of the justices in Washington.

Religious Preferences

The Christian Right has become a major force in American politics, and its strength derives in part from the large number of adherents who live throughout the United States. Its presence is particularly substantial in the South; indeed, one of the reasons why the South has had such high levels of social conservatism is its disproportionate number of Evangelical Christians (Boles 1996). In the southern states, Christian fundamentalists have adhered to a more conservative brand of Evangelical doctrine, including a strong belief in biblical literalism and a rejection of evolution (Wilcox 1991; Wilcox and Robinson 2010).

Like any organized interest, the religious right seeks public policy consistent with its preferences by advocating its agenda to relevant policy-makers. As representatives, legislators are attentive to the various predilections of their constituents (see Jewell 1985), and the religious preferences of the electorate can be especially salient to office-seekers (Yamane and Oldmixon 2006). Thus, the presence of a large number of conservative Christians, particularly in the South, should have obvious relevance for public officials who make decisions about the role of religion within society.

For their part, judges on state supreme courts who know that their jobs depend, at least to some extent, upon satisfying Evangelicals within their state have good reason to favor conservative principles when resolving questions about the meaning of the Establishment Clause. To be sure, the influence of conservative Christians may be more relevant for judges who must appeal directly to the voters for support—indeed, recent research suggests that elected judges are no less affected by the wishes of the voters than their legislative counterparts (Brace and Boyea 2008)—but regardless of how they are chosen, judges of all stripes want their decisions to be taken seriously by relevant publics. After all, judges do not possess any power beyond their ability to render opinions in individual cases. As a consequence, judges are motivated to maintain the credibility that is necessary for their decisions to be carried out by elected officials; they are dependent upon different constituencies to give force to their edicts (Murphy 1964). Members of state supreme courts who run afoul of the religious convictions of their fellow citizens face a loss of standing within their respective communities and should, therefore, take such religious preferences into account.

Citizen Ideology

Religious preferences may naturally be important when resolving cases that have religious implications. But if judges are concerned about preserving their legitimacy, religious convictions alone may not capture the full effect of local opinion. The ideological orientations of a state more generally might well be a consideration. Those orientations vary widely across the country: southern states (e.g. Alabama, Georgia, and Mississippi) and western states (e.g. Idaho, Utah, and Wyoming) have some of the most conservative populations, while liberal preferences are more common in the northeast (Massachusetts, Rhode Island, and Vermont) (Berry et al. 1998). Whatever the preferences of the state's citizenry, they establish an important context in which judges must operate.

When faced with applying a precedent of the U.S. Supreme Court, a strategic judge might ask herself, "What will be the likely popular reaction from a decision to limit the scope of religion in the public sphere?" Such a judge, if she is at all savvy, will be able to anticipate the response to a separationist decision. Some decisions, of course, are unlikely to resonate with the public at large; for example, a ruling declaring unconstitutional a prison policy that offers special privileges to religious inmates will likely be greeted with indifference by residents within a state. Other decisions that limit more traditional practices—like a decision that strikes down prayer before a football game—might generate substantial public ire. In those cases, however, the level of public anger will necessarily be tempered by how liberal or conservative the citizens of the state may be. Texans, for example, could vehemently oppose such a decision, while Vermonters might be more circumspect. Stated differently, the decision about how high to build the wall separating church and state may be driven by what local residents are willing to tolerate.

Governmental Ideology

Of course, a judge's standing in the eyes of her citizens is not the only factor that contributes to her professional legitimacy. In fact, a judge may attach even greater value to how she is evaluated by her contemporaries within state government. Judges pay a good deal of attention to how they are viewed by other elites (Baum 2006). So, the political ideology of state officials, such as legislators and the governor, might likewise constrain the choices that a judge makes. Consider a judge who, in applying the relevant precedents of the U.S. Supreme Court, decides that a Christmas display on public property is designed to promote the Christian faith, as opposed to, say, acknowledging the historical origins of a national holiday. Or consider a judge who, again taking her cues from the Supreme Court, concludes that local officials have placed a copy of the Ten Commandment in a courthouse, not as a means of highlighting an important source of Western law, but rather to promote Judeo-Christian values. The consequences in either case could be severe.

Judges whose decisions are inconsistent with the preferences of other policy-makers may find themselves subjected to withering public criticism from elected officials, legislative efforts to limit the implementation of their decisions, and even outright defiance from those charged with giving force to the court's rulings. In the extreme, decisions that fly in the face of the popularly elected officials can be the impetus for attempts to overturn the court's decisions and even oust judges from office (see, for example, Clark 2010).

Just as a strategic judge should consider citizen preferences, so too should that judge estimate how state policy-makers will respond to a decision that limits religion in the public sphere. The more conservative a state's legislative and executive officials, the greater the incentive to avoid strict adherence to the U.S. Supreme Court's policies.

Precedential Characteristics

In a number of different ways, the U.S. Supreme Court's religious precedents themselves create pressures on state supreme courts. Under the doctrine of *stare decisis*, judges are obligated to adhere to the relevant policies of higher courts. As the nation's highest court on matters of federal law, the Supreme Court authoritatively construes the meaning of the Establishment Clause, and lower courts are bound by their judgments.

For the most part, lower courts make good faith efforts to abide by those precedents. Judges in both state supreme courts and federal courts of appeals make policies that are consistent with the guidance given them by the Supreme Court in Washington (Comparato and McClurg 2007; Hoekstra 2005; Songer, Segal, and Cameron 1994). Following that guidance is not always a straightforward matter, however. There are often a good many precedents that, in one way or another, represent legal principles that a judge might consider in a case. In light of the sheer volume of prior decisions—some of which may well point a judge in different directions—how might a judge decide whether to follow a specific precedent?

One obvious way is to consider the precedent's compatibility with the particular facts of a case. If a decision of the Supreme Court speaks to the issue before a state supreme court, the judges on that court would be obliged to honor it, all else being equal. One should bear in mind, however, that the nature of a precedent's influence is not obvious. In drafting a written opinion, a judge may follow the Supreme Court's rulings because that judge has a strong sense of fidelity to the law. At the same time, judges can be selective about which prior decisions they will follow and which they will minimize or ignore (Segal and Spaeth 1999, 2002). So, a judge may simply select a precedent that provides convenient justification for a decision. A precedent in which the Supreme Court found a violation of the Establishment Clause, for instance, is obviously more pertinent to a decision limiting religion in the public sphere than in one permitting it. Stated differently, liberal precedents are appealing justifications for judges making similarly liberal policy, less desirable when rendering a conservative judgment. It may be that a judge feels constrained to follow that precedent, or it may be that the judge first made a decision and then found a precedent to support it. Whatever the motive, supreme courts should cite the precedents that point in the same ideological direction.

Quite apart from the ideological compatibility between a precedent of the Supreme Court and the decision of a lower court, a number of characteristics of the precedents themselves affect how judges evaluate and employ them. Precedents that are decided by a wide margin (say, 9–0 or 8–1) are generally afforded greater respect than those decided by a bare majority of justices. Similarly, as precedents age, they are given less consideration. The reasons are easy to understand. When making a decision in an Establishment Clause case, a state supreme court will find it hard to ignore a recent decision decided unanimously by the U.S. Supreme Court; there is little doubt about the meaning of the law. Decisions that are the product of sharp divisions on the Supreme Court suggest a higher degree of uncertainty and the possibility of the Court revisiting the issue. Likewise, older precedents, which may have been well adapted to the past, often appear less compelling in the present; they lose some of their currency, especially as their specific case facts are overtaken by more recent decisions. Consequently, both the size of the majority coalition and the age of a precedent tend to affect its subsequent treatment in other cases (Benesh and Reddick 2002; Brenner and Spaeth 1995; Hansford and Spriggs 2006).

Explaining Support for the Supreme Court's Precedents

To test the impact of local political pressures on state supreme courts, I began by collecting data on all Establishment Clause cases rendered by state supreme courts from 1960 through 2010. This exercise yielded a total 335 cases.[6] Next, I identified all cases in which the U.S. Supreme Court decided an issue related to the First Amendment's Establishment Clause from 1946 through 2010, a period covering the chief jusiceships of Fred Vinson, Earl Warren, Warren Burger, William Rehnquist, and John Roberts.[7] Across this time frame, the Supreme Court decided some 56 cases involving questions of religious establishments, 29 of which were "separationist." It is these decisions—the ones that place limits on religion in the public sphere—that typically carry symbolic weight with the mass population and are therefore the cases in which state judges are most likely to be constrained by popular preferences.

My analytic strategy is to determine when and why a state supreme court favorably cited any of the U.S. Supreme Court's "separationist" precedents. To do that, I generated a series of dyads, or matched pairs, in which each state supreme court decision was matched with each of the Supreme Court's decisions. By this means, I created multiple observations for each state court decision, one for each precedent of the Court. With these data in hand, I then collected citation information by determining, in each opinion of a state supreme court, whether that opinion cited any of the precedents of the Supreme Court. Obviously, many state court decisions predated various Supreme Court precedents—i.e., a court cannot cite a case that has yet to be decided—so I dropped all observations in which it was not possible, chronologically speaking, for the state court to cite the Supreme Court. This process resulted in 2,910 usable observations. The virtue of this approach is that it enables one to gather information relevant to both the state court decision at the time it was rendered and the available precedents of the Supreme Court that might be cited.

To assess the political pressures that are specific to each state, I assembled a variety of measures. These include whether a state employed judicial elections for choosing its judges (coded as 1; otherwise 0), whether a state was located in the South (coded as 1; otherwise 0), and the percentage of each state's religious adherents that could be classified as Evangelical Christians.[8] To assess the political preferences of a state's citizens as well as its state legislators and governor, I rely upon the composite annual estimates calculated by Berry and his colleagues (1998). Each score ranges from a minimum of 0 (i.e., most conservative) to 100 (i.e., most liberal).[9] In addition, to capture the "precedential pull" of a Supreme Court decision, I coded in each dyad whether the outcome of the state supreme court was ideologically compatible with the Supreme Court decision available for citation (i.e., 1 if both decisions were separationist or if both decisions was accommodationist; otherwise 0).[10] Finally, for each precedent of the U.S. Supreme Court, I determined the size of the majority coalition as well as the age of each precedent at the time of the state court's decision.[11]

How might one evaluate whether a state supreme court followed a particular precedent of the U.S. Supreme Court? Although scholars have approached this question in a number of different ways, I rely upon Westlaw's KeyCite information. For any given Supreme Court decision, Westlaw determines whether a case was cited in a favorable fashion in the written opinions of federal and state courts. Although Westlaw also reports the relative amount of discussion a case receives in an opinion, I employ a more basic indicator for the sake of simplicity: did the state supreme court cite the U.S. Supreme Court's precedent in a positive fashion? (coded as 1; otherwise 0).[12] This categorization has a straightforward interpretation. It is a simple assessment of adherence to the Court's separationist decisions.

By this definition, state supreme courts positively cited a Supreme Court precedent in roughly 10% of their opportunities to do so. Stated differently, in 10% of the case-to-precedent dyads did a state supreme court rely upon the available precedent to justify its decision. Whether this represents a large or small degree of reliance upon precedent cannot be known without knowing how frequently state courts cite the Court's precedents in other areas of the law. No matter what the legal issue, however, it would probably be unusual for any appellate court to cite all, or even most, available precedents. The principle of *stare decisis* requires legal principles from prior cases to be applied in cases that raise the same basic questions as those posed in the precedent-setting cases. The Supreme Court's Establishment Clause jurisprudence covers a good deal of ground—aid to religious schools, prayer in public schools, the public display of religious symbols, and so on—and thus the relevance of those decisions varies from one state court case to the next.

My principal concern is explaining *why* state supreme courts cite any given case. To do that, I construct a statistical model of the citation behavior of state supreme courts. Since a court's decision is either to cite a precedent or not to cite a precedent—speaking more methodologically, since my dependent variable is dichotomous—I employ a technique known as probit analysis. This method can estimate the independent effect of possible explanations (i.e., independent variables) on the likelihood, or probability, that a precedent is cited. Because it is a form of multiple regression, it has the virtue of determining the influence of one variable while controlling for other possible explanations that might compete for explanatory power; it can reveal what is genuinely important (from a statistical standpoint) and what is not.

The probit model explains the decision to cite a precedent as a function of the various political pressures outlined above, including whether states utilize competitive elections for judges, the regional norms of the South, and a state's religious preferences. In order to differentiate the effects of the more conservative Evangelicals in the South from those in other parts of the country, I utilize two separate variables; one measure is a state's percentage of religious adherents who are Evangelical Christians, calculated only for southern states (0 otherwise), and the other is a comparable percentage, calculated for all remaining states (0 otherwise). The model also accounts for the political preferences of a state's citizenry, the ideology of a state's elected representatives, and the characteristics of the Supreme Court's precedent. The results of this analysis are presented in Table 13.1.

In general, the model provides confirmatory evidence for several of the hypotheses. In particular, judges who seek and maintain their offices in competitive elections are significantly less likely to cite a separationist precedent of the U.S. Supreme Court than are judges chosen through some form of appointment. The negative sign on the coefficient for supreme courts with elected judges (−0.12) means that those judges have a lower probability of citing the Court's liberal doctrine relating to the Establishment Clause. As expected, judges who must appeal directly to the voters will avoid providing ammunition to their political opposition. Whatever number and type of precedents elected judges do rely upon—for example, they might cite decisions of state supreme courts or federal courts of appeals—their written opinions are less likely to be grounded in the U.S. Supreme Court's policies that limit

Table 13.1 Probit Model of Citation to Precedent of the U.S. Supreme Court

Variable	Coefficient	Standard error
Judges chosen by competitive election	–0.12*	0.05
Southern state	0.82*	0.40
Evangelicals, southern state	–2.26*	1.07
Evangelicals, non-southern state	0.003	0.309
State citizen ideology	0.58*	0.26
State government ideology	0.17	0.17
Ideological compatibility	0.61*	0.09
Size of precedent's majority coalition	0.02	0.07
Age of precedent	–0.004	0.004
Constant	–1.95	0.43

Note
N = 2,190; Wald Chi^2 = 124.59 ($p<0.001$); standard errors are clustered on U.S. Supreme Court decision; dependent variable equals 1 if the state supreme court positively cited the Supreme Court's "separationist" precedent, 0 if the supreme court did not positively cite the precedent; * indicates $p<0.05$ or better (two-tailed test).

the role of religion in society than are the opinions of judges who do not have to face a possible re-election challenge.

The concentration of Evangelical Christians in a state also reduces its supreme court's support for separationist precedent, at least for those states located in the South. Not surprisingly, the more fundamentalist strain of Evangelical Christianity that has pervaded the South creates community pressure on judges to avoid basing their decisions on the kind of policies that run counter to the beliefs of a large number of their fellow citizens. No judge, elected or appointed, wants to be subjected to public ridicule or criticism, and relying upon decisions that could be regarded as, say, favoring evolution or criticizing biblical values can provided the basis for a spirited public rebuke.

By contrast, outside of the southern states, the number of Evangelicals has no effect on the opinion writing of supreme courts. True, the coefficient of 0.003 is positive, meaning that Evangelicals outside the South increase the probability of citing the Court's precedents, but the magnitude of the effect is minuscule—and, statistically speaking, it has *no* effect.[13]

With respect to the ideological dispositions of a state's citizens and elected officials, only the political preferences of a state's mass public affects the behavior of its judges. The more liberal the citizens within a state, the less constrained its judges will be in deciding whether to base their decisions on precedents that limit the role of religion in society. Alternatively, the more conservative a state, the more reluctant its judges will be to highlight precedents that grate upon the local population's ideological sensibilities.[14] At the same time, the members of state supreme courts display no concern for the preferences of their executive and legislative counterparts. If state judges are sensitive to outside political pressures, it is the state's residents that are the source of their concern, not the governors and state legislators whom those residents elect.

It is no surprise that the ideological congruence between a state court's policy and the Supreme Court's precedent is strongly related to citation behavior. All else being equal, liberal (or, alternatively, conservative) precedents probably have more intellectual bearing upon similarly liberal (or conservative) outcomes in state supreme courts. In a state court decision permitting the public display of the Ten Commandments, for example, a Supreme Court precedent upholding the legitimate secular uses of the Commandments (*Van Orden v. Perry* 2005) obviously has greater relevance than a decision that struck down a similar display that was motivated by a religious purpose (*McCreary County v. ACLU of Kentucky* 2005). Although both precedents might well be cited, one would simply have a higher probability of justifying the decision than the other.

This relationship needs to be interpreted with caution. Although it establishes a clear and perhaps obvious link between state court decisions and Supreme Court precedents, it tells us nothing about the motives behind the citation behavior. It may be a function of judges conscientiously applying the law, or it could just as easily reflect judges picking and choosing among available precedents to provide a justification for decisions that state judges are making for reasons of their own.

Apart from ideological compatibility, the other variables measuring the characteristics of precedents are not significant predictors. In other contexts, the age of a Supreme Court precedent or the number of justices supporting the outcome may be important. Insofar as Establishment Clause cases are concerned, though, these variables provide no additional explanatory power.

One unexpected finding in these results is that judges from southern states appear to be significantly more likely, not less likely, to derive authority from the U.S. Supreme Court for their written opinions. This runs exactly contrary to the expectation that the more traditional cultural norms of the South would depress reliance upon liberal church–state precedents. One cannot interpret this finding in isolation, however, because the statistical model also accounts for regional differences in the measure of southern Evangelicals. Stated differently, to evaluate the impact of southern judges, one has to consider all variables in the analysis that measure their "southernness." As I have explained, larger numbers of the Christian Right in a southern state reduce the probability of its supreme court citing the Court's precedents, but increasing numbers of Evangelicals outside the South have no discernible impact. Taken together, these results mean that, although courts within the South evince a (surprisingly) higher level of support for the Court's precedents than judges outside the South, that support declines significantly in the South in response to the size of the Christian Right. Stated differently, outside the South, judges are not especially supportive of the Court, no matter how many Evangelicals live within their state. Southern judges, by contrast, may be more—or less—supportive than other judges, depending upon the number of conservative Christians.

A helpful way to see how these various predictors work in combination with one another is to use the statistical model to predict the likelihood of a court citing Establishment Clause precedent under different conditions. Figure 13.1, for example, graphs the impact of the Christian Right on southern judges, and it compares that impact by charting separate estimates for competitively elected and appointed judges.[15]

Two features of Figure 13.1 merit discussion. First, these data illustrate that, regardless of whether they are elected or appointed, southern judges are well aware of the concentration of Evangelicals within their respective states. A more conservative, fundamentalist strand of the Evangelical community has typified the South (Wilcox 1991), and as those religious conservatives assume greater numbers within a court's decisional environment, judges are increasingly aware of the need to avoid antagonizing this segment of the local population. In southern states with fewer Evangelicals—say, 20% of their religious adherents—courts actually have a fairly substantial likelihood of citing the liberal precedents of the Supreme Court, a probability of roughly 0.25. (The comparable probability for non-southern states, not shown in Figure 13.1, is only 0.10.)[16] That probability quickly declines, however, as a state becomes more religiously homogeneous.

Second, Figure 13.1 illustrates that religious pressures in the South are greater for elected than for non-elected judges. Regardless of the number of Evangelicals within their states, judges who must regularly stand for re-election—and therefore face a possible challenge—are more aware of the consequences of making church–state decisions that alienate voters. Of course, the differences between elected and appointed judges are not dramatic, and indeed the gap between them narrows with increases in the level of Evangelicals.

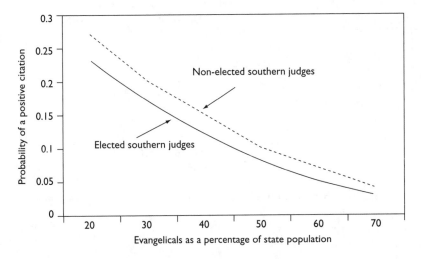

Figure 13.1 Estimated impact of Evangelicals on southern courts.

A more direct illustration of the importance of the voters can be found in Figure 13.2. These data represent the impact of the political ideology of a state's citizenry on a state court's reliance upon the Supreme Court's precedent.[17] As in Figure 13.1, these data distinguish between elected and appointed judges. These probabilities tell a similar tale; elected judges are consistently more reticent about citing liberal church–state precedent, regardless of the preferences of the voting population. Concerned about the need to preserve political capital, elected judges in highly conservative states are loathe to base their written opinions on what many voters will inevitably regard as attacks on their traditional convictions, propagated by the justices in Washington. As the state's demographic profile changes from red to blue, however, judges have less to fear from invoking the Supreme Court to justify their case outcomes. Again, judges who do not face the specter of a re-election challenge are generally more disposed to invoke the liberal orthodoxy of the Court, a tendency that is more pronounced for judges in liberal states. As was the case with Figure 13.1, however, one should not make too much of these differences; the actual probabilities are fairly similar. The general picture that emerges from both figures is that judges on state supreme courts are concerned about exposing themselves to criticism and thus are strategic in the formulation of their written opinions—especially if that criticism might come in the context of a re-election campaign.[18]

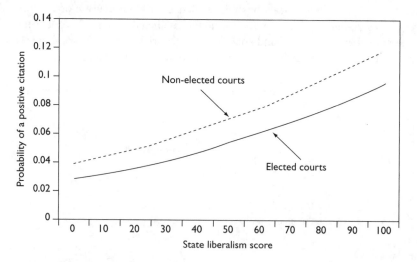

Figure 13.2 Estimated impact of state ideology on elected and non-elected courts.

Conclusion

Like all policy-makers, judges want their decisions to be respected and valued. Indeed, their effectiveness in office depends upon their legitimacy. Consumers of judicial policies—those who must abide by them, those who must put them into effect, and so on—will adhere to those policies only to the extent that they are held in sufficiently high regard. Courts, therefore, are not isolated from community pressures. Indeed, the separation of powers adopted by both the national and state governments ensures that courts are inherently weak institutions, wholly dependent upon other actors to put their decisions into effect. Of necessity, state judges (especially those who must calculate how to remain in office) must approach the business of resolving disputes with a strategic eye.

Church–state litigation provides an interesting context in which to analyze those strategic calculations. The nature of decision-making by appellate courts demands that judges justify their decisions through written opinions that are based upon appropriate legal authority, not the least of which are the precedents of a higher court. In interpreting the First Amendment's Establishment Clause, therefore, state supreme courts are obliged to consider and, where appropriate, to follow the rulings of the United States Supreme Court. Because the craft of opinion writing is not a mechanical exercise—because the meaning and correct application of precedents is something over which judges may reasonably differ—judges enjoy a good deal of discretion in deciding how best to frame and formulate their policies.

Faced with Supreme Court decisions that cut against the grain of the values of many Americans, judges on state supreme courts must estimate the costs of using those decisions to substantiate the choices that they make. For many judges, those costs are substantial. Regional variation in public opinion, different religious convictions, and the ideological patterns that map across state lines all combine, in one way or another, to affect how judges determine whether to invoke those precedents to support their own decisions. For some judges, the prospect of competitive elections only magnifies such concerns.

There are limits, of course, to what can be inferred from these data. The analysis presented in this chapter is restricted to a particularly salient area of the law, one which matters a great deal to many Americans. There is no reason to think, therefore, that the effects documented here would extend more generally to other areas of policy-making by state courts. If one were to conduct a similar analysis of cases involving questions of insurance or labor law, tax policy, or banking regulation, for example, community preferences would probably have little or no impact. (At the same time, the ideological orientations of other elected officials might, unlike here, turn out to be quite important.)

Still, these results underscore the need to consider the context in which judges make decisions. Judges must reflect on the consequences of their choices, and in church–state cases—where decisions can challenge local culture and inflame passionate public reaction—they must think with particular care about how their policies will be received by different segments of society. By anticipating those reactions and by making strategic adjustments to their decisions, they promote both electoral security and institutional legitimacy.

Notes

1 See, respectively, *Mueller v. Allen* (1983), *Zobrest v. Catalina Foothills School District* (1993), *Good News Club v. Milford* (2001), and *Zelman v. Simmons-Harris* (2002).
2 *Engel v. Vitale* (1962); *Wallace v. Jaffree* (1985).
3 *Edwards v. Aguillard* (1987).
4 *Lee v. Weisman* (1992); *Santa Fe Independent School District v. Doe* (2000).
5 The results of the polls summarized here may be found at www.pollingreport.com/religion.htm.
6 These cases were identified by a Westlaw search, searching the headnotes—or summaries—of opinions for terms such as "Establishment Clause," "religious establishment," "religion," "First Amendment," and so on. This process was somewhat over-inclusive, in that upon closer inspection I determined that issues relating to the Establishment Clause were not actually addressed in a good many cases. Those cases were excluded from the analysis.
7 These data are available from The Supreme Court Database, which is housed at http://scdb.wustl.edu/.
8 Although the method of selection is usually constant across all cases, a few states altered their methods during the time period covered. So, each observation reflects the method at the time of the decision. These data were taken from the American Judicature Society's website, "Judicial Selection in the States (www.judicialselection.us/). Although it can be defined in different ways, the South is coded here, following the conventions of Brewer and Stonecash (2009), as the states of the Confederacy plus Kentucky (i.e., Alabama, Arkansas, Florida, Georgia, Kentucky, Louisiana, Mississippi, North Carolina, South Carolina, Tennessee, Texas, and Virginia). The religious preferences of the states are taken from the various surveys housed at The Association of Religion Data Archives (www.thearda.com), and I rely upon their classification of Evangelical faiths. Most of these surveys have been conducted decennially by the Glenmary Research Center and titled *Churches and Church Membership in the United States*. So, for each state supreme court decision, I code the percentage of Evangelicals as the percentage reported in the survey closest to the date of the supreme court's decision.
9 These scores, which have been updated to cover the years 1960 through 2008, may be accessed at Professor Richard C. Fording's website at www.uky.edu/~rford/stateideology.html.
10 The Supreme Court Database codes decisions as either liberal (i.e., separationist) or conservative (i.e., accommodationist). Using that database's same coding rules, I classified the outcomes of the state court cases.
11 The number of justices in the majority was derived from the Supreme Court Database, and the age of the precedent was calculated by subtracting the year of the state supreme court's decision (as reported in Westlaw) from the year in which, again according to the Supreme Court Database, the precedent was decided.
12 In the analysis reported here, I could substitute Westlaw's ranking of positive analysis—where 0 indicates that the case receives no positive treatment; 1 means that

the opinion "[c]ontains a brief reference to the cited case"; 2 indicates that it "[i]ncludes some discussion of the cited case, usually less than a paragraph; 3 means that the opinion "[c]ontains a substantial discussion of the cited case, usually more than a paragraph"; and 4 denotes that it "[c]ontains an extended discussion of the cited case, usually more than a printed page of text" (see http://west. thomson.com/westlaw/advantage/keycite/symbols/default.aspx)—and the results would look substantially the same. Of course, discussion of a case may be negative, but since my interest is in whether state courts follow the Supreme Court's precedent, I examine the positive assessment.

13 This is because the coefficient is not statistically significant. Coefficients that are not significantly related to the dependent variable cannot be differentiated from zero, and thus their "effects" can be ignored.

14 To a certain extent, of course, the preferences of a state's population will be reflected in the political preferences of its judges; regardless of the selection mechanism, liberal states are apt to choose liberal judges, just as conservative states will be likely to elevate conservatives to the bench. A measure to control for the ideology of a state's supreme court (Brace, Langer, and Hall 2000), however, is not significant when included in this model, nor does it alter the results and interpretations presented here.

15 For these other estimates, all other variables were set to their median values.

16 Perhaps when southern supreme courts make liberal decisions on church–state issues, they engage in "buck-passing," going out of their way to cite the Supreme Court and, by implication, to attribute blame to the justices in Washington. At some point, though, the concentration of the Christian right would become sufficiently large that the cost of perturbing such a significant segment of the community outweighed the strategic benefits.

17 As in Figure 13.1, these estimates are calculated by setting other predictors to their median values.

18 It is worth noting that many judges who are appointed must still be re-elected in retention elections. In retention elections, however, judges do not face an opposing candidate—voters decide only whether a judge will be permitted to remain in office—and judges are retained at very high rates (Hall 2001).

Part V

Implementation and Impact

Chapter 14

Lower Court Compliance with Precedent

Sara C. Benesh and Wendy L. Martinek

Americans appear to be complacent in the belief that the courts—and the U.S. Supreme Court in particular—constitute a powerful branch of government. We rarely consider the degree to which the courts actually possess power, and the public continues to come to the courts with its problems assuming that an effective judicial remedy will be forthcoming (Scheingold 2004). Indeed, some even lament the "excessive power" that this unelected branch wields in society (Ely 1980). However, as Hamilton famously put it, the Court has "no influence over either the sword or the purse ... It may truly be said to have neither force nor will, but merely judgment" (Hamilton). Though there is a Supreme Court police force, the mission of that force is to protect the justices, the Court, and visitors to the Court, not to compel other actors to follow the will of the Court.[1] In other words, the Court makes decisions but those decisions are not self-executing; the Court's rulings are given effect only through the actions of others, and the reaction of those other actors is not always perfectly in concert with the Court's rulings (Baum 2002). This is reflected in the famous quote attributed to President Andrew Jackson regarding a decision of the Court under Chief Justice Marshall: "John Marshall has made his decision, now let him enforce it!" The historical evidence indicates that Jackson made no such statement (Boller and George 1989, 53). However, it persists in the political folklore, certainly in part because it reflects the Court's predicament when it comes to enforcement of its decisions (if not the accuracy of the president's words). How, then, in the absence of the usual carrots and sticks relied upon to induce others to "fall in line," has the Supreme Court become such a significant player in American politics? How does it have impact in American society?

Our focus in this chapter is on one key dimension of the Court's power: its ability to induce lower courts to abide by its precedents, hence increasing its influence and impact. As a preliminary matter, we note that the question of what *impact* the Supreme Court has is certainly much broader than the extent to which the nation's high court can command lower court *compliance*. Understanding the impact of the Court requires understanding the ability of the Court to exert influence in society *writ large*.[2] Accordingly, alternative foci for the study of the Court's impact include, for example, the Court's influence on congressional behavior (Martin 2001), the development and administration of higher education admissions policies (Taylor, Haynie, and Sill 2008), or the presence of small-town displays of religious symbols in late December (Segal, Spaeth, and Benesh 2005, 368).[3] Scholars vigorously debate whether the Court can indeed exert a broad impact in society given its enforcement challenges (Hall 2011; Rosenberg 2008; cf. McCann 1994), and some even suggest that the Court, when it makes controversial decisions in a given issue area, can make matters worse by creating a backlash (Keck 2009). Nonetheless, lower court compliance certainly affects Supreme Court impact—without compliance by lower courts and other actors affected by Supreme Court decisions and without their responsiveness to changes in Supreme Court doctrine, the Court can have no impact.[4] Thus, the appeal of focusing on lower court compliance lies in the fact that the lower courts constitute "the first link in the chain of events that gives a judicial decision its impact" (Canon and Johnson 1999, 29).

We begin our consideration of compliance by examining the leading models of lower court compliance. We then discuss the legitimacy of the Supreme Court and its power as derived from that support, considering the extent to which the mere moral force of Supreme Court authority might compel compliance with its rulings by the lower state and federal courts, its most important of agents. Our inquiry is ultimately directed at the compelling question of whether it is inevitable that the lower courts will faithfully implement the precedents of the Supreme Court.

Compliance with the Supreme Court

Scholars studying the Supreme Court originally paid little heed to how the Court's rulings were treated by lower courts. Lower court compliance was simply taken as a given. As students of the Court became aware that compliance was not, in fact, a given (perhaps prompted by the Court's efforts to desegregate public schools), they devoted increasingly more time and attention to understanding whether and how lower courts responded to the rulings of the nation's highest court. Not surprisingly, then, early analyses of lower court compliance centered on evident noncompliance on the part of lower courts with Supreme Court precedents in controversial areas of the law, such as civil rights and liberties (see, for example, Murphy 1959; Peltason 1961). In contrast, most contemporary research on compliance has found that lower courts (as well as other actors, for that matter) generally comply with Supreme Court rulings across a variety of issue areas and under a variety of circumstances (see, for example, Benesh and Reddick 2002; Luse et al. 2009; Songer and Sheehan 1990). Of course, a lower court need not completely or overtly thwart Supreme Court precedent in order to provide a less-than-faithful application of it. Indeed, the lower courts have several options available to them should they find themselves faced with a Supreme Court precedent they find unappealing. They can interpret the decision narrowly, limiting the application of the precedent based on very specific factual differences between the precedential case and the case to which the precedent ostensibly applies (Canon and Johnson 1999, 92–114). They may cite their own opinions in lieu of citing the "offending" precedent (Manwaring 1968).[5] They may attempt to distinguish their case from the one for which Supreme Court precedent is available (Caminker 1994). They may dispose of the case on procedural grounds (e.g., finding that the parties do not have standing to bring suit) (Canon and Johnson 1999, 92–114). They may criticize the Supreme Court while following it (Tarr 1977). Or, the lower courts may simply ignore the existence of the offending precedent (Reddick and Benesh 2000).

Given the wealth of tools at the disposal of lower courts to avoid adherence to Supreme Court precedents, the widespread compliance that has been documented seems like an enigma. To unravel that puzzle, scholars have employed a variety of frameworks for understanding the relationship between the Supreme Court and the lower courts and the dynamics of compliance. Communications theory, for example, draws attention to the clarity of the transmission of precedent from superior to inferior courts (Canon 1999, 442–443). An obvious prerequisite for compliance in that theory is that those responsible for complying are aware of the precedents with which they are to comply. Awareness of a decision, however, is unlikely to be problematic for lower court judges, as litigants (through their attorneys) and law clerks will likely call all relevant cases to the judges' attention. Judges also have enhanced abilities to conduct their own online searches for case law, making it quite unlikely that a judge will not know about an applicable precedent (Cross et al. 2010). Indeed, given modern technology, lower courts probably hear of Supreme Court decisions immediately, long before they consider cases to which they may apply.

Alternatively, organizational theories conceptualize the relationship between the Supreme Court and lower courts as an organization, applying theories of organizational behavior borrowed from the public administration literature. A key concept in this line of research is the notion of decisional (or organizational) inertia, which is the tendency of organizational routines and standard operating procedures to be sticky; i.e., slow to change (Baum 1976). In this framework, precedents from the Supreme Court can be seen as disruptive forces, requiring lower courts to change their own standard operating procedures. How compliant lower courts are, then, is a function of how different the edicts contained in new Supreme Court precedents are from those embedded in old Supreme Court precedents or the precedent of the lower court itself. The common law nature of the American legal system,[6] however, means that courts (both inferior and superior) are always engaged in some level of adjustment in their decisions over time. Hence, a new precedent may well be adopted far more easily than a new regulation may be by an administrative agency.

Though theoretical frameworks drawn from communications theory and organizational behavior have appealing aspects to them, they do not explicitly take into account the hierarchical nature of the judiciary. The Supreme Court is the institution at the apex of the federal judiciary and the only court created explicitly by the Constitution.[7] The most compelling frameworks for understanding compliance, then, pay particular attention to this hierarchy of justice.[8] Principal–agent theory and team theory take this hierarchical perspective into account, and are the theories most employed in recent research on lower court compliance with Supreme Court precedent. We discuss each in turn.

Principal–Agent Theory

Principal–agent theory originated as a way of understanding the relationship between buyers and sellers in economic transactions (see, for example, Ross 1973). Buyers are the principals who wish to obtain the highest quality goods or services at the lowest possible cost. Sellers, on the other hand, wish to maximize profits. Profit maximization may take the form of selling more goods or services than the principal needs or maximizing prices while minimizing quality. Note that the principals and agents have different goals and that these goals may, in fact, conflict with one another. To illustrate this theory, consider the relationship between an individual in the market for a used car (a principal) and an individual who sells used cars (an agent). The buyer wants to obtain the best car possible for the lowest price possible, while the seller wants to obtain the biggest profit possible from the sale. The problem for the buyer is that she does not have access to the same information about the used cars for sale that the seller does. Given the differences in goals between the buyer and the seller—the buyer wants to get the best deal while the seller wants to make the most profit—that difference in information gives an advantage to the seller. The seller (the agent), after all, knows about the histories of the cars on sale while the buyer (the principal) does not. In short, there is an information asymmetry that benefits the seller.

This concept of information asymmetry led political scientists to adopt the principal–agent framework to illuminate the relationship between bureaucracies and the legislatures that create and maintain them (Mitnick 1975). Legislators delegate authority to bureaucrats to implement policies, but bureaucratic interests may diverge from those of the legislators because they develop independent expertise about policy implementation or attract constituencies with preferences that diverge from those of the legislators (Waterman and Meier 1998, 176). This permits bureaucratic agents to shirk, that is, to direct their efforts at goals that differ from those of their legislative principals (Brehm and Gates 1997, 21). Principals can reduce shirking by monitoring the behavior of their agents, but monitoring is costly in terms of time and energy. And, if taken to an extreme, monitoring can be costly enough to obviate any benefit from delegation; if a principal must monitor each and every action of an agent, then the principal might as well do the tasks herself! The first scholars to explicitly apply the principal–agent framework to the study of the judicial hierarchy were Songer, Segal, and Cameron (1994) but it has been used by numerous scholars since then (see, for example, Benesh 2002; Benesh and Martinek 2002; Brent 2003; Westerland *et al.* 2010). As Brent (2003) notes:

> That judicial scholars should be attracted to principal–agent theory is not surprising, because it accurately describes many of the essential features of the American judiciary. The judiciary is a hierarchy in which the subordinate actors (agents) are charged with the responsibility of implementing policy devised by actors at higher levels (principals). Judicial principals engage in only sporadic, inconsistent oversight of their agents ..., permitting those agents to pursue their own goals when those goals conflict with those of the principal.
>
> (p. 560)

The Supreme Court—by both practice and design—is not intended to "right every wrong" or adjudicate every dispute. It explicitly disavows the role of error corrector. Indeed, it hears few cases each year and exercises virtually unrestricted discretion in determining which, of the thousands of appeals it receives, to hear (Pacelle 1995; H.W. Perry 1991). As a consequence, the Court has few opportunities to monitor the thousands of cases decided by the lower federal courts and state courts of last resort,[9] and it embraces even fewer of the opportunities it does have. In short, lower courts may have a good deal of latitude to shirk in the application of Supreme Court precedents, should they choose to do so.[10]

Of course, a principal's need to minimize shirking by monitoring agents is lessened the more information the principal has when it comes to picking agents. This leads to the concept of adverse selection, which refers to the conditions under which a principal selects the agent. Ideally, a principal should have complete information about the skills, abilities, and preferences of the agent(s) it is selecting. This would permit the principal to select the agent that is least likely to act contrary to the principal's interests (i.e., the lower court judges most likely to faithfully apply Supreme Court precedents, in the context of the judiciary). Here, the utility of the principal–agent framework for understanding superior–inferior court interactions is compromised in that the Supreme Court has nothing to do with the selection of its agents (the lower courts) at either the state or the federal level. Like their superiors on the Supreme Court, lower federal court judges undergo selection via a constitutionally-mandated process in which the president makes a nomination that must be confirmed by the Senate.[11] With regard to state court judges, the majority of such judges are elected by state or sub-state electorates, and those that do come to the state bench via a non-elective mechanism are still in no way beholden to the members of the Supreme Court for their appointments (see American Judicature Society 2011). In short, the Supreme Court faces an extreme adverse selection problem: it must rely on agents chosen for it by others, and, additionally, it is powerless to remove wayward agents from office.

The fit of the judicial hierarchy to the principal–agent framework, while sometimes argued to be uncomfortable, nonetheless is of considerable value for understanding lower court compliance given the explicit hierarchical setup of the judiciary. The Supreme Court *is* "the boss" of the lower courts,[12] and it is an authoritative one at that. Accordingly, lower court judges should, for the most part, heed the policy prescriptions of the Supreme Court precisely because the Supreme Court is their superior. From this perspective, the judiciary is much like an administrative agency, with the lower courts acting as bureaucrats, implementing to the best of their ability the policy enactments of the Supreme Court, and using their expertise to fill in gaps where they arise.

Team Theory

An alternative to principal–agent theory is *team theory*. Like principal–agent theory, team theory has its origins in economics (Marschak and Radner 1972). Specifically, team theory was advanced as a model of decision-making in organizations. The basic logic of the team model is that different members of a team (an organization) possess different information relevant to the achievement of the team's goals and, further, that different team members control different decisions of the organization. In short, both information and decision-making authority are decentralized. "But all team-theoretic models share one key feature: they ignore the interests of the team members—there is no shirking, free-riding, lying, lobbying or strategizing of any kind" (Gibbons 2003, 761). The interests of team members can be ignored because they are assumed to be identical (i.e., each member of the team desires the same thing—namely, the success of the organization). To illustrate the team theory framework, consider a firm with a central production manager and a set of unit managers. The central production manager controls the allocation of resources among the units, deciding, for example, how much manpower is allocated to each unit. Each unit manager, however, makes decisions regarding how the manpower allocated to his unit will be deployed. Further, each unit manager has specialized knowledge about his own particular unit and what is necessary for it to function best. That is, both decision-making authority (except for the resource allocation made by the central manager) and information are spread throughout the organization. All of the managers—including the central production manager—want the company to maximize profits across all units since performance bonuses at the firm are determined by overall company performance. That is, each manager gets the same share of the available bonus money and the available bonus money is a straight-forward function of the company's total profits. In effect, all of the managers have an incentive to share information and take cues from one another to enhance the likelihood of each unit manager making the decisions for his unit that will reap the biggest profit for the company (and, hence, the biggest bonuses for the managers).

Various scholars—primarily, but not exclusively, legal scholars situated in law schools—imported team theory to describe and explain lower court compliance (Cross 2005; Kornhauser 1995; Staudt 2004). The basic assumption of the team model—the assumption of a shared organizational goal—is useful for thinking about the fidelity of lower courts to higher court rulings because it implies that adherence to precedent is simply a matter of enhancing the likelihood of correctly deciding a case. Judges at higher levels of the judicial hierarchy presumably have greater levels of expertise to select good vehicles for articulating guiding precedents and, given the luxury of discretionary dockets, more time and judicial energy to craft such precedents (Kornhauser 1995; Westerland et al. 2006). This allows lower court judges—with presumably less expertise and less time—to use precedents as a short cut that will permit them, on average, to render more "correct" rulings simply by relying on the relevant precedent in each case. Hence, while lower court judges comply with Supreme Court precedent because the Supreme Court is their superior under the principal–agent framework, lower court judges comply with Supreme Court precedent because that precedent is most likely to be the "correct" legal interpretation under the team theory framework. Of course, this perspective is sometimes criticized due to its lack of regard for the policy preferences of the lower court judges themselves, which have been shown to be influential on their decision-making.[13]

The Mechanism of Compliance

In both of the above accounts of how compliance works, there are a number of potential mechanisms through which the Supreme Court can gain compliance. In the framework of team theory, compliance is a natural consequence of clear precedents, as the only obstacles to compliance are a lack of understanding on the part of the lower courts as to the requirements of precedent.[14] The key mechanism, then, is well-articulated and clearly communicated rules of law embedded in Supreme Court opinions, applied perfectly by lower courts desiring only to "get it right."

In the principal–agent model, the Supreme Court can obtain compliance via monitoring, e.g., the lower courts will comply with the Supreme Court in order to avoid review and reversal. Songer and his colleagues examined this possibility in the context of compliance by the U.S. courts of appeals and found it to be an important consideration for lower courts (Songer, Segal, and

Cameron 1994). Indeed, these scholars found evidence that litigants make rational calculations as to the likelihood of Supreme Court review when they make decisions regarding appeals, and so the lower courts have an incentive to consider the Supreme Court's precedents to lessen the likelihood of appeal.[15] The essential mechanism, then, would appear to be rational litigants who are willing to appeal cases to call to the Court's attention deviant behavior by the lower courts (coupled with lower courts that wish to avoid reversal).[16]

Other scholars argue that, to the contrary, the lower courts do not fear reversal—or, at least, not sufficiently to induce compliance against their will (Klein and Hume 2003). While it may be that lower court judges worry about the effects of reversal on their personal reputations or aspirations for elevation to a higher bench (Caminker 1994), or that they are concerned about having policies with which they disagree etched into the law of the land by the Supreme Court (McNollgast 1994–1995), reversal is such a rare event that it is difficult to see it as a threat with the teeth to induce compliance (Benesh 2002). The Supreme Court hears so few cases—a scant 100 cases per term in recent years—in comparison to the volume of cases heard in the U.S. courts of appeals and state courts of last resort that a lower court judge can assume that the likelihood of any particular decision being reviewed is minimal at best (Bowie and Songer 2009).[17] Empirically speaking, Klein and Hume demonstrate that, in the cases most likely to attract the Supreme Court's attention, the circuit courts[18] are no more likely to decide search and seizure questions as the Supreme Court would than they are in the cases least likely to attract the Court's attention; under both situations, circuit courts are very likely to comply.[19]

An alternative mechanism for inducing compliance—whether from the perspective of principal–agent theory or team theory—is the Court's legitimacy. The Court's power, as Hamilton suggests, rests in its authority to make decisions. Its legitimacy, as most call it, also has the potential to be *the* driving force in compliance by lower courts.[20]

The Court is widely considered to be the most popular branch of American government. Indeed, Gibson and Caldeira (2011) go so far as to use the word "love" to label the high regard in which the public holds the Court. The potential reasons for the Court's legitimacy advantage over other institutions of government are many. Hibbing and Theiss-Morse (2002) suggest that the Court is more highly regarded due to its processes: it does not engage in open political debate the way that Congress does.[21] Casey (1974) offers "myth" as the reason for the Court's strong performance on measures of public approval and support: people approve of the Court because they know little about it, and the information they do have is couched in its many symbols. As Perry (1999) documents, the Court is awash with symbols—from the black robes to the temple-like architecture—that contribute to the myth of the Court. Gibson and Caldeira (2009c) agree that symbols are powerful, but they also find knowledge of the Court to be positively related to how individuals view the legitimacy of the Court. Further, the Court is seen as the embodiment of the rule of law, and Americans highly value the rule of law (Gibson 2007). Other scholars detail the ways in which the courts, because they are held in such high esteem, are not only legitimate policy-makers, but also make policy more legitimate by ruling on it (Clawson, Kegler, and Walternburg 2001; Stoutenborough, Haider-Markel, and Allen 2006).[22]

The justices themselves note that both their association with "the law" and the fact that they are "above politics" are important to maintaining the Court's legitimacy (Clark 2010). Justices also frequently warn their colleagues (presumably to influence their choices) of the damaging consequences certain courses of action can have upon the Court's legitimacy (Farganis 2009). Recall, for example, Justice Stevens' dissent in *Bush v. Gore* (2000):

> The endorsement of that position [that is, the position articulated in the opinion of the Court] by the majority of this Court can only lend credence to the most cynical appraisal of the work of judges throughout the land. It is confidence in the men and women who administer the judicial system that is the true backbone of the rule of law. Time will one day heal the wound to that confidence that will be inflicted by today's decision. One thing, however, is certain. Although we may never know with complete certainty the identity of the winner of this year's Presidential election, the identity of the loser is perfectly clear. It is the Nation's confidence in the judge as an impartial guardian of the rule of law.
>
> (pp. 128–129)

In fact, warnings about legitimacy by the justices have risen dramatically in recent years, meaning that it is not only political commentators and law professors who suggest that some of the decisions made by the Court may well influence perceptions of the authority of the Court. Indeed, the justices themselves are sensitive to (and work to protect) the Court's legitimacy (Farganis 2009).

Members of the Court care about legitimacy because it is a valuable resource. Clark (2010) argues that inter-branch relations are influenced by the amount of legitimacy the Court possesses at any given time, as well. To wit, Congress passes "court-curbing" legislation when the Court's legitimacy is comparatively low, which acts as a signal to the Court. The Court, in turn, responds to Congress' message and backs down from the legal policy that agitates Congress. Clark agrees that the Court is aware of its legitimacy, but argues that Congress is more so—by virtue of the close relationship between Congress and the public via the electoral connection—and so the Court uses congressional action against it as a signal that, should it continue on its course, it risks losing its legitimacy—something about which the Court cares deeply. Hence, legitimacy, while seemingly an abstract concept, is quite real and has the potential to constrain very powerful institutional actors.

We argue that the Court's legitimacy is powerful enough to serve as another, perhaps the key, mechanism for inducing compliance. The Court is an extremely authoritative policy-maker, especially among judges of the lower courts, who are socialized—via their education at our nation's leading law schools and via their experience on the bench—into a legal culture that regards Supreme Court decisions as the source of the true meaning of the Constitution and precedent to require deference. Comparing monitoring and legitimacy as competing mechanisms of compliance under the principal-agent framework, Benesh argues, "The impetus to comply comes from what the Supreme Court *is* rather than what it *does*" (Benesh 2002; emphasis in original). This notion is corroborated by interviews with courts of appeals judges, who, in noting their constitutional position (as judges on "such inferior courts," as they are explicitly called in the language of the Constitution) characterize compliance with Supreme Court decisions as a given; they see it as their role to implement higher court precedents.[23] Indeed, this legitimacy (or acceptance of the Supreme Court as the arbiter of the Constitution) may be the mechanism for compliance in both the team model, in which getting it "right" is the operative value (Klein and Hume 2003),[24] and in the principal-agent model, as lower court judges defer to their authoritative boss. In the team model, the higher court's precedent is the best evidence of the correct legal ruling; in the principal–agent model, that precedent is a command as to how the lower court ought to make its decision in an applicable case.

Whatever the mechanism, even somewhat casual orders from the Supreme Court are considered carefully by the courts of appeals (Benesh *et al.* 2007),[25] and lower court judges, when interviewed, note quite simply that complying with the Supreme Court is their job (Baum 1978; Benesh 2008). Although one might expect different levels of courts to comply to a greater or lesser extent with Supreme Court decisions—given their differential distance from the Supreme Court, levels of professionalism, and positions in the system—even trial courts and state courts seemingly comply (Benesh and Martinek 2009; Stidham and Carp 1982). In short, nearly all of the scholarly evidence shows that courts are compliant with Supreme Court precedent. We spend some time in the next section discussing how scholars have come to this conclusion. More specifically, we examine the various ways one might measure compliance.

Measuring Compliance

How can a social scientist determine whether a given lower court decision is compliant with Supreme Court precedent? This is an admittedly difficult question given that the Court has many precedents, often on both sides of an issue, and that its precedents are not necessarily designed to completely structure decision-making by the lower courts under every circumstance. Indeed, the Supreme Court sometimes muddles the issues because the nine justices themselves cannot agree over every aspect of the decision. Recent research shows that concurring opinions—that is, opinions written by those justices who agree with the disposition of the case (reverse or affirm) but disagree over the reason for that decision—can influence the likelihood of compliance by the lower courts.[26] And, the Court cannot possibly anticipate every factual situation that may arise.

In addition, the lower courts operate under different constraints than does the Supreme Court, and so comparing trends in decision outcomes between the Supreme Court and the lower courts—such as percentage of cases decided liberally—is not necessarily a relevant measure of compliance, given that the lower courts may simply be deciding different cases. For example, because the U.S. courts of appeals have little control over their dockets, they hear a good many of less-than-compelling appeals:

> The common law principle that every litigant should have the opportunity for at least one review means that many of the cases that come before the U.S. Courts of Appeals, although no doubt terribly important to the litigants in the case, are legally frivolous in the sense of raising no important issues of law, a marked difference from the situation at the U.S. Supreme Court.
>
> (Martinek 2009)

When it comes to the criminally accused or convicted, the stakes are sufficiently high for the defendant that most avail themselves of the right to an appeal. But, the vast majority of those appeals are, as a result, simply meritless. Because scholars generally consider decisions as being "conservative" if a court decides against the criminal defendant (Segal and Spaeth 2002; Songer, Sheehan, and Haire 2000), the circuits make far more conservative decisions, regardless of their own ideological preferences, than does the Supreme Court. If the Supreme Court is particularly liberal in its criminal cases, then the lower courts will look noncompliant without necessarily being so (Eisenberg, Miller, and Perino 2009).

One scholar offers a useful definition from which we may derive measures of compliance: Compliance entails the "proper application of standards enunciated by the Supreme Court in deciding all cases raising similar or related questions," while noncompliance "involves a failure to apply—or properly apply—those standards" (Tarr 1977, 35). How, then, have scholars implemented that definition, or, in social-science speak, how have they operationalized compliance? Some earlier studies, as mentioned previously, merely sought to discern whether liberal Supreme Court rulings were followed in time by liberal lower court rulings. More recently, scholars have found what appears to be a better tool to measure compliance in the legal research resource known as *Shepard's Supreme Court Citations*.

Shepard's Supreme Court Citations is a commercial service offered by Lex-isNexis and is widely used in the legal community. The attorney coders who work for *Shepard's* read every Supreme Court and lower court decision and compile a list of all the cases cited by those opinions, classifying them into one of several categories as to the legal treatment of the cited case.[27] Some decisions merely cite another case and are not classified as having legally treated the cited case. It is likely that these citations are more offhand, likely in a string of citations, and hence are not considered a substantive treatment of the cited case. Other cases are categorized as having "followed" the cited case. These are cases in which the second court considers the precedent and employs its logic, applying it faithfully to the facts of its case. Still others are categorized as "criticizing" the cited case, in that they express some disagreement with the resolution of and opinion in the cited case. Scholars have placed each of the nine ways *Shepard's* codes cases into "positive" and "negative" categories.[28] The positive group includes "followed," as discussed above. Negative treatments include "overruled," "questioned," "limited," and the above-mentioned "criticized." Hence, scholars can identify each lower court opinion that has been rendered after a Supreme Court decision, and then use the *Shepard's* code as a way to operationalize compliance; e.g., if the lower court "followed" the Supreme Court decision, it has properly applied the "standards enunciated by the Supreme Court" in a case "raising similar or related questions" (Tarr 1977, 35).

Several authors have used this approach. Benesh and Reddick (2002), for example, consider how long it takes a circuit court to start complying with a new Supreme Court precedent that overrules a previous Supreme Court decision. Using *Shepard's*, supplemented with additional independent coding, the authors ascertain whether, in its first case, a circuit complies with ("follows") the new precedent. The authors then trace the reaction of each circuit to each Supreme Court decision over time. They find that, although most circuits comply at their very first or second opportunity, some aspects of the Supreme Court's decision (unanimity, the age of the overruled precedent, complexity, and whether it was a criminal procedure case) and the Supreme Court's ideology (in particular, its ideological proximity from the Court when the precedent was set), as well as some aspects of the circuit itself (whether it was affirmed by the Supreme Court), influence the speed of compliance.

Westerland and his colleagues (2010) also employ *Shepard's* to determine why circuit courts positively or negatively treat Supreme Court decisions. They find that change in ideology from the Court that decided a given case to the contemporary Court depresses the likelihood of a positive treatment of precedent by the circuit court, as does the precedent's age. Interestingly, precedents with concurring opinions are more likely to be positively treated, as are those cases that have been positively treated by the Supreme Court over time. What their study most importantly adds, though, is that the lower court's own precedent also matters; the circuit's prior positive treatments of a precedent increase the likelihood of subsequent positive treatment, while the circuit's own negative prior treatment decreases the likelihood of later positive treatment. The lower courts did, however, more frequently treat the Supreme Court's decisions positively, a finding that leads the authors to conclude that the principal–agent model works well to explain lower court compliance decisions.

Not all of the extant research about compliance relies upon *Shepard's*, however. Much of it relies, instead, upon coding of case-specific facts to discern the extent to which Supreme Court precedent is relied upon by lower courts. The basic logic is that, by coding lower court decisions for facts influential to the Supreme Court in setting its precedent, one can measure the influence of those precedential facts on lower court decision-making. Benesh (2002), for example, compares the factors that structure decision-making in the Supreme Court in cases involving challenges to the admissibility of confessions to those that structure decision-making in the U.S. courts of appeals. (Was there physical or psychological coercion? Were *Miranda* warnings given? How old is the defendant?, and so on.) She then compares the patterns evident in the Supreme Court's confession jurisprudence with those evident in the courts of appeals and finds striking similarities. The preferences of the courts of appeals judges also matter, however, with more liberal judges inclined to strike challenged confessions and more conservative judges inclined to permit them to stand. Building on this work, Benesh and Martinek (2002) conduct a similar comparison of confession case decision-making between the Supreme Court and state courts of last resort; they find a high degree of correspondence between the factors that are influential on the Supreme Court and those that matter to the state supreme courts.[29]

A more recent analysis that simultaneously considers the correspondence of both court of appeals and state court of last resort decision-making with Supreme Court precedent (also in the area of challenged confessions) led Benesh and Martinek (2009) to conclude that

> both the federal courts of appeals and state supreme courts are compliant ... But state courts are evidently less compelled than the circuit courts to make certain decisions as a consequence of the factual configuration of the case under consideration.
>
> (p. 816)

These authors attribute the lesser "attentiveness" of state high courts to the fact that judges on those courts must be sensitive to their state political contexts—particularly if they are elected judges—as well as the Supreme Court. Indeed, elected judges may find themselves between the Scylla of upsetting their constituents and the Charybdis of frustrating Supreme Court precedent. Comparato and McClurg (2007), in their examination of decision making in search and seizure cases by state courts of last resort (i.e., cases involving challenges to evidence claimed to have been obtained in violation of Fourth Amendment protections against unreasonable search and seizure), also find Supreme Court precedent to have a substantial influence on the choices of state supreme court judges. Of particular note is their finding that judges selected via appointment (rather than election) are more likely to conform their decision-making to Supreme Court precedent, regardless of their own personal ideology.

A variant of the basic fact pattern analysis relies upon the concept of jurisprudential regimes. Students of the courts have struggled for decades—some would say for over a century (Hettinger, Lindquist, and Martinek 2006)—to disentangle the relative influence of traditional legal factors and the preferences and attitudes of judicial decision-makers in the choices they make. Richards and Kritzer (2002) offer the concept of jurisprudential regimes as part of an effort to quantify legal influence and allow for an analysis of the relative impact of legal and extra-legal factors. Rather than seeing Supreme Court opinions as necessitating particular outcomes, the jurisprudential regimes approach conceptualizes precedents as enumerating relevant factors to be considered and indicating how those factors are to be weighed in the adjudication of future cases. In explaining this concept, Richards and Kritzer note that one reason the Supreme Court adheres to these blueprints is to guide lower courts in their decision-making in relevant cases, thereby promoting consistency in the law. In a similar vein, Luse and her colleagues (2009) investigated decisions in the U.S. courts of appeals to see whether the Supreme Court's decisions interpreting the First Amendment's clause on religious establishments structure decision-making in those lower courts. They ask, in effect, whether an appeals court would decide a given case in the same way that the Supreme Court would, if it were to consider the case. They found that, indeed, the courts of appeals were attentive to the Supreme Court's precedent in that they were influenced by the law's purpose, its primary effect, and the extent to which it induced government entanglement, even after accounting for the preferences of the court of appeals judges themselves. In addition, they present evidence that this reliance on the Court's jurisprudential regimes indicates compliance borne of a desire to make law well; since the ideology of the contemporaneous Supreme Court was not a significant influence on decisions of the circuit courts, it is unlikely that these judges were motivated by a desire to avoid reversal.[30]

Conclusion

Stare decisis—literally translated as "to stand by things decided"—is a powerful principle that infuses common law legal systems with a sense of continuity and stability in the law. Not only does *stare decisis* mean that the Supreme Court's jurisprudence is generally marked by only slow and incremental change, it also means that lower courts should (at least in principle) be faithful in their application of the law as interpreted by the Supreme Court. Accordingly, from a normative perspective, for *stare decisis* to be a robust legal principle, lower courts at both the state and federal level must be compliant. Compliance on the part of lower courts is also of abiding interest for two very practical reasons. First, if the lower courts are not obedient, then the meaning of the Constitution will literally vary from one jurisdiction to the next. Of course, the 50 separate state judiciaries are not intended to be the mere appendages of the federal judiciary; the principle of federalism prohibits that. And, the geographic organization of the federal courts also suggests at least some play for regional influences in the interpretation of the law (Carrington 1999). But ultimately, the Supreme Court is supposed to be the final arbiter as to the meaning of the Constitution. And, second, the Supreme Court as a governing institution is only as powerful as its ability to induce compliance with its judgments: "If the Supreme Court cannot instill its policy prescriptions in its own judicial agents, what influence can it have on society?" (Benesh and Reddick 2002, 535).

Given the importance of lower court compliance, then, it is not surprising that a host of scholars have expended considerable time and energy to better understanding both the extent of compliance (and noncompliance) and what accounts for the patterns of lower court compliance that are evident. All of the various methods of measuring compliance we detail above, even those that use the most imprecise measures, have come to a similar conclusion: lower courts do a pretty good job of complying with the Supreme Court. Hence, the Court does indeed have impact, at least among its judicial compatriots. But, to return to the question posed at the start of the chapter, is such compliance *inevitable*? Given our argument that the strongest mechanism for compliance is the Supreme Court's legitimacy, it is unlikely that the extent to which the lower courts comply will change much over time. The Court is and has been the most legitimate institution of national government for most of its history. Were that to change, then perhaps the impetus to comply would be lessened. But none of the scholars who study the Court's legitimacy see it slipping away any time soon (Gibson, Caldeira, and Spence 2003; Kritzer 2001). Even considering other potential mechanisms of compliance—clear communication (Canon 1999), organizational inertia (Baum 2002), the desire to avoid reversal by the Supreme Court (Baum 1978), professional socialization into a norm of compliance (Tarr 1977), self-interest to preserve integrity and enhance respect (Baum 1976; Caminker 1994), simple ideological compatibility between inferior and superior courts (Baum 1976; Reddick and Benesh 2000)—there is no reason to expect levels of compliance to decrease. This does not, of course, mean that compliance will be perfect, and commentators will continue to notice those aberrant cases of noncompliance. But compliance will surely remain the norm, and the Supreme Court will continue to exert a strong influence over decisions made by inferior courts. Whether the Supreme Court has or will continue to have influence in other circles and on society in general is a question that has also been considered by many scholars, but is here left to the reader to explore.

Notes

1 The Supreme Court of the United States Police was created in 1949, its precursor being a Supreme Court security force selected from among the ranks of the U.S. Capitol Police. The Supreme Court Police was originally only given the authority to patrol the Supreme Court building and grounds. The protection of the justices remained the responsibility of the U.S. Marshals Service (as it was in the infamous case of *In re Neagle* [1890]) until the early 1980s.

2 Canon and Johnson (1999) identify four primary populations or audiences that the Court, by necessity, relies upon for the implementation of its decisions and, hence, its impact: the interpreting population, which tells others what the decision means (e.g., judges and attorneys); the implementing population, which puts decisions into action on a day-to-day basis (e.g., bureaucrats and school officials); the consumer population, which includes virtually every citizen of the country at one time or another, depending on the issue area under consideration (i.e., the affected population of a specific decision); and the secondary population, which includes anyone who knows about and learns about, and perhaps debates the merits of, a Supreme Court decision (e.g., public office holders, interest groups, the media, the public at large).

3 The existence of such displays demonstrates one roadblock to impact noted by Baum (2002, 229): either no citizen is offended by the religious symbol, or none is willing to incur the personal and financial costs of challenging it.

4 With regard to compliance, scholars have distinguished between compliance as congruence and compliance as responsiveness. Congruence is simply the extent to which the lower courts act consistently with the dictates of the Supreme Court. Responsiveness refers to the situation in which decisional trends in the Supreme Court are mirrored in the lower courts. Of course, a lower court that is perfectly congruent with the Supreme Court (i.e., one that makes decisions exactly as the Supreme Court would) will also be perfectly responsive. However, a lower court may be responsive without being entirely congruent if, for example, the lower court makes more conservative decisions as the Supreme Court renders more conservative precedents but does not faithfully apply those precedents exactly as the Supreme Court would (Songer, Segal, and Cameron 1994).

5 Interestingly, the Supreme Court itself readily acknowledges and accepts this as a possibility, as evidenced in the opinion in *Michigan v. Long* (1983, 1040–1041).

6 A common law legal system is one in which judges make law in the decisions they render, law that is considered binding on later and lower courts.

7 The Supreme Court is created by Article III of the Constitution. Congress has the authority to create additional courts under the auspices of both Article I and Article III.

8 But see Baum (1976, 232), who argues that hierarchy may have little to do with compliance with Supreme Court precedent.

9 The majority of states designate their highest state-level court as a "supreme court." There are notable exceptions, however, including New York, whose court of last resort is the New York Court of Appeals, while the New York Supreme Court is the major trial court in the state judiciary. Here, we use "court of last resort" and "supreme court" interchangeably to refer to the highest court in a state's judicial system.

10 In the language of principal–agent theory, the Supreme Court faces the challenge of moral hazard in that it cannot observe all of the actions of its agents (i.e., the lower courts) and therefore runs the risk of the agents behaving contrary to the interests of the Court (i.e., not faithfully applying Supreme Court precedents).

11 The exception to this procedure is for nominations to courts created by Congress under its authority specified in Article I, rather than in Article III. The selection of judges for so-called Article I courts can be arranged however Congress sees fit. While the major trial courts (U.S. district courts) and major intermediate appellate courts (U.S. courts of appeals) at the federal level are Article III courts, the U.S. Court of Appeals for Veterans Claims and the U.S. Court of Appeals for the Armed Forces, for example, are Article I courts.

12 Technically, on issues involving the interpretation of state statutes or state constitutional provisions, the high court of the respective state is the final authority. However, state high court interpretations are subject to review by the Supreme Court if federal regulations, rules, or constitutional provisions are implicated.

13 Though the so-called "attitudinal model" has received the most definitive support in the context of the Supreme Court (Segal and Spaeth 1993), there is ample evidence that judicial attitudes matter considerably for decision-making in lower federal (e.g., Hettinger, Lindquist, and Martinek 2006) and state courts (e.g., Hall and Brace 1999), as well.

14 In this regard, the team theory shares the logic of communication theories of compliance that focus on clarity in the transmission of precedent.

15 This fear of reversal is also assumed to drive compliance in other scholarship, for example Baum (1978). On rational litigants, see also Cameron and Kornhauser (2006).

16 An alternative that shares the same logic is the existence of fellow appellate court judges who are willing to invest the time and energy into serving as "whistleblowers" and alerting the Supreme Court to unfaithfulness on the part of their fellow judges through separate opinions (e.g., dissenting opinions) (Cross and Tiller 1998).

17 Of course, not all lower court cases are equally likely to be selected for review, and several scholars have argued that the Court can and does engage in strategic monitoring; see, for example, Cameron, Segal, and Songer (2000), Lax (2003).

18 The U.S. courts of appeals are colloquially referred to as circuit courts, reflecting the fact that the precursors to the U.S. courts of appeals (created in 1891) were the U.S. Circuit Courts (which finally ceased to operate on January 1, 1912) as well as the fact that they are organized into 11 geographically-based circuits.

19 Klein and Hume (2003) use "importance," inter-circuit conflict, circuit caseload, the number of cases heard by the Supreme Court in the two previous terms, and the propensity of the circuit to be reviewed by the Supreme Court in the past to define the likelihood of review.

20 This linkage between legitimacy and compliance or impact was made by Canon, but was not vigorously pursued by other scholars (Canon 1999). Some of Vanberg's (2005) intuitions, however, are quite similar, as are those of Clark (2010). Baum (2002) also speaks of institutional authority as driving compliance.

21 Concerns about eroding the legitimacy of the Court in the eyes of the public have been a strong motivating force behind opposition to introducing cameras into Supreme Court proceedings (Cohn 2007–2008).

22 These (and other) scholars have shown that policies emanating from the Supreme Court are perceived to be more legitimate than policies emanating from other institutions. In other words, regardless of the content of the policy, the language used in making it, or the ideological preferences of the individual judging the

legitimacy of it, things the Supreme Court says are paid more heed than things said by other institutions.

23 Anonymous interview with circuit judge, conducted by Sara Benesh on April 16, 2007. For a more detailed discussion, see Benesh (2008). This idea is corroborated by earlier interviews conducted by Baum (1978) and in surveys of trial judges conducted by Gibson (1977).

24 Klein's (2002) interviews suggest that the goal of getting cases "right" in a legal sense is an important one to judges. Baum (2006), however, notes that, for any given case, another audience may be of greater concern than the Supreme Court and legal commentators.

25 The term "GVR" refers to a decision by the Supreme Court to grant certiorari, vacate the lower court's decision, and remand the case to the lower court in light of some intervening event, usually a related Supreme Court decision. These orders are no more than five lines long, most often, but occasion a great deal of consideration by the circuit courts. Indeed, in some circuits, briefs are filed and oral arguments made over the applicability of the "in light of" case to the original case result. That these short orders are paid such attention lends credence to the seriousness with which the lower courts regard Supreme Court actions.

26 The influence goes both ways: concurrences critical of the majority opinion lessen compliance, while concurrences that reaffirm the majority opinion enhance compliance (Corley 2010). Elsewhere, Corley (2009) demonstrates that plurality decisions—e.g., those that do not enjoy majority support—are especially vulnerable to noncompliance. Baum (1976) similarly discusses the influence of decisional clarity on implementation (but see Johnson 1979; Benesh and Reddick 2002).

27 *Shepard's* also indexes federal and state laws and regulations. The widespread usage of *Shepard's* for legal research has led to the use of the term "to Shepardize" as a generic verb that refers to the process of determining if a given precedent, law, or statute remains "good law."

28 Spriggs and Hansford (2000) find that the *Shepard's* coding is quite reliable (e.g., it includes all cases cited in a given case, includes nearly all subsequent cases that legally treat an earlier case, and nearly always assigns the same treatment code that the authors of the article would have assigned) and, in most cases, also valid (e.g., the categories measure the kind of legal treatment they purport to measure).

29 Benesh and Martinek also find, however, that state legal factors matter as well. In particular, they find that challenges to the admissibility of confessions are less successful in states in which the state constitution provides less protection against self-incrimination.

30 If fear of reversal were driving compliance, presumably the ideology of the Supreme Court would have affected the circuit court's decision; as the Supreme Court became more conservative, the lower court would be less likely to strike down laws as violating the Establishment Clause; e.g., they would have been more likely to rule in an accommodationist (conservative) direction (Luse *et al.* 2009).

Chapter 15

Why Strict Scrutiny Requires Transparency

The Practical Effects of *Bakke*, *Gratz*, and *Grutter*[1]

Richard Sander

As the 2002–2003 term of the United States Supreme Court unfolded, few if any of its pending cases received as much media attention as the twin bill of affirmative action cases. In *Grutter v. Bollinger* and *Gratz v. Bollinger*, the Court had taken on two distinct challenges to affirmative action policies at the University of Michigan (UM). Barbara Grutter was challenging a racial preference system built into UM's School of Law, and Jennifer Gratz was challenging the use of racial preferences by UM's undergraduate admissions. Through the briefing, oral argument, and subsequent Court deliberations, most of the betting ran against the university. Recent Supreme Court decisions had struck down affirmative action plans in employment and contracting; a majority of the justices had records hostile to racial preferences in nearly all contexts. Moreover, most elite colleges and professional schools had been using racial preferences to favor minorities in admissions for over 30 years, and nearly everyone conceded that such programs should not persist indefinitely. On June 27, 2003, the Court announced both decisions. In *Gratz v. Bollinger*, a 6–3 majority of the Court ruled that UM's undergraduate admissions system was patently unconstitutional; in *Grutter v. Bollinger*, the Court held by a slender 5–4 vote that the law school's system survived constitutional scrutiny, but only subject to a number of constraints and only temporarily. On its face, this seemed like a stinging rebuke to the university's policies and a considerable narrowing of the scope of affirmative action. Yet the front pages of newspapers across the country the next day showed a gleeful Mary Sue Coleman—the president of the university—literally jumping for joy on news of the decisions. The question must be asked: why was this woman smiling?

The remarkably simple answer is this: President Coleman knew that, in practice, the *Grutter* and *Gratz* decisions would have little effect on the scale and effects of the university's affirmative action policies. Indeed, as I will discuss in this chapter, *Grutter* and *Gratz*—along with their progenitor, *Bakke v. University of California*—have collectively had effects almost directly opposite to those articulated in the decisions. At least among public law schools in the United States, and at the University of Michigan's undergraduate college itself, racial preferences became larger, not smaller, after *Grutter* and *Gratz*; particular racial classifications became more, not less, determinative of admissions decisions; and for most schools, the entire process—far from doing away with "mechanical" admissions processes—became more mechanical than ever. An era when higher education would embrace race neutrality, which Justice O'Connor (the architect of *Grutter*) confidently predicted would arrive in the 2020s, now seems further away than ever.

This is unusual: while Supreme Court decisions do not always have the sweeping effects implied by their words (Canon and Johnson 1999; Rosenberg 2008), they do tend to push on-the-ground behavior in the direction laid down by the Court. At worst, one would think, a Court holding would have no effect at all. So producing effects *opposite* to those pronounced by the Court is a remarkable, if dubious, legacy of *Grutter* and *Gratz*, and it makes these cases, along with their legal forebearers, interesting material for a case study in the exercise of judicial authority. Examining the on-the-ground effects of these decisions also helps us think about how the Court can operationalize the idea of strict scrutiny—the standard that, in theory, governs affirmative action law.

A Few Facts About Admissions Preferences

Grutter, *Gratz*, and *Bakke* are intrinsically interesting because most readers have experienced the remarkable opacity of college and university admissions. Elite and advanced-degree schools thrive on the allure of selectivity, and like all allurements, this one depends on a certain air of mystery. Listen to any admissions officer's speech on "how to get in" and you will know exactly what I mean. The mystique of higher education admissions is also quite important in understanding the challenge of judicial regulation. Let us begin, then, with a brief glimpse behind the veil.

Both elite universities and professional schools introduced "pro-minority" racial preferences in the late 1960s, an innovation that capped a very turbulent generation of change in admissions. Before World War II, very few schools in the United States were truly "selective" in the modern sense (Karabel 2005; Lemann 1999). Nearly all schools admitted the bulk of their applicants. A few elite ones had admission exams, and a number of prestigious schools placed various social obstacles in the path of admission.[2] Postwar America, however, witnessed an explosive growth in college enrollment,[3] and middle-class Americans began to think their smart children could legitimately aspire to attend famous schools and pursue elite professions. The elite schools themselves, faced with unprecedented demand and the rapid emergence of science, technology, and quantitative social science as subjects of intense national interest, were rapidly injecting an ethos of meritocracy into many aspects of their operations, including admissions. The schools embraced standardized tests as a means of reducing "class" prejudice, and embraced the idea that competitive admissions should be based primarily on objective "merit." To protect the children of alumni and college sports, schools used "legacy" and athletic preferences as well, but meritocratic criteria were dominant by the 1960s, as elite schools found themselves admitting only a third, a quarter, or even a fifth of their applicants.[4]

Part of the new meritocratic vision embraced greater ethnic and racial diversity, and both elite college campuses and professional schools undoubtedly became more open and welcoming places in the early 1960s. But by the mid-1960s, many colleges realized they would have very small black enrollments without special efforts. Unprecedented levels of college activism, initially focused on the Vietnam War but soon spreading to other issues, also put an intense spotlight on the "racial climate" on campuses and the paucity of black students. Consequently, over a relatively short period between 1967 and 1970, dozens of elite and professional schools adopted special minority admissions programs. These usually involved some special outreach efforts, but always also included "preferential" admissions for blacks (and soon, Hispanic) applicants, meaning that low or middling test scores and grades were discounted.

College administrators initially based racial preference programs on three key premises. First, they believed it was essential for colleges to do their part to foster the development of national minority leadership in politics, in the professions, and in the technocratic elite. Second, they believed that it would take some time, perhaps a generation, for the effects of civil rights programs to kick in and correct the effects of poverty and poor education on black students. Third, they knew colleges would be accused of hypocrisy if they could not generate reasonably significant numbers of minority students, since they obviously had no qualms about using preferences for athletes and (in private colleges, at least) legacies. Under these circumstances, instituting preferences large enough to generate substantial minority enrollments (i.e., very large race preferences) seemed like an obvious step, and one they hoped would rapidly fade as racial gaps in academic preparedness declined.

As a significant number of schools instituted minority preferences, still others felt compelled to follow suit, in part because the preferences of other schools tapped all the readily available minority students who could be admitted on race-neutral grounds. By the mid-1970s, preferences were pervasive at the top 200 undergraduate programs outside the South and in most law and medical schools, and continued to spread in subsequent years.

After several decades of rapid evolution, higher education admissions systems had reached a kind of stasis by the late 1970s. Although there have been some subtle changes since then, almost any important, substantive fact one could adduce about elite and professional-school admissions in 2012 would have held 35 years ago. The irony is that it is this exact era when an array of schools have faced legal challenges, and, in the perception of outsiders at least, universities have had to pass through one gauntlet after another. A question to keep in mind as we proceed is whether the net effect of this legal ferment has been to solidify, rather than disrupt, the ways that universities factor race into admissions.

The essential, continuing elements of racial preferences have been these:

1   Racial preferences are driven by gaps in levels of academic preparedness. Ever since college admissions officers started thinking seriously about race in the 1960s, they have realized that the median black applicant has academic credentials (e.g., test scores and grades) dramatically below the median white student. In the mid-1970s, for example, the median black typically had credentials around the 10th percentile of the typical white[5]). Any specific threshold of credentials established as an academic target (say, presumptively admitting students at the 70th percentile and above) would have the effect, then, of admitting whites at 10 times the rate of blacks. (Smaller but analogous gaps exist between Hispanics and whites.) Nearly all university preference systems are driven by this fundamental conundrum. And all predictions that racial preferences would fade over time have been premised on the belief that these racial credential gaps would themselves largely disappear. But while access has increased dramatically (black college enrollment, for example, increased nearly tenfold from 1968 to 2008 (Statistical Abstract 1981, 2010)), the relative level of minority preparation has improved only modestly (the median black credentials in most higher education application pools is now at about the 15th or 20th percentile of the white distribution). Thus, the absolute number of high-credential blacks and Hispanics has increased sharply over time, but race-neutral methods would still tend to produce results that disproportionately exclude blacks and Hispanics.

2   Consequently, racial preferences are not "tie-breakers," but rather a central factor that transforms the application of the typical affected candidate. Most admissions officers more or less "race-norm" applicants— that is, they consider the academic preparedness of each candidate relative not to the general admissions pool, but relative to the preparedness of other candidates of the same race. This does not necessarily mean that admissions decisions are racially segregated; it does mean that the admissions officer is at least making a mental adjustment of test scores and grades based on the race of the applicant.

3   Since the "preparedness gap," relative to whites, is on average different for Hispanics, blacks, and American Indians, the size of racial preferences are, usually, correspondingly different for each of these groups. Especially where there are large numbers of both Hispanic and black applicants, administrators are careful to calibrate preferences to roughly correspond to the relative size of their applicant pools. For example, suppose that 10% of a school's

applicants were black, and 5% were Hispanic. Using the same size preference for both groups would produce something like a 2:1 ratio of Hispanic-
to-black admits; since the school wants admissions to be reasonably close to
application ratios, race-specific calibration of preferences is adopted.[6]

4   Preferences come with costs, especially for the beneficiaries. In the early
     days of affirmative action, there was much speculation (and hope) that
     minority students admitted with large preferences would "catch up" in
     academic skills and achieve levels of academic distinction comparable to
     their classmates. Scholars now agree that this happens occasionally, but is
     not the typical outcome. The median black student admitted with a large
     preference tends to end up with grades that put her somewhere near the
     10th percentile of the GPA distribution (this holds in both colleges and
     graduate schools), and median Hispanic student (who receives a smaller
     preference) tends to end up around the 25th percentile of GPA. (Minor-
     ity students admitted without preferences, in contrast, perform pretty
     much the same as everyone else.) More controversial is the question of
     whether the low grades that result from preferences are associated with
     other problems—less learning, stigma, loss of academic self-confidence, a
     tendency to switch into less rigorous academic majors, lower graduation
     or professional certification rates, and worse earnings in the long-term.

Although many of the ideas in point (4) above—often clumped together as
the "mismatch hypotheses"—are disputed, there is not much disagreement,
especially among admissions officers themselves, that (1) through (3) accurately characterize university preference programs. Indeed, over the years
enough data about admissions systems has leaked out that these basic features
can hardly be denied.

The Structure of Preferences

The Supreme Court's first substantive decision on university preferences came in
Bakke. The University of California at Davis School of Medicine had an unusually rigid preference system; the school set aside 16 out of 100 spots in its medical
school for minority applicants. This was a true "quota" system. Since "quota" is
such a lightning-rod term in affirmative action discourse, it is worth discussing
its meaning in some detail, and distinguishing it from other preference systems.
Indeed, since the Supreme Court's efforts to regulate affirmative action have
often been suffused with ambiguity, some conceptual and terminological preci-
sion now will pay large dividends when we examine the Court's decisions.

Consider two similar schools that each enroll 100 new students every fall.
School A has a rigid quota of 16 minority spots, while School B has a flexible
"goal" of enrolling 16 minorities per year, on average, over many years. The
rigid quota puts School A at two disadvantages. First, if the pool of minority

applicants is particularly thin in some years, School A must admit some particularly weak applicants to meet its annual quota. School B, in contrast, can admit extra minorities in years with strong applicant pools, and fewer minorities in lean years, thus maximizing the quality of its minority students over time. Second, School A must make admissions in waves, since it cannot predict its yield rate exactly (especially with a group as small as its minority quota). It will admit some students in April, see how it fares in yield, and then admit additional students off its wait-list over the summer. These students will tend to be significantly weaker, since the strongest wait-list students will probably have accepted offers from other schools to nail down their plans. School B does not need to play this inefficient game. It can admit its strongest minority candidates based on average yield rates over time; if in the end it falls short this year, it will make it up next year or the year after.

Thus, regardless of how one feels about preference policies, quotas are not very good ways to implement them because of their rigidity. They are likely to exist only if a school's administration is so bureaucratic, or so dysfunctional, that policy-makers cannot trust policy implementers to pursue a flexible goal in good faith over a period of time. A quota guarantees results at the cost of efficient implementation.

From a legal standpoint, quotas are particularly troublesome. They imply a spoils system, in which politicians or administrators simply carve up state benefits into racial "shares." They also make explicit a process in which applicants of different races are not directly compared with one another. Under the Davis quota, it didn't matter whether there were 100, or 5,000, white applicants with stronger credentials than the 16th enrolled minority.

Consider, by way of contrast, a "point" system. Suppose that School B considers a combination of factors in admitting students: SAT scores, high school grades, work experience, community service, letters of reference, leadership qualities, and so on. Suppose that it awards points depending on the level of achievement in each of these areas, and admits students who pass some threshold of total points—say, 800 points out of 1,000 possible. Finally, suppose that under this system, only an average of 5% of the admitted students are minorities, but that if School B adds 100 points to each minority student's file, then an average of 16% of its admitted students are minorities.[7] To achieve the racial diversity it seeks, School B adopts this point system.

Even though the two systems produce identical results over the long term, School B's "point system" has several advantages over School A's quota. The point system will produce rising and falling numbers of minority students from year to year as the strength of the minority pool fluctuates. There is no chance under the point system that the school will be forced to admit an extraordinarily weak minority applicant just to meet the quota; every admitted minority must have at least 700 points on the "non-racial" admissions criteria. Moreover, under the point system majority and minority students are not completely isolated from competition with one another; if the majority pool gets stronger, so that the school raises its admissions threshold to 820 from 800, then minority students will now have to meet a higher (720) threshold as well. Very importantly, the point system is transparent—at least to those administering it. In this design, admissions officers understand how race trades off with other factors, and it is easy to predict such things as the SAT credential gap between admitted majority and minority students.

Now consider a third system, which uses neither points nor quotas, but rather relies on an admissions officer to read the files of all the applicants, to make mental note of all the relevant factors in admission and all the characteristics of all the applicants, and to decide who should be admitted. Such a system used to be called "discretionary" (i.e., based on the discretion of the admitting officer) but has now come to be known as "holistic." Although a holistic system sounds quite different from a point system, the difference is more apparent than real. If professors are evaluating a few candidates for a new faculty position, or a department chair is comparing a handful of applicants for a graduate fellowship, it is possible to think of the selection as "holistic," in the sense that dozens of individual characteristics are weighed and compared in an overall, largely intuitive judgment. But when a college or professional school is considering thousands of applicants for hundreds of spots, the process is necessarily algorithmic—the admissions officer or officers have *some* methodology for weighing the various elements of a file against one another. The only question is whether the algorithm is applied systematically (with an explicit formula) or capriciously. An internally inconsistent system wouldn't serve anybody's interests, so no matter whether a school considers its decisions to be formulaic or not they almost certainly are. Given enough time and patience, an investigator could reconstruct the implicit algorithm used by an admissions officer, even one who thinks her admissions decisions are purely intuitive.[8]

Of course, even in a point system, not every element is objective; determining the strength of a candidate's writing or the quality of a recommendation ordinarily involves both objective and subjective assessments. The distinction between a "point system" and a "holistic" approach is not really about whether "objective" elements of an application, like test scores, are given more weight, but whether the various elements of applications are compared consistently.

This extended discussion of admissions methods may seem tedious, but as we shall see, it goes to the heart of Supreme Court jurisprudence on affirmative action in higher education.

Bakke v. University of California at Davis

Lawsuits challenging racial preferences in college and university admissions are difficult to bring. Few students know much about how preferences or college admissions work; even fewer know whether they were in the ideal "zone," where they can show they would have been admitted to a school "but for" the school's use of racial preferences.[9] Still fewer want to put their education on hold while pursuing expensive, complex, and difficult litigation.[10] Given the relative handful of challenges that have been brought, a remarkable number of them have turned into major cases.

The first pivotal case was brought by Allan Bakke, a young engineer and Marine veteran who wanted to become a doctor. His challenge to the University of California, Davis Medical School had all the right ingredients: Bakke was a strong candidate; he did not enter another medical school after starting his suit, and, as mentioned above, Davis used an explicit set-aside, or quota, for minorities in selecting medical students. The issue deeply divided a Court which was, on the whole, more liberal than the present Court. Justices Brennan, White, Marshall, and Blackmun held that racial preferences to correct general societal discrimination should be permitted, temporarily, in higher education. Justices Stevens, Stewart, Burger, and Rehnquist held that any consideration of race violated Title VI of the 1964 Civil Rights Act. The ninth Justice, Lewis Powell, wrote the deciding opinion, siding with the conservative camp to find the University of California's racial quota illegal, but siding with the liberal camp to hold that universities were not completely precluded from considering race in admissions decisions. Race, he found, could be used as one of many factors taken into account by a university in pursuit of its legitimate desire to create a diverse student body:

> Race or ethnic background may be deemed a "plus" in a particular applicant's file, yet it does not insulate the individual from comparison with all other candidates for the available seats. The file of a particular black applicant may be examined for his potential contribution to diversity without the factor of race being compared, for example, with that of an applicant identified as an Italian-American if the latter is thought to exhibit qualities more likely to promote beneficial educational pluralism. Such qualities could include exceptional personal talents, unique work or service experience, leadership potential, maturity, demonstrated compassion, a history of overcoming disadvantage, ability to communicate with the poor, or other qualifications deemed important. In short, an admissions program operated in this way is flexible enough to consider all pertinent elements of diversity in light of the particular qualifications of each applicant, and to place them on the same footing for consideration, although not necessarily according them the same weight.[11]

Powell's holding thus precluded quotas—which clearly did insulate minorities from direct competition—but seemed consistent with either a "point" system or a "holistic" approach. The critical ambiguity in Powell's opinion concerned just how much weight might be given to race. Powell's words, in the paragraph above and other passages, seemed to envision a system in

which colleges first determined (using test scores and past school performance) who met an academic threshold sufficient to make success at the school
probable. From the resulting field of candidates, the school would pick a mix
of students reflecting a diverse set of non-academic or quasi-academic qualities. But at the vast majority of professional schools and elite colleges, admissions officers faced a great dearth of strong minority students in their
applicant pools. The schools routinely admitted minority students at great
risk of failure. And race was not simply another diversity characteristic. The
weight given to race at a great many schools far exceeded the weight given to
all other diversity factors *combined*. Such practices were obviously in tension
with the spirit of Powell's words, but his decision only explicitly banned
quotas.

Powell seems to have been well aware of this problem. According to John
Jeffries's (1994) excellent biography, Powell approached *Bakke* pragmatically.
He felt that merely affirming the California Supreme Court—and prohibiting
racial preferences in education—would be too dramatic a step to take in 1978;
some time was needed to give blacks a foothold in the leadership rungs of
society. But he found outright quotas offensive, and thought explicit set-asides
would become rigid and divisive. He wanted a solution that seemed to curtail
preferences while not precluding them, and he wanted a rationale that did not
empower every college to engage in broad social engineering.

For more than a generation, the Supreme Court had consistently applied
"strict scrutiny" to racial classifications; under this standard, governments
using racial classifications must show that they have a "compelling interest"
motivating the use of race, and that the means employed to achieve that interest are not merely reasonable, but "narrowly tailored" to achieve the government's purpose. Virtually all forms of public-sector racial discrimination
prevalent in the 1950s and early 1960s fell before such a standard, but many
argued that "strict scrutiny" was not the proper standard for "benign" discrimination programs, like the Davis quotas, where politically weak groups
were favored. But in keeping with his view that minority preference programs
should be temporary, and not become entrenched, Powell thought it essential
to keep the "strict scrutiny" standard. By defining a public university's interest
in diversity as a "compelling interest," and by suggesting that race could be
only one of many factors in the diversity mix, Powell found a rationale that
simultaneously (a) worked as a legal argument, (b) achieved his various goals
in the case, and (c) achieved a compromise on a socially divisive issue.

The cost of these successes was an opinion that was hopelessly vague. Powell's opinion laid out no timetables, no test of how a university would demonstrate its "compelling interest" in diversity, and no guidance on when the size
of a racial preference crossed an impermissible line. He even suggested that
an attraction of a "diversity" program, like the one used by Harvard College,
was that there was no "facial" (e.g., declared) intent to discriminate. As Jeffries
points out,

This was pure sophistry. Harvard did not – and could not – deny that race was a factor in admissions. By refusing to look beyond "facial intent" in situations where the fact of racial preference was open, acknowledged, and indisputable, Powell simply penalized candor. Stripped of legalisms, the message amounted to this: "You can do whatever you like in preferring racial minorities, so long as you do not say so."

(Jeffries 1994, 484)

Universities got the message. Quotas disappeared after *Bakke*, but as noted above, strict numerical quotas were almost invariably foolish and inefficient methods of implementing policy anyway. In their place came "diversity" programs that usually listed many student characteristics of interest to the school, and did not mention that race was pre-eminent among these. Schools maintained racial goals, but were generally careful not to articulate these as specific numbers. An admissions officer would understand from general administrative discussions that racial diversity was very important; she would then produce a student body that reflected, racially, the makeup of the applicant pool. Administrators could then signal that the weight given to race should go up ("we need better representation") or go down ("we need to pay closer attention to minimum credentials") at the margins.

Substantively, *Bakke* left racial preferences perfectly intact. An exhaustive study by political scientists Susan Welch and John Gruhl (1998) found that *Bakke* had no noticeable effect on minority enrollments at either law or medical schools. A survey of law school admissions officers found that only one in 100 respondents felt that *Bakke* had a "significant" impact on their own school's policies (even though a large majority conceded that *other* law schools had had racial quotas before *Bakke*). I am aware of no similar study done at the undergraduate level, but the available evidence shows black enrollments rising, not falling, at elite colleges after *Bakke* (Bowen and Bok 1998). Thirty years after the decision, the proportion of "underrepresented minorities" at the UC Davis Medical School was 16.8%.[12]

Although the advent of the Reagan administration in the 1980s portended a new assault on affirmative action, nothing of the sort happened in the realm of higher education. Frank Dobbin (2009) has argued in his fascinating book, *Inventing Equal Opportunity*, that by the 1980s, a diversity ideology had taken firm hold in much of the corporate United States; human resource directors evolved a language that legitimated hiring preferences as a strategy that increased efficiency and diminished the threat of litigation. So federal prodding—once important in pushing firms to hire minorities—was now irrelevant. Whatever zeal existed in the corporate sector for diversity, it paled in comparison to the thorough embrace of this ideal in higher education (Maranto, Redding, and Hess 2009). Preference policies solidified at flagship state universities, elite colleges, professional schools, and many doctoral programs, and spread through the South, where preferences had not been much used in the 1970s. Accreditation agencies increasingly added diversity standards to their criteria for evaluating higher education programs, which often, in effect, required a school to have racial goals comparable to those of its peers (U.S. Civil Rights Commission 2008).

Nonetheless, a second wave of challenges to higher education preferences gained traction in the 1990s. Appointments by Presidents Reagan and Bush had nudged the Supreme Court to the right, and in areas other than education the Court had sharply narrowed the permissible scope of preferences. Intellectual debate about the continued logic of, and need for, racial preferences surfaced even among centrists and progressives in a way it had not in the 1980s (Jencks 1992; Thernstrom and Thernstrom 1997). Affirmative action showed signs of becoming a national political issue. President Clinton anticipated public restiveness on the issue with his 1995 initiative to "mend" rather than "end" affirmative action, and in 1996 California, by popular initiative, became the first of a series of states to ban racial preferences at public universities.

Into this environment came the second major court challenge to university preferences. In 1992, Cheryl Hopwood and (ultimately) three other applicants who had been rejected by the University of Texas School of Law filed suit in federal court, alleging both statutory and constitutional violations of their civil rights. After a district court opinion that, Powell-like, offered half a loaf to each party, the Fifth Circuit Court of Appeals ruled strongly against the use of racial preferences, even finding that *Bakke* was no longer good law because of subsequent Supreme Court decisions in areas outside higher education. This decision effectively banned the use of race in public university admissions throughout the Fifth Circuit (Texas, Louisiana, and Mississippi). When the Supreme Court declined to grant certiorari in *Hopwood*, many observers concluded that a national prohibition was only a matter of time.

A coalition of anti-preference lawyers and nonprofits decided to put this idea to the test with two lawsuits in federal court challenging different admissions practices at the University of Michigan. *Gratz v. Bollinger* challenged the use of race by Michigan's undergraduate college, and *Grutter v. Bollinger* challenged racially preferential admissions at Michigan's law school. In both suits, the plaintiffs focused on the two key facts: administrators at both schools used racial preferences openly, and the weight given to race was rather large.

The battle was joined on an epic scale, for observers on all sides saw the case as the last stand for state-sponsored affirmative action policies. The University of Michigan commissioned significant internal research on the benefits of the preference programs; media coverage was intense; and, as the case progressed, amici briefs poured into the courts in record numbers.

The plaintiffs won victories in both cases in the lower court, though the judge in *Gratz* held that amendments to Michigan's undergraduate policy, undertaken since the commencement of litigation, had rendered it constitutional. On appeal, the Sixth Circuit took *Grutter* up *en banc* and reversed in favor of the university. The Supreme Court then took the unusual step of not only granting cert to *Grutter*, but taking *Gratz* directly from the district court, so that it could hear both appeals together.

The Court faced two cases that had a few differences but were dominated by similarities. Both Michigan's undergraduate program and its law school were elite programs, and were therefore highly selective.[13] Both schools drew many of their students from out-of-state, though again the law school had a more genuinely "national" student body. In both schools, black and Hispanic applicants had much lower average credentials than white and Asian applicants, and under most conceivable color-blind policies, would be admitted at significantly lower rates.

There were three significant differences between the two programs. The College was a much larger program, and thus received many more applications—between 15,000 and 20,000 each year, compared with between three and four thousand for the law school. And the College, like most undergraduate colleges, took significant account of a larger number of factors in its admissions decisions than did the law school. As in most of legal education, Michigan Law School's admissions decisions could be largely predicted by simply knowing a student's LSAT score, college GPA, and race. At the college, in contrast, many different test scores were relevant (SAT I, achievement tests, AP exams), and more attention was paid to the student's area of interests, essays, socioeconomic status, and so on. The scale and complexity of the undergraduate admissions process led to a third difference: the College used an explicit point system, while the Law School did not.

As in *Bakke*, the Supreme Court was closely divided on the question of racial preferences at a public university. Three justices (Ginsburg, Souter, and Stevens) considered both programs to be constitutional; four justices (Rehnquist, Kennedy, Thomas, and Scalia) considered both to be unconstitutional. Of the two justices in the middle (Breyer and O'Connor), Breyer wrote only a brief and not very revealing opinion to explain the distinction between the two. Thus, O'Connor's opinion proved to be as important in this round as Powell's opinion was in *Bakke*.

Justice O'Connor followed Justice Powell's footsteps, at least to a certain point. Like Powell, she viewed the pursuit of "diversity" as the key rationale for racial preferences; she held that public universities have a compelling interest in fostering this diversity, which meant that even under the "strict scrutiny" triggered by a racial classification, it might survive. The question was how race could be used, and here, O'Connor spelled out a seemingly challenging list of criteria for a valid racial preference system:

1   A university must, in good faith, determine that a diverse student body is essential to its educational mission and that race is an essential element of this diversity.

2   Each student given a racial preference must be selected because of the student's unique ability to contribute to the school's diversity; race by

itself, in other words, should never be "the defining feature of his or her application"; the school should instead use race only when it intersects with other diversity-enhancing characteristics.

3   No group of minority students can be "insulated" from competition with all other students; rather, if a school chooses to consider race at all it must "consider all pertinent elements of diversity in light of the particular qualification of each applicant."

4   Numerical targets for race representation were not permissible, though schools could seek a broad "critical mass" of minority students. "Racial balancing" was "patently unconstitutional."

5   Schools using race must demonstrate that race-neutral methods of achieving their diversity objectives are inadequate, and that race consideration itself is only a "temporary" expedient.

With these principles in hand, O'Connor rather easily struck down the College's racial preference system. Clearly, giving a large point boost to every black and Hispanic student violates at least the second of the above principles, and arguably the third as well. But O'Connor simultaneously, and rather mysteriously, concluded that the Law School easily met these same criteria.

On some counts, it was obvious that O'Connor went out of her way to find the Law School in compliance with her tests. On the first criteria, she found that "'good faith' ... is 'presumed' absent 'a showing to the contrary.'" Since the test itself came from her opinion, it was hard to see how the plaintiff could have been expected to show, at the trial phase of the case, the university's "bad faith." On the fifth criteria, she wrote that "we take the Law School at its word that it would 'like nothing better than to find a race-neutral admissions formula' and will terminate its race-conscious admissions program as soon as practicable," even though there was no evidence in the record that the Law School had experimented with race-neutral methods or reduced (rather than expanded) the scope of its racial preferences over time. O'Connor expressed confidence, again without citing evidence, that preferences would be gone by the year 2028.

But the greatest difficulty with O'Connor's opinion was her seeming confusion about the effect of a point system and her belief that the Law School "actually gives substantial weight to diversity factors besides race." To see the difficulties in her views, it is helpful to inspect the data in Tables 15.1 and 15.2, which are calculated from the UM College and Law School's admissions decisions in 1999—information that was before the Court but not presented in this way. The two tables use a simple academic index: a scale that runs from 0 to 1000 and is calculated for each student from her test scores (SAT I for the College; LSAT for the Law School) and her recent grades (high school GPA

Table 15.1 Undergraduate admissions rates at the University of Michigan, nonresidents only, 1999 (by academic "index" and race)

Admissions rate for non-minority applicants (%)		Admissions rate for underrepresented-minority applicants (%)	
900 and above	99.6	800 and above	98.4
850–899	93	750–799	90
800–849	68	700–749	89
750–799	30	650–699	48
700–749	7	600–649	21
Under 700	5.4	Under 600	7

Table 15.2 Comparative admissions rates at the University of Michigan Law School, 1999 (by academic "index" and race)

Admissions rate for white applicants (%)		Admissions rate for black applicants (%)	
850 and above	97	710 and above	96
830–849	91	690–709	90
810–829	70	670–689	72
790–809	44	650–669	38
750–789	16	610–649	22
710–749	5	570–609	11
Under 710	2	Under 570	0

for the College; college GPA for the Law School).[14] The index is simple, but it powerfully illustrates some basic dynamics of the two admissions systems.

Note, first, that for the "majority" race, the index is more closely related to admissions outcomes at the Law School than at the College. At the College, there is a difference of at least 150 index points between the ranges where non-minorities have a very low chance of admission (i.e., the "under 750" index range) and a very high chance of admission (i.e., the "900 and above" range). At the Law School, there is an analogous swing in admission probabilities over a mere 100-point range (compare "710–749" for whites with "850 and above").[15] This implies that the Law School is placing great weight on this simple index, and less weight on other factors (a conclusion that can also be demonstrated mathematically).

Second, and more important, the overall weight given to race is evidently greater in the Law School data than in the College data. As close inspection of these tables will suggest, and as more complex analysis confirms, being "black" is equivalent, in Law School decisions, to being awarded an extra 140 index points; at the College, the 15-point boost given to minorities translates to about 120 points on the academic index shown here (Ayres and Foster 2006).

If we put these two observations together, a third conclusion follows: blacks at the Law School were operating on a completely different admissions track from whites, one more different (more segregated) than the separate tracks created by the College's "point" system. In the academic index range at the Law School where white admissions rates varied (710 and above), blacks were essentially guaranteed admission. And at the admission categories where blacks were actually in competition for spots (709 and below), whites had virtually no chance of admission. O'Connor's claim that "the Law School frequently accepts non-minority applicants with grades and test scores lower than URM applicants who are rejected" is simply untrue, unless she is using "frequently" in absolute terms and half-a-dozen instances in each admissions cycle qualify. Certainly it happened *much less* often at the Law School than at the College, in both absolute and relative terms. The College, meanwhile, obviously took greater account of diversity factors other than race; indeed, the school's point system gave roughly the same weight to socioeconomic background as to race, making it a comparatively rare oasis of class diversity in a nation full of elite colleges serving only affluent students (Kahlenberg 1996; Sander 2011).

Like Justice Powell, O'Connor plainly wanted to give half a loaf to both the critics and the proponents of racial preferences at universities. But, even more so than in Powell's case, O'Connor's lack of analytic rigor made a mess of her opinion; she simply did not understand the actual operation of either the College or the Law School admissions systems. She invalidated "point" systems without any substantive or logical reason for doing so, and she approved a system—the Law School's "holistic" method—that embodied the actual harms that most concerned her.[16] The net message for anyone paying close attention seemed to be that schools could do what they liked, so long as they sounded the right intentions and did not sufficiently quantify their work so that an outsider could readily determine how their preferences worked. No wonder Mary Sue Coleman was smiling.

Impact of *Grutter* and *Gratz*

University of Michigan

If *Grutter* and *Gratz* mattered anywhere, they should have mattered at the University of Michigan. After all, the College's methods of using race in undergraduate admissions had been specifically ruled unconstitutional by the Supreme Court. One might have expected dramatic changes in both methods and outcomes. Can we tell what happened?

Table 15.3 replicates the analysis presented in Table 15.1 on Michigan's undergraduate college—except it uses admissions data from 2006, three years after *Grutter*.[17] Since post-*Gratz*, the university was no longer treating race as a two-category phenomenon (URMs vs. non-URMs), Table 15.3 compares two specific racial groups: blacks and Asians.

In the 2006 regime, things have changed, but not necessarily in the way Justice O'Connor may have envisioned. There is still a broad range of index

Table 15.3 Undergraduate admissions rates at the University of Michigan, nonresidents only, 2006 (by academic "index" and race)

Admissions rate for Asian applicants (%)		Admissions rate for black applicants (%)	
900 and above	75	800 and above	96
850–899	36	750–799	72
800–849	11	700–749	43
750–799	5	650–699	27
Below 750	3	Under 650	14

scores within which blacks are guaranteed admission. And, in the lower index categories, there are much greater disparities between black and Asian admission rates in 2006 than existed between URM and non-URMs in 1999. There are thus many more cases in 2006 where race appears to be "the determining factor" in admissions. Not surprisingly, statistical analysis shows race was given more weight in 2006 than in 1999.

Even more ironic is the emergence of "racial balancing" in UM College admissions after *Gratz*. Under the school's challenged system, applicants got points if they were "underrepresented minorities" ("URMs")—that is, black, Hispanic, or American Indian. Race did not otherwise factor into admissions, so URMs got one type of preference, and anyone of another race got none. By 2006, however, the College was engaged in full-scale racial engineering: blacks received much larger preferences than Hispanics, who received large preferences over whites, who received preferences over Asians. The tendency, if not the motive, of this multi-tiered discrimination was to keep admissions closely aligned with the racial composition of applicants. If this was not racial balancing, what could be?

In the 2006 data, we have information on the socioeconomic status ("SES") of each applicant. Strikingly, many Asians and whites with relatively low SES are denied admission in index ranges where many blacks with high SES are admitted. There is no evidence in these data that black applicants are evaluated individually to determine what special contribution their race might make to UM's educational environment. Rather, blacks are evaluated to see which ones with relatively low index scores can be admitted with the least chance of academic failure.

In other words, the College's move to a "holistic" system in the wake of *Gratz* produced outcomes in which race was a more pervasive and heavily weighted factor, where every race was treated differently, and where socioeconomic diversity played a thoroughly subordinate role to race. None of these developments, of course, were known to Michigan voters, who approved by large margins a ballot initiative at the end of 2006 that sought, like California's Proposition 209, to ban the use of race altogether in state programs (including the University of Michigan). The enforceability of that ban is still unresolved at this writing (summer 2011).

Patterns at Law Schools

Next to the University of Michigan itself, the part of higher education that might have been most introspective after *Grutter* and *Gratz* were the nation's public law schools. For one thing, it was a law school admissions system that had received particularly intense scrutiny; one might have expected law schools to examine their own systems to make sure these had the character-istics vouchsafed by the Court. For another, *Grutter* marked the third chal-lenge in a decade to racial preference systems used by law schools; these institutions were clearly unusually vulnerable to attack. One might thus have expected admissions systems to (a) become less mechanical, (b) institute smaller racial preferences, (c) grant racial preferences more inconsistently, and (d) avoid signs of "racial balancing."

Yet, so far as we can tell, public law schools tended to do exactly the oppos-ite. Racial preferences generally became more mechanical, more consistent, larger, and continued to treat Hispanics and blacks differently.

I make these claims with the aid of unusually good data on law school admis-sions both before and after *Grutter*. In 2003, a research assistant and I wrote to a number of law schools with public records requests, and secured anonymized, individual-level admissions data from seven schools. In 2007, my staff and I made a more systematic effort, contacting nearly all the 70-odd public law schools in the United States. In this round we secured data from 40 law schools, including six that had responded in 2003. These 40 are broadly representative of public law schools in the United States. The number of variables we obtained varied from school to school, but for all applicants at all schools, we have LSAT scores, undergraduate grades, race, and application outcome—the data needed to do the sort of basic analyses illustrated in Tables 15.1, 15.2, and 15.3.

In Table 15.4, I present four summary measures of how law school admis-sions systems operated before and after *Grutter*. The first two rows show esti-mates of how "mechanical" the admissions processes are. To measure this, I use the simple device of the Somers' D, which is a measure of how well one can predict a binary outcome. Admissions decisions are "binary" because there are essentially two possibilities: accept or reject the applicant. With these data, one can run a logistic regression analysis and predict who is admitted, and one can measure how accurate are the predictions. Suppose, for example, that a law school admits half of its applicants. If asked to predict the outcome of "application 3759," with no knowledge of the applicant's individual charac-teristics, any guess one made has a 50/50 chance of proving correct. But sup-pose that if one knows each applicant's LSAT score and undergraduate GPA ("UGPA"), one can make correct guesses 80% of the time. The error rate has fallen from 50 out of 100 to 20 out of 100, a 60% reduction. The Somers' D would thus be 0.60. Note that with *all* of the information used in admissions decisions, one could in principle achieve a Somers' D of 1.00. With the few pieces of data we do have, any Somers' D over 0.80 suggests a simple and fairly mechanical system. Indeed, the explicity mechanical, pre-*Grutter* under-graduate admissions system at University of Michigan has a Somer's D of 0.81, when analyzed by the same methods used in Table 15.4 for law schools.

With the same regression analysis, one can determine the relative importance of various admissions factors. For example, if we predict admissions outcomes and include LSAT, UGPA, in-state residency, and race, the resulting regression equation will tell us the association between a change in any factor and the change in admission probability. This is not conclusive, because there are other factors not in the equation that shape admissions (e.g., college quality, letters of recommendation, public service, the application essay). However, the closer the Somers' D gets to 1.00, the less scope there is for unmeasured factors to have any influence. In other words, if one can predict admissions outcomes, knowing only a few characteristics of each applicant, from these factors with a high degree of accuracy, one can infer that no other factors figured importantly in admissions decisions.

Table 15.4 also includes averages calculated from the "odds ratio" for black admissions (relative to white admissions) at each law school. The odds ratio is a descriptive statistic generated by a logistic regression. In very approximate, intuitive terms, the square root of an odds ratio indicates how much more likely a black is, relative to a white, to be accepted by a law school, at a credential range where both groups have a non-zero chance of admission or rejection.

The patterns shown in Table 15.4 are striking. By all four measures, law school admissions became, on average, more mechanical and more focused on race after the *Grutter* decision. Notably, the increase in Somers' D is particularly large and abrupt for black applicants. (Recall that, to Justice O'Connor, the sine qua non of a constitutional use of race was considering the *unique* contributions particular minority students could make to a school's diversity.) The average

Table 15.4 Characteristics of law school admissions before and after *Grutter*

Characteristic	Six public law schools		40 law schools post-Grutter, 2005, 2006, and 2007 admissions cycles
	Pre-Grutter: 2002 and 2003	Post-Grutter: 2005, 2006, 2007	
Somers' D, all decisions	0.82	0.85	0.86
Somers' D, decisions on black applicants	0.76	0.85	0.88
Preference size (in LSAT points), black applicants	11.2	12.7	13.1
Median "odds" ratio, black-to-white admissions	102	138	150

Note
All figures are averages for the observed admissions cohorts across schools, unless otherwise noted.

Somers' D for blacks of 0.88 in our 40-school sample means that, at many law schools, admissions officers are effectively segregating admissions and simply admitting all but two or three of the highest-credential black applicants, while rejecting hundreds or thousands of applicants of other races with identical credentials.[18] These data suggest very narrow definitions of diversity indeed.

Of the six law schools for which we have before-and-after data, only the University of Michigan Law School—the subject of *Grutter*—showed significant signs of moving towards a significantly less mechanical admissions process in the years following the decision, with Somers' D scores for all admittees falling below 0.75. This is no accident; Dean Evan Caminker has told me that the school deliberately tried to make its admissions more multi-factored even before the Supreme Court's decision in *Grutter*. The data on preference size and odds ratios show an increased focus on race after *Grutter*, and an increasing tendency to insulate black admissions from other admissions decisions.

Law schools also showed no sign of reducing practices that looked like racial balancing. Both before and after *Grutter*, nearly all law schools used admissions preferences for both blacks and Hispanics, but applied systematically larger preferences to blacks; preference size seems to be most heavily influenced by the strength or weakness of a particular group's applicant pool, rather than by a general quest to maximize diversity.

What are the reasons for these patterns? At these we really can only guess, since any law school dean (or head of admissions) would obviously act at her great peril in candidly discussing admissions rationales. But a variety of evidence supports these hunches about the several institutional forces at work:

1   As Mary Sue Coleman's reaction in front of the Supreme Court illustrated, most of the higher education establishment felt much more relief than concern about the *Gratz/Grutter* framework. Even before analysts demonstrated that Michigan's law school gave greater weight to race than Michigan's undergraduate program, it was obvious that O'Connor, like Powell before her, had placed much more emphasis on matters of form than substantive outcomes.

2   The advantages of formulas, as a means of efficiently summarizing complex information about individual applicants, were too great to be dispensed with by many (and perhaps the great majority) of universities, colleges and professional schools. The key to staying out of trouble was to not give a specific assignment of points to race. Schools consequently moved to one of two methods: (a) informally segregated admissions, or (b) "holistic" processes that were carefully cultivated to produce specific and predictable racial results.

3   All admissions officers realized if they increased the level of "individualized assessment" they gave to minority candidates, it would be necessary

to delve further down (credential-wise) into the minority pool to admit the requisite number of students. In other words, factoring in more "soft" considerations, such as a student's community service or socioeconomic status, would necessarily mean giving less weight to "hard" credentials, like LSAT and college grades. Yet admissions officers were usually aware that admitting students with lower hard credentials would hurt their school's graduation and bar passage rates. This logic led them to resist the holistic approach most doggedly when considering minority students, even though it was with racially-preferred students that O'Connor envisioned the most individualized assessment.

4   Schools felt themselves more than ever pulled into a competitive process in which eliteness ratings were importantly influenced by both the credential level of their students (median LSATs and college grades) and by the school's "diversity" (URM) numbers. Both pressures pushed them toward admissions that were simpler—driven by scores, grades, and race—rather than more complex.

5   A guiding principle of Justice O'Connor's decision—and a value clearly shared by most of the Court—was that universities should have the autonomy to decide whether diversity is necessary to their educational mission, and—within limits—what form that diversity should take. This implies that accreditation bodies—external agencies that decide whether schools are meeting minimum standards—should not judge the diversity policies of schools (aside, of course, from making sure civil rights law are not violated). Yet the available evidence suggests that these bodies continue to be quite heavy-handed in mandating and enforcing "diversity" policies that cannot be met without the use of large racial preferences (U.S. Civil Rights Commission 2008).

Affirmative Action and Judicial Policy-Making

Over the past generation, the impact of judicial decisions has become an intellectually rich and active area of research (Canon and Johnson 1984, 1999; Rosenberg 1991). Courts have very limited capacity, and not much inclination, to insure that decisions are actually implemented. A great deal depends on whether decision-makers affected by the decision (in this case, university administrators) are in sympathy with a holding, believe that disobedience can be readily detected, and fear the consequences of an enforcement lawsuit (White 2001).

When addressing matters that rivet and deeply divide American society, the Supreme Court has usually treaded with caution. As Michael Klarman (2004) argues in his insightful history of the Court's civil rights decisions, Supreme Court decisions often reflected public opinion at least as much as they shaped it. Justices were wary of issuing decisions that were unlikely to be implemented;

and when the Court did lead, it usually avoided getting very far in front of emerging social consensus. In affirmative action, the Court faced an unusual kind of public division. Opinion polls and popular votes on "preference bans" showed that a majority of Americans opposed racial preferences (and would be even more opposed if they knew how large and mechanical these preferences were at many universities). But institutional leaders in the United States strongly favored them—not just at universities, but in the corporate world and even the American military. The briefs submitted to the Court, which provide a rough index of at least how "elites" weigh in upon an issue, ran overwhelmingly in favor of racial preferences for both *Bakke* and *Grutter/Gratz*.

Powell and O'Connor both presumably knew that, given the high allegiance of university administrators to preference systems, obedience to a sweeping restriction of affirmative action was not a foregone conclusion (Lipson 2007, 2011).

Under the circumstances, it is not surprising that Powell and O'Connor both hit upon the idea of banning some very visible *symbol* of affirmative action—quotas in *Bakke* and point-systems in *Gratz*—while remaining somewhat vague about what sort of preferences *were* permitted. In this way, the justices struck politically viable compromises and made it likely that at least on the face of things, practices would appear to change.

But a steep price was paid. As others have shown, Supreme Court decisions that set vague standards are particularly likely to be half-heartedly implemented, or even completely ignored, by the government actors with relevant operational responsibilities (Staton and Vanberg 2008). But in the affirmative action cases, the stakes were higher; the Court was interpreting the application of its most exacting standard—strict scrutiny—to the delicate issue of reverse discrimination. In not only allowing preference programs to survive strict scrutiny, but creating vague standards, the justices sent a double message: not only were the particulars vague, but the underlying standard was made soft, rather than formidable.

From what we know of Justice Powell's motivations in *Bakke*, he did seek a meaningful curtailment of preferences; certainly he wanted to avoid the long-term entrenchment of race as a central criterion for allocating university spaces. But *Bakke* led to just that type of entrenchment. We know less, for now, about Justice O'Connor's motives, but it is hard to imagine she secretly hoped her decision would move on-the-ground practices in the opposite direction from her stated principles. Indeed, remarks O'Connor has made since her retirement suggest she regrets the vagueness of *Grutter*. In both cases, the central error made in these decisions was to make the operation of preference systems more opaque, rather than more transparent.

Transparency in this context means two things: first, that those monitoring university behavior can readily measure the size of racial preferences; and second, that the standards governing the use of preferences be concrete enough so that monitors can determine with some confidence whether a standard is violated. Point systems are obviously helpful in attaining these goals, but they are not essential. Justice Powell could have, for example, held that racial preferences could be no larger than those extended based on socioeconomic disadvantage. Justice O'Connor could have made her vague 25-year timeline more concrete by requiring that universities cut the size of their racial preferences at least in half every 10 years. So long as these sorts of standards are accompanied by a require-ment that universities engaging in racial preferences create anonymized, public datasets that record key applicant characteristics and admission decisions, the decisions become almost self-executing. Without transparency, "strict scrutiny" becomes literally a contradiction in terms.

Transparency would have collateral benefits, as well. A requirement that uni-versities provide data on other types of diversity factored into admissions would make far more public the extraordinary lack of socioeconomic diversity at nearly all professional schools and elite colleges (Kahlenberg 1996, 2004; Sander 2011). Data on student outcomes would make it far easier to document the extent of the "mismatch" phenomenon. Transparency would not only help make the Supreme Court's holding tangible and enforceable; it would also lead to a common empirical understanding of affirmative action, and a level of accounta-bility in higher education, that has been sought, but missing, for many years.

Notes

1 I am especially grateful to Jane Yakowitz for doing the underlying analysis for Table 15.4, *infra*, as well as discussing with me in detail most of the concepts explored in this chapter. I have also received valuable input from Kevin McGuire, Stuart Taylor, Jon Varat, Eugene Volokh, and Steve Yeazell.

2 Jewish quotas, preference for established schools, etc.

3 College enrollment rose by a factor of five between the eve of World War II and the late 1960s (see Carter *et al.* 2006, *Historical Statistics of the United States, Mille-nial Edition*, 2–441).

4 Admissions at elite schools have continued to become more competitive, albeit at a slower rate (and in part simply because more students strategically apply to many uni-versities). Most elite schools today admit only 10–12% of their applicants (*US News*).

5 "Percentile" is a distributional term, in which the lowest ranking student is said to be at the 1st percentile, and the top ranking student at the 99th percentile. If some-one is at the 10th percentile, that means that 10% of the students are ranked below him, and 90% are ranked above him.

6 Among Hispanics, Cuban-Americans tend to substantially outperform other His-panic groups on standardized tests; many schools will therefore have different preferences for Hispanic sub-groups. Similarly, on the West Coast, many schools have different ethnic-specific preferences for various Asian ethnicities.

7 For purposes of simplicity in this example, I assume yield rates are similar across races.

8 For example, the investigator could first collect all the avowedly quantitative information used by the officer, such as test scores and grades. Next, the investigator would give the officer pairs of applicant files, and ask her to say which file has the stronger letters of recommendation, the greater hardship to overcome, and so on. With enough pairwise rankings, the investigator could create an ordinal ranking of

the files according to the various subjective criteria used by the officer. With this information, the investigator could create and run a logistic regression in which the admissions decision is the outcome, and the various quantitative data and the subjective ordinal rankings are the independent variables. The coefficients produced by this regression would tell us the relative weight given to each factor, and the "score" each applicant earns on each factor. If the admissions officer made internally consistent distinctions among applicants, then the regression equation would be able to "predict" the officer's decisions with perfect accuracy.

9　Employment discrimination cases are more common than other types of civil rights cases because the plaintiff is usually an "insider" who is fired or denied a promotion, and thus has lots of inside knowledge and, probably, a large number of specific grievances (Donohue and Siegelman 1991). Potential affirmative action challenges, in contrast, are just the opposite—they have little knowledge of any specific university, and tend to view a rejection from any one school as relatively inconsequential.

10　This is the moral of *DeFunis v. Odegaard*, a suit challenging preferences that made it all the way to the Supreme Court in 1974. The Court ultimately declined to issue a substantive ruling on the ground that the plaintiff, Marco DeFunis, had nearly finished law school by the time the case reached the Court, thus mooting the question of whether he should have been admitted to the University of Washington.

11　Powell drew this account of a "permissible" use of race from a brief submitted by Harvard College; he even explicitly endorsed a Harvard-like admissions system as constitutional.

12　This figure, unlike the 16% quota litigated in *Bakke*, did not include Asians (*Princeton Review*, 2009 at 244).

13　Michigan's undergraduate college was (and is) considered among the top three or four undergraduate public universities in the nation; its law school was (and is) generally ranked first among public law schools, and even including private schools like Yale and Harvard, ranked among the top six or seven.

14　The relative weights for each school's academic index were determined by regressing applicant characteristics on admissions outcomes, and using these coefficients to determine weights. In other words, the weights reflect, as best we can determine, the relative weight given to test scores and grades by admissions officers.

15　The same distinction applies to minority admissions: at the College, there is a 200-point gap between "almost certain" admits and "almost certain" rejections among underrepresented minorities; at the law school an analogous swing occurs over merely 140 index points.

16　Note that Ayres and Foster (2006) reach the same analytic conclusions I did in Sander (2004).

17　This is the year Michigan voters passed Proposition 2, which prohibited the use of preferences; while the constitutionality of Prop 2 is still being litigated, the 2006 data offer the best chance to see how UM's undergraduate program implemented *Gratz* and *Grutter*. In calculating the 2006 index, I have used a slightly different formula to reflect changes in the relative weight UM gave to the SAT (and the shift of the SAT to a 2,400-point scale). Note also that both Table 15.1 and Table 15.3 focus on out-of-state admissions, to control for the significant effect in-state residency has on admissions of all groups (the racial disparities reported here are not very different for in-state than out-of-state applicants).

18　Recall that a Somers' D of 0.88 means that about 94% of all admissions decisions can be predicted knowing only the LSAT, UGPA, and race of the applicant. Keep in mind, too, that these figures are minimums; if we knew about other factors considered in admissions (e.g., recommendations, disciplinary records, etc.) we would get still closer to perfect prediction.

References

Abraham, Henry J. 1999. *Justices, Presidents, and Senators: A History of the U.S. Supreme Court Appointments from Washington to Clinton.* Lanham: Rowman & Littlefield.

Achen, Christopher H. 1986. *The Statistical Analysis of Quasi-Experiments.* Berkeley: University of California Press.

Ah How (alias Louie Ah How) v. United States. 1904. 193 U.S. 65.

Aldrich, John H., and Forrest D. Nelson. 1984. *Linear Probability, Logit, and Probit Models.* Beverly Hills: Sage Publications.

Allen, Carleton Kemp. 1964. *Law in the Making,* 7th ed. New York: Clarendon Press.

American Judicature Society. 2011. "Judicial Selection in the States." Available at: www.judicialselection.us (accessed June 1, 2011).

Anastasoff v. U.S. 2000. 223 F.3d 898.

Angell, Marcia. 1997. *Science on Trial: The Clash of Medical Evidence and the Law in the Breast Implant Case.* New York: W.W. Norton.

Apple, R.W. 1990. "Sununu Tells How and Why He Pushed Souter for Court," *The New York Times,* July 25, A12.

Applebome, Peter. 1994. "Prayer in Public Schools? It's Nothing New for Many." *New York Times,* November 22, A1.

Arceneaux, Kevin T., Chris W. Bonneau, and Paul Brace. 2008. "Judging Under Constraint: Institutions and State Supreme Court Decisionmaking." Paper Presented at the Annual Meeting of the Midwest Political Science Association, April 3–6, Chicago.

Ayres, Ian, and Sydney Foster. 2006. "Don't Tell, Don't Ask: Narrow Tailoring After Grutter and Gratz." *Texas Law Review* 85(3): 517–583.

Bach, Stanley, and Steven S. Smith. 1988. *Managing Uncertainty in the House of Representatives: Adaptation and Innovation in Special Rules.* Washington, DC: Brookings Institution.

Bailey, Michael A. 2007. "Comparable Preference Estimates Across Time and Institutions for the Court, Congress, and Presidency." *American Journal of Political Science* 51(3): 433–448.

Bailey, Michael A., and Forrest Maltzman. 2008. "Does Legal Doctrine Matter Unpacking Law and Policy Preferences on the U.S. Supreme Court." *American Political Science Review* 102(3): 369–384.

Bailey, Michael A., and Forrest Maltzman. 2011. *The Constrained Court: Law, Politics and the Decisions Justices Make.* Princeton: Princeton University Press.

Bailey, Michael A. and Albert Yoon. 2011. "While there's a Breath in My Body: The Systemic Effects of Politically Motivated Retirement from the Supreme Court." *Journal of Theoretical Politics* 23(3): 293–316.

Bailey, Michael A., Brian Kamoie, and Forrest Maltzman. 2005. "Signals from the Tenth Justice: The Political Role of the Solicitor General in Supreme Court Decision-making." *American Journal of Political Science* 49(1): 72–85.

Bailey, William C., and Ruth D. Peterson. 1994. "Murder, Capital Punishment, and Deterrence: A Review of the Evidence and an Examination of Police Killings." *Journal of Social Issues* 50: 53–74.

Bailis, David S., and Robert J. MacCoun. 1996. "Estimating Liability Risks with the Media as Your Guide: A Content Analysis of Media Coverage of Civil Litigation." *Law and Human Behavior* 20: 419–429.

Baldus, David C., George G. Woodworth, and Charles A. Pulaski, Jr. 1990. *Equal Justice and the Death Penalty: A Legal and Empirical Analysis*. Boston: Northeastern University Press.

Baldus, David C., George Woodworth, David Zuckerman, Neil Adam Weiner, and Barbara Broffitt. 1998. "Racial Discrimination and the Death Penalty in the Post-Furman Era: An Empirical and Legal Overview, with Recent Findings from Philadelphia." *Cornell Law Review* 83(6): 1638–1770.

Banner, Stuart. 2003. "The Myth of the Neutral Amicus: American Courts and Their Friends, 1790–1890." *Constitutional Commentary* 20: 111–130.

Barnes, Jeb. 2007. "Bringing the Courts Back In: Interbranch Perspectives on the Role of Courts in American Politics and Policy Making." *Annual Review of Political Science* 10(June): 25–43.

Baum, Lawrence. 1976. "Implementation of Judicial Decisions: An Organizational Analysis." *American Politics Quarterly* 4: 86–114.

Baum, Lawrence. 1978. "Lower-Court Response to Supreme Court Decisions: Reconsidering a Negative Picture." *Justice System Journal* 3: 208–219.

Baum, Lawrence. 1998. *The Supreme Court*, 6th ed. Washington, DC: CQ Press.

Baum, Lawrence. 1999. "Recruitment and the Motivations of Supreme Court Justices." In Cornell W. Clayton and Howard Gillman, eds. *Supreme Court Decision-making: New Institutionalist Approaches*. Chicago: University of Chicago Press, pp. 201–213.

Baum, Lawrence. 2002. "The Implementation of United States Supreme Court Decisions." In Ralf Rogowski and Thomas Gawron, eds. *Constitutional Courts in Comparison: The U.S. Supreme Court and the German Federal Constitutional Court*. New York: Berghahn Books, pp. 219–238.

Baum, Lawrence. 2006. *Judges and Their Audiences: A Perspective on Judicial Behavior*. Princeton: Princeton University Press.

Baumgartner, Frank, Suzanna De Boef, and Amber Boydstun. 2008. *The Decline of the Death Penalty and the Discovery of Innocence*. Cambridge: Cambridge University Press.

Bedau, Hugo Adam. 2004. *Debating the Death Penalty*. New York: Oxford University Press.

Beiser, Edward N. 1968. "A Comparative Analysis of State and Federal Judicial Behavior: the Reapportionment Cases." *American Political Science Review* 62(3): 788–795.

Benesh, Sara C. 2002. *The U.S. Court of Appeals and the Law of Confessions: Perspectives on the Hierarchy of Justice*. New York: LFB Scholarly Publishing.

Benesh, Sara C. 2008. "Supreme Court Monitoring via GVR." *Southern Illinois Law Review* 32: 659–681.

Benesh, Sara C., and Wendy L. Martinek. 2002. "State Supreme Court Decision Making in Confession Cases." *Justice System Journal* 23: 109–133.

Benesh, Sara C., and Wendy L. Martinek. 2009. "Context and Compliance: A Comparison of State Supreme Courts and the Circuits." *Marquette Law Review* 93: 795–824.

Benesh, Sara C., and Malia Reddick. 2002. "Overruled: An Event History Analysis of Lower Court Reaction to Supreme Court Alteration of Precedent." *Journal of Politics* 64(2): 534–550.

Benesh, Sara C., Saul Brenner, and Harold J. Spaeth. 2002. "Aggressive Grants by Affirm-Minded Justices." *American Politics Research* 30(3): 219–234.

Benesh, Sara C., Jennifer K. Luse, Amanda Schaeffer, and Nicole Simmons. 2007. "Supreme Court Monitoring via GVRs." Paper Presented at the Annual Meeting of the Midwest Political Science Association, April 12–15, Chicago.

Berman, Harold, and William R. Greiner. 1966. *The Nature and Function of Law*, 2nd ed. Brooklyn: The Foundation Press.

Berry, Jeffrey M. 1997. *The Interest Group Society*, 3rd ed. New York: Longman.

Berry, William D., Evan J. Ringquist, Richard C. Fording, and Russell L. Hanson. 1998. "Measuring Citizen and Government Ideology in the American States, 1960–1993." *American Journal of Political Science* 42: 327–348.

Binder, Sarah A. 1996. "The Partisan Basis of Procedural Choice: Allocating Parliamentary Rights in the House, 1789–1990." *American Political Science Review* 90(March): 8–20.

Binder, Sarah A. 1997. *Minority Rights, Majority Rule: Partisanship and the Development Of Congress*. New York: Cambridge University Press.

Binder, Sarah A., and Forrest Maltzman. 2002. "Senatorial Delay in Confirming Judges, 1947–1998." *American Journal of Political Science* 46: 190–199.

Birkby, Robert H. 1966. "The Supreme Court and the Bible Belt: Tennessee Reaction to the 'Schempp' Decision." *Midwest Journal of Political Science* 10: 304–319.

Biskupic, Joan. 2009. "Supreme Court Mulls Judicial Bias," March 3, *USA Today*. Available at: www.usatoday.com/news/washington/2009-03-03-scotus-judges_N. htm.

Black, Earl, and Merle Black. 2002. *The Rise of Southern Republicans*. Cambridge, MA: Harvard University Press.

Black, Ryan C., and Ryan J. Owens. 2009a. "Agenda-Setting in the Supreme Court: The Collision of Policy and Jurisprudence." *Journal of Politics* 71(3): 1062–1075.

Black, Ryan C., and Ryan J. Owens. 2009b. "Join-3 Votes and Supreme Court Agenda Setting." Unpublished manuscript.

Black, Ryan C., and Ryan J. Owens. 2009c. "Analyzing the Reliability of Supreme Court Justices' Agenda Setting Records." *Justice System Journal* 30(3): 254–264.

Black, Ryan C., and James F. Spriggs, II. 2008. "An Empirical Analysis of the Length of U.S. Supreme Court Opinions." *Houston Law Review* 45(3): 621–683.

Blalock, Hubert M. 1967. *Towards a Theory of Minority Group Relations*. New York: Capricorn.

Blume, John, Theodore Eisenberg, and Martin T. Wells. 2004. "Explaining Death Row's Population and Racial Composition." *Journal of Empirical Legal Studies* 1: 165–207

Bogus, Carl T. 2001. *Why Lawsuits Are Good for America: Disciplined Democracy, Big Business, and the Common Law*. New York: New York University Press.

Boles, John B. 1996. *The Great Revival: Beginnings of the Bible Belt.* Lexington: University of Kentucky Press.

Boller, Paul F., Jr., and John George. 1989. *They Never Said It: A Book of Fake Quotes, Misquotes, and Misleading Attributions.* New York: Oxford University Press.

Bonneau, Chris W. 2005. "What Price Justice(s)? Campaign Spending in State Supreme Court Elections." *State Politics and Policy Quarterly* 5(2): 107–125.

Bonneau, Chris W. 2007. "The Effects of Campaign Spending in State Supreme Court Elections." *Political Research Quarterly* 60(3): 489–499.

Bonneau, Chris W., and Damon M. Cann. 2009. "The Effect of Campaign Contributions on Judicial Decisionmaking." Unpublished manuscript.

Bonneau, Chris W., and Melinda Gann Hall. 2009. *In Defense of Judicial Elections.* New York: Routledge.

Bonneau, Chris W., Brent D. Boyea, Damon M. Cann, and Victoria A. Farrar-Myers. 2010. "Campaign Contributions in State Supreme Court Elections." Paper Presented at the Annual Meeting of the Midwest Political Science Association, April 22–25, Chicago.

Bonneau, Chris W., Thomas H. Hammond, Forrest Maltzman, and Paul J. Wahlbeck. 2007. "Agenda Control, the Median Justice, and the Majority Opinion on the U.S. Supreme Court." *American Journal of Political Science* 51(4): 890–905.

Boucher, Jr., Robert L., and Jeffrey A. Segal. 1995. "Supreme Court Justices as Strategic Decision Makers: Aggressive Grants and Defensive Denials on the Vinson Court." *Journal of Politics* 57(3): 824–837.

Bowen, William G., and Derek Bok. 1998. *The Shape of the River: The Long-Term Consequences of Considering Race in College and University Admissions.* Princeton: Princeton University Press.

Bowers v. Hardwick. 1986. 478 U.S. 186.

Bowie, Jennifer Barnes, and Donald R. Songer. 2009. "Assessing the Applicability of Strategic Theory to Explain Decision Making on the Courts of Appeals." *Political Research Quarterly* 62: 393–407.

Brace, Paul, and Brent D. Boyea. 2008. "State Public Opinion, the Death Penalty, and the Practice of Electing Judges." *American Journal of Political Science* 52(2): 360–372.

Brace, Paul, and Melinda Gann Hall. 1990. "Neo-Institutionalism and Dissent in State Supreme Courts." *Journal of Politics* 52(1): 54–70.

Brace, Paul, and Melinda Gann Hall. 1993. "Integrated Models of Judicial Dissent." *Journal of Politics* 55(4): 914–935.

Brace, Paul, and Melinda Gann Hall. 1995. "Studying Courts Comparatively: The View from The American States." *Political Research Quarterly* 48: 5–29.

Brace, Paul, and Melinda Gann Hall. 1997. "The Interplay of Preferences, Case Facts, Context, and Rules in the Politics of Judicial Choice." *Journal of Politics* 59: 1206–1231.

Brace, Paul, Laura Langer, and Melinda Gann Hall. 2000. "Measuring the Preferences of State Supreme Court Judges." *Journal of Politics* 62(2): 387–413.

Brehm, John, and Scott Gates. 1997. *Working, Shirking, and Sabotage.* Ann Arbor: University of Michigan Press.

Brenner, Saul. 1979. "The New Certiorari Game." *Journal of Politics* 41(2): 649–655.

Brenner, Saul, and Harold J. Spaeth. 1995. *Stare Indecisis: The Alteration of Precedent on the Supreme Court, 1946–1992.* New York: Cambridge University Press.

Brent, James. 2003. "A Principal-Agent Analysis of U.S. Courts of Appeals Responses to *Boerne v. Flores*." *American Politics Research* 31: 557–570.

Brewer, Mark D., and Jeffrey M. Stonecash. 2009. *Dynamics of American Political Parties*. New York: Cambridge University Press.

Breyer, Stephen. 1998. "The Interdependence of Science and Law." *Judicature* 82(1): 24–27.

Brigham, John. 1996. *The Constitution of Interests: Beyond the Politics of Rights*. New York: New York University Press.

Brodie, Ian. 2002. *Friends of the Court: The Privileging of Interest Group Litigants in Canada*. Albany: State University of New York Press.

Brown v. Board of Education. 1954. 347 U.S. 483.

Bueno de Mesquita, Ethan, and Matthew Stephenson. 2002. "Informative Precedent and Intrajudicial Communication." *American Political Science Review* 96(December): 755–766.

Burnside, Fred. 1999. "Dying to Get Elected: A Challenge to the Jury Override." *Wisconsin Law Review* 5: 1015–1049.

Bush v. Gore. 2000. 531 U.S. 98.

Bush v. Vera. 1996. 517. U.S. 952.

Bush, George W. 2010. *Decision Points*. New York: Crown Publishers.

Calabresi, Steven, and James Lindgren. 2006. "Term Limits for the Supreme Court: Life Tenure Reconsidered." *Harvard Journal of Law and Public Policy* 29(3): 770–877.

Caldeira, Gregory A. 1987. "Public Opinion and the U.S. Supreme Court: FDR's Court-Packing Plan." *American Political Science Review* 81(December): 1139–1153.

Caldeira, Gregory A., and John R. Wright. 1988. "Organized Interests and Agenda Setting in the U.S. Supreme Court." *American Political Science Review* 82(4): 1109–1127.

Caldeira, Gregory A., and John R. Wright. 1990. "Amici Curiae Before the Supreme Court: Who Participates, When, and How Much?" *Journal of Politics* 52(3): 782–806.

Caldeira, Gregory A., and John R. Wright. 1998. "Lobbying for Justice: Organized Interests Supreme Court Nominations, and United States Senate." *American Journal of Political Science* 42(2): 499–523.

Caldeira, Gregory A., John R. Wright, and Christopher J.W. Zorn. 1999. "Sophisticated Voting and Gate-Keeping in the Supreme Court." *Journal of Law, Economics, & Organization* 15(3): 549–572.

Cameron, Charles M. 1993. "New Avenues for Modeling Judicial Politics." Paper Presented at the Conference on the Political Economy of Public Law, Wallis Institute of Political Economy, Rochester University.

Cameron, Charles M., and Lewis A. Kornhauser. 2006. "Appeals Mechanisms, Litigant Selection and the Structure of Judicial Hierarchies." In Jon Bond, Roy Fleming, and James Rogers, eds. *Institutional Games and the U.S. Supreme Court*. Charlottesville: University of Virginia Press, pp. 173–204.

Cameron, Charles M., Albert D. Cover, and Jeffrey A. Segal. 1990. "Senate Voting on Supreme Court Nominees: A Neoinstitutional Model." *American Political Science Review* 84: 413–524.

Cameron, Charles, Jeffrey Segal, and Donald Songer. 2000. "Strategic Auditing in a Political Hierarchy: An Informational Model of the Supreme Court's Certiorari Decision." *American Political Science Review* 94(1): 101–116.

Caminker, Evan H. 1994. "Why Must Inferior Courts Obey Supreme Court Precedents?" *Stanford Law Review* 46(April): 817–873.

Cann, Damon M. 2002. "Campaign Contributions and Judicial Behavior." *American Review of Politics* 23(Fall): 261–274.

Cann, Damon M. 2007. "Justice for Sale? Campaign Contributions and Judicial Decisionmaking." *State Politics and Policy Quarterly* 7(3): 281–297.

Cann, Damon M., and Jeff Yates. 2008. "Homegrown Institutional Legitimacy: Assessing Citizens' Diffuse Support for State Courts." *American Politics Research* 36(2): 297–329.

Canon, Bradley C. 1999. "Courts and Policy: Compliance, Implementation, and Impact." In John B. Gates and Charles A. Johnson, eds. *The American Courts: A Critical Assessment.* Washington, DC: CQ Press, pp. 435–466.

Canon, Bradley C., and Charles A. Johnson. 1999. *Judicial Policies: Implementation and Impact,* 2nd ed. Washington, DC: CQ Press.

Caplan, Lincoln. 1987. *The Tenth Justice: The Solicitor General and the Rule of Law.* New York: Knopf.

Carrington, Paul D. 1999. "The Obsolescence of the United States Courts of Appeals: Roscoe Pound's Structural Solution." *Journal of Law & Policy* 15: 515–529.

Carrington, Paul D., Daniel J. Meador, and Maurice Rosenberg. 1976. *Justice on Appeal.* St. Paul: West Publishing.

Carroll, James. 2004. "Americans and the Death Penalty: Gallup Reviews Public Opinion on the Death Penalty in Wake of Scott Peterson Case." *Gallup Organization,* December 15.

Carrubba, Clifford J., and Tom S. Clark. 2010. "Rule Making in a Political Hierarchy." Paper Presented at the Midwest Political Science Association, Chicago.

Carrubba, Clifford, Barry Friedman, Andrew D. Martin, and Georg Vanberg. 2007. "Does the Median Justice Control the Content of Supreme Court Opinions?" Paper Presented at the Second Annual Conference on Empirical Legal Studies.

Carter, Susan B., Scott Sigmund Gartner, Michael R. Haines, Alan L. Olmstead, Richard Sutch, and Gavin Wright, eds. 2006. *Historical Statistics of the United States, Earliest Times to the Present, Millennial Edition.* New York: Cambridge University Press.

Casey, Gregory. 1974. "The Supreme Court and Myth: An Empirical Investigation." *Law & Society Review* 8: 385–419.

Cawley, Jared B. 2004. "Friend of the Court: How the WTO Justifies the Acceptance of the Amicus Curiae Brief from Non-Governmental Organization." *Penn State International Law Review* 23(1): 47–78.

CBS News/*New York Times* Poll. 2006. Retrieved May 19, 2011 from the iPOLL Databank, The Roper Center for Public Opinion Research, University of Connecticut. January.

Center for Responsive Politics. 2010. "Background: Tobacco." Available at: www.opensecrets.org/industries/background.php?cycle=&ind=A02 (accessed December 13, 2010).

Center for Responsive Politics. 2011. "Influence and Lobbying: Tobacco." Available at: www.opensecrets.org/industries/indus.php?ind=a02 (accessed January 15, 2011).

Champagne, Anthony. 1988. "Judicial Reform in Texas." *Judicature* 72(3): 146–159.

Chase, Harold W. 1972. *Federal Judges: The Appointing Process.* Minneapolis: University of Minnesota Press.

Choi, Stephen J., Mitu Gulati, and Eric Posner. n.d. "What do Federal District Court Judges Want? An Analysis of Publication, Citations, and Reversals." *Journal of Law, Economics & Organization* (forthcoming).

Clark, Tom S. 2009. "The Separation of Powers, Court Curbing and Judicial Legitimacy." *American Journal of Political Science* 53(4): 971–989.

Clark, Tom. 2010. *The Limits of Judicial Independence.* New York: Cambridge University Press.

Clark, Tom S., and Benjamin Lauderdale. 2010. "Locating Supreme Court Opinions in Doctrine Space." *American Journal of Political Science* 54(4): 871–890.

Clawson, Rosalee A., Elizabeth R. Kegler, and Eric N. Waltenburg. 2001. "The Legitimacy-Conferring Authority of the U.S. Supreme Court: An Experimental Design." *American Politics Research* 29: 566–591.

Clayton, Cornell, and Howard Gillman, eds. 1999. *Supreme Court Decision Making: New Institutional Approaches.* Chicago: University of Chicago Press.

Clayton, James E. 1962. "Wave of Protests Follows Ruling on Prayers in School." *New York Times,* June 27, A1.

Cleary, Edward L., and Allen D. Hertzke. 2005. *Representing God at the Statehouse: Religion and Politics in the American States.* Lanham, MD: Rowman & Littlefield.

Clermont, Kevin M., and Theodore Eisenberg. 2000. "Anti-Plaintiff Bias in the Federal Appellate Courts." *Judicature* 84: 128–134.

Clermont, Kevin M., and Theodore Eisenberg. 2001. "Appeal from Judge or Jury Trial: Defendant's Advantage." *American Law and Economics Review* 3: 125–164.

Clermont, Kevin M., and Theodore Eisenberg. 2002. "Plaintiphobia in the Appellate Courts: Civil Rights Really Do Differ From Negotiable Instruments." *University of Illinois Law Review* 2002: 947–978.

Cohen, Jonathan M. 2002. *Inside Appellate Courts.* Ann Arbor: University of Michigan Press.

Cohn, Marjorie. 2007–2008. "Let the Sun Shine on the Supreme Court." *Hastings Constitutional Law Quarterly* 35: 161–168.

Collier, D., and J. Mahon, Jr. 1993. "Conceptual 'Stretching' Revisited: Adapting Categories in Comparative Politics." *American Political Science Review* 87(4): 845–855.

Collins, Paul M., Jr. 2004. "Friends of the Court: Examining the Influence of Amicus Curiae Participation in U.S. Supreme Court Litigation." *Law & Society Review* 38(4): 807–832.

Collins, Paul M., Jr. 2007. "Lobbyists before the U.S. Supreme Court: Investigating the Influence of Amicus Curiae Briefs." *Political Research Quarterly* 60(1): 55–70.

Collins, Paul M., Jr. 2008. *Friends of the Supreme Court: Interest Groups and Judicial Decision Making.* New York: Oxford University Press.

Collins, Paul M., Jr., and Wendy L. Martinek. 2010. "Friends of the Circuits: Interest Group Influence on Decision Making in the U.S. Courts of Appeals." *Social Science Quarterly* 91: 397–414.

Collins, Paul, M., Jr., and Lisa A. Solowiej. 2007. "Interest Group Participation, Competition, and Conflict in the U.S. Supreme Court." *Law & Social Inquiry* 32(4): 955–984.

Comiskey, Michael. 2004. *Seeking Justices: The Judging of Supreme Court Nominees.* Lawrence: University of Kansas Press.

Commonwealth of Pennsylvania v. Labron. 1997. 690 A. 2d. 228.

Commonwealth of Pennsylvania v. Matos. 1996. 749 A. 2d. 468.

Comparato, Scott A. 2003. *Amici Curiae and Strategic Behavior in State Supreme Courts*. Westport: Praeger.

Comparato, Scott A., and Scott D. McClurg. 2007. "A Neo-Institutional Explanation of State Supreme Court Responses in Search and Seizure Cases." *American Politics Research* 35(5): 726–754.

Corley, Pamela C. 2009. "Uncertain Precedent: Circuit Court Responses to Supreme Court Plurality Opinions." *American Politics Research* 37: 30–49.

Corley, Pamela. 2010. *Concurring Opinion Writing on the U.S. Supreme Court*. Albany: SUNY Press.

Cortner, Richard C. 1988. *A Mob Intent on Death: The NAACP and the Arkansas Riot Cases*. Middletown, CT: Wesleyan University Press.

Crawford, Vincent, and Joel Sobel. 1982. "Strategic Information Transmission." *Econometrica* 50(6): 1431–1451.

Cross, Frank. 2005. "Appellate Court Adherence to Precedent." *Journal of Empirical Legal Studies* 2: 369–405.

Cross, Frank B., and Emerson H. Tiller. 1998. "Judicial Partisanship and Obedience to Legal Doctrine: Whistleblowing on the Federal Courts of Appeals." *Yale Law Journal* 107: 2155–2175.

Cross, Frank B., James F. Spriggs II, Timothy R. Johnson, and Paul J. Wahlbeck. 2010. "Citations in the U.S. Supreme Court: An Empirical Study of Their Use and Significance." *University of Illinois Law Review* 2010(2): 489–575.

Dahl, Robert A. 1957. "Decision-Making in a Democracy: The Supreme Court as a National Policy-Maker." *Journal of Public Law* 6: 279–295.

Degler, Carl N. 1972. "Racism in the United States: An Essay Review." *Journal of Southern History* 38: 101–108.

Derthick, Martha. 2010a. *Up in Smoke: From Legislation to Litigation in Tobacco Politics*, 3rd ed. Washington, DC: CQ Press.

Derthick, Martha. 2010b. "From Litigation to Legislation in Tobacco Politics: The Surrender of Philip Morris." Paper Presented at the APPAM Research Conference, November, Boston.

Devins, Neal, and Louis Fisher. 2004. *The Democratic Constitution*. New York: Oxford University Press.

Dickson, Del. 1994. "State Court Defiance and the Limits of Supreme Court Authority: *Williams v. Georgia*." *Yale Law Journal* 103: 1423–1481.

District of Columbia v. Heller. 2008. 171 L. Ed. 2d 637.

Dobbin, Frank. 2009. *Inventing Equal Opportunity*. Princeton: Princeton University Press.

Donohue, John, and Peter Siegelman. 1991. "The Changing Nature of Employment Discrimination Litigation." *Faculty Scholarship Series*. Paper 42. Available at: http://digitalcommons.law.yale.edu/fss_papers/42.

Draper, Robert. 2007. *Dead Certain: The Presidency of George W. Bush*. New York: Free Press.

Dubois, Philip L. 1986. "Penny for Your Thoughts? Campaign Spending in California Trial Court Elections, 1976–1982." *Western Political Quarterly* 39(2): 265–284.

Dunne, Gerald. 1977. *Hugo Black and the Judicial Revolution*. New York: Simon & Schuster.

Duverger, Maurice. 1954. *Political Parties*. New York: Wiley Press.

Edmonson v. Leesville Concrete Company. 1991. 500 U.S. 614.

Edwards v. Aguillard. 1987. 482 U.S. 578.

Ehrlich, Isaac. 1975. "The Deterrent Effect of Capital Punishment: A Question of Life and Death." *American Economic Review* 65: 397–417.

Eisenberg, Theodore, Geoffrey Miller, and Michale A. Perino. 2009. "A New Look at Judicial Impact: Attorney's Fees in Securities Class Actions After Goldberger v. Integrated Resources, Inc." *Washington University Journal of Law and Policy* 29: 5–35.

Ellsworth, Phoebe C., and Samuel R. Gross. 1994. "Hardening of the Attitudes: Americans' Views on the Death Penalty." *Journal of Social Issues* 50: 19–52.

Ely, John Hart. 1980. *Democracy and Distrust: A Theory of Judicial Review.* Cambridge, MA: Harvard University Press.

Emmert, Craig F. 1992. "An Integrated Case-Related Model of Judicial Decisionmaking: Explaining State Supreme Court Decisions in Judicial Review Cases." *Journal of Politics* 54(2): 543–552.

Emmert, Craig F., and Carol Ann Traut. 1994. "The California Supreme Court and the Death Penalty." *American Politics Quarterly* 22(1): 41–61.

Employment Division, Department of Human Resources of Oregon v. Smith. 1990. 494 U.S. 872.

Engel v. Vitale. 1962. 370 U.S. 421.

Epstein, Lee, and Jack Knight. 1998. *The Choices Justices Make.* Washington, DC: CQ Press.

Epstein, Lee, and Jack Knight. 1999. "Mapping Out the Strategic Terrain: The Informational Role of Amici Curiae." In Cornell W. Clayton and Howard Gillman, eds. *Supreme Court Decision Making: New Institutionalist Approaches.* Chicago: University of Chicago Press, pp. 215–235.

Epstein, Lee, and Joseph F. Kobylka. 1992. *The Supreme Court and Legal Change: Abortion and the Death Penalty.* Chapel Hill: University of North Carolina Press.

Epstein, Lee, and Jeffrey A. Segal. 2005. *Advice and Consent: The Politics of Judicial Appointments.* New York: Oxford University Press.

Epstein, Lee, Jeffrey A. Segal, and Harold J. Spaeth. 2007. "Digital Archive of the Papers of Harry A. Blackmun." Available at: http://epstein.law.northwestern.edu/research/BlackmunArchive/.

Epstein, Lee, Rene Lindstadt, Jeffrey A. Segal, and Chad Westerland. 2006. "The Changing Dynamics of Senate Voting on Supreme Court Nominees." *Journal of Politics* 68(2): 296–307.

Epstein, Lee, Andrew D. Martin, Jeffrey A. Segal, and Chad Westerland. 2007a. "The Judicial Common Space." *Journal of Law, Economics, & Organization* 23(2): 303–325.

Epstein, Lee, Jeffrey A. Segal, Harold J. Spaeth, and Thomas G. Walker. 1996. *The Supreme Court Compendium: Data, Decisions, and Developments.* 2nd ed. Washington, DC: CQ Press.

Epstein, Lee, Jeffrey A. Segal, Harold J. Spaeth, and Thomas G. Walker. 2007b. *The Supreme Court Compendium: Data, Decisions, and Developments,* 4th ed. Washington, DC: CQ Press.

Epstein, Lee, Thomas G. Walker, Nancy Staudt, Scott Hendrickson, and Jason Roberts. 2007. "The U.S. Supreme Court Justices Database." Chicago: Northwestern University School of Law, March 8. Available at: http://epstein.law.northwestern.edu/research/justicesdata.html.

Farganis, Dion. 2009. "Do Supreme Court Justices Play the Legitimacy Card? Preliminary Evidence of an Emerging Strategic Tactic." Unpublished paper on file with the
authors.

Feeley, Malcolm, and Edward Rubin. 1998. *Judicial Policy-Making And The Modern
State: How The Courts Reformed America's Prisons.* New York: Cambridge University Press.

Ferejohn, John, and Charles Shipan. 1990. "Congressional Influence on Bureaucracy."
Journal of Law, Economics, & Organization 6, Special Issue: 1–21.

Ferejohn, John, and Barry Weingast. 1992. "A Positive Theory of Statutory Interpretation." *International Review of Law and Economics* 12(2): 263–279.

Flaherty, David H. 1969. "An Introduction to Early American Legal History." In David
H. Flaherty, ed. *Essays in the History of Early American Law.* Chapel Hill: The University of North Carolina Press, pp. 3–38.

Flemming, Roy B., and B. Dan Wood. 1997. "The Public and the Supreme Court: Individual Justice Responsiveness to American Policy Moods." *American Journal of
Political Science* 41(2): 468–498.

Florida v. White. 1995. 664 So. 2d. 442.

Fordham, Michael. 2009. "Public Interest Interventions in the UK Supreme Court:
Ten Virtues." Paper Presented at the Symposium on the Role of Interveners in
Public Interest Litigation at the David Asper Centre for Constitutional Rights, Uni-
versity of Toronto Faculty of Law, November 6, Toronto.

Fowler, James H., Timothy R. Johnson, James F. Spriggs, II, Sangick Jeon, and Paul J.
Wahlbeck. 2007. "Network Analysis and the Law: Measuring the Legal Importance
of Precedents at the U.S. Supreme Court." *Political Analysis* 15(Summer): 324–346.

Frankfurter, Felix. 1935. Letter to Franklin D. Roosevelt. Franklin D. Roosevelt Presidential Library, Hyde Park, New York. May 29.

Frankfurter, Felix. 1938. *Mr. Justice Holmes and the Supreme Court.* Cambridge, MA:
Harvard University Press.

Friedman, Barry. 1990. "A Different Dialogue: The Supreme Court, Congress and
Federal Jurisdiction." *Northwestern University Law Review* 85(1): 1–61.

Friedman, Barry. 1998. "The History of the Countermajoritarian Difficulty, Part One:
The Road to Judicial Supremacy." *New York University Law Review* 73(2): 333–433.

Friedman, Barry. 2006. "Taking Law Seriously." *Perspectives on Politics* 4(2): 261–276.

Friedman, Barry. 2009. *The Will of the People: How Public Opinion Has Influenced the
Supreme Court and Shaped the Meaning of the Constitution.* New York: Farrar,
Straus and Giroux.

Friedman, Lawrence M. 1985. *A History of American Law.* New York: Simon & Schuster.

Friedman, Lawrence M., Robert A. Kagan, Bliss Cartwright, and Stanton Wheeler.
1981. "State Supreme Courts: A Century of Style and Citation." *Stanford Law Review*
33(May): 773–818.

Furman v. Georgia. 1972. 408 U.S. 238.

Garber, Steven, and Anthony G. Bower. 1999. "Newspaper Coverage of Automotive
Product Liability Verdicts." *Law and Society Review* 33: 93–122.

Garfinkel, Harold. 1949. "Research Notes on Inter- and Intra-racial Homicides." *Social
Forces* 27: 369.

Garland, David. 1990. *Punishment and Modern Society.* Chicago: University of
Chicago Press.

Gelman, Andrew, and Thomas C. Little. 1997. "Poststratification into Many Categories Using Hierarchical Logistic Regression." *Survey Methodology* 23(2): 127–135.

George, Tracey E., and Lee Epstein. 1992. "On the Nature of Supreme Court Decision Making." *American Political Science Review* 86: 323–327.

Geyh, Charles Gardner. 2001. "Publicly Financed Judicial Elections: An Overview." *Loyola of Los Angeles Law Review* 34: 1467–1487.

Gibbons, Robert. 2003. "Team Theory, Garbage Cans and Real Organizations: Some History and Prospects of Economic Research on Decision-Making in Organizations." *Industrial and Corporate Change* 12: 753–787.

Gibbs, Robert. 2009. White House Press Briefing. Available at: www.whitehouse.gov/the_press_office/Press-Briefing-By-Press-Secretary-Robert-Gibbs-5-1-09. May 1.

Gibson, James L. 1977. "Discriminant Functions, Role Orientations and Judicial Behavior: Theoretical and Methodological Linkages." *Journal of Politics* 39: 984–1007.

Gibson, James. 1983. "From Simplicity to Complexity: The Development of Theory in the Study of Judicial Behavior." *Political Behavior* 5: 7–49.

Gibson, James L. 2007. "Changes in American Veneration for the Rule of Law." *DePaul Law Review* 56: 593–607.

Gibson, James L. 2008. "Challenges to the Impartiality of State Supreme Courts: Legitimacy Theory and 'New Style' Judicial Campaigns." *American Political Science Review* 102(1): 59–75.

Gibson, James L., and Gregory Caldeira. 2009a. "Knowing the Supreme Court? A Reconsideration of Public Ignorance of the High Court." *The Journal of Politics* 71(2): 429–441.

Gibson, James L., and Gregory Caldeira. 2009b. "Confirmation Politics and the Legitimacy of the U.S. Supreme Court: Institutional Loyalty, Positivity Bias, and the Alito Nomination." *American Journal of Political Science* 53(1): 139–155.

Gibson, James L., and Gregory A. Caldeira. 2009c. *Citizens, Courts, and Confirmations: Positivity Theory and the Judgments of the American People.* Princeton: Princeton University Press.

Gibson, James L., and Gregory A. Caldeira. 2011. "Has Legal Realism Damaged the Legitimacy of the U.S. Supreme Court?" *Law & Society Review* 45: 195–219.

Gibson, James L., Gregory A. Caldeira, and Lester Kenyatta Spence. 2003. "The Supreme Court and the U.S. Presidential Election of 2000: Wounds, Self-Inflicted or Otherwise?" *British Journal of Political Science* 33: 535–556.

Gibson, James L., Jeffrey A. Gottfried, Michael X. Delli Carpini, and Kathleen Hall Jamieson. 2011. "The Effects of Judicial Campaign Activity on the Legitimacy of Courts: A Survey-Based Experiment." *Political Research Quarterly* 64(3): 545–558.

Gifford, Donald G. 2010. *Suing the Tobacco and Lead Pigment Industries: Government Litigation as Public Health Prescription.* Ann Arbor: University of Michigan Press.

Giles, Michael W., Bethany Blackstone, and Richard L. Vining, Jr. 2008. "The Supreme Court in American Democracy: Unraveling the Linkages between Public Opinion and Judicial Decision." *Journal of Politics* 70(2): 293–306.

Giles, Michael W., Virginia A. Hettinger, and Todd Peppers. 2001. "Picking Federal Judges: A Note on Policy and Partisan Selection Agendas." *Political Research Quarterly* 54: 623–641.

Giles, Michael W., Virginia A. Hettinger, and Todd Peppers. 2002. "Measuring the

Preferences of Federal Judges: Alternatives to Party of the Appointing President." Emory University. Typescript.

Gimpel, James G., and Robin M. Wolpert. 1996. "Opinion Holding and Public Attitudes Toward Controversial Supreme Court Nominees." *Political Research Quarterly* 49(1): 163–176.

Ginsburg, Ruth Bader. 2004. "Speaking in a Judicial Voice: Reflections on *Roe v. Wade*." In David M. O'Brien, ed. *Judges on Judging: Views from the Bench*, 2nd ed. Washington, DC: CQ Press, pp. 194–200.

Glendon, Mary Ann. 1993. *Rights Talk: The Impoverishment of Political Discourse*. New York: The Free Press.

Goepp, Katharine. 2002. "Presumed Represented: Analyzing Intervention as of Right When the Government is a Party." *Western New England Law Review* 24: 131–175.

Goldberg, Deborah, Sarah Samis, Edwin Bender, and Rachel Weiss. 2005. *The New Politics of Judicial Elections, 2004*. Washington, DC: Justice at Stake Campaign.

Goldfield, David R. 2004. *Still Fighting the Civil War: The American South and Southern History*. Baton Rouge, LA: Louisiana State University Press.

Good News Club v. Milford. 2001. 533 U.S. 98.

Goodhart, Arthur L. 1930. "Case Law in England and America." *Cornell Law Quarterly* 15(2): 173–193.

Goodman, Walter. 1984. "Strongest Effort Yet to Put Organized Prayer in Schools." *New York Times*, March 8, A1.

"G.O.P Blocks Judicial Nominee in a Sign of Battles to Come." 2011. *New York Times*, May 19.

Graddy, Elizabeth. 2001. "Juries and Unpredictability in Products Liability Damage Awards." *Law & Policy* 23: 29–45.

Gratz v. Bollinger. 2003. 539 U.S. 244.

Greenburg, Jan Crawford. 2007. *Supreme Conflict: The Inside Story of the Struggle for Control of the United States Supreme Court*. New York: Penguin Books.

Greene, William H. 2000. *Econometric Analysis*, 4th ed. Upper Saddle River: Prentice Hall.

Greenhouse, Linda. 2003. "Bush and Affirmative Action: News Analysis; Muted Call in Race Case." *New York Times*, 17 January, A1.

Gregg v. Georgia. 1976. 428 U.S. 123.

Gross, Samuel R., and Robert Mauro. 1989. *Death & Discrimination: Racial Disparities in Capital Sentencing*. Boston: Northeastern University Press.

Gruhl, John. 1980. "The Supreme Court's Impact on the Law of Libel: Compliance by Lower Federal Courts." *Western Political Quarterly* 33(4): 502–519.

Grutter v. Bollinger. 2003. 593 U.S. 306.

Gryski, Gerard S., Gary Zuk, and Sheldon Goldman. n.d. "A Multi-User Data Base on the Attributes of U.S. District Court Judges, 1789–2000." Available at: http://web.as.uky.edu/polisci/ulmerproject/auburndata.htm.

Haines, Charles Grove. 1944. *The Role of the Supreme Court in American Government and Politics 1789–1835*. Berkeley: University of California Press.

Hall, Kermit L. 1989. *The Magic Mirror: Law In American History*. New York: Oxford University Press.

Hall, Matthew E.K. 2011. *The Nature of Supreme Court Power*. New York: Cambridge University Press.

Hall, Melinda Gann. 1992. "Electoral Politics and Strategic Voting on State Supreme Courts." *Journal of Politics* 54: 427–446.

Hall, Melinda Gann. 1995. "Justices as Representatives: Elections and Judicial Politics in the American States." *American Politics Quarterly* 23: 485–503.

Hall, Melinda Gann. 2001. "State Supreme Courts in American Democracy: Probing the Myths of Judicial Reform." *American Political Science Review* 95(2): 315–330.

Hall, Melinda Gann, and Chris W. Bonneau. 2006. "Does Quality Matter? Challengers in State Supreme Court Elections." *American Journal of Political Science* 50(1): 20–33.

Hall, Melinda Gann, and Chris W. Bonneau. 2008. "Mobilizing Interest: The Effects of Money on Citizen Participation in State Supreme Court Elections." *American Journal of Political Science* 52(3): 457–470.

Hall, Melinda Gann, and Paul Brace. 1999. "State Supreme Courts and Their Environments: Avenues to General Theories of Judicial Choice." In Cornell W. Clayton and Howard Gillman, eds. *Supreme Court Decision-Making: New Institutionalist Approaches.* Chicago: University of Chicago Press, pp. 1–14.

Haltom, William, and Michael McCann. 2004. *Distorting the Law: Politics, Media, and the Litigation Crisis.* Chicago: University of Chicago Press.

Hamilton, Alexander. "Federalist #78." *The Federalist Papers.*

Hammond, Thomas H., Chris Bonneau, and Reginald Sheehan. 2005. *Strategic Behavior and Policy Choice on the U.S. Supreme Court.* Palo Alto: Stanford University Press.

Handler, Joel, Ellen Jane Hollingsworth, and Howard S. Erlanger. 1998. *Lawyers and the Pursuit of Legal Rights.* New York: Academic Press.

Hansen, Mark. 1991. "The High Cost of Judging." *ABA Journal* 77(9): 44–47.

Hansford, Thomas G. 2004. "Information Provision, Organizational Constraints, and the Decision to Submit an Amicus Curiae Brief in a U.S. Supreme Court Case." *Political Research Quarterly* 57(2): 219–230.

Hansford, Thomas G., and James F. Spriggs, II. 2006. *The Politics of Precedent on the U.S. Supreme Court.* Princeton: Princeton University Press.

Harlan, John Marshall. 1964. Dissenting Opinion in *Reynolds v. Sims* (377 U.S. 533).

Harvey, Anna, and Barry Friedman. 2006. "Pulling Punches: Congressional Constraints on the Supreme Courts Constitutional Rulings, 1987–2000." *Legislative Studies Quarterly* 31(4): 533–562.

Harvey, Anna, and Barry Friedman. 2009. "Ducking Trouble: Congressionally-Induced Selection Bias in the Supreme Court's Agenda." *Journal of Politics* 71(2): 574–592.

Harvey, Paul. 2007. *Freedom's Coming: Religious Culture and the Shaping of the South from the Civil War through the Civil Rights Era.* Chapel Hill: University of North Carolina Press.

Haskins, George L., and Herbert A. Johnson. 1981. *History of the Supreme Court of the United States: Foundations of Power: John Marshall, 1801–1815.* New York: Macmillan.

Hausegger, Lori, and Lawrence Baum 1999. "Inviting Congressional Action: A Study of Supreme Court Motivations in Statutory Interpretation." *American Journal of Political Science* 43(1): 162–185.

Healy, Thomas. 2001. "Stare Decisis as a Constitutional Requirement." *West Virginia Law Review* 104(Fall): 43–121.

Heiner, Ronald A. 1986. "Imperfect Decisions and the Law: On the Evolution of Legal Precedent and Rules." *Journal of Legal Studies* 15(June): 227–261.

Heise, Michael. 2003. "Mercy by the Numbers: An Empirical Analysis of Clemency and Its Structure." *Virginia Law Review* 89: 239–310.

Hettinger, Virginia A., Stefanie A. Lindquist, and Wendy L. Martinek. 2003. "The Role and Impact of Chief Judges on the United States Courts of Appeals." *The Justice System Journal* 24: 91–117.

Hettinger, Virginia, Stefanie A. Lindquist, and Wendy L. Martinek. 2004. "Comparing Attitudinal and Strategic Accounts of Dissenting Behavior on the U.S. Courts of Appeals." *American Journal of Political Science* 48: 123–137.

Hettinger, Virginia, Stefanie A. Lindquist, and Wendy L. Martinek. 2006. *Judging on a Collegial Court.* Charlottesville: University of Virginia Press.

Hibbing, John R., and Elizabeth Theiss-Morse. 2002. *Stealth Democracy: Americans' Belief about How Government Should Work.* New York: Cambridge University Press.

Hilliker, Donald. 1981. "Rule 24: Effective Intervention." *Litigation* 7: 21–23.

Hoekstra, Valerie J. 2005. "Competing Constraints: State Court Responses to Supreme Court Decisions and Legislation on Wages and Hours." *Political Research Quarterly* 58(2): 314–328.

Hojnacki, Marie, and Lawrence Baum. 1992. "'New-Style' Judicial Campaigns and the Voters: Economic Issues and Union Members in Ohio." *Political Research Quarterly* 45(4): 921–948.

Holdsworth, W.S. 1934. "Case Law." *Law Quarterly Review* 50(April): 180–195.

Hopwood v. Texas. 1996. 78 F.3d 932.

Horowitz, Donald L. 1977. *The Courts and Social Policy.* Washington, DC: Brookings Institution Press.

Horwitz, Morton J. 1977. *The Transformation of American Law, 1780–1860.* Cambridge, MA: Harvard University Press.

Howard, J. Woodford. 1968. "On the Fluidity of Judicial Choice." *American Political Science Review* 62(1): 43–56.

Howe, M.D. 1953. *Holmes–Laski Letters: The Correspondence of Mr. Justice Holmes and Harold J. Laski: 1916–1935.* Cambridge, MA: Harvard University Press.

Hulbary, William E., and Thomas G. Walker. 1980. "The Supreme Court Selection Process: Presidential Motivations and Judicial Performances." *Western Political Quarterly* 33: 185–197.

Humphries, Martha Anne, and Donald R. Songer. 1999. "Law and Politics in Judicial Oversight of Federal Administrative Agencies." *The Journal of Politics* 61: 207–220.

Illinois v. Gates. 1983. 462 U.S. 213.

Jeffries, John J. 1994. *Justice Lewis F. Powell, Jr.: A Biography.* New York: Fordham University Press.

Jencks, Christopher. 1992. *Rethinking Social Policy: Race, Poverty and the Underclass.* Cambridge, MA: Harvard University Press.

Jenkins, Jeffrey, Michael Crespin, and Jamie Carson. 2005. "Parties as Procedural Coalitions in Congress: An Examination of Differing Career Tracks." *Legislative Studies Quarterly* 30(August): 365–389.

Jewell, Malcom E. 1985. "Legislators and Constituents in the Representative Process." In Gerhard Loewenberg, Samuel C. Patterson, and Malcolm E. Jewell, eds. *Handbook of Legislative Research.* Cambridge, MA: Harvard University Press, pp. 97–131.

Johnson v. Transportation Agency of Santa Clara County, California. 1987. 480 U.S. 616.

Johnson, Charles A. 1979. "Lower Court Reactions to Supreme Court Decisions: A Quantitative Examination." *American Journal of Political Science* 23(4): 792–804.

Johnson, Charles A. 1987. "Law, Politics, and Judicial Decision-Making: Lower Federal Court Uses of Supreme Court Decisions." *Law and Society Review* 21: 325–340.

Johnson, Dirk. 2000. "Schools Seeking to Skirt Rules That Bar Ten Commandments." *New York Times,* February 27, p. 24.

Johnson, Guy. 1941. "The Negro and Crime." *Annals* 217: 92–110.

Johnson, Timothy R. 2003. "The Supreme Court, the Solicitor General, and the Separation of Powers." *American Politics Research* 31(4): 426–451.

Johnson, Timothy R., and Jason M. Roberts. 2004. "Presidential Capital and the Supreme Court Confirmation Process." *Journal of Politics* 66(3): 663–683.

Johnson, Timothy R., Paul J. Wahlbeck, and James F. Spriggs, II. 2006. "The Influence of Oral Argumentation Before the U.S. Supreme Court." *American Political Science Review* 100(1): 99–113.

Jones, Edith Holan. 1990. Letter to C. Boyden Gray. George Bush Presidential Library, College Station, TX. July 24.

Jones, Harry W. 1975. "Our Uncommon Common Law." *Tennessee Law Review* 42(Spring): 443–463.

Kagan, Robert A. 2001. *Adversarial Legalism: The American Way of Law.* Cambridge, MA: Harvard University Press.

Kahan, Dan M., Donald Braman, and John Gastil. 2006. "A Cultural Critique of Gun Litigation." In Timothy D. Lytton, ed. *Suing the Gun Industry: A Battle at the Crossroads of Gun Control and Mass Torts.* Ann Arbor: University of Michigan Press, pp. 105–126.

Kahlenberg, Richard D. 1996. *The Remedy: Class, Race, and Affirmative Action.* New York: Basic Books.

Kahlenberg, Richard D. 2004. *America's Untapped Resource: Low-Income Students in Higher Education.* New York: Twentieth Century Fund.

Karabel, Jerome. 2005. *The Chosen: The Hidden History of Admission and Exclusion at Harvard, Yale, and Princeton.* New York: Houghton Mifflin.

Karsten, Peter. 1997. *Heart versus Head: Judge-Made Law in Nineteenth-Century America.* Chapel Hill: University of North Carolina Press.

Kastellec, Jonathan P., Jeffrey R. Lax, and Justin Phillips. 2010. "Public Opinion and Senate Confirmation of Supreme Court Nominees." *Journal of Politics* 72(3): 767–784.

Katcher, Leo. 1967. *Earl Warren: a Political Biography.* New York: McGraw-Hill.

Kearney, Joseph, and Thomas Merrill. 2000. "The Influence of Amicus Curiae Briefs on the Supreme Court." *University of Pennsylvania Law Review* 148(3): 743–854.

Keck, Thomas M. 2009. "Beyond Backlash: Assessing the Impact of Judicial Decisions on LGBT Rights." *Law & Society Review* 43: 151–186.

Keil, Thomas J., and Gennaro F. Vito. 1992. "The Effects of the Furman and Gregg Decisions on Black-White Execution Ratios in the South." *Journal of Criminal Justice* 20: 217–226.

Kellstedt, Lyman, and Mark Noll. 1990. "Religion, Voting for President, and Party Identification, 1948–1984." In Mark Noll, ed. *Religion and American Politics: From the Colonial Period to the 1980s.* New York: Oxford University Press, pp. 355–379.

Kempin, Frederick G. 1959. "Precedent and Stare Decisis: The Critical Years, 1800 to 1850." *American Journal of Legal History* 3: 28–54.

Kessler, David. 2002. *A Question of Intent: A Great American Battle with a Deadly Industry.* New York: Public Affairs.

Key, V.O. Jr. 1949. *Southern Politics.* New York: Alfred A. Knopf.

King, Gary, Robert O. Keohane, and Sidney Verba. 1994. *Designing Social Inquiry: Scientific Inference in Qualitative Research.* Princeton: Princeton University Press.

Klarman, Michael. 2004. *From Jim Crow to Civil Rights: The Supreme Court and the Struggle for Racial Equality.* New York: Oxford University Press.

Kleck, Gary. 1981. "Racial Discrimination in Criminal Sentencing: A Critical Evaluation of the Evidence with Additional Evidence on the Death Penalty." *American Sociological Review* 46: 783–805.

Klein, David E. 2002. *Making Law in the United States Courts of Appeals.* Cambridge: Cambridge University Press.

Klein, David E., and Robert Hume. 2003. "Fear of Reversal as an Explanation for Lower Court Compliance." *Law & Society Review* 37: 579–581.

Knight v. Commissioner of the Internal Revenue Service. 2008. 552 U.S. 181.

Knight, Jack. 1992. *Institutions and Social Conflict.* New York: Cambridge University Press.

Knight, Jack, and Lee Epstein. 1996a. "The Norm of Stare Decisis." *American Journal of Political Science* 40(November): 1018–1035.

Knight, Jack, and Lee Epstein. 1996b. "On the Struggle for Judicial Supremacy." *Law and Society Review* 30(1): 87–120.

Koenig, Thomas H., and Michael L. Rustad. 1998. "'Crimtorts' as Corporate Just Deserts." *University of Michigan Journal of Law Reform* 31: 289–352.

Koenig, Thomas H., and Michael Rustad. 2001. *In Defense of Tort Law.* New York: New York University Press.

Koenig, Thomas H., and Michael L. Rustad. 2004. "Toxic Torts, Politics, and Environmental Justice: The Case for Crimtorts." *Law & Policy* 26: 189–207.

Kohn, Abigail A. 2005. *Shooters: Myths and Realities of America's Gun Cultures.* New York: Oxford University Press.

Kornhauser, Lewis A. 1992. "Modeling Collegial Courts: Legal Doctrine." *Journal of Law, Economics & Organization* 8(3): 441–470.

Kornhauser, Lewis A. 1995. "Adjudication by a Resource-Constrained Team: Hierarchy and Precedent in a Judicial System." *Southern California Review* 68: 1605–1629.

Krislov, Samuel. 1963. "The Amicus Curiae Brief: From Friendship to Advocacy." *Yale Law Journal* 72: 694–721.

Kritzer, Herbert M. 2001. "Impact of Bush v. Gore on Public Perceptions and Knowledge of the Supreme Court." *Judicature* 85: 32.

Lambert, Frank. 2010. *Religion in American Politics: A Short History.* Princeton: Princeton University Press.

Landes, William M., and Richard A. Posner. 1976. "Legal Precedent: A Theoretical and Empirical Analysis." *Journal of Law & Economics* 19: 249–307.

Langbein, Laura I. 1986. "Money and Access: Some Empirical Evidence." *Journal of Politics* 48(4): 1052–1062.

Lax, Jeffrey R. 2003. "Certiorari and Compliance in the Judicial Hierarchy: Discretion, Reputation, and the Rule of Four." *Journal of Theoretical Politics* 15: 61–86.

Lax, Jeffrey R. 2007. "Constructing Legal Rules on Appellate Courts." *American Political Science Review* 101(3): 591–604.

Lax, Jeffrey R. 2011. "The New Judicial Politics of Legal Doctrine." *Annual Review of Political Science* 14: 131–157.

Layton, Lyndsey. 2009. "Chances Bright for Legislation Seeking FDA Regulation of Tobacco," *Washington Post,* May 11.

Lee v. Weisman. 1992. 505 U.S. 577.

Lee, Thomas R. 1999. "Stare Decisis in Historical Perspective: From the Founding Era to the Rehnquist Court." *Vanderbilt Law Review* 52(April): 647–735.

Lemann, Nicholas. 1999. *The Big Test: The Secret History of the American Meritocracy.* New York: Ferrar Strauss.

Levinson, Sanford. 1977. "Review of *From the Diaries of Felix Frankfurter* by Joseph P. Lash." *American Journal of Legal History* 21(1): 80–83.

Lindquist, Stefanie A. 2007. "Bureaucratization and Balkanization: The Origin and Effects of Decision Making Norms in the Federal Courts of Appeals." *University of Richmond Law Review* 41: 659–705.

Lindquist, Stefanie A., and David E. Klein. 2006. "The Influence of Jurisprudential Considerations on Supreme Court Decisionmaking: A Study of Conflict Cases." *Law & Society Review* 40(1): 135–162.

Lindquist, Stefanie A., David A. Yalof, and John A. Clark. 2000. "The Impact of Presidential Appointments to the U.S. Supreme Court: Cohesive and Divisive Voting within Presidential Blocks." *Political Research Quarterly* 53: 795–814.

Lipson, Daniel N. 2007. "Embracing Diversity: The Institutionalization of Affirmative Action as Diversity Management at UC-Berkeley, UT-Austin, and UW-Madison." *Law & Social Inquiry* 32(4): 985–1026.

Lipson, Daniel. 2011. "The Resilience of Affirmative Action in the 1980s: Innovation, Isomorphism, and Institutionalization in University Admissions." *Political Research Quarterly* 64(1): 132–144.

Liptak, Adam. 2007. "Carefully Plotted Course Propels Gun Case to Top," *New York Times,* December 3, A16.

Lockett v. Ohio. 1978. 438 U.S. 586.

Lott, John R. 2010. *More Guns, Less Crime: Understanding Crime and Gun Control Laws,* 3rd ed. Chicago: University of Chicago Press.

Luse, Jennifer K., Geoffrey McGovern, Wendy L. Martinek, and Sara C. Benesh. 2009. "'Such Inferior Courts …': Compliance by Circuits with Jurisprudential Regimes." *American Politics Research* 37: 75–106.

Lynch, Kelly J. 2004. "Best Friends? Supreme Court Law Clerks on Effective Amicus Curiae Briefs." *Journal of Law and Politics* 20(1): 33–75.

McCall, Madhavi M. 2008. "The Politics of Judicial Elections: The Influence of Campaign Contributions on the Voting Patterns of Texas Supreme Court Justices, 1994–1997." *Politics and Policy* 31(2): 314–343.

McCall, Madhavi M., and Michael A. McCall. 2006. "Campaign Contributions, Judicial Decisions, and The Texas Supreme Court: Assessing the Appearance of Impropriety." *Judicature* 90(5): 214–225.

McCann, Michael W. 1994. *Rights At Work: Pay Equity Reform and The Politics Of Legal Mobilization.* Chicago: University of Chicago Press.

McCann, Michael W., and William Haltom. 2004. "Framing the Food Fights: How Mass Media Construct and Constrict Public Interest Litigation." Center for the

Study of Law and Society Jurisprudence and Social Policy Program. Available at: http://repositories.cdlib.org/csls/lss/19 (accessed May 17, 2011).

McCann, Michael W., William Haltom, and Shauna Fisher. 2009. "Criminalizing Big Tobacco: Legal Mobilization and the Politics of Responsibility for Health Risks in the United States." Paper Presented at the Annual Meeting of the Western Political Science Association, March, Vancouver. Available at: www.pugetsound.edu/faculty-sites/bill-haltom/ (accessed May 14, 2011).

McCarty, Nolan, and Rose Razaghian. 1999. "Advice and Consent: Senate Response to Executive Branch Nominations 1885–1996." *American Journal of Political Science* 43: 1122–1143.

McCleskey v. Kemp. 1987. 481 U.S. 279.

MacCoun, Robert J. 2006. "Media Reporting of Jury Verdicts: Is the Tail (of the Distribution) Wagging the Dog?" *DePaul Law Review* 55: 539–562.

McCreary County v. ACLU of Kentucky. 2005. 545 U.S. 844.

McCubbins, Mathew, Roger G. Noll, and Barry R. Weingast. 1987. "Administrative Procedures as Instruments of Political Control." *Journal of Law, Economics, and Organization* 3(Fall): 243–277.

McCulloch v. Maryland. 1819. 4 Wheat. 316.

McDaniel, Patricia A., and Ruth E Malone. 2005. "Understanding Phillip Morris's Pursuit of U.S. Government Regulation of Tobacco." *Tobacco Control* 14: 193–200.

McFadden, Daniel. 2004. "Conditional Logit Analysis of Qualitative Choice Behavior." In Paul Zarembka, ed. *Frontiers in Econometrics.* New York: Academic Press, pp. 105–142.

McGrory, Mary. 1992. "Thomas Fallout Begins Out of Chicago." *The Washington Post,* March 29.

McGuire, Kevin. 1998. "Explaining Executive Success in the U.S. Supreme Court." *Political Research Quarterly* 51(2): 505–526.

McGuire, Kevin T. 2004. "The Institutionalization of the U.S. Supreme Court." *Political Analysis* 12(2): 128–142.

McGuire, Kevin T. 2005. "An Assessment of Tenure on the U.S. Supreme Court." *Judicature* 89: 8–15.

McGuire, Kevin T. 2009. "Public Schools, Religious Establishments, and the U.S. Supreme Court: An Examination of Policy Compliance." *American Politics Research* 37: 50–74.

McGuire, Kevin T., and Gregory A. Caldeira. 1993. "Lawyers, Organized Interests, and the Law of Obscenity: Agenda Setting in the Supreme Court." *American Political Science Review* 87(3): 717–726.

McGuire, Kevin T., and James A. Stimson. 2004. "The Least Dangerous Branch Revisited: New Evidence on Supreme Court Responsiveness to Public Preferences." *Journal of Politics* 66: 1018–1035.

McIntosh, Wayne V., and Cynthia L. Cates. 2010. *Multi-Party Litigation: The Strategic Context.* Vancouver: University of British Columbia Press.

McNollgast. 1994–1995. "Politics and the Courts: A Positive Theory of Judicial Doctrine and the Rule of Law." *Southern California Law Review* 68(6): 1631–1683.

Maddala, G.S. 1983. *Limited-Dependent and Qualitative Variables in Econometrics.* New York: Cambridge University Press.

Maltese, John Anthony. 1995. *The Selling of Supreme Court Nominees.* Baltimore: Johns Hopkins University Press.

Maltzman, Forrest, James F. Spriggs, and Paul J. Wahlbeck. 2000. *Crafting Law on the Supreme Court: The Collegial Game.* New York: Cambridge University Press.

Manwaring, David R. 1968. "The Impact of *Mapp v. Ohio.*" In David H. Everson, ed. *The Supreme Court as Policy-Maker,* 2nd ed. Carbondale: Public Affairs Research Bureau, pp. 1–43.

Maranto, Robert, Richard E. Redding, and Frederick M. Hess. 2009. *The Politically Correct University: Problems, Scope, and Reforms.* Washington, DC: AEI Press.

Marbury v. Madison. 1803. 1 Cranch 137.

Marschak, Jacob, and Roy Radner. 1972. *Economic Theory of Teams.* New Haven: Yale University Press.

Marshall, Thomas R. 1993. "Symbolic versus Policy Representation on the U.S. Supreme Court." *Journal of Politics* 55: 140–150.

Martin v. Hunter's Lessee. 1816. 1 Wheat. 304.

Martin, Andrew D. 2001. "Congressional Decision Making and the Separation of Powers." *American Political Science Review* 95: 361–378.

Martin, Andrew D., and Kevin M. Quinn. 2002. "Dynamic Ideal Point Estimation via Markov Chain Monte Carlo for the U.S. Supreme Court, 1953–1999." *Political Analysis* 10(2): 134–153.

Martinek, Wendy L. 2009. "Appellate Workhorses of the Federal Judiciary: The U.S. Courts of Appeals." In Mark C. Miller, ed. *Exploring Judicial Politics.* New York: Oxford University Press, pp. 125–139.

Massaro, John. 1990. *Supremely Political: The Role of Ideology and Presidential Management in Unsuccessful Supreme Court Nominations.* Albany: State University of New York Press.

Mather, Lynn. 1998. "Theorizing About Trial Courts: Lawyers, Policymaking, and Tobacco Litigation." *Law and Social Inquiry* 23: 897–940.

Mathews, Donald G. 1979. *Religion in the Old South.* Chicago: University of Chicago Press.

Mayhew, David. 1974. *Congress: The Electoral Connection.* New Haven, CT: Yale University Press.

Melnick, R. Shep. 1983. *Regulation and the Courts: The Case Of The Clean Air Act.* Washington, DC: Brookings Institution Press.

Michigan v. Long. 1983. 463 US 1032.

Michigan v. Mosley. 1975. 423 US 96.

Mishler, William, and Reginald S. Sheehan. 1993. "The Supreme Court as a Counter-majoritarian Institution? The Impact of Public Opinion on Supreme Court Decisions." *American Political Science Review* 87(1): 87–101.

Mishler, William, and Reginald S. Sheehan. 1994. "Response: Popular Influence on Supreme Court Decisions." *American Political Science Review* 88(3): 716–724.

Mitnick, Barry M. 1975. "The Theory of Agency: The Policing 'Paradox' and Regulatory Behavior." *Public Choice* 24: 27–42.

Montana v. Bullock. 1995. 901 P. 2d. 61.

Moore v. Dempsey. 1923. 261 U.S. 86.

Moraski, Byron J., and Charles R. Shipan. 1999. "The Politics of Supreme Court Nominations: A Theory of Institutional Constraints and Choices." *American Journal of Political Science* 43: 1068–1095.

Mueller v. Allen. 1983. 463 U.S. 388.

Murdock v. City of Memphis. 1875. 20 Wall. 590.

Murphy, Walter F. 1959. "Lower Court Checks on Supreme Court Power." *American Political Science Review* 53: 1017–1031.

Murphy, Walter F. 1964. *Elements of Judicial Strategy.* Chicago: University of Chicago Press.

Nakell, Barry, and Kenneth A. Hardy. 1987. *The Arbitrariness of the Death Penalty.* Philadelphia: Temple University Press.

In re Neagle. 1890. 135 U.S. 1.

Nemacheck, Christine L. 2007. *Strategic Selection: Presidential Nomination of Supreme Court Justices from Herbert Hoover through George W. Bush.* Charlottesville: University of Virginia Press.

Newmyer, R. Kent. 1985. *Supreme Court Justice Joseph Story: Statesman of the Old Republic.* Chapel Hill: University of North Carolina Press.

Nicholson, Chris, and Paul M. Collins, Jr. 2008. "The Solicitor General's Amicus Curiae Strategies in the Supreme Court." *American Politics Research* 36: 382–415.

North, Douglass C. 1990. *Institutions, Institutional Change and Economic Performance.* New York: Cambridge University Press.

Oldmixon, Elizabeth Anne. 2005. *Uncompromising Positions: God, Sex, and the U.S. House of Representatives.* Washington, DC: Georgetown University Press.

Overby, L. Marvin, Beth M. Henschen, Julie Strauss, and Michael H. Walsh. 1994. "African-American Constituents and Supreme Court Nominees: An Examination of the Senate Confirmation of Thurgood Marshall." *Political Research Quarterly* 47(4): 839–855.

Overby, Marvin L., Beth M. Henschen, Michael H. Walsh, and Julie Strauss. 1992. "Courting Constituents? An Analysis of the Senate Confirmation Vote on Justice Clarence Thomas." *American Political Science Review* 86: 997–1002.

Owens, Ryan. 2010. "The Separation of Powers and Supreme Court Agenda Setting." *American Journal of Political Science* 54(2): 412–427.

Owens, Ryan J., and Lee Epstein. 2005. "Amici Curiae During the Rehnquist Years." *Judicature* 89: 127–132.

Owens, Ryan J., David R. Stras, and David A. Simon. n.d. "Explaining the Supreme Court's Docket Size." *William and Mary Law Review* (Forthcoming).

Pacelle, Richard L., Jr. 1995. "The Dynamics and Determinants of Agenda Change in the Rehnquist Court." In Lee Epstein, ed. *Contemplating Courts.* Washington, DC: CQ Press, pp. 251–274.

Palmer, Jan. 1982. "An Econometric Analysis of the U.S. Supreme Court's Certiorari Decisions." *Public Choice* 39: 387–398.

Parents Involved in Community Schools v. Seattle School District No. 1. 2007. 551 U.S. 701.

Park, David K., Andrew Gelman, and Joseph Bafumi. 2006. *State Level Opinions from National Surveys: Poststratification using Multilevel Regression,* vol. 12. Palo Alto: Stanford University Press, pp. 375–385.

Paternoster, Raymond, Robert Brame, Sarah Bacon, and Andrew Ditchfield. 2004. "Justice by Geography and Race: The Administration of the Death Penalty in Maryland 1978–1999." *Margins: Maryland's Law Journal on Race, Religion, Gender, and Class* 4: 1–97.

Peltason, Jack. 1961. *Fifty-Eight Lonely Men: Southern Judges and School Desegregation.* New York: Harcourt, Brace, and World.

Peppers, Todd C. 2006. *Courtiers of the Marble Palace: The Rise and Influence of the Supreme Court Law Clerk.* Palo Alto: Stanford University Press.

Perry, Barbara. 1991. A "Representative" Supreme Court? The Impact of Race, Religion, and Gender on Appointments. New York: Greenwood.

Perry, Barbara A. 1999. The Priestly Tribe: The Supreme Court's Image in the American Mind. Westport, CT: Praeger.

Perry, H.W., Jr. 1991. Deciding to Decide: Agenda Setting in the United States Supreme Court. Cambridge, MA: Harvard University Press.

Pickerill, J. Mitchell. 2004. Constitutional Deliberation in Congress: The Impact of Judicial Review in a Separated System. Durham, NC: Duke University Press.

Planned Parenthood v. Casey. 1992. 505 U.S. 833.

Posner, Richard. 2005. "The Supreme Court 2004 Term, Foreword: A Political Court." Harvard Law Review 119(1): 31–102.

Posner, Richard. 2008. How Judges Think. Cambridge, MA: Harvard University Press.

Powell v. State of Georgia. 1998. 510 S.E. 2d 18.

Powell, Lewis F., Jr. 1990. "Stare Decisis and Judicial Restraint." Washington and Lee Law Review 47(Spring): 281–290.

Price, Polly J. 2000. "Precedent and Judicial Power After the Founding." Boston College Law Review 42(December): 81–121.

Radelet, Michael L., and Glenn L. Pierce. 1985. "Race and Prosecutorial Discretion in Homicide Cases." Law & Society Review 19: 587–621.

Rasmusen, Eric. 1994. "Judicial Legitimacy as a Repeated Game." Journal of Law, Economics, & Organization 10(April): 63–83.

Reddick, Malia, and Sara C. Benesh. 2000. "Norm Violation by the Lower Courts in the Treatment of Supreme Court Precedent: A Research Framework." Justice System Journal 21: 117–142.

Regents of the University of California v. Bakke. 1978. 438 U.S. 265.

Republican Party of Minnesota v. White. 2002. 536 US 765.

Rheinstein, Max. 1995. "Max Weber on Law in Economy and Society." In Stuart Macaulay, Lawrence M. Friedman, and John Stookey, eds. Law and Society: Readings on the Study of Law. New York: W.W. Norton & Co.

Richards, Mark J., and Herbert M. Kritzer. 2002. "Jurisprudential Regimes in Supreme Court Decision Making." American Political Science Review 96(2): 305–320.

Richardson, Elmo. 1979. The Presidency of Dwight D. Eisenhower. Lawrence: Regents Press of Kansas.

Riker, William H. 1988. Liberalism Against Populism: A Confrontation Between The Theory Of Democracy And The Theory Of Social Choice. Prospect Heights, IL: Waveland Press.

Roberts, John C. 2003. Confirmation Hearings on Federal Appointments. United States Senate Committee on the Judiciary, serial no. J-108-1, part 3.

Roberts, John G. 2010. "2010 Year-End Report on the Federal Judiciary." Available at: www.supremecourt.gov/publicinfo/year-end/2010year-endreport.pdf.

Roper v. Simmons. 2005. 543 U.S. 551.

Rosenberg, Gerald. 1991. The Hollow Hope: Can Courts Bring About Social Change? Chicago: University of Chicago Press.

Rosenberg, Gerald N. 2008. The Hollow Hope: Can Courts Bring About Social Change? 2nd ed. Chicago: University of Chicago Press.

Ross, Stephen A. 1973. "The Economic Theory of Agency: The Principal's Problem." American Economic Review 62: 134–139.

Rubin, Edward, and Malcolm Feeley. 2003. "Judicial Policy-Making and Litigation against the Government." *University of Pennsylvania Journal of Constitutional Law* 5: 617–663.

Ruckman, P.S., Jr. 1993. "The Supreme Court, Critical Nominations, and the Senate Confirmation Process." *Journal of Politics* 55: 793–805.

Rustad, Michael, and Thomas Koenig. 1993. "The Supreme Court and Junk Social Science: Selective Distortion in Amicus Briefs." *North Carolina Law Review* 72: 91–162.

Rutkus, Denis Steven, and Maureen Bearden. 2006. "Supreme Court Nominations, 1789–2005: Actions by the Senate, the Judiciary Committee, and the President." Congressional Research Service Report, January 5.

Sack, Kevin. 1997. "In South, Prayer is a Form of Protest: A Ruling is Opposed in Classrooms, Courtroom and Statehouse." *New York Times*, November 8, A1.

Salisbury, Robert H. 1984. "Interest Representation: The Dominance of Institutions." *American Political Science Review* 78(1): 64–76.

Samuels, Suzanne Uttaro. 2004. *First among Friends: Interest Groups, the U.S. Supreme Court, and the Right to Privacy*. Westport, CT: Praeger.

Sander, Richard. 2004. "A Systemic Analysis of Affirmative Action in American Law Schools." *Stanford Law Review* 54: 367–484.

Sander, Richard. 2011. "Class in American Legal Education." *Denver University Law Review* 88(4): 631–682.

Sandler, Ross, and David Schoenbrod. 2003. *Democracy By Decree: What Happens When Courts Run Government*. New Haven: Yale University Press.

Santa Fe Independent School District v. Doe. 2000. 530 U.S. 790.

Sarat, Austin, and Stuart Scheingold. 1998. *Cause Lawyering: Political Commitments and Professional Responsibilities*. New York: Oxford University Press.

Savage, Charlie. 2009. "A Judge's View of Judging Is on the Record." *New York Times*, May 14, A21.

Savelsberg, Joachim J. 1994. "Knowledge, Domination, and Capital Punishment." *American Journal of Sociology* 99: 911–926.

Schauer, Frederick. 1987. "Precedent." *Stanford Law Review* 39(February): 571–605.

Scheingold, Stuart A. 1974. *The Politics of Rights: Lawyers, Public Policy and Political Change*. New Haven, CT: Yale University Press.

Scheingold, Stuart. A. 1984. *The Politics of Law and Order: Street Crime and Public Policy*. New York: Longman.

Scheingold, Stuart A. 2004. *The Politics of Rights: Lawyers, Public Policy, and Political Change*, 2nd ed. Ann Arbor: University of Michigan Press.

Schlozman, Kay Lehman. 1984. "What Accent the Heavenly Chorus? Political Equality and the American Pressure System." *Journal of Politics* 46(4): 1006–1032.

Schneider, Anne, and Helen Ingram. 1993. "The Social Construction of Target Populations: Implications for Politics and Policy." *American Political Science Review* 87: 334–347.

Schotland, Roy A. 2001. "Financing Judicial Elections, 2000: Change and Challenge." *Detroit College of Law at Michigan State University Law Review*: 849–899.

Schubert, Glendon. 1965. *The Judicial Mind*. Evanston: Northwestern University Press.

Schubert, Glendon. 1974. *The Judicial Mind Revisited*. New York: Oxford University Press.

Schuck, Peter. 1986. *Agent Orange on Trial: Mass Toxic Disaster in Courts*. Cambridge, MA: Belknap Press.

Schwartz, Edward P. 1992. "Policy, Precedent, and Power: A Positive Theory of Supreme Court Decision-Making." *Journal of Law, Economics & Organization* 8(2): 219–252.

Scigliano, Robert. 1971. *The Supreme Court and the Presidency*. New York: Free Press.

Scott, Kevin N., and Theodore Eisenberg. 2002. "Appeal from Jury or Judge Trial: Defendant's Advantage." *American Law and Economics Review* 3: 125–164.

Segal, Jeffrey. 1984. "Predicting Supreme Court Cases Probabilistically: The Search and Seizure Cases (1962–1981)." *American Political Science Review* 78: 891–900.

Segal, Jeffrey A. 1987. "Senate Confirmations of Supreme Court Justices." *Journal of Politics* 49: 998–1015.

Segal, Jeffrey A. 1988. "Amicus Curiae Briefs by the Solicitor General during the Warren and Burger Courts." *Western Political Quarterly* 41: 135–144.

Segal, Jeffrey A., and Albert D. Cover. 1989. "Ideological Values and the Votes of U.S. Supreme Court Justices." *American Political Science Review* 83(2): 557–565.

Segal, Jeffrey A., and Harold J. Spaeth. 1993. *The Supreme Court and the Attitudinal Model*. Cambridge: Cambridge University Press.

Segal, Jeffrey A., and Harold J. Spaeth. 1994. "The Attitudinal Model: The Authors Respond." *Law and Courts Newsletter* 4(1): 10.

Segal, Jeffrey A., and Harold J. Spaeth. 1996. "The Influence of *Stare Decisis* on the Votes of United States Supreme Court Justices." *American Journal of Political Science* 40 (4): 971–1003.

Segal, Jeffrey A., and Harold J. Spaeth. 1999. *Majority Rule or Minority Will: Adherence to Precedent on the U.S. Supreme Court*. Cambridge: Cambridge University Press.

Segal, Jeffrey A., and Harold J. Spaeth. 2002. *The Supreme Court and the Attitudinal Model Revisited*. Cambridge: Cambridge University Press.

Segal, Jeffrey A., Charles M. Cameron, and Albert D. Cover. 1992. "A Spatial Model of Roll Call Voting: Senators, Constituents, Presidents, and Interest Groups in Supreme Court Confirmations." *American Journal of Political Science* 36: 96–121.

Segal, Jeffrey A., Harold J. Spaeth, and Sara C. Benesh. 2005. *The Supreme Court in the American Legal System*. Cambridge: Cambridge University Press.

Shapiro, Martin. 1972. "Toward a Theory of 'Stare Decisis.'" *Journal of Legal Studies* 1(January): 125–134.

Shelton, Dinah. 1994. "The Participation of Nongovernmental Organizations in International Judicial Proceedings." *American Journal of International Law* 88(4): 611–642.

Shepsle, Kenneth. 1986. "The Positive Theory of Legislative Institutions: An Enrichment of Social Choice and Spatial Models." *Public Choice* 50 (Carnegie Papers in Political Economy): 135–179.

Shepsle, Kenneth A., and Barry R. Weingast. 1987. "The Institutional Foundations of Committee Power." *American Political Science Review* 81(1): 85–104.

Shipan, Charles R. 1995. "Looking for a Smoking Gun: Committee Jurisdictions and Congressional Voting Decisions." *Public Choice* 83(April): 65–79.

Shipan, Charles R. 1996. "Senate Committees and Turf: Do Jurisdictions Matter?" *Political Research Quarterly* 49(March): 177–189.

Shipan, Charles R. 1997. *Designing Judicial Review: Interests Groups, Congress, and Communications Policy*. Ann Arbor: University of Michigan Press.

Shipan, Charles R., and Megan L. Shannon. 2003. "Delaying Justice(s): A Duration Analysis of Supreme Court Confirmations." *American Journal of Political Science* 47: 654–668.

Silverstein, Gordon. 2009. *Law's Allure: How Law Shapes, Constrains, Saves, and Kills Politics.* Cambridge: Cambridge University Press.

Simard, Linda Sandstrom. 2008. "An Empirical Study of Amici Curiae in Federal Court: A Fine Balance of Access, Efficiency, and Adversarialism." *The Review of Litigation* 27(4): 669–711.

Simon, Jonathan, and Christina Spaulding. 1999. "Tokens of Our Esteem: Aggravating Factors in the Era of Deregulated Death Penalties." In Austin Sarat, ed. *The Killing State: Capital Punishment in Law, Politics, and Culture.* New York: Oxford University Press, pp. 81–113.

Simons, Kenneth W. 2008. "The Crime/Tort Distinction: Legal Doctrine and Normative Perspectives." *Widener Law Journal* 17: 720–732.

Sitz v. Michigan Department of State Police. 1993. 506 N.W. 2d. 209.

Smith, Kevin B. 2004. "The Politics of Punishment: Evaluating Political Explanations of Incarceration Rates." *Journal of Politics* 66: 925–938.

Songer, Donald R. 1987. "The Impact of the Supreme Court on Trends in Economic Policy Making in the United States Courts of Appeals." *Journal of Politics* 49(3): 830–841.

Songer, Donald R., and Susan Haire. 1992. "Integrating Alternative Approaches to the Study of Judicial Voting." *American Journal of Political Science* 36: 963–982.

Songer, Donald R., and Reginald S. Sheehan. 1990. "Supreme Court Impact on Compliance and Outcomes: *Miranda* and *New York Times* in the United States Courts of Appeals." *Western Political Quarterly* 43(2): 297–316.

Songer, Donald R., and Reginald S. Sheehan. 1992. "Who Wins on Appeal? Upperdogs and Underdogs in the United States Courts of Appeals." *American Journal of Political Science* 36: 235–258.

Songer, Donald R., and Reginald S. Sheehan. 1993. "Interest Group Success in the Courts: Amicus Participation in the Supreme Court." *Political Research Quarterly* 46(2): 339–354.

Songer, Donald R., Ashlyn Kuersten, and Erin Kaheny. 2000. "Why the Haves Don't Always Come Out Ahead: Repeat Players Meet Amici Curiae for the Disadvantaged." *Political Research Quarterly* 53: 537–556.

Songer, Donald R., Jeffrey A. Segal, and Charles M. Cameron. 1994. "The Hierarchy of Justice: Testing a Principal-Agent Model of Supreme Court-Circuit Court Interactions." *American Journal of Political Science* 38(August): 673–696.

Songer, Donald R., Reginald S. Sheehan, and Susan Brodie Haire. 1999. "Do the 'Haves' Come Out Ahead over Time? Applying Galanter's Framework to Decision of the U.S. Courts of Appeals." *Law & Society Review* 33:811–832.

Songer, Donald R., Reginald Sheehan, and Susan Haire. 2000. *Continuity and Change on the United States Courts of Appeals.* Ann Arbor: University of Michigan Press.

Songer, Michael J. and Isaac Unah. 2006. "The Effect of Race, Gender, and Location in Prosecutorial Decision to Seek the Death Penalty in South Carolina." *South Carolina Law Review* 58: 161–210

Sotomayor, Sonia. 2009. Opening Statement before the Senate Judiciary Committee. United States Senate Committee on the Judiciary, July 13.

Spaeth, Harold J. 2002. *The Vinson–Warren Supreme Court Judicial Database,*

1946-1968 Terms. East Lansing: Department of Political Science, Michigan State University.

Spaeth, Harold J. 2009. *The Original United States Supreme Court Database, 1953-2007 Terms.* East Lansing: Department of Political Science, Michigan State University.

Spohn, Cassia C., and J.W. Spears. 1997. "Gender and Case Processing Decisions: A Comparison of Case Outcomes for Male and Female Defendants Charged with Violent Felonies." *Women and Criminology* 8: 29-59.

Spriggs, James F., II, and Thomas G. Hansford. 2000. "Measuring Legal Change: The Reliability and Validity of *Shepard's Citations.*" *Political Research Quarterly* 53(2): 327-341.

Spriggs, James F., II, and Thomas G. Hansford. 2001. "Explaining the Overruling of Supreme Court Precedent." *Journal of Politics* 63(4): 1091-1111.

Spriggs, James F., II, and Thomas G. Hansford. 2002. "The U.S. Supreme Court's Incorporation and Interpretation of Precedent." *Law & Society Review* 36: 139-159.

Spriggs, James F., and Paul J. Wahlbeck. 1995. "Calling It Quits: Strategic Retirement on the Federal Courts of Appeals, 1893-1991." *Political Research Quarterly* 48(September): 573-597.

Spriggs, James F., and Paul J. Wahlbeck. 1997. "Amicus Curiae and the Role of Information in the Supreme Court." *Political Research Quarterly* 50(2): 365-386.

State of Connecticut v. Kimbro. 1985. 496 A. 2d. 498, 507-508.

Staton, Jeffrey K., and Georg Vanberg. 2008. "The Value of Vagueness: Delegation, Defiance, and Judicial Opinions." *American Journal of Political Science* 58(3): 504-519.

Staudt, Nancy. 2004. "Modeling Standing." *New York University Law Review* 79: 612-684.

Stern, Robert L., Eugene Gressman, Stephen M. Shapiro, and Kenneth S. Geller. 2002. *Supreme Court Practice*, 8th ed. Washington, DC: Bureau of National Affairs.

Stevens, John Paul. 1983. "The Life Span of a Judge-Made Rule." *New York University Law Review* 58(April): 1-21.

Stidham, Ronald, and Robert A. Carp. 1982. "Trial Courts' Responses to Supreme Court Policy Changes." *Law and Policy Quarterly* 4: 215-234.

Story, Joseph. 1833. *Commentaries on the Constitution of the United States.* Cambridge: Brown, Shattuck.

Stoutenborough, James W., Donald P. Haider-Markel, and Mahalley D. Allen. 2006. "Reassessing the Impact of Supreme Court Decisions on Public Opinion: Gay Civil Rights Cases." *Political Research Quarterly* 59: 419-433.

Strieb, Victor L. 2006. "Rare and Inconsistent: The Death Penalty for Women." *Fordham Urban Law Journal* 33: 609-625.

Sugarman, Stephen D. 2006. "Comparing Tobacco and Gun Litigation." In Timothy D. Lytton, ed. *Suing the Gun Industry: A Battle at the Crossroads of Gun Control and Mass Torts.* Ann Arbor: University of Michigan Press, pp. 196-222.

Sulam, Ian. 2011. "Precedent, Policy, Indeterminacy: Using Doctrine Space to Bridge Across Circuits." Paper Presented at the 2011 Annual Meeting of the Midwest Political Science Association, Chicago.

Surrency, Erwin C. 1981. "Law Reports in the United States." *American Journal of Legal History* 25(January): 48-66.

Tanenhaus, Joseph, Marvin Schick, and David Rosen. 1963. "The Supreme Court's

Certiorari Jurisdiction: Cue Theory." In Glendon A. Schubert, ed. *Judicial Decision-Making*. New York: Free Press, pp. 111–132.

Tarr, G. Alan. 1977. *Judicial Impact and State Supreme Courts*. Lexington: Lexington Books.

Taylor, Jamal, Stacia L. Haynie, and Kaitlyn Sill. 2008. "Affirmative Action, Appellate Court Decisions and Minority Enrollment in Institutions of Higher Education, 1990–2005." Paper Presented at the Annual Meeting of the Southern Political Science Association, January 9–12, New Orleans.

Thayer, James. 1893. "The Origin and Scope of the American Doctrine of Constitutional Law." *The Harvard Law Review* 7(3): 129–156.

Thernstrom, Stephan, and Abigail Thernstrom. 1997. *America in Black and White: One Nation, Indivisible*. New York: Simon & Schuster.

Thornburg, Thomas H. 1995. *North Carolina Crimes: A Guidebook on the Elements of Crime*, 4th ed. Chapel Hill, NC: Institute of Government, the University of North Carolina at Chapel Hill.

Tobias, Carl. 1991. "Standing to Intervene." *Wisconsin Law Review*: 415–463.

Toobin, Jeffrey. 2007. *The Nine: Inside the Secret World of the Supreme Court*. New York: Anchor Books.

Traut, Carol Ann, and Craig F. Emmert. 1998. "Expanding the Integrated Model of Judicial Decision Making: The California Justices and Capital Punishment." *Journal of Politics* 60: 1166–1180.

Tsebelis, George. 1990. *Nested Games: Rational Choice In Comparative Politics*. Berkeley: University of California Press.

Unah, Isaac. 2009. "Choosing Those Who Will Die: The Effect of Race, Gender, and Law in Prosecutorial Decision to Seek the Death Penalty in Durham County, North Carolina." *Michigan Journal of Race and Law* 15: 135–179.

Unah, Isaac. 2011. "Empirical Analysis of Race and the Process of Capital Punishment in North Carolina." *Michigan State Law Review*, vol. 3, forthcoming.

Unah, Isaac, and John Charles Boger. 2001. "Preliminary Report on the Finding of the North Carolina Death Penalty Study." Available at: www.unc.edu/~iunah/NC_death_penalty_project.html.

Unah, Isaac, and K. Elizabeth Coggins. 2011. "Punishment Politics: Gubernatorial Rhetoric, Political Conflict, and the Instrumental Explanation of Mass Incarceration in the American States." Available at: http://ssrn.com/author=635772.

United States Bureau of the Census, Statistical Abstract of the United States: 1981.

United States Bureau of the Census, Statistical Abstract of the United States: 2011.

United States Commission on Civil Rights. 2008. *Affirmative Action in American Law Schools: Briefing Report*. Washington, DC.

Van Orden v. Perry. 2005. 545 U.S. 677.

Vanberg, Georg. 2005. *The Politics of Constitutional Review in Germany*. Cambridge: Cambridge University Press.

Vasquez v. Hillery. 1986. 474 U.S. 254.

Voices for Choices v. Illinois Bell Telephone Company. 2003. 339 F.3d 542.

Wagner, Wendy E. 2007. "When All Else Fails: Regulating Risky Products through Tort Litigation." *Georgetown Law Journal* 95: 693–732.

Wahlbeck, Paul J. 1997. "The Life of the Law: Judicial Politics and Legal Change." *Journal of Politics* 59(August): 778–802.

Wahlbeck, Paul J., James F Spriggs, II, and Forrest Maltzman. 1998. "Marshalling the

Court: Bargaining and Accommodation on the United States Supreme Court." *American Journal of Political Science* 42: 294–315.

Wald, Patricia M. 1995. "The Rhetoric and the Results of Rhetoric: Judicial Writings." *University of Chicago Law Review* 62(Fall): 1371–1419.

Walker, Thomas G., and Lee Epstein. 1993. *The Supreme Court of the United States: An Introduction*. New York: St. Martin's Press.

Wallace v. Jaffree. 1985. 472 U.S. 38.

Waltenburg, Eric N., and Charles S. Lopeman. 2000. "Tort Decisions and Campaign Dollars." *Southeastern Political Review* 28(2): 241–263.

Ward, Artemus. 2003. *Deciding to Leave: the Politics of Retirement from the United States Supreme Court*. Albany: State University of New York Press.

Ward, Artemus, and David L. Weiden. 2006. *Sorcerers' Apprentices: 100 Years of Law Clerks at the United States Supreme Court*. New York: New York University Press.

Ware, Stephen J. 1999. "Money, Politics, and Judicial Decisions: A Case Study of Arbitration Law in Alabama." *Journal of Law and Politics* 25(4): 645–686.

Warren, Charles. 1911. *A History of the American Bar*. Boston: Little, Brown.

Waterman, Richard W., and Kenneth J. Meier. 1998. "Principal–Agent Models: An Expansion?" *Journal of Public Administration Research and Theory* 8: 173–202.

Watson, George, and John A. Stookey. 1995. *Shaping America: The Politics of Supreme Court Appointments*. New York: HarperCollins.

Way, H. Frank, Jr. 1968. "Survey Research on Judicial Decisions: The Prayer and Bible Reading Cases." *Western Political Quarterly* 21(2): 189–205.

Webster v. Reproductive Health Services. 1989. 492 U.S. 490.

Wechsler, Herbert. 1959. "Toward Neutral Principles of Constitutional Law." *Harvard Law Review* 73(1): 1–35.

Welch, Susan, and John Gruhl. 1998. *Affirmative Action and Minority Enrollments in Medical and Law Schools*. Ann Arbor: University of Michigan Press.

Westerland, Chad, Jeffrey A. Segal, Lee Epstein, Charles M. Cameron, and Scott Comparato. 2010. "Strategic Defense and Compliance in the U.S. Courts of Appeals." *American Journal of Political Science* 54: 891–905.

Westerland, Chad, Jeffrey A. Segal, Lee Epstein, Scott Comparato, and Charles M. Cameron. 2006. "Lower Court Defiance of (Compliance with) the U.S. Supreme Court." Paper Presented at the Annual Meeting of the Midwest Political Science Association, April 20–23, Chicago.

White, Welsh S. 2001. *Miranda's Waning Protections: Police Interrogation Practices after Dickerson*. Ann Arbor: University of Michigan Press.

Whitford, Andrew, and Jeffrey Yates. 2009. *Presidential Rhetoric and the Public Agenda*. Baltimore: Johns Hopkins University Press.

Whittington, Keith. 1999. *Constitutional Construction: Divided Powers and Constitutional Meaning*. Cambridge, MA: Harvard University Press.

Wilcox, Clyde. 1991. *God's Warriors: The Christian Right in Twentieth-Century America*. Baltimore: Johns Hopkins University Press.

Wilcox, Clyde, and Carin Robinson. 2010. *Onward Christian Soldiers? The Religious Right in American Politics*, 4th ed. Boulder: Westview Press.

Wilson, James Q. 1985. *Thinking About Crime*. New York: Vintage Books.

Wisconsin v. Mitchell. 1993. 508 U.S. 476.

Wolfgang, Marvin, and Mark Riedel. 1973. "Race, Judicial Discretion, and the Death Penalty." *Annals* 407: 119.

Wolpert, Robin M., and James G Gimpel. 1997. "Information, Recall, and Accountability: The Electorate's Response to the Clarence Thomas Nomination." *Legislative Studies Quarterly* 22(4): 535–550.

Wood, Robert S. 2006. "Tobacco's Tipping Point: The Master Settlement Agreement as a Focusing Event." *The Policy Studies Journal* 34: 419–436.

Wright, John R. 1989. "PAC Contributions, Lobbying, and Representation." *Journal of Politics* 51(3): 713–729.

Wright, Ronald F. 2009. "How Prosecutor Elections Fail Us." *Ohio State Journal of Criminal Law* 6: 581–610.

Yalof, David A. 1999. *Pursuit of Justices: Presidential Politics and the Selection of Supreme Court Nominees.* Chicago: University of Chicago Press.

Yamane, David, and Elizabeth A. Oldmixon. 2006. "Affiliation, Salience, Advocacy: Three Religious Factors in Public Policy-Making." *Legislative Studies Quarterly* 31: 433–460.

Yates, Jeffrey, and Richard J. Fording. 2005. "Politics and State Punitiveness in Black and White." *Journal of Politics* 67: 1099–1121.

Youngdale, Elizabeth. 2008. "Reviewing the Law Reviews." *Defense Counsel Journal.* October 1. Available at: www.allbusiness.com/legal/torts-business-torts/11700027–1. html (accessed February 19, 2009).

Ysursa v. Pocatello Education Association. 2009. 172 L. Ed. 2d 770.

Zelman v. Simmons-Harris. 2002. 536 U.S. 639.

Zobrest v. Catalina Foothills School District. 1993. 509 U.S. 1.

Index

Page numbers in *italics* denote tables, those in **bold** denote figures.